Praise for *Agent*

"A valuable window on both sides in a letha...
— ... *York Times Book Review*

"A rare look inside the mindset of the most dangerous jihadis of the past decade."   —*New York Post*

"[A] gripping firsthand account . . . Storm's work provides valuable and fascinating insight into the quiet battle being waged between clandestine national agencies and various terrorist organizations."
—*Christian Science Monitor*

"*Agent Storm* feels like a James Bond story or one of John Le Carré's marvelous spy thrillers. Yet the story written by CNN's Paul Cruickshank and Tim Lister is a true account . . . First-rate."   —War on the Rocks

"Storm's tale of dodging drones and navigating alliances may read like a great espionage thriller . . . but his deeply personal struggle with extremism and atonement is the real story."   —*Maxim*

"Morten Storm has done the Western world a great service . . . And by the way, the CIA owes him five million dollars."
—Brian Kilmeade, Fox News

"*Agent Storm* is the remarkable memoir of a Danish convert-turned-extremist who managed not only to infiltrate al Qaeda's ranks but would later become one of West's most valued human intelligence assets in the war on terrorism. As a true spy story, this book brings you incredibly close to what it actually takes to be an extremist and get into a terrorist group while balancing loyalty and treachery in the world of intelligence. Essential reading for everyone interested in how the war on terrorism is actually fought in the shadows."

—Dr. Magnus Ranstorp, a leading expert on
international terrorism and research director
of the Centre for Asymmetric Threat Studies
at the Swedish National Defence College

AGENT STORM

AGENT STORM

My Life Inside al Qaeda and the CIA

MORTEN STORM WITH
PAUL CRUICKSHANK
AND TIM LISTER

Grove Press
New York

First published in Great Britain in 2014 by the Penguin Group

Published simultaneously in Canada
Printed in the United States of America

ISBN 978-0-8021-2429-6
eISBN 978-0-8021-9236-3

Grove Press
an imprint of Grove Atlantic
154 West 14th Street
New York, NY 10011

Distributed by Publishers Group West

groveatlantic.com

15 16 17 18   10 9 8 7 6 5 4 3 2 1

CONTENTS

Contents

Contents

27. A Spy in the Cold

Map of Yemen

Red Sea

Dammaj

AL-JAWF

Sana'a

MARIB

Y E

SHABWA

Ataq

Al-Hota

Taiz

Lawdar

Azzar

ABYAN

Shaqra

Jaar Zinjibar

Aden

DJIBOUTI

Gulf of Aden

SOMALIA

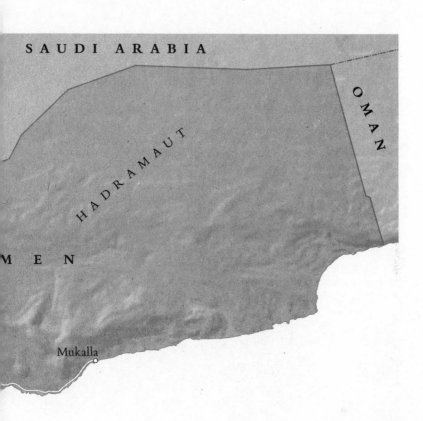

SAUDI ARABIA

OMAN

HADRAMAUT

MEN

Mukalla

Arabian Sea

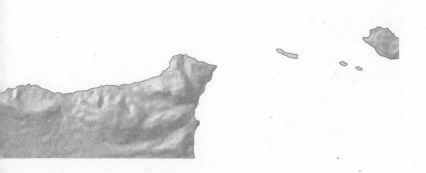

AUTHORS' NOTE

Any spy who goes public will inevitably face scrutiny, especially one claiming to have worked as a double agent for four Western intelligence services on some of their most sensitive counter-terrorism operations after 9/11.

What makes Morten Storm's story unique is the extraordinary amount of audiovisual evidence and electronic communications he collected during his time as a spy, which both corroborate his story and enrich his account.

This material, to which he gave us unfettered access, includes:

- emails exchanged with the influential cleric Anwar al-Awlaki;
- videos recorded by Awlaki and the Croatian woman who travels to Yemen to marry the cleric, a marriage arranged by Storm even as Awlaki was being hunted by the US;
- dozens of encrypted emails between Storm and terrorist operatives in Arabia and Africa that are still on the hard drives of his computers;
- records of money transfers to a terrorist in Somalia;
- text messages with Danish intelligence officers still stored on his mobile phones;
- secret recordings made by Storm of conversations with his Danish and US intelligence handlers, including a thirty-minute recording of a meeting with a CIA agent in Denmark in 2011 during which several of Storm's missions targeting terrorists were discussed;
- handwritten mission notes;
- video and photographs of Storm driving through Yemen's tribal areas just after meeting Awlaki in 2008;
- video of Storm with British and Danish intelligence agents in northern Sweden in 2010.

Unless otherwise stated in the endnotes all emails, letters, Facebook exchanges, text messages and recordings of conversations quoted in the book are reproduced verbatim, including spelling and grammatical mistakes. Some have been translated into English from Danish.

Storm also provided photographs taken with several of his Danish intelligence handlers in Iceland. Reporters at the Danish newspaper *Jyllands-Posten* were able to confirm the identity of the agents through their sources.

Several individuals mentioned in the book corroborated essential elements of Storm's story. We have not disclosed the full identity of some of them for their own safety. No Western intelligence official was willing to go on the record.

Storm provided us with his passports, which include entry and exit visas for every trip outside Europe described in the book from the year 2000 onwards. He also shared hotel invoices paid by 'Mola Consult', a front company used by Danish intelligence, which according to Denmark's business registry was dissolved just before he went public. Additionally he provided dozens of Western Union receipts cataloguing payments by Danish intelligence (PET). His PET handlers listed Søborg – the district in which PET is located in Copenhagen – on the paperwork.

We used pseudonyms for three people in the book to protect their safety or identity, which we make clear at first reference. We have used only the first name of several others for security or legal reasons. A *dramatis personae* is attached at the end of the book. The book includes Arabic phrases and greetings; a translation is given at first reference.

We have added a number of photographs and other visual testimonies of Storm's work in an archive at the end of the book and a colour picture section. These include a photograph of a briefcase containing a $250,000 reward from the CIA, handwritten notes from a meeting with Awlaki, decrypted emails, money transfer receipts, and video images and pictures taken in Yemen's Shabwa province on trips to meet the cleric.

Paul Cruickshank and Tim Lister, April 2014

CHAPTER ONE
DESERT ROAD

Mid-September 2009

I sat in my grey Hyundai peering into the liquid darkness, exhausted and apprehensive. Exhausted because my day had started before dawn in Sana'a, Yemen's capital, some 200 miles to the north-west. Apprehensive because I had no idea who was coming to meet me or when they would arrive. Would they greet me as a comrade or seize me as a traitor?

The desert night had an intensity I had never seen in Europe. There were no lights on the road that led from the coast into the mountains of Shabwa province, a lawless part of Yemen. At times there hadn't been much of a road either. A fine coating of sand had drifted on to the baking tarmac. Long after sunset, a humid breeze wafted in from the Arabian Sea.

My apprehension was fed by guilt: I had only been able to drive into this no-man's-land, where al-Qaeda's presence was growing as the government's authority waned, because my young Yemeni wife, Fadia, was beside me.[1] On the pretext of visiting her brother we had negotiated one checkpoint after another on a dangerous route south.

In my quest to reconnect with Anwar al-Awlaki, an American-Yemeni cleric who had become one of al-Qaeda's most influential and charismatic figures, I knew I was risking my life. Yemen's military and intelligence services had recently stepped up their attempts to combat al-Qaeda in the Arabian Peninsula (AQAP), one of the most active and

---

1 Fadia is not her real name. For her safety and that of her family, I have given her a pseudonym.

dangerous franchises of Osama bin Laden's group. There was the risk of an ambush, a shoot-out at a checkpoint or just a lethal misunderstanding.

There was also the danger that Awlaki – now dubbed 'al-Qaeda's rock star' by Western newspapers – might no longer trust me. My trip had been at his request. In an email he had saved in the draft folder of an anonymous email account we shared, he had told me:

'Come to Yemen. I need to see you.'

It had been nearly a year since I had seen Awlaki and in that time he had continued a remorseless and fateful journey. The radical preacher sympathetic to al-Qaeda had become an influential figure within its leadership, aware of and involved in its plans to export terror.

I had already missed one rendezvous. Awlaki had invited me to come out to a meeting of Yemen's leading jihadis in a remote part of Marib, a desert province that had reputedly been the home of the Queen of Sheba centuries earlier. Awlaki's younger brother, Omar, was meant to organize my travel to Marib, but had insisted I dress as a woman in a full veil, or niqab, so that we could get through the checkpoints. At 6 foot 1 inch tall and weighing nearly eighteen stone, I was dubious. I had declined the offer, even though the driver who would take me to meet these wanted men was a police officer. Such were the contradictions of Yemen. My absence from such an important gathering of al-Qaeda's leaders in Yemen had gnawed at me. So a few days later my wife and I undertook this odyssey to Shabwa.

After a few minutes I heard the muffled growl of a distant engine, then saw headlights and the approach of a Toyota Land Cruiser packed with serious young men brandishing AK-47s. The escort party had arrived. I grasped my wife's hand. If things were about to go very wrong, we would know in the next few moments.

All day we had followed curt directions texted from Awlaki, as if they were clues in some bizarre treasure hunt. 'Take this road, turn left, pretend to the police that you are going to Mukalla along the coast.'

I could hardly blend in with the locals. As a heavy-set Dane with a shock of ginger hair and a long beard, I might as well have been an alien life form in a country of wiry, dark-skinned Arabs. In a land where kidnapping and tribal rivalries, trigger-happy police and militant jihadis made travelling an unpredictable venture, the sight of someone like me, with a petite Yemeni woman at my side, crammed into a hired car heading towards the rebellious south was – to say the least – an unusual one.

The day had started well enough. The morning cool before the intense heat took hold was invigorating. There had been a hold-up at the first checkpoint outside Sana'a, always the most troublesome. Why would anyone want to leave the relative security of the capital for the badlands of the south? I chatted in Arabic, which always impressed my inquisitors, while my wife – her face and hair covered in the black niqab – sat mutely in the passenger seat. It was no accident that a CD in the car was playing verses from the Koran. I told them we were going to see my wife's brother and join a wedding party on the coast and would be travelling via Aden – Yemen's main port on the Arabian Sea and the hub of commercial life.

The police at the roadblock had difficulty deciphering my passport. Few of them were likely to read Arabic well, let alone be able to understand the Roman alphabet. They seemed to think I was Turkish – perhaps because the very idea of a European travelling across Yemen was so unfathomable. My broad smile and apparent ease with my surroundings were enough for them. It probably helped that it was not only September – a scorching month in Arabia – but also the middle of Ramadan. The men were tired from fasting.

Once we were clear of that first checkpoint, the challenge was to stay on the road, or at least to prevent others from driving us off it. Several times I caught a glimpse down sheer cliffs of the rusting carcass of a truck or bus. Roads in Yemen seemed to attract pedestrians with a death wish, whether camels, dogs, cows or kids. As vehicles hurtled towards them they would wander into the middle.

The colours of the morning gave way to the white heat of the mid-afternoon, and I struggled to stay focused on the road and on the risks of our journey. At last the mountains began to give way to the coastal lowlands – the Tehama. In the distance lay the port of Aden. The city had suffered since the collapse of South Yemen and the ruthless military campaign of the North's President, Ali Abdullah Saleh, to unify the two halves of Yemen in the 1990s. The people of the south saw themselves as neglected. A separatist movement was gaining strength, compounding the challenge to the Yemeni government from al-Qaeda militants.

In my rear-view mirror, the mountains were swallowing the glowering sun. I tried to navigate my way around Aden's chaotic fringe – to join the long coastal road that I had been instructed to take by another of Awlaki's text messages.

Anwar al-Awlaki was from a powerful clan in the mountainous Shabwa province. His father had been a respected academic and a minister in Yemen's government who had gone to America on a Fulbright fellowship and had a Ph.D. from the University of Nebraska. The younger Awlaki had himself been a university lecturer in Sana'a after abandoning the United States in the wake of 9/11, worried (with justification) he was being targeted by the FBI. He had met two of the hijackers in California months before the attack, though there was no evidence that he knew their plans.

Seven years on, the landscape – and Awlaki – had changed. President Saleh was ever more desperate for US aid and was under growing pressure to take a harder line against al-Qaeda sympathizers. There had already been a suicide bomb attack on the US embassy in September 2008, which killed ten, and mass breakouts of al-Qaeda inmates from supposedly top-security prisons. Yemen was al-Qaeda's favourite recruiting ground – it had provided a pipeline of young men with little education who were dispatched to Osama bin Laden's training camps before 9/11. Some of them had become bin Laden's bodyguards before being caught escaping from the Tora Bora mountains of Afghanistan and sent to Guantanamo Bay.

Now Yemen was the base for al-Qaeda's affiliate in Yemen, AQAP, and a top destination for European and American militants dreaming of jihad. And Awlaki's militancy had hardened. His sermons – carried around the world on YouTube – were a guiding light for would-be jihadis. In rural townships in Pennsylvania, cramped flats in England, the suburbs of Toronto, young men were consuming his every word.

For the CIA and MI6, Awlaki represented the future of al-Qaeda. His knowledge of Western societies, his fluent English and his command of social media posed a new and more lethal threat than grainy videos and arcane statements from bin Laden.

In 2006 he had been arrested and charged with being involved in a vague kidnapping conspiracy. He had spent eighteen months in jail in Sana'a and had even received a visit from FBI agents wanting to know more about his meetings with the 9/11 hijackers. And then he had vanished into Yemen's vast and unforgiving interior.

And so I found myself heading east out of Aden, on the last leg of my mystery tour of Yemen. We arrived at another rudimentary checkpoint, a couple of battered 'STOP' signs either side of a shed of corrugated metal that only concentrated the searing heat. In some ways this shed was a frontier, marking the effective limit of the state's authority. Beyond was a road that foreigners could only travel if escorted by soldiers, forbidding lands roamed by al-Qaeda fighters and bandits.

We repeated the wedding story; how I knew the route to Mukalla along the coast and could converse in Arabic. Should we decline protection, we were told, we would have to return to Aden and sign a document absolving the authorities of all responsibility for our safety.

An hour later the sun had gone but its red rays still illuminated the dusk. We returned to the checkpoint, document in hand. By then, the guards were about to break their Ramadan fast with the meal known as *iftar*. They couldn't care less what happened to this crazy European and his silent Yemeni bride.

The southern coast of Yemen could be the perfect vacation destination: endless beaches of soft sand, warm waters, superb fishing. It was untouched but sadly untouchable, the fringe of a failing state – interrupted only by scruffy coastal towns like Zinjibar, where scattered breeze blocks spoke of projects unfinished or not yet begun.

As we drove, now free of the last barrier, our spirits lifted. Adrenalin coursed through me.

The final text instruction from Awlaki arrived. I should tell the police I needed petrol and then head north.

Shaqra was little more than a fishing village. On this steamy night it was deserted, the occasional dog hobbling across the main street. If anything it was more dilapidated than when we had passed through a year before on our previous voyage to meet Awlaki.

Outside the town, a grandiose junction with signs showing a

smiling President marked the point at which the road divided, one branch going inland and up into the rebellious interior, the other continuing along the coast. I knew I would never be allowed to head inland, so my instructions were to tell the police checkpoint that I was going along the coast but needed fuel from the petrol station a couple of miles in the other direction. It was a ruse that had clearly worked before. The police, rendered dozy by *iftar*, waved us on. They would not see us return.

Now I sat with Fadia – our pulses racing on a lonely desert road – dazzled by the headlights of a vehicle packed with armed men.

A bearded man in his mid-thirties with sharp, dark eyes, and a red-chequered scarf around his head, emerged from a cloud of dust drifting across the beam of the Land Cruiser's headlights. The way the rest of the group fell in behind him made it clear that Abdullah Mehdar was their leader. He was known as being fearless, and having militant leanings. I scrutinized his face as he walked towards us.

'*As salaam aleikum* [Peace be with you],' he said at last, greeting me in Arabic and breaking into a broad smile. The tension left my body as if a fever had broken. In my relief I hugged every one of Mehdar's companions. They had brought food – bananas, bread – and we broke the Ramadan fast together. I felt safe for the first time that day. I was with some of Yemen's most wanted, a group of armed men I did not know, in the dead of night, heading towards the wilderness of Shabwa. But it was as if I were in a cocoon, admitted to a brotherhood of simple beliefs and unquestioned loyalties.

Mehdar was Awlaki's personal emissary, like him a member of the Awalik tribe – and Yemen was a country where tribal loyalties trumped all others. Knowing that I had been invited here by Awlaki and was the cleric's friend, he was deeply respectful and courteous.

After a few minutes, he said we should move. This was an area where highway robbery was all too common, and where criminals were as well armed as militants. It must have been gone 9 p.m. by the time the convoy arrived at its destination: the Land Cruiser followed my little Hyundai – surely the first hire car ever to have puttered through this remote corner of Shabwa. The vehicles threw up a cloud of dust as we sped down a track outside an unlit hamlet. Mountains loomed beyond, though on this moonless night there was no telling where the land ended and the vast sky began.

I could not know it then but I was in the vicinity of al-Hota, a settlement nestled in the shadow of a towering rocky plateau in the Mayfa'a district of Shabwa – the heart of al-Qaeda country.

We arrived at an imposing two-storey house inside a compound with high walls. The gates were opened and swiftly closed by two men with AK-47s slung over their shoulders. I felt a surge of panic. My journey to meet Anwar al-Awlaki was complete, but what if Yemen's security services knew of my plans and had let me make this journey, or Awlaki himself no longer trusted me? And then there was Fadia. She knew Awlaki, and knew we were friends, but had no inkling of my true purpose.

I glanced up at the constellations before climbing the steps. My feet were made of lead; the few paces up to the house felt like an eternity. There was no way out now. Images of Nick Berg and Daniel Pearl, two Americans who had met gruesome deaths at the hands of al-Qaeda, beheaded on video, flashed through my mind.

Fadia was escorted to the back, where the tribesmen's womenfolk were waiting. In this part of Yemen the sexes would never mix socially. Later she told me about the stoicism of the women, many of whose husbands had been killed in the cause of jihad. It was common for the widows to marry another jihadi – but hardly a recipe for domestic tranquillity.

The large unfurnished hall led to an even larger reception room, and the first thing I noticed was a line of weapons neatly propped against the wall – more AK-47s, vintage rifles, even a rocket-propelled-grenade launcher. This was a group ready to fight at a moment's notice, but its enemy was as likely a rival tribe as the Yemeni security services.

A dozen men were gathered around a big silver bowl laid on the floor and piled high with chicken and saffron rice. They were young; some had been village boys just a few years ago. And in the middle of them was Anwar al-Awlaki, slim, elegant, with those intelligent eyes that had already seduced so many restless souls in Europe and America. He rose with a warm smile and embraced me.

'*As salaam aleikum*,' he said with affection. He exuded natural authority, gesturing at the room as if to underline that he was master of this
place and these people.

Awlaki was wearing his trademark white robes, immaculate despite
the dust and heat, and the glasses that seemed to confirm his intellect.
I was struck by the contrast between the simple and uneducated country boys gathered here and this scholar of Islam, a philosopher turned
spiritual guide of jihad. After his greeting, the entire party rose to welcome me. They were all in awe of 'the Sheikh', whose magnetism was
undimmed despite his seclusion.

'Come, eat,' Awlaki said, his American accent tinged by several
years back in his Arab homeland.

He seemed delighted to have my company, a welcome interruption
to his intellectual solitude. But first he must see to his guest's needs.
After introducing me to the men sitting on the floor, Awlaki found me
space among them as the communal meal began. The guests were
devouring the chicken and rice with their hands – and for all my familiarity with Yemeni ways I could not help but ask for a spoon. This was
a source of huge amusement. I found that a couple of self-deprecating
remarks and my Arabic – honed over more than a decade visiting and
living in Yemen – set them at ease.

Scrutinizing Awlaki, I saw a detachment, a melancholy about him –
as if his isolation in Shabwa and the American-led pressure on him
were beginning to take a toll. It had been almost two years since his
release from prison, thanks to the intervention of his powerful family.
In the early months of 2008 he had left Sana'a and taken refuge in his
ancestral homeland. The motto of the Awalik tribe was reputed to be:
'We are the sparks of Hell; whoever interferes with us will be burned.'

In the year since I had last seen him, Awlaki's movements had
become more furtive – hence my odyssey for the sake of this brief
encounter. The Sheikh was constantly on the move from one safe
house to the next, occasionally retreating to mountain hideouts around
the fringes of the 'Empty Quarter' – the ocean of sand that stretched
into Saudi Arabia.

Despite the preacher's seclusion, he continued to deliver online sermons and communicate with followers through email accounts and

texts. His messages had grown more strident – perhaps because of his months in detention, where he was held in solitary confinement most of the time, perhaps because his reading of Islamist scholarship had led him to a more radical outlook. And maybe his banishment to the mountain wilderness had fed a growing hostility to the world.

When the meal was done, Awlaki stood and asked me to accompany him to a smaller room.

I studied his face.

'How are you?' I asked, at a loss for anything more substantial.

'I am here,' Awlaki said, with a hint of fatalism. 'But I miss my family, my wives, my children. I cannot go to Sana'a, and it is too dangerous for them to come here. The Americans want me dead. They are putting pressure on the government all the time.'

Drones wandered the skies, he said, but he was not scared of them.

'This is the path of the Prophets and the pious men: jihad.'

He said the 'brothers' were disappointed that I had not made it to Marib; they had heard much about me. As we talked it became clear that Awlaki felt little threat from the Yemeni government, which would rather box the al-Qaeda problem into Shabwa and hope it went away than try to tackle the tribal feuds that had allowed militants space to settle and organize.

Awlaki told me he wanted to see the end of the Saleh government, regarding it as secular and a pawn of America. With relish he described how a recent ambush of government forces had netted heavy weapons, including anti-tank rockets, and inflicted severe casualties. Perhaps they could be transferred to Islamists in Somalia, who were badly in need of such weapons, he mused.

The spiritual guide had become the quartermaster.

A few months earlier, Awlaki had sent a message to al-Shabaab, the militant Islamist group that had brought Sharia to much of Somalia. They were, he said, setting Muslims an example on how to fight back.

'The ballot has failed us, but the bullet has not,' Awlaki had written. 'If my circumstances had allowed, I would not have hesitated in joining you and being a soldier in your ranks.'

The man who had once condemned the 9/11 attacks as un-Islamic when he lived in America had recently written on his blog, 'I pray that

Allah destroys America and all its allies . . . We will implement the rule of Allah on Earth by the tip of the sword whether the masses like it or not.'

He had also begun to convey this message to Muslims living in the West, likening their situation to that faced by the Prophet Mohammed and his followers in pre-Islamic Mecca, where they were persecuted and forced to make the journey – the *hijra* – north to Medina.

And just weeks before my visit, writing from his Shabwa oupost, Awlaki had attacked the cooperation of Muslim countries with the US military, saying 'the blame should be placed on the soldier who is willing to follow orders . . . who sells his religion for a few dollars.'

It was an argument that would have a deep impact on an officer in the United States army, Major Nidal Hasan, who had already exchanged emails with Awlaki.

Awlaki told me that in jihad it was acceptable that civilians would suffer and die. The cause justified the means. I swiftly disagreed, knowing that my plain-spoken views were part of my appeal to Awlaki, who was prepared to argue the point based on his reading of the Koran and *Hadith*.

Several months before, a young man who had attached himself to Mehdar had travelled to a neighbouring province and killed himself and four South Korean tourists in a suicide attack.

'He is now in paradise,' one of his friends had told me over dinner. It wasn't clear to me whether Mehdar himself had any role in the attack or even condoned it – but the commitment of these fighters went far beyond the rhetorical.

I told Awlaki I supported attacks on military targets, but informed him flatly that I could not and would not help him obtain anything that would be used against civilians. I did not want to be scouring Europe for bomb-making equipment that would ultimately result in civilian deaths.

'So you disagree with the mujahideen?' Awlaki asked.

'On this, we will have to disagree.'

I also detected a more toxic animosity towards America, as if Awlaki felt he had been victimized there as a Muslim. He had been arrested in San Diego – though never charged – for soliciting prostitutes. The humiliation still gnawed at him: the way the FBI had 'let it be known' that Awlaki's personal conduct was sometimes not that expected of an imam, a nod and a wink aimed at besmirching his character.

The subject of women was very much on Awlaki's mind as we conversed into the small hours. Awlaki's self-imposed exile meant that he no longer had any personal contact with his two wives. One he had known since childhood; they had married in their teens. More recently he had taken a second wife, not yet twenty when they were married. But, he told me, he needed the company of a woman who understood and would share the sacrifices of a jihadi's life, someone who would be married to the cause.

'Perhaps you can look out for someone in the West, a white convert sister,' he suggested.

It was the second time he had broached marrying a woman from Europe and I knew he was now serious. It would not be easy and there would be risks. But I knew there were plenty of women who saw Awlaki as a gift from Allah.

There were other requests. He asked me 'to find brothers to work for the cause and to get money from Europe and some equipment'.

He also wanted me to recruit militants to come to Yemen for training and 'then return home – ready to wage jihad in Europe or America'. He did not specify the training – nor what they would be expected to do. But in our two-hour conversation I was left with the impression that Awlaki wanted to begin a campaign of terror attacks in Europe and the US.

The next morning, Awlaki was gone – whether for his own security or because of some meeting I was not told. Instead I spent some time with Abdullah Mehdar, the tribal leader who had met me the previous night. I could not help but admire this apparently honourable man, his unquestioning loyalty to Awlaki. He seemed to have no interest in attacking the West, but wanted Yemen to become an Islamic state with Sharia law. His commitment was so intense that he wept as one of the young fighters leading prayers spoke of the promise of paradise.

They might have a warped world-view, I thought, but these people were not hypocrites. Their loyalty was simple, intense.

I was in a hurry to get away: our flight was due to leave Sana'a for Europe the next evening, and who knew how long the journey back would take? Fadia emerged from the women's quarters and we prepared to leave.

As those forbidding gates swung open, I discovered our car had a puncture – which was perhaps not surprising after the high-speed drive through the mountains.

Abdullah ran out and helped me change the tyre. There were again tears in his eyes: he seemed to sense an incipient danger.

'If we don't meet again, we will see each other in paradise,' he said, the tears now running down his cheeks.

The mujahideen escorted us to the main road and bid us goodbye. We had left the cocoon.

I knew that in three Western capitals there were people waiting to hear every detail of the hours that I had spent with Anwar al-Awlaki. I needed to get to Sana'a – and then out of Yemen, fast.

CHAPTER TWO
GANGS, GIRLS, GOD

1976–1997

The path to my meeting with Anwar al-Awlaki in the mountains of Yemen was – to put it mildly – an unlikely one. I was born on the second day of 1976 in a windswept town on the coast of Denmark. Korsør, with its neat red-brick bungalows, could not be more different from the outer reaches of Yemen. At the edge of undulating farmland on Zeeland, it looks westwards across the grey waters of the Great Belt towards the island of Funen.

Korsør belies the conventional image of Scandinavian tolerance and progressiveness. It's a gritty, working-class town of 25,000 people, including a sprinkling of immigrants from Yugoslavia, Turkey and the Arab world.

My family was lower middle class – but we were not really a family at all. My alcoholic father left home when I was four. In fact he vanished. There were no weekend visits, no fishing trips or days out. My mother, Lisbeth, seemed to have a weakness for flawed men. She remarried, and my stepfather was a brooding, menacing presence, exploding into fits of violence. It might be the way I was holding my fork or just a word. There was no warning, just a fist delivered with force. My mother did not escape the violence, and a few times left home only to return when promised that things would change. They never did, yet she stayed with him for nearly twenty years.

'I'm not proud of the childhood you got,' she would say with sadness years later. 'I actually feel that it is my fault that you became what you did.'

As a child I roamed the shoreline, woods and fields around Korsør. I had plenty of time to myself and wanted to be away from home from dawn till dusk. I would build camps with friends, swing ropes over the frigid waters and drop in, yelling.

The few photographs I have from those days show a face full of uncertainty. There is a wariness about my eyes that brings back a host of unwelcome memories. But I also had a manic energy – energy that seemed to invite trouble.

I celebrated turning thirteen by attempting my first armed robbery with two friends, Benjamin and Junior. It was not a triumph of planning or execution. We chose a small store run by an elderly man renowned for his meanness and his cheap cigars. Clad in balaclavas, we waited in the gloom for the shop to close and then tried to burst in as the shopkeeper began to lock up. Benjamin brandished a .22 revolver that belonged to his father.

The man's strength belied his age as he tried to force the door shut. Perhaps it was the fear of losing the contents of the till that inspired his resistance. Somehow he managed to lock us out.

Humiliated, we turned to a takeaway restaurant nearby. This time I was sent in with the gun.

My heart sank the moment I pulled out the weapon. I recognized the young woman behind the counter, a family friend. I tried to sound older than I was, lowering my voice in a way that must have come across like a record playing at the wrong speed.

'This is a robbery.'

It did not sound convincing.

The woman peered over the counter, more puzzled than alarmed.

'Morten, is that you?'

I turned and fled. We took out our frustrations on an elderly woman in the street by snatching her bag. But she fell and broke her hip, and the police soon beat a path to my home.

It was the start of a spiral. In school I enjoyed history, music and the discussion of religion and cultures but was bored by the demands of classwork. None of my teachers really connected with me – or even seemed to notice me – and I would taunt them. They would respond by throwing chalkboard dusters at me – or by breaking down in tears – as the classroom was reduced to chaos.

I was sent to a 'special school' – one for wayward, hyperactive boys – which concentrated on sports and activities, and where students were confined to the classroom for just two hours a day. I was entrusted with a chainsaw in the woodlands and allowed to wear myself out on the football field. There was no shortage of adventure. The school organized trips abroad for the children they were trying to mould into citizens. The intention was well-meaning but the results were less rewarding. A visit to Tunisia triggered my love of travel and adventure, but we reduced the teachers to emotional wrecks, even stealing their clothes and selling them to some locals.

By fourteen I was an unstoppable force. An immigrant from the former Yugoslavia called Jalal and I unravelled water hoses in the school corridors and fired hundreds of gallons into every corner of the building. The school from which it was supposedly impossible to get expelled could take no more.

I had one last chance – at a high school near Korsør, where a maths teacher who saw my sports potential took me under his wing. I was soon playing junior football at a high level. There were mutterings that scouts for professional teams were checking my progress. But my school record, bulging with disciplinary notices, preceded me. One teacher in particular wanted me out of the school. When I was selected to play for a Danish schools' football team at a tournament in Germany, she took me to one side. Her eyes narrowed and with an expression of grim satisfaction she told me I would not be going because my academic record was not good enough. She knew that going to the tournament was the one thing I craved. I kicked a cup of coffee out of her hand.

It was the last thing I would ever do inside a school. At sixteen, just weeks before my final exams, my formal education was finished. But my street education was just beginning. I joined up with a group branded the 'Raiders' by local police because we roamed the town wearing Oakland Raiders baseball hats and baggy trousers.

The Raiders were mainly Palestinians, Turks and Iranian Muslims.

We made an unlikely group: the young Dane with red hair and thick biceps (looking like a Norse raider) and his Muslim friends. I gravitated to the Raiders because like many of the immigrant kids I felt like an outsider in Korsør, and I always identified with the underdog. We had few prospects and a lot of time on our hands; most of our energy was devoted to drinking as much cheap beer as we could afford and scoring with as many girls as would let us. My teenage Muslim friends wore their faith lightly. They drank and partied like the rest of us. They would defend Islam in the face of a growing anti-Muslim mood, but did not feel bound by its more demanding restrictions.

Their families had come to settle in Denmark – escaping violence or poverty in their homelands. By 1990, Denmark, like other Scandinavian countries, had a sizeable immigrant population. It had granted refugee or guest-worker status to thousands of families from Turkey, Yugoslavia, Iran and Pakistan. In the first dozen years of my life, Denmark's immigrant population from 'non-Western' countries more than doubled. The influx had begun to test Denmark's reputation as a liberal and progressive society. Skinhead gangs would descend on Korsør with sticks and bats but the Raiders were ready for them. I was never far from the action and found the rush addictive.

It helped that I had a talent for boxing and spent plenty of time in the gym. One of Korsør's few claims to fame was that it had been the point of departure for Viking raids on England a millennium ago. So it seemed appropriate that one of its more recent sons was Denmark's best-known boxer, Brian Nielsen, who would fight Evander Holyfield and Mike Tyson.

Nielsen was involved with a thriving amateur boxing club in Korsør, where the youth programme was run by a professional boxer named Mark Hulstrøm. A heavyweight in his late twenties, Hulstrøm was still fighting. Built like an ox, balding with a goatee, he was a man of few emotions. But he was excited by my potential as a young welterweight. I was quick on my feet, with a fast jab, a solid right-hook and a strong jaw. And I loved the physical exertion. Boxing – as well as jujitsu – was a release for the anger I felt, towards my brutal stepfather and against every attempt to make me conform.

I went to the gym – an anonymous grey building on the edge of Korsør – for three years. One day, soon after my sixteenth birthday, Mark took me aside.

'You have real class,' he said – his dark-brown eyes gleaming. 'You could make the Olympic squad, even turn pro.'

Mark visited my mother to explain why I should get more boxing training. Young enough to remember how chaotic a teenager's life could be, he was also old enough to be a figure of authority. He was as close to a surrogate father as I would get.

My talent took me to tournaments in Czechoslovakia and Holland. Denmark's national coach came to watch me and I was selected for the national school sports squad. The Korsør club had provided several of Denmark's Olympic boxers; there seemed every possibility that I could join that elite.

For a while I dreamt of making it as a boxer. But, to Hulstrøm's disappointment, the discipline demanded was beyond me and I spent as much time using my boxing training in brawls as I did in the ring.

My mother, the essence of lower-middle-class Danish propriety, had long given up on me, and by the age of sixteen I was rarely at home. Rather than face her disapproving looks I bunked down at the homes of my Raider friends. I was never quite sure where I would lay my head the next night. Frequently it was long after midnight, because by now I had discovered the down-at-heel pubs and clubs of Korsør.

Shortly before my seventeenth birthday, there was a big street festival in Korsør. A thug confronted me and accused me of trying to take his girlfriend. With one blow I floored him, knocking him nearly unconscious. It would prove a busy weekend. Another girl's boyfriend threatened me with a carving knife. With the blade against my throat, my welterweight training kicked in. I stepped back quickly and delivered a right-hook. Two punches; two knockouts. Maybe the Olympics were not such a pipedream after all.

On weekdays I would visit Hulstrøm's boxing club. At weekends the action would continue, but without gloves. I was rarely hurt, thanks to my speed and a sense of when I was about to be hit. To combine partying, drinking and fighting was far more fun than nine minutes in the ring. And I could look after my friends whenever racist baiting erupted at the clubs. 'Paki', 'black pig' . . . the insults would fly. And I would step forward and put the assailant on the deck with a couple of punches.

Hulstrøm was a man of many parts. Beside the boxing club, he ran a Korsør disco called Underground. I could be found there several nights a week, even though my musical tastes were more Metallica and death metal than Abba. It was at Underground that I met my first love – a slim, red-haired girl called Vibeke.

Vibeke was a postal worker but her passion was dance and she took ballet lessons in Copenhagen with the sort of dedication that I lacked. She was a calming influence. I found work as an apprentice in a furniture workshop, and with time Vibeke might have tamed my wilder side.

But trouble seemed to follow me. One evening, after plenty of beer, I made out with another girl at a Korsør youth club. Unfortunately her boyfriend heard about our connection. He threatened me with a Danish army assault rifle and was subsequently picked up by the police. Incredibly, they released him without charge after a few hours. Perhaps they reasoned that such a threat was understandable if the target was Morten Storm.

I decided to take matters into my own hands. The boyfriend had supposedly turned up at a party in a grim apartment block on the outskirts of Korsør. When I arrived with three friends the host insisted he had not been there. Convinced he was lying, we beat him with pots and pans we found in the kitchen.

I never found the boyfriend, but the Korsør police found me. I was convicted of aggravated assault and sentenced to four months in a juvenile remand centre.

My prospects were not exactly blossoming. I had been kicked out of five schools and my mother had washed her hands of me. I also had a criminal record. The chances of my choosing the 'straight and narrow' were diminishing by the day. And far from leading me away from crime, my apprenticeship inside the remand centre made me harder.

My eighteenth birthday – spent in jail – offered little to celebrate. But at least when I came out I was eligible to drive, and that proved a passport to easy money. Mark Hulstrøm was supplementing his income from the gym with a thriving business smuggling cigarettes from Poland through Germany and into Denmark. We called it the 'Nicotine Triangle'.

By the mid-1990s cigarette smuggling had become the third-largest illegal business in Germany behind drugs and gambling. The business model was simple. Low taxes and no custom duty meant that a carton of cigarettes in Poland was one third the price of a carton in Germany or Denmark.

Our cover story was that we were buying spare car parts in Germany, where they were cheaper, and bringing them to Denmark. Hulstrøm saw me as a loyal, fearless operator. I spoke some German and was trusted to exchange currencies. We used hired cars – to minimize losses in case the driver was stopped and the vehicle impounded. The cars picked up a few dents – but it was a lucrative circuit.

The distribution centre was a remote farmhouse near the Polish border. At the gates of the farm, an unkempt guard who smelt of sour cabbage would wave me in. I would place a pile of Deutschmarks on the table, and a few minutes later an entire toilet would be moved to one side, revealing a cellar crammed with cartons of cigarettes.

On the drive back, I would look out for foreigners – preferably dark-skinned ones – approaching the Danish border and then follow them. The Danish border police were usually far more interested in questioning them and examining their passports than stopping a young Dane in a van. Occasionally I would cross from Germany into Denmark on tracks or unmarked roads. It was tradecraft that would prove useful when I moved on.

Sometimes I was making the trip two or three times a week and earning the equivalent of $1,000 each time. Not only was the money good: I loved feeling like an apprentice gangster, alert for the police, hiding the contraband, keeping my nerve at border crossings, handling large piles of crisp banknotes.

Just months after emerging from a remand centre penniless and homeless, I had wads of cash, wore smart clothes and was living the high life. Mark Hulstrøm entrusted me with the keys to Underground – now frequented by escorts from Copenhagen who had smelt the money. For the first time in my life I felt important, part of something big. I may have given up making it as a boxer, but I still enjoyed sparring and wanted to stay in shape. I continued to train in Hulstrøm's gym, and as I bulked up I moved into the light-heavyweight bracket.

My biological father had moved across the Great Belt to Nyborg. I had not seen him in well over a decade but now I was an adult and felt obliged to try to reconnect with him, even if not wildly enthusiastic about what would at best be an awkward encounter. My cousin Lars agreed to come with me and we took the ferry one slate-grey morning from Korsør across to Nyborg.

My apprehension was justified. My father was gruff and unrepentant about abandoning me and my mother. His breath, at midday, reeked of alcohol. We left him after less than an hour; I felt deeply depressed and angry.

Lars and I dropped by a bar in Nyborg to recover. A mistake. A drunk man disrupted our game of pool and then tried to pick a fight. I did my best to ignore him, but when he shaped up to strike me, I responded with a sharp upper cut. The bartender said he was calling the police and closing the place, and Lars and I left. We split up but Lars was arrested almost immediately, and so was I soon after returning to Korsør.

Convicted of assault, I was sentenced to my second spell behind bars – this time six months in Helsingør. The fact that I was provoked made no difference. By now I had what they call 'form' – a record of violence. From jail I wrote a confession to Vibeke. This was the person I was, I wrote, suggesting trouble followed me like a dog. But we could still make a life together, I added. Casting us as American gangsters, I imagined Vibeke as my 'Bonnie' and signed my letters 'Your Clyde'.

I could not see much alternative to a life of crime, with jail time an occupational hazard and violence never far away. I rarely derived pleasure from hitting anyone; none of my friends would have ever called me vicious. But I was loyal to a fault and would defend others and myself if threatened. I was not the sort who would walk away from a confrontation.

I did have one score to settle, one that had been a long time waiting.

At a family birthday party soon after my release from jail in April

1995, tensions flared between my mother and stepfather. He had a venomous tongue and knew how to wound her. I saw tears well in her eyes. I warned him to back off but the sniping continued. Without thinking, I stepped forward and struck him hard in the face. He looked stunned, as if suddenly realizing the boy he had so long abused was now a man – and much stronger than him. His glasses shattered and he fell backwards across a table. I watched him go, a tablecloth wrapping itself like a shroud around him.

There was stunned silence. My mother looked at me with a mixture of horror and gratitude; it was perhaps the strangest expression I have ever seen. I walked out of the hall, my knuckles throbbing but my eyes gleaming with pride.

It wasn't easy to find work after my release from prison. I had two convictions, no qualifications, few skills – but I also had some useful contacts. During my time inside I had met a senior member of the Bandidos biker gang, Michael Rosenvold. I think he liked me because I was the only inmate who wasn't scared of him.

Denmark had thriving motorbike gangs, and the Bandidos were locked in a violent struggle with the Hell's Angels. The Bandido motto was: 'We are the people our parents warned us about.' I would surely fit in perfectly.

Across Scandinavia, the 'Great Nordic Biker War' had been raging for more than a year. At least ten people had been murdered and many more seriously injured. In Sweden an anti-tank rocket was fired at a Hell's Angels clubhouse. The conflict was fuelled by the trade in drugs coming from southern Europe.

Rosenvold introduced me to other gang members as 'Denmark's youngest psychopath'. It was meant in jest but I certainly cut a formidable figure, tall with broad shoulders and thick biceps. I quickly warmed to the camaraderie, the supply of drugs and girls. By then I had got my first tattoo, on my right bicep: 'STORM'. It did not take me long to become accepted: reliable in a fight, ready to party. The Bandidos were the Raiders on steroids.

Despite my time inside, Vibeke had stuck with me. In a town where thrills were few and far between, she found my links to the underworld exciting and liked how I mimicked the life of a high-roller. Even so she was taken aback by some aspects of the lifestyle. At one party in Korsør she turned up in a black turtleneck with her hair neatly tied back. Most Bandidos women were pneumatic (if not natural) blondes, who wore minimalist outfits of tiger and leopard prints.

When Vibeke found a sports bag full of guns, explosives, hashish and speed that I had hidden under her bed, she erupted in anger. She threw the bag out of the window and yelled at me to get out of her apartment and never come back.

In March 1996, Hell's Angels gang members opened fire on a group of Bandidos outside Copenhagen airport with machine guns and other weapons, killing one.

Rosenvold called me.

'I want you to organize a group in Korsør, people we can rely on, who can hold territory,' he said. 'And I'm going to need you as one of the guys around me. I'm a target now.'

At twenty I was the youngest chapter leader for the Bandidos in Denmark. It was like I had found a family. Loyalty to the cause was everything.

For the next few months I was Rosenvold's bodyguard and we 'held' Korsør and its surroundings. There were street battles, nightclub brawls. An evening would not be complete without a fight and we knew how to pick them, whether the Angels were down the street or nowhere to be seen.

To begin with, I relished the adrenalin rush and the sense of importance. But as 1996 drew to a close, I worried that the lifestyle was making me an addict – to a cycle of drugs, gratuitous violence and hardcore partying. There was no space left for relationships, for peace of mind.

Two episodes crystallized my unease. On a freezing night shortly before New Year's Eve, a fight broke out between two big guys and some Bandidos at a Korsør dive. It was normal enough. But this time a bouncer intervened, dragged one of the Bandidos out on to the street and pummelled him. We were not about to let it pass.

The next morning, along with another member of the gang, I paid a visit to the bouncer. The icy grey was giving way to darker gloom when we arrived. I had a baseball bat hidden in my jacket. We donned balaclavas and knocked at his door, pushing him to the floor as he answered. Wielding the bat I swung it at his hips and knees.

In the days after the beating I couldn't get the sound of his moaning out of my head. I could still hear the crack of his knee fracturing and see his limp broken arm. I began to feel ashamed. Perhaps Rosenvold was right and I was a psychopath.

Occasionally I would look at other young men turning twenty-one, studying for a degree, starting a job, owning a car, going steady. I knew I couldn't handle routine, but I was beginning to worry that the constant fixes of violence and drugs could kill me. And that made me start questioning the purpose of my life and what might come after it. Deep down I didn't like the person I was turning into. Was I becoming an even more vicious version of my stepfather?

The second thing to feed my doubts was a meeting in one of Korsør's clubs with a twenty-year-old woman called Samar. After being evicted by Vibeke I badly needed a lover. I soon imagined a relationship with Samar, and not only because she had the exotic looks of a gypsy with wild, dark eyes, full lips and raven-dark hair, and a presence that I found irresistible.

A Palestinian-Christian, Samar came from a large immigrant family. Her mother soon treated me as a son. I felt wanted, and not just because I could tip the balance in a brawl.

It wasn't long before I proposed, and her family threw an engagement party. It began as a polite affair at a local hall until some Bandidos turned up. Samar's grandmother looked on as the guys leapt about to Arabic pop songs in their leather jackets and snorted lines of coke among the couscous and baklava.

Samar's family remained fond of me. The possibility of having her as a partner made me reconsider the Bandidos. Exhaustion had seeped into my soul. For all the highs my life in the gang had become meaningless.

We spent the night of my twenty-first birthday together, and I was happy: a feeling so rare that it almost shocked me. I was frightened of losing it. In the following weeks, when I wasn't with Samar, I would lie awake at night. I imagined getting into another fight that would land me behind bars again, or overdosing or getting stabbed. There were plenty of ways to be taken out of circulation. And then Samar would be gone.

On an unusually bright morning a few weeks after my birthday, I found myself in the town's library. I felt empty and needed sanctuary.

The library, a two-storey building of corrugated steel and concrete, was close to the water's edge. That morning it provided warmth from the chill breeze that found every corner of Korsør. For a while I stared at the choppy waters and the span of the Great Belt Bridge. I browsed aimlessly among the shelves, vaguely aware of the chatter from the children's section, but gravitated towards history and religion, subjects that had always fascinated me despite my wasted school days.

I had never felt religious – I had even been expelled from confirmation classes. The priest had told my mother that I was too much of a troublemaker, even for God. But I thought there must be some sort of afterlife. I had had some contact with Islam through my immigrant friends – Palestinians, Iranians and Turks – and had always envied the strength of their families, the way they always had dinner together, the bonds that united them while facing poverty and discrimination.

Perhaps that was why I sat down in an alcove with a book about the life of the Prophet Mohammed. Within minutes I was so absorbed in the story that the world outside evaporated.

The book laid out the tenets of Islam and the life of its founder with seductive simplicity. Mohammed's father had died before he was born. As his mother, Aminah, gazed at her first son, she heard a voice. 'The best of mankind has been born, so name him Mohammed.'

She had sent him into the desert to learn self-reliance and to master Arabic as spoken by the Bedouin. But Aminah had died when Mohammed was just seven, and he was passed into the care first of his grandfather and then of his uncle.

What immediately appealed about his life was its dignity and simplicity. As a young man, Mohammed would be called 'al-Saadiq' (the Truthful One) and 'al-Amin' (the Trustworthy One). He had granted freedom to a slave who had been given to him and declared him his own son.

I learned Mohammed was a successful trader who travelled through Arabia and as far as Syria. But he was also a deeply spiritual man, and in his thirties he would retreat to meditate in a cave on Mount Hira near Mecca. It was there that the Archangel Gabriel visited him and declared he was God's messenger.

'Proclaim in the name of your Lord who created! / Created man from a clot of blood.'

As the sun slanted across the Scandinavian sky, I became immersed in the events of the seventh century. I imagined Mohammed taking refuge in a cave as his enemies, the Quraish of Mecca, searched for him. By a divine miracle, it was said, a spider had spun its web over the mouth of the cave and a bird had laid eggs nearby, so the place looked undisturbed and was not searched. The episode was recounted in the Koran. 'When Disbelievers drove him out, he had no more than one companion; they were two in the cave and he said to his companion, "Have no fear, (for) Allah is with us."'

I did not notice the approach of dusk. Mohammed's story was one of battling the odds, as he sought to propagate Islam in the face of persecution. Here was a man – with his small band of followers – prepared to fight for his beliefs. In the words of the Koran:

'Permission to fight is granted to those against whom war is made, because they have been wronged, and God indeed has the power to help them. They are those who have been driven out of their homes unjustly only because they affirmed: Our Lord is God.'

Fighting for a cause appealed to me; it brought a sense of solidarity and loyalty.

I pictured the migration from Mecca to Medina, the desert battles that Mohammed and his few hundred followers waged and his triumphant return to the holy city, where he showed clemency to the Quraish despite their many attempts to stifle the young religion.

I felt I could relate to Mohammed's struggles as a man better than to some vague deity with a beard. As Allah's messenger he seemed a more plausible historical figure than Jesus. It seemed ludicrous to me that God should have a son. I was also struck that Mohammed's words provided for every aspect of life, from marriage to conflict to obligation. Good intentions were recognized and rewarded. The book cited the Prophet: 'Certainly, Allah does not look at your shapes [appearance] or wealth. But He only looks at your hearts and deeds.'

Here was a prescription that was both merciful and compassionate and offered absolution for sins. A pathway to a more fulfilling life. Islam could help me rein in my instincts and gain some self-discipline.

I was still reading when a librarian approached me to announce that the library was about to close. I had been sitting in that same alcove for six hours and had read some 300 pages about the life of the Prophet.

The chill wind took my breath away as I stepped out of the library into the cobblestoned streets. Nearby the beacon of a lighthouse rotated. After being steeped in the Arabian desert and consumed by divine revelations, I found it disorientating to be back in the Scandinavian winter. But my mind and my soul were still far away.

CHAPTER THREE
THE CONVERT

Early 1997–Summer 1997

I was far from the only young man in Europe or America at the end of the twentieth century to find meaning in a different way of life and code of conduct, to find faith and fellowship where there had been none.

In the weeks after reading about Mohammed I engaged several of my Muslim friends in debates about Islam, and I read more about the religion and its founding generations. I borrowed another of the library's few books on Islam and bought a copy of the Koran. At first I found it difficult to understand the Holy Book and felt overwhelmed by the demands of Islamic culture. But I was encouraged by a Turkish friend, Ymit, who was thrilled that for once a Dane wanted to embrace rather than sneer at his religion.

Ymit had been one of the 'Raiders' and we had remained friends despite my encounters with the Danish criminal-justice system and graduation to the Bandidos. He had a sharp wit and was intelligent, genuinely interested in the world beyond Korsør. He was knowledge-able about Islam and took it seriously, even if he was also familiar with alcohol and cocaine. Ymit told me that Mohammed's illiteracy was a blessing and made the faith purer.

'It meant that everything he said was a revelation from God, untainted by man. It meant the Koran was a miracle.'

'But if you are a real Muslim, Ymit, how come you drink and do drugs like me?'

'Because I can still repent if I go to Friday prayers and seek forgiveness for my sins.'

Others tried to dissuade me. A Christian Lebanese friend called Milad, who owned a small grocery across from the library, was stunned.

Morten Storm – biker, boozer and boxer – had found religion, and the wrong religion at that.

'Why do you want to follow that ignorant pervert? Mohammed was a fool, a Bedouin who could not read or write.'

'At least he was a human being, someone who really existed and received messages from God. No one pretended he was the Son of God,' I shot back.

A couple of weeks after my epiphany in Korsør library, Ymit asked me to come to the mosque in a nearby town for Friday prayers. The building was not what I expected – there was no golden dome, nor a minaret from which the muezzin would call the faithful. It was a nondescript bungalow in a side street. But the intensity of the congregation and the warmth of their welcome to me, a stranger, a pale European, was moving.

The imam was an elderly man with watery eyes and a thick, powder-white beard. He spoke in a low soft voice that trailed into a whisper as he asked me about the Prophets and the Pillars of Islam. He had little Danish and Ymit translated for me. Did I accept the Five Pillars of Islam – that there is no God but God and Mohammed is His messenger, performing prayer, paying the *Zakat* (charity to the poor), fasting in the month of Ramadan and performing *Hajj* (the pilgrimage to Mecca)?

Did I accept that Jesus was not the Son of God?

I answered yes, even though the finer points of theology and doctrine were beyond my understanding.

At the end of this series of questions, I had to recite the Declaration of Faith, the *shahada*.

'There is no God but God, and Mohammed is the messenger of God.'

There was a pause. And then the imam said, 'You are now a Muslim. Your sins are forgiven.'

Ymit translated and then embraced me.

'Now you are truly my brother,' he said, his eyes glistening. 'But you are not really a convert, more a revert. In Islam, we believe that every person is born a Muslim because we are all created by God and there is only one God.

'You should be circumcised,' he said with a grin, 'but it's not compulsory. It's more important that you now take a Muslim name.'

My life had undergone a momentous change. It was uplifting; I had been purged. Guilt evaporated, a fresh start beckoned.

'I think you should be "Murad",' Ymit said. 'It means "goal" or "achievement".'

It seemed appropriate.

I did not become a strictly observant Muslim immediately. In fact, my friends had an unconventional way of celebrating. We converged on an apartment to consume several six-packs of beer. It was my first communion – Korsør style. I could always repent later, they laughed.

To begin with, the forgiving of sins, absolution through prayer, was a large part of Islam's appeal to me. I soon learned and would cite a saying of the Prophet:

'Suppose there is a river that flows in front of your house and you take a wash five times in it. Then would there remain any dirt and filth on you after that? Performing daily prayers five times a day is similar to that which washes away sins.'

The Koran and the sayings attributed to the Prophet were especially generous to the dedicated 'revert' who took his religion seriously. In the words of one such saying – or *hadith*: 'If a servant accepts Islam and completes his Islam, Allah will record for him every good deed that he performed before [adopting Islam]; and will erase for him every evil deed that he did before.'

I did not leave the Bandidos immediately and even took several members along with me to the mosque. This did not go down well with senior members of the gang, who called me to a meeting to tell me to keep my beliefs to myself.

Samar, even though she was from a Christian family, was more accepting. She thought my conversion showed a maturity that was a welcome departure from my gang lifestyle. She did not seem to harbour any anti-Muslim feelings and we continued to make plans together.

It was – of all people – the Korsør police who inadvertently pushed me towards a much stricter adherence to my new religion.

On a glorious June evening, days after the summer solstice and with the sun still high in the sky, I joined some friends at a Kurdish restaurant in Korsør to watch the world heavyweight title fight – the bizarre bout in Las Vegas between Mike Tyson and Evander Holyfield.

A police car passed and then came back to the restaurant. Two officers got out.

'Morten Storm,' one said, with a look of smugness, 'you are under arrest in connection with the attempted robbery of a bank.'

I had nothing to do with the break-in and thought they were just trying to annoy me. Expecting that I would be back at the restaurant in a matter of minutes, I shouted to my friends: 'Keep the beers cold.'

I was wrong. I never tasted the beer and never saw Tyson bite off part of Holyfield's ear.

Instead I spent the night in a police waiting room, studying the bare walls and reflecting on my situation. Once again, just as I seemed to be getting ahead, sensing progress and even stability, my past and my reputation had pulled me back.

It's never going to end, I thought. They're just going to keep coming after me. So long as I am in Korsør I'll be a marked man, rotating between life in a gang on the outside to life in a much worse gang inside. I don't want to spend half my life in prison.

The next morning, waiting for yet another court appearance, I said to myself, very simply: 'It's over.'

It was time to change my life, not just its trappings, before I was dragged into a never-ending cycle of court appearances, jail sentences and attempts at rehabilitation. I was remanded in custody for ten days. I knew several Bandidos who had been involved in the bank job but refused to give names. Loyalty still mattered. But my brief stay in Køge prison was a landmark because it reinforced the values and self-discipline I was beginning to learn as a new Muslim.

My first act was symbolic. I declared myself a Muslim to the prison authorities and refused to eat pork. Then I met a fellow convert, Suleiman, who had a profound and immediate impact on me. Suleiman, with his shaven head, looked like Bruce Willis. He was inside on weapons charges, but that did not prevent him from lecturing me about Islam and membership of the Bandidos being irreconcilable.

'You have to choose,' he said one afternoon as we wandered through the exercise yard. 'Allah cannot accept you as a true Muslim if you are going to drink and do drugs and go through your life without good intentions. The heart is the sanctuary of Allah; so do not allow anyone to dwell therein except Allah.'

Suleiman's words rang true. It was time to put the Bandidos behind me. Islam was already beginning to change me, not as a weekly or even daily rite but as a belief system that would influence and soon dictate my every action.

A Palestinian friend had given me a key ring with 'Allah' inscribed on it; I treasured it. I began keeping the Koran in the highest place in the room, out of respect.

Another inmate I met in Køge was a Palestinian Dane named Mustapha Darwich Ramadan. His trade was armed robbery in the cause of jihad. He was in solitary confinement and I could hear him praying. I managed to slip him some fruit and we were able to talk briefly. He would later resurface in one of the most brutal videos to emerge in Iraq.

No charges were brought against me over the robbery and I walked out of Køge determined to leave Denmark as soon as possible – and to avoid Bandidos members. Some could not accept that I had left the gang and even suspected that I was planning to join the Hell's Angels. I felt like I was on the run; I kept a loaded gun on me at all times, moving from place to place.

Suleiman was released from jail soon after. His wife's family were Pakistanis and had settled in central England. He was planning to join them – and his old van represented my escape route to a new life.

On an overcast early summer day we set off for Calais and then crossed the English Channel. The white cliffs of Dover – more a dirty eggshell – invited me towards a new adventure. I was leaving behind some angry bikers and a chaotic love life. I had discovered that Samar, whose sex drive was apparently insatiable, had been less than angelic while I was behind bars. I had even begun seeing Vibeke again but had soon realized that I wanted Samar back. She had visited me during my brief stay in Køge jail and we had talked about Islam. She even said that she was ready to become a Muslim.

A job, somewhere to live, new horizons – and then I would call her. She had promised she would join me.

My new home was in Milton Keynes in England. A town created on an architect's master plan, it was a bland collection of housing estates surrounded by countryside. Suleiman's in-laws helped me find accommodation and a warehouse job. For the first time in my life – guided by Islam – I saved a little money. I hoped Samar would see that I'd turned a corner and come to live with me.

Every day Suleiman prodded me towards being a conscientious Muslim. I was a project; he was the proselytizer. He encouraged me to pray five times a day and wear an Islamic cap.

'The companions of the Prophet Mohammed were never seen without their heads covered,' he explained to me one day as we drove to one of the mosques that were popping up across the English Midlands.

Soon I was praying on my own. I had the zeal of a convert, soaking up the customs and prescriptions of Islam. I felt a sense of stability I had never had before.

Several weeks after arriving I plucked up the courage to call Samar and ask her to come over. I hoped I could sell my new setting, a fresh start.

I was not normally given to nerves, but as I jammed pound coins into a public phone I realized my palms were sweating and my stomach turning.

After a few tones she picked up.

'Darling, it's Murad, er, Morten. How are you?'

She was subdued. I pressed on.

'I have a good job. I'm making some money. And I've got a decent place to live. Milton Keynes isn't very exciting, but it's not far from London.'

I sounded like a telemarketer. There was silence at the other end. I soldiered on.

'I have enough to plan a good wedding for us, and a honeymoon. I know people here who can help organize a proper Muslim wedding ceremony.'

She cut me off and poured pure venom down the line.

'Fuck you and fuck Islam. I don't want to live in England and I don't want to live with you.'

I reeled.

'Samar . . .'

'Don't call me again.' The line went dead.

I stared through the grimy glass panes. Without any explanation the engagement was over – for good. I stumbled into the street. My first attempt to build something with someone had crumbled to dust. I was on my own.

There was a call from across the street.

'*As salaam aleikum.*'

A middle-aged Pakistani recognized me as a fellow Muslim, thanks to my cap. His name was G. M. Butt and he owned a kiosk near a cinema complex called The Point.

We had exchanged greetings on my occasional visits to his little shop. He was a man of good intentions, who saw pleasing Allah as one of his duties on earth.

I told him a bit about the phone call. He was sympathetic.

'Brother! Come and help me and I will try to help you. I am not the young man I used to be – I need help with all the boxes and deliveries.'

So my fianceé had rejected me because of my religion, but a man who scarcely knew me had embraced me for it.

G.M. was a good man. Soon I told him how I cried at night, my longing for Samar. One day I asked him for a day off so that I could go to London and pray.

London's most famous mosque is on the edge of Regent's Park, set among the rose gardens and graceful Edwardian terraces. Since its construction in the 1970s, largely with Saudi money, it has somehow blended into this leafy corner of London. The gold of its dome flickers through the plane trees; the call to prayer wafts across the traffic.

I went to the mosque's bookshop. Perhaps if I sent Samar some books about Islam she would understand better. The attendant directed me towards the office, or *dawa*, where a tall and venerable Saudi with dark skin and a long salt-and-pepper beard greeted me.

'*Masha'Allah* [God has willed it],' he exclaimed, delighted that a European convert had come to his mosque.

He introduced himself as Mahmud al-Tayyib.

'Where are you from?' he asked.

I told him that I had recently arrived from Denmark and had converted to Islam just a few months earlier.

'Are you married?'

I launched into my sad tale about Samar, how she had promised to join me, my plans for a Muslim wedding.

Tayyib was sympathetic. In his gentle way he was also persuasive. Like Suleiman he had a passion for conveying his faith. He was a man of deep learning.

'Would you like to study Islam? Why not travel to a Muslim country?'

It was a soft but earnest sell.

'I can get you to Yemen. It's the easiest Muslim country to get a visa to study – do you have a passport?'

I did. But I had never heard of Yemen. And I had little notion of what Tayyib regarded as the authentic expression of Islam. He was one of the many well-funded envoys sent around the world by wealthy Saudi interests to bring Muslims into the Wahhabi fold. Ever since the Islamic Revolution in Iran, the Saudis had spent lavishly promoting their 'authentic' brand of Islam in the face of the challenge posed by Ayatollah Khomeini. To the puritanical Wahhabis – Sunni fundamentalists – the Shia were heretics guilty of polluting Islam.

Of this battle for the soul of Islam, being waged in mosques around the world, I knew little. But I was about to become one of its foot soldiers.

'There is a seminary in Yemen. It is remote and it is primitive by European standards,' Tayyib continued. 'But it is pure. Many foreigners seeking truth in Islam go there. It is called Dammaj. I can organize a plane ticket for you and people to look after you when you arrive.'

His eyes were sparkling.

'The imam at Dammaj is a great scholar, Sheikh Muqbil. He is returning Yemen to the true path of the Sunnah. But you should know that the day is long and you will have to get a grasp of Arabic.'

I was excited. I loved to travel and the thought of visiting Arabia had been beyond my wildest imagination. Now I was being offered a return ticket, a place to stay and a chance to become immersed in my new faith.

I accepted Tayyib's offer and said it would take me a couple of weeks to wrap up my affairs in England. He was delighted.

'But don't become a Sufi or a Shia,' he said with a wry grin, 'and don't shave any more.'

CHAPTER FOUR
ARABIA

Late Summer 1997–Summer 1998

For a 21-year-old Dane, the searing heat of Sana'a was an assault on the senses. Before I flew into Yemen's capital in the late summer of 1997 I had no sense of my destination. I had vaguely imagined that Sana'a was actually in Oman, where Western oil companies were established and a moderate Sultan ruled a peaceful kingdom. I could not have been more wrong.

I was shocked by the ramshackle building that passed for Yemen's welcome to the world. Flies drifted in the arrivals hall as wiry Yemeni men jostled for position at passport control.

Tayyib had organized for me to be picked up. I was greeted by a couple of young men of Somali background (a lot of Somalis had crossed the Gulf of Aden to settle in Yemen). I was overwhelmed by the noise and chaos, the mountains rising above the city.

Sana'a filled the senses: the medieval buildings of mud brick in Sana'a's old quarter decorated like outsize marzipan confections, the air full of dust but also of the scent of herbs and spices, the shabby appearance of the men, the women shrouded in black, the call of the muezzin and the guttural Arabic. I was taken aback at the sight of men holding hands. Above all I was amazed by the Kalashnikovs; people even carried them while visiting the supermarket.

My first two weeks were spent in a poor district of Sana'a, living in a house without furniture, sitting cross-legged on the floor, eating Somali food. It was a halfway house as well as a half-built house. Tayyib had warned me that it might take some time to reach Dammaj, which was in a valley some 100 miles north from Sana'a. Depending on the political climate, the Yemeni government frequently put up roadblocks to prevent foreigners from travelling there, concerned that it was becoming a magnet for militants.

Within days I realized that Yemen was the destination of choice for a growing number of Western converts to Islam – including several Americans in search of what they imagined was the authentic (and austere) Salafi interpretation of Islam. Among those I encountered in Sana'a was a Vietnam veteran close to the firebrand preacher Louis Farrakhan. There were also British, French and Canadian converts.

Salafism was capturing the imagination of a generation of Muslims and converts. It derived from the Arabic *'al-salaaf al-salih'* – meaning the pious forefathers, the first three generations of Muslims. As such, it represented a return to the pure and original core of Islam, free of interpretation or revisionism. But Salafism was far from coherent; its adherents derived different messages from those forefathers. Some eschewed politics and loathed the Muslim Brotherhood for its political activism; only God could legislate through the application of Sharia law. Others reviled 'non-believers' and non-Salafi Muslims (especially the Shia), and disavowed rulers who allied themselves with the hated West.

I was not prepared for this ferment among Muslims. In my naivety I had imagined a religion whose followers were united in obedience to Allah. The books I had read in Denmark said nothing of the schisms and hatreds that ran through Islam like faultlines. And I was not familiar with the one concept that would come to dominate the next decade of my life: jihad.

Getting to Dammaj would be the first trial of my faith and dedication. I decided to travel with one of the Americans I had met – Rashid Barbi, an African-American convert from North Carolina – and a Tunisian.

After an hour in a battered Peugeot, Rashid, the Tunisian and I – along with a Yemeni guide – had to climb out to avoid a military checkpoint. This was an area of tribal rivalries and frequent clashes between Sunni and Shi'ite groups.

We began walking through the mountains in the blazing sun, but were ill-prepared. We had no water and no protection, either from the heat or later from the cold as night fell. I was wearing cheap sandals and soon my feet were a forest of blisters.

At dusk we stopped to pray at the edge of a cliff, but it was too dark to make any further progress. A burst of monsoon rain further dampened our spirits. I began to feel feverish and more than once I asked myself what on earth I had done. I had left Milton Keynes just two weeks ago, but its bland comforts suddenly seemed very appealing.

It would be a night and half a day before we finally traipsed into the valley of mud houses and date-palm trees, which were overlooked by a massive escarpment. The whitewashed-brick complex of the Dammaj Institute was snuggled into an oasis of greenery. The chugging of diesel water-pumps in the surrounding fields was the only sound in the torpid afternoon heat.

Sheikh Muqbil thought our little group must have been arrested and was relieved to hear of our arrival. He approached us with a whole chicken, exclaiming that the man from 'Benimark' had finally made it. He had little sense of European geography. Rashid and I devoured the food while the Sheikh and his bodyguards laughed at our sunburned and bedraggled appearance.

I was taken aback by the Sheikh's appearance; it was the first time I had seen a man with a long, straggly hennaed beard, a custom among distinguished preachers and tribal figures in Yemen.[2]

---

2 Sheikh Muqbil bin Haadi was a local preacher from the Wadi'a tribe who had studied for two decades in Saudi Arabia before being imprisoned and then expelled from the country. He had been suspected of links to the jihadist group that had briefly and violently occupied the Grand Mosque in Mecca in 1979. Despite his persistent criticism of the relatively secularist government of President Ali Abdullah Saleh in Yemen, Muqbil continued teaching unhindered. This was in part because he taught that rebellion against rulers was only permissible if they acted as disbelievers. Muqbil had rejected the overtures of Osama bin Laden, who was recruiting many of al-Qaeda's foot soldiers from Yemen, frequently poor and illiterate young men who were easily persuaded to travel for jihad. He had asked Muqbil to provide shelter and guns for his fighters, but Muqbil had refused, wary that too close an embrace of bin Laden could provoke unwelcome consequences. Muqbil wrote polemics against aspects of popular culture such as television and against other Islamic sects. He saw equality of the

I was entrusted to the care of Abu Bilal, a bookish Swedish-Ghanaian student in his mid-twenties, who gave me a tour of the complex. He spoke fluent English as well as Arabic. During my first weeks in Dammaj, he or Rashid was almost always at my side translating for me.

The intensity of the place was difficult to take in. Like a new boy at a big school I felt intimidated by the collective emotion of Dammaj and its size. On the tour Abu Bilal told me the Institute – or Masjid – had started as a small collection of mud-brick buildings, but had expanded as its reputation spread. Now it had a library and a mosque capable of accommodating several hundred worshippers. Loudspeakers blared to announce the start of classes and lectures. The complex was surrounded by intensively cultivated and irrigated plots.

Abu Bilal explained to me the rules: single male students were strictly prohibited from going into areas of the complex reserved for married men. The five daily prayers were compulsory: each student was required to arrive on time and in silence. In between, students were required to attend lessons on the Koran and lessons from the life of the Prophet Mohammed. The mosque was the only one in the Muslim world in which students were required to keep their shoes on. A *hadith* viewed as authoritative by Sheikh Muqbil stated the Prophet had prayed in this way, and he was not about to let a practice built up over the centuries get in the way of his students following the true path.

Dammaj was a place of religious ferment. There were perhaps 300 young men there when I arrived, almost every one of them bearded, with the ardent expression of those convinced they had found righteousness. They came from many places but were united by a rejection of the modern world.

Despite my lack of Arabic, I soon found out what was driving these young men – and most were under thirty. They felt Muslims – and especially Arab Muslims – had been betrayed by their own leaders and exploited by the West. Dictators had robbed the people in a sea of

---

sexes and democracy as un-Islamic. And the enemies of Islam included both communists and America.

corruption but done nothing to help the Palestinians. The original religion had been corrupted by Western modes of thinking. And so it was time to return to the purest and most authentic expression of Islam.

Dammaj was a place of few comforts. I was given a bare room made of breeze blocks as my quarters, which I shared with Abu Bilal. We slept on blankets on the concrete floor, which was a luxury because most students were sleeping on mud floors. Food was frequently rice, beans and ginger tea. An egg was an extravagance. The toilet was a hole in the ground in the washroom. I had to learn how to clean myself with water with my left hand. The drainage system had not kept pace with the expansion of the Institute and a whiff of raw sewage would often interrupt our studying. But for all the discomforts, it was a haven of calm, self-discipline and devotion after my biker years.

The great question of the day was when and how Muslims should take up jihad in defence of their religion. Sheikh Muqbil refused to support violence against rulers and most Salafis saw education as the way to restore Islam. But some of his students would later criticize him for not speaking out against the presence of US troops on Saudi soil. This had been a cataclysm for Salafis: how could the infidel be allowed to set foot in the kingdom that protected Islam's holiest sites?

Under a date-palm one autumn afternoon one student – an Egyptian – spoke for most when we discussed the evils that Islam must grapple with.

'How can it be that the Custodian of the Two Holy Sites allows American troops to defile our lands? How can it be that our governments spend billions on American planes and tanks? They turn their back on Islam, allow alcohol, allow women to dress as prostitutes. Muslims have lost their way and it is up to us to re-educate them in Allah's way.'

Many of Dammaj's students had already returned home to set up similar institutes and schools across the Muslim world. Part of the appeal of this radical philosophy was that it bypassed the religious establishment and went directly to the fount of Islam. In that sense it empowered the poor and the persecuted and allowed them to spread the word, even if they had not benefited from decades of religious learning in the schools of Islamic law.

Sheikh Muqbil regarded the *Hadith*, accounts of the actions and sayings of the Prophet recorded by his early followers, as the core of his teaching. The crisis of Islam, he held, could only be addressed by returning to the original texts and rejecting 'innovators' – mere mortals who had the temerity to interpret God's word: 'There is no God except God and Mohammed is His messenger.' The spirit of Dammaj could be summed up by a *hadith*: 'The most evil matter is novelty, and every novelty is an innovation, and every innovation is an error, and every error leads to hellfire.' It did not leave much room for argument.

It was a bare but liberating message. And for someone like me who hated elites and establishments, it was intoxicating. I was now a witness to the multiple and overlapping struggles within Islam: between Salafis and others, among the Salafis themselves. And I was soon a willing participant in these struggles, soaking up scholarly texts, plunging into debates with other students.

It was in Dammaj that I began to get a sense at first hand of the violent rivalry between Sunni and Shia Muslims. The day I arrived, I saw rows of AK-47 rifles neatly lined against the walls of the Institute; and a number of students were on security duty, with weapons slung over their shoulders. The Institute was in a part of Yemen dominated by a Shia sect known as the Houthis.[3] The Sheikh made no attempt to hide his loathing of the Shia, and there were frequent clashes between his tribe and the Houthis.

The students at Dammaj did everything together – learning, eating, praying. Life revolved around the mosque. The day began before dawn with the first prayers of the day, and we received hours of Koranic instruction in the shade of the palms. We would spend long periods memorizing the Koran.

---

3 Some Houthis in northern Yemen subscribe to a form of Shi'ism that is close to that of Iranian Shia. Others subscribe to a Zaydi Shia revivalist movement that is strongest around Saa'da. Until the 1962 revolution Zaydi imams – who claimed they were directly descended from the Prophet Mohammed – ruled North Yemen. Despite the fact that the Zaydi creed is closer to Sunni Islam than any other branch of Shia Islam, hardline Sunnis in Yemen regarded them as apostates.

We never received anything amounting to paramilitary training but like many young Yemenis we did learn to fire guns, including AK-47s, at makeshift targets in the hills. A couple of Americans with military backgrounds played a leading part in the training, among them Rashid Barbi, who had been in the US army in Kuwait.

The Sheikh said such training was commanded by a *hadith* that stressed a strong believer was of greater value than a weak one and that all Muslims had to be prepared for jihad. Several students approached him to ask for permission to travel to Chechnya or Somalia to fight; but he only granted permission to those less than whole-hearted in their studies. It was a way to winnow out the thinkers from the men of action.

I embraced the purity of the lifestyle, the absence of mobile phones or music, drugs and alcohol. I began teaching boxing to some of my fellow students and took them running. In return I sensed their respect. It felt far more satisfying than any knockout I had delivered on the streets of Korsør. By night, as I gazed up at the stars, I felt I belonged.

Occasionally I would write to Samar, but I never mailed any of the letters. As I became submerged in the rituals of Dammaj there seemed less and less point. One day, sorting through the few belongings I had brought, I was surprised to find photographs of our engagement party. Without much feeling I shredded them one by one. When I wanted a wife, she would have to be a good Muslim.

The Sheikh, for all his learning, had a mischievous sense of humour, and for some reason I became one of his favourite students. He would take me by the hand and walk through the oasis, talking to me in Arabic. I would grasp only one word in every ten, but he went on talking.

He would also single me out during his lectures.

'Beni-marki,' he would exclaim, grinning broadly, before command-ing me to stand up and read *hadith*. I had begun to learn a few phrases of Yemeni Arabic but was unable to recite *hadith*, and would mumble apologies. A Libyan student took pity on me and taught me one *hadith* in Arabic. When I stood and recited it, Sheikh Muqbil was delighted – and began pounding the desk. He told the several hundred assembled students that my diligence showed Islam would spread throughout the world.

'This is the sign that Allah promised us,' he said. 'We must take care of our new Muslim brothers and teach them Islam and be patient with them.'

Despite the best efforts of the Yemeni government, there were plenty of foreign students at Dammaj, among them British Pakistanis from Birmingham and Manchester, Tunisians, Malaysians and Indonesians. There was also a second African-American called Khalid Green. A few had been in Bosnia, fighting with its Muslim population against the Serbs and Croats in the mid-1990s. Some would later become prominent militants in their own countries.

To begin with I was the only fair-skinned Caucasian at Dammaj. That made me an object of curiosity for many of the students and the local tribes. Yet I never felt excluded or ostracized because of my ethnicity.

I was later joined by a soft-spoken American convert from Ohio, called Clifford Allen Newman, and his four-year-old son, Abdullah. Newman went by the name Amin. He looked and sounded like what some Americans would call a 'redneck', but he spoke Arabic well and had spent time in Pakistan before moving to Yemen. We struck up a friendship. Like me he seemed to be fleeing a bad relationship. US authorities had a warrant for his arrest on international kidnapping charges because he had brought Abdullah with him to Yemen after a judge awarded custody to his ex-wife in their divorce the year before. Newman had wanted his son to have a strict Muslim upbringing.

I spent four months in Dammaj. In early 1998 I left the isolation of the seminary and travelled back to the capital, where I found myself a basic apartment. Newman and his son moved in with me briefly, while they looked for a place of their own.

I was serious about my faith; it was my compass and I planned to return to Dammaj. By the time I travelled back to Sana'a I was a hardcore Salafi. I could argue against the accursed 'innovators'.

In Sana'a I was introduced to some radical preachers, including one Mohammed al-Hazmi – who three years later would take to the pulpit and welcome the events of 9/11 as 'justified revenge' against America.

Another was Sheikh Abdul Majid al-Zindani, one of the most powerful religious figures in Yemen and prominent in the main opposition party, which he had co-founded. Al-Zindani, who was in his late fifties, had thousands of followers. He ran a university in Sana'a – al-Iman – whose mosque was crammed with several thousand worshippers every Friday.[4]

When my first experience of Ramadan as a devout Muslim came about, I was invited to break the fast with him one evening. Al-Zindani wanted me to enrol in al-Iman University.

A man of great wealth, he had a fabulous library at his house in Sana'a.

'What can I do to help you?' he asked.

He was not expecting my answer.

'Is it true you are with the Muslim Brotherhood?' I asked. 'If that is so, you will lead me to hellfire.'

We had been taught at Dammaj that the Muslim Brotherhood, a political movement that was one of the few sources of dissent in Arab countries, had abandoned true Sharia and were innovators where it suited their political ends, in some countries supporting the concept of democratic elections. This was anathema to true Salafis, because it pretended that mere mortals could make laws.

I did not ask the question with any animosity but al-Zindani looked stunned. Despite his radical profile, the Sheikh was not sufficiently militant for my taste. And as a strident Salafist and no respecter of status, I was not afraid to tell him as much.

He was clearly not used to being challenged by a novice but recovered his composure.

'It seems that if you come to al-Iman, we will have many interesting debates. But you must not believe everything you are told. Even good Muslims are sometimes confused or misguided,' he said, smiling.

To show he had no hard feelings about my insolence, al-Zindani let

---

4 Al-Zindani would later be described by some as the spiritual leader of al-Qaeda in Yemen. In 2004 the US designated him as a 'global terrorist', noting his long-standing connection to Osama bin Laden. In reality he was his own man, sympathetic to bin Laden's world-view but jealous of his status – and freedom. For example, in the early 1990s he had refused to support a plan by bin Laden to overthrow the Saleh regime.

me see some of his most precious volumes, and we talked more about the early days of Islam. I was learning fast.

A friend from Dammaj introduced me to a network of young Salafis in the city. Some were veterans of jihad who had fought the Soviets in Afghanistan in the 1980s and more recently had been in the Balkans. Of the growing pool of militants in Yemen, some were beginning to see the West, and especially America, as the enemy of Islam. There had already been bomb attacks against US interests in Saudi Arabia; and more were being planned. One of this circle was an Egyptian named Hussein al-Masri. Although he did not acknowledge it directly he was very likely a member of the Egyptian group Islamic Jihad. Al-Masri was a wanted man in his homeland. In his mid-thirties, he had a diffident manner and soft voice that belied his experience as a militant with extensive contacts. He was also the first person I heard utter the name Osama bin Laden.

At that time – in early 1998 – bin Laden was building al-Qaeda's presence in south and eastern Afghanistan, in Kandahar and around Jalalabad. Welcomed by the Taliban, his organization was already plotting attacks against Western targets, including a deadly bombing it would carry out months later on US embassies in Nairobi and Dar es Salaam.[5] Al-Masri told me of the training camps al-Qaeda had established in Afghanistan and how to travel there via Pakistan. He said he could arrange passage if I ever wanted to go.

I was in two minds: the adventurer in me was tempted, but as a Salafi I had not yet accepted that waging such a jihad was legitimate. Pure Salafis also looked down on groups like the Taliban, whose practices we saw as unorthodox.

To Western eyes, such differences might seem like semantics, but to teachers at Dammaj or in Riyadh, the Taliban's philosophy bordered on heresy. They encouraged 'excessive' praying beyond the five times a day mandated by the Prophet. Sheikh Muqbil had taught that one should not even countenance sitting down with such men. While they might be Muslims, they could lead you to damnation.

---

5 The near simultaneous 7 August 1998 bombings of the US embassies in Nairobi and Dar es Salaam killed over 200, including twelve Americans.

In making this point he liked to quote a famous *hadith* of the Prophet: 'My Ummah [nation] will break into seventy-three sects – only one will be in paradise and the rest will be in hell.'

For now, my sense of ideological purity won out.

Among my companions in Sana'a was a dark-skinned seventeen-year-old Yemeni with a generous smile and a shy courtesy. Abdul had curly, short-cropped hair and the beginnings of a beard. He can't have weighed more than seven stone; his legs were like stalks. But even at his age he was well connected with militants in Sana'a – men who had fought the communists in Afghanistan, the Serbs in Bosnia. Abdul and I often talked late into the night at his home, fuelled by endless glasses of sugary mint tea. I loved his natural enthusiasm and curiosity. He was full of questions about Europe, amazed and delighted that Islam had gained a foothold in these northern heathen lands. He yearned to travel and enjoyed practising his rudimentary English on me. I was impressed by his deep religious commitment. He was not unusual in knowing the Koran by heart but his voice was so melodic that he was often asked to recite prayers in the mosque.

My time in Yemen had deepened my faith. It had been little more than a year since I had entered a mosque for the first time and mumbled my Declaration of Faith. Now I knew the Koran, could recite *hadith* and discuss Islamic law. The man who had sent me, Mahmud al-Tayyib, had probably expected I would return home within weeks, unable to cope with the hardships of the poorest country in the Arab world.

But after the best part of a year in Yemen I was ready for a change. I had endured two bouts of dysentery, had no money and was beginning to tire of being stared at in the streets of Sana'a. I dug out my return ticket to London.

CHAPTER FIVE
LONDONISTAN

Summer 1998–Early 2000

I arrived at Heathrow airport on a muggy late summer's day in 1998, relieved to be free of the dust and heat of Sana'a and faintly amused by the orderly appearance of suburban London. I was soon reunited with Mahmud al-Tayyib at the Regent's Park mosque and regaled him with stories of Dammaj and Sana'a.

I helped teach Muslims who came to the mosque and began accompanying an elderly Iraqi preacher and several converts to Speakers' Corner in Hyde Park, where we would try to spread the word of Islam. We must have been a strange sight in our long Islamic *thawbs*, the ankle-length robe. Sometimes we would get into heated debates with evangelical Christians.

'The Koran is the pure word of God,' I would shout, remembering to quote a famous verse from the Koran. 'Had it issued from any but God, they would surely have found in it many a contradiction.'

We were usually greeted by a mixture of indifference and suspicion, which only reinforced our determination to continue proselytizing.

For radical Muslims London had become a cauldron of debate and rivalry. There were many echoes of the discussions that had occupied our afternoons under the date-palms of Dammaj. And the gritty district of Brixton, south of the River Thames, had become the centre of this tussle for the soul of Islam.

Brixton had seen riots in the early 1980s, pitching Afro-Caribbean youth against the Metropolitan Police. Disturbances had then spread to a dozen cities. The area had since become somewhat gentrified, but its housing was rundown and there was still plenty of poverty. Even on a bright summer's day in 1998 the high street was gloomy – a collection of down-at-heel stores and roads strewn with escaped plastic bags. But Brixton mosque was thriving and its reputation for Salafism was attracting devotees from across Europe. I had first heard about the mosque from British Muslims who had come to Yemen.

Most of my friends and flatmates were of a similar outlook. My experiences in Yemen and especially my time at Dammaj fascinated them. I even met the singer Cat Stevens several times. He had changed his name to Yusuf Islam and become a Sufi Muslim; I had some animated conversations with him about the true path of Islam. Salafis scorned Sufi Muslims for their veneration of saints and other perceived distortions of the faith.

I picked up temporary jobs, mostly driving, which helped me find radical mosques throughout London: in Hounslow, Shepherd's Bush and Finchley. None was as grand as Regent's Park; some were no more than shabby basements. But they were energized by a fervour which was by then challenging – and worrying – more moderate preachers, as well as the British security services.

The new circle I had entered included plenty of angry young men looking to inflict revenge on the West for its persecution of Muslims. A few clearly had emotional or psychological issues, displaying wild mood swings or budding paranoia, but most were driven by an unshakable belief that they had found the true way to obey Allah and that obedience called for waging jihad. A surprising number of French converts had come to Brixton, including one called Mukhtar. We talked about everything, shared a passion for martial arts and attended the mosque together.

Mukhtar was a French convert in his thirties, with a lean physique and close-set dark eyes. He reminded me a little of the French footballer Zinedine Zidane. We had met at Brixton mosque and he told me he had come to London to get away from police brutality in the rundown suburb of Paris where he had lived.

I soon met his French-Moroccan flatmate, one Zacarias Moussaoui. They lived in a decrepit 1960s council tower block that reeked of decay.

Their apartment was bare: no beds or sofas, just a couple of mattresses and rough hessian mats on the floor. It was a typical Salafists' pad.

Moussaoui had just turned thirty. He was well-built but beginning to put on weight. A thin black beard ran from his sideburns down his jaw and petered out at his chin. His receding hair was swept back. He would often cook tagine and couscous for everyone.

Moussaoui was clearly intelligent and had recently received a Master's degree at London's South Bank University, which was not far from Brixton. Most of the time he was quiet and unassuming, but brooding. He rarely talked about himself and never about his family. He did, however, have a passion for martial arts, especially Filipino knife-fighting.

Occasionally he would talk in general terms about jihad in Afghanistan and especially in Chechnya, which was at that time the cause célèbre of jihadis. Islamist rebels were battling the might of the Russian army. We all agreed that there was an obligation to support the rebels, through prayer, money or even waging jihad ourselves.

'It would be sinful if we don't at least raise money,' Moussaoui once said in his soft French-accented voice, as we sat cross-legged on the floor.

The age of online videos had dawned and we would watch stuttering, blurry images on websites which championed the Chechen struggle: ambushes of Russian troops, but more often human rights atrocities by the Russians against Chechen civilians in the Chechen capital, Grozny. Moussaoui would stare at the screen, his eyes glistening and his head shaking.

'*Kuffar* [infidel] Russians,' he muttered one day. 'I would happily die in Grozny if I could take a platoon of them with me.'

What he never told us was that he had already been to Chechnya and worked for the rebels – helping tell the world of their cause with his IT skills. He had also helped recruit others from abroad to join the Chechen war. Nor did he tell us he had spent time in one of al-Qaeda's camps in Afghanistan in the spring of 1998. While the rest of us debated jihad, Moussaoui had already lived it.

In October 1999 the Russians began a ground offensive against

Grozny. Television coverage and videos posted online revealed the true horror of what amounted to a scorched-earth campaign, with tens of thousands of civilians forced to flee their homes.

Thousands of miles away, my small Salafist circle in Brixton could not contain its anger. One bright autumn morning we emerged from the Brixton mosque furious that the preachers had never called for prayers let alone action in support of the Chechen resistance. Their battle against overwhelming odds made them heroes to us. We also knew that hundreds of foreign fighters, including graduates from Dammaj, had made their way to the Russian Caucasus.

'You see,' I said to Moussaoui and others, 'once again the establishment has deserted us, allowing the atheists to murder and maim our people without even raising a murmur. Our preachers are terrified they will fall foul of the police; they are so comfortable with their London life.'

We picketed the mosque, appealing for money and support for the Chechen resistance.

On 21 October Russian rockets rained down on a market in Grozny, killing dozens of women and children. I was instantly reminded of the Bosnian Serbs' shelling of the Sarajevo market, which had killed dozens of Muslims in 1995. The television footage was heartbreaking and enraging – and we redoubled our efforts to shame the mosque establishment into acknowledging the Chechens' suffering. Sometimes we would register our anger by attending a nearby mosque run by Nigerians that openly supported jihad in Chechnya.

In autumn 1999 Moussaoui's demeanour changed. The brooding became anger. He began to turn up at the Brixton mosque wearing combat fatigues and embraced the more militant environment at the Finsbury Park mosque in North London. Among those who trailed in his wake was a tall Jamaican-Englishman called Richard Reid, who had a long, thin face, a straggly beard and unkempt, curly hair held together in a ponytail. In another era he might have been a hippy. Reid was a petty criminal and Muslim convert, and he always looked like he needed a decent meal.

It was clear that Reid was in awe of Moussaoui. He attached himself to our group but said little; he seemed lonely. I lost contact with both men late in 1999 and thought little more of them, especially Reid – who seemed weak, impressionable. There were rumours that they had gone to Afghanistan – and I wondered whether the two of them had trained with al-Qaeda. Even so, I was stunned when their names and faces were splashed on television and newspapers two years later.

Moussaoui would be arrested shortly before 9/11 in Minnesota. He had entered the United States to get flying lessons, and would soon become known as the 'twentieth hijacker'. Reid would board a flight from Paris to Miami on 22 December 2001 with explosive powder hidden in his shoes. Restrained by flight attendants and passengers as he tried to light fuses hidden in his shoes, he would become known as the 'shoe-bomber'.

As my associations with radical Islamists expanded, I was often surprised by who among them crossed the Rubicon from talk to terror. They were rarely the obvious ones. But it was clear even in 1999 that London – and especially the mosque at Finsbury Park – was becoming the clearing-house for dozens of militants intent on acts of terrorism. And they often had similar backgrounds: with difficult or violent childhoods, little education and few prospects; unemployed, unmarried and seething with resentments.

Aware of the militant rhetoric emerging from places like the Finsbury Park mosque, the British security services were beginning to pay more attention to London's jihadist scene. But like many Western agencies they seemed to be playing catch-up, trying to grasp the extent of the problem, find out more about the leading lights, travel and funding, the rivalries among radical circles. Brixton and Finsbury Park became the battlegrounds for Londonistan, pitching the pro-Saudi Salafis like old Tayyib against a generation of angry jihadis that wanted to bring down the Saudi royal family, fight the Russians in Chechnya and purify the Muslim world of Western influences.

For my own part, books, lectures and conversations late into the night all helped prod me towards support for jihad, for taking up arms to defend the faith. I could not understand why the imams of most London mosques, including Abdul Baker at Brixton, studiously avoided mention of jihad let alone issue fatwas, commands to action. In Dammaj the duty of jihad as part of our religion had been our daily fare.

In the dying days of 1999 I went to a lecture in Luton, a town north of London, by Shaikh Yahya al-Hajuri, one of the teachers at Dammaj. He was surprised to see me.

'What are you doing here?' he asked me as I greeted him afterwards. 'You are supposed to be back in Yemen.'

I was taken aback by his tone. Had I abandoned the true path? Was my faith being adulterated in Europe? I went home and prayed for guidance, for a sign from Allah that I should return to what in many ways was the cradle of my devotion.

It came on a Friday morning just weeks later. I had dropped into the basement kitchen at the Regent's Park mosque for a cheap meal. A dark-skinned woman approached me, looking anxious.

'Brother, please can you come to help my husband. He wants to pray but he can't walk from the car.'

I went upstairs with her. The couple were from Mauritius. Her elderly husband looked so fragile that I thought to move him might break him. He was sitting in the driver's seat of an ancient Mercedes.

'I'm all right, brother,' he said. 'I just need to rest and get my breath back.'

I picked up an inhaler from the floor of the car. But he only became paler; it was almost as if he were vanishing before my eyes. His breathing became laboured, a quiet heaving scarcely audible amid the rush of traffic. His eyes closed and he fell back in the seat. There was a faint gurgling in his throat and his eyes reopened, staring vacantly through the front window.

I thought for a moment that he had recovered from some sort of spasm but soon found myself muttering in Arabic 'There is no God but Allah' to aid his passage to paradise. He coughed weakly and was gone.

As his wife screamed hysterically, I lifted the man out of the car and was struck for an instant by how surreal the scene must seem: a large Viking carrying a sliver of an African across lanes of London traffic. A park warden ran over to tell me that he had radioed for an ambulance. But it was too late.

It shook me. How we all hang by a thread. I helped prepare the man's corpse for burial at the Wembley mosque in keeping with Islamic practice. As I washed the grey skin I thought about how I had seen him leave this world – and how fortunate he had been that a fellow Muslim had been on hand to pray for him as he passed.

It was a sign. I could not die here among the *kuffar*. I had to be surrounded by people of my faith. Allah had prescribed it. If you died among disbelievers it was a sin. In the words of one *hadith*: 'Whoever settles among the disbelievers, celebrates their feasts and joins in their revelry and dies in their midst will likewise be raised to stand with them on the Day of Resurrection.'

The world was divided into believers and non-believers, and the worst Muslim was better than the best Christian.

But to return to the Muslim world would require a passport. Mine had been ruined during my travels. I went to the Danish embassy in London to try to get a replacement. But they had other business with me – an outstanding criminal conviction. Back in 1996 I had been involved in a scrap in a bar over a spilt drink. I had head-butted one of my assailants and then punched another. I was arrested on the way home and later sentenced to a six-month term, to be served in typically Danish fashion when cell space became available. Before it did, I had left Denmark, and under the date-palms in Dammaj I had forgotten the whole episode. Now the sentence was overdue – and I would only get a new passport if I returned to Denmark to face the music.

I would spend the first months of the new millennium behind bars.

CHAPTER SIX

DEATH TO AMERICA

Early 2000–Spring 2002

After negotiation with the Danish authorities, I returned home to serve my delayed sentence in early 2000. I had only one condition: I would not return to a prison where any Bandidos were held. The prison service ignored the agreement and I thought I would have to fight for my life – but discovered that other Muslims in the prison in Nyborg had formed a gang for mutual protection.

I served my penance, spending the time weightlifting and running, but it was a time of frustration. I was desperate to return to Yemen but I had to make money. And to make money I had to gain some sort of qualification. With the help of counsellors who worked with released prisoners, I signed up for business studies at a college in Odense (which included a monthly stipend for living expenses from the Danish state) and began worshipping at the Wakf mosque. It was a lively place full of Somalis, Palestinians and Syrians that would degenerate into violence over theological disputes. During one Friday prayers I grabbed the microphone from a preacher whom I thought misguided – he had the temerity to wear his trousers below the ankles, a practice scorned by Salafis.

'Don't listen to him. He's an innovator who belongs to one of the seventy-two sects destined for hellfire!' I yelled.

Odense is the home-town of Hans Christian Andersen, and its old streets and quaint gabled houses would fit neatly into a children's story.

It is a model of Danish progressiveness – bicycle paths, pedestrianized streets, green spaces. But its outskirts are less evocative. Many Muslims – first- and second-generation immigrants – had moved into its less salubrious social housing in the suburb of Vollsmose, and as in London there was a drumbeat of jihadism.

After I was released from prison I learned that Sheikh Muqbil, my mentor at Dammaj, had issued a fatwa calling for Holy War against Christians and Jews in the Moluccan Islands of Indonesia, where sectarian fighting was raging. He urged non-Indonesian Muslims to help establish Islamic law there.

The leader of Laskar Jihad, the al-Qaeda-affiliated group at the centre of the fighting, was Ja'far Umar Thalib. He had been a fellow student at Dammaj. And some of my friends there – including the former American soldier Rashid Barbi – had gone to Indonesia to join the battle.[1]

I made a trip over to England with a Pakistani friend, Shiraz Tariq[2] – to raise money in mosques for the mujahideen in the Moluccas. Once again I was angered by the feeble response of many Salafist imams to this gross assault on our faith.

To me, jihad was still a defensive duty rather than a right to wage offensive warfare against disbelievers. I took the words of the Koran as my guide: 'Fight in the cause of Allah those who fight you, but do not transgress, for Allah loves not the transgressor. Fight in the way of Allah against those who fight against you, but begin not hostilities. Lo! Allah loves not aggressors.'

These words brought an obligation to fight or support the fight – whether in the Balkans, Chechnya or the Moluccan Islands of Indonesia. But jihad without such a foundation was illegitimate.

The boundaries between defensive and offensive jihad were not

---

1 Barbi eventually returned to North Carolina. The last time I heard from him was around 2009. He had married a Somali woman and was working in a factory.

2 Tariq claimed he had connections to the Pakistani terrorist group Lashkar e Taiba and that he had taken several young men to train in Pakistan. He was killed fighting with al-Qaeda-linked jihadists in Syria in late 2013.

always clear and would blur further as al-Qaeda began its campaign of global jihad. They were at the heart of animated debates I had with friends in Odense such as Mohammad Zaher, a Syrian-Palestinian immigrant who had a strong Middle Eastern nose, a close-cropped beard and deep-set, solemn eyes.

Zaher like me was unemployed and with time on our hands we often went fishing together. He would bombard me with questions about Dammaj and Sheikh Muqbil. I explained the fatwas he and other imams had issued making jihad lawful in Indonesia, but also stressed that random acts to 'terrorize the disbelievers' were not allowed. In evidence I summoned the words of an eminent Saudi cleric who had said that the obligation of jihad 'must be fulfilled by Muslims at different levels in accordance with their different abilities. Some must help with their bodies, others with their property and others with their minds.'

Zaher seemed ordinary, sympathetic to the idea of jihad but not as extreme as some I knew. Yet again I would be dumbfounded when the ordinary did the extraordinary. In September 2006 he would be arrested for what Danish authorities at the time called the 'most serious' plot ever discovered in the country.

I had not forsaken my goal of returning to the Muslim world but as usual was short of cash, trying to complete my studies on a modest stipend. My talents as an enforcer would once more come to the rescue.

Odense had a substantial and volatile Somali community. One afternoon I received a call from a Somali friend asking me to intervene at a local wedding where a row had broken out.

When I reached the venue, I saw what was becoming an all too familiar dispute playing out. Against the wishes of the presiding imam, the sexes were mixing and music was blaring from speakers. Such Western practices were anathema to Salafis.

The argument escalated as I intervened and a wedding guest lunged at the imam with a knife. Thankfully, reflexes honed in the clubs of Korsør did not desert me and I knocked the knife out of his hand. What I did not see was his accomplice, who struck me on the back of the head with a bottle. As blood streamed down my neck, the man was dragged away.

Anxious that the disturbance not be reported to the police, community leaders assured me that they would apply Sharia law to my assailant. I was given the options of breaking a bottle over his head, forgiving him or taking blood money of nearly $3,000. I wasn't inclined to forgive him and did not want to return to prison for breaking a bottle over someone's head. But the blood money meant that suddenly I could travel again.

I had recently taken to browsing Muslim 'matrimonial' sites on the internet, hopeful of finding a suitably religious but also suitably attractive partner. They would never be referred to as dating sites and were rather more prim than their American counterparts. The women who had posted their details had little to say of their personal likes and dislikes, more often promising to be good, obedient and faithful wives. Every one of them wore the hijab and a meek expression. Even so, one living in the Moroccan capital had attracted my attention. Karima spoke English, was well-educated and religiously observant, and had approached me with a simple online question: would I like to marry her?[3]

Flush with cash thanks to a broken bottle, with a clean Danish passport and my debt to society paid in full, I was soon airborne.

I was met by her brother in Rabat – the vetting committee. Even before I met Karima I went to a couple of the more radical mosques in Salat, a poorer neighbourhood of Rabat. Here too Salafism was thriving: the fact that I had been to Yemen and knew Sheikh Muqbil opened doors. It also impressed Karima's family.

Karima was petite with olive skin, almond eyes and a demure manner that complemented her deep faith. I found her both attractive and intelligent. She was already thinking about emigrating to Yemen or Afghanistan with me to seek a purer existence. Within days we were married at her family's house. It may seem ridiculous that two people

---

3 Karima is a pseudonym. I am not using her real name to protect her identity for security reasons.

could marry days after meeting each other, but it was the way dictated by our faith. There was no question of dating, of discreet dinners to explore each other's thoughts and emotions. Allah would take care of everything.

And the Danish state would take care of relocating me to Yemen. Youth education grants were just one aspect of its overarching social welfare system. I applied to learn Arabic at the CALES language institute in Ṣana'a and received a grant – no questions asked. Karima remained in Morocco while I set about preparing for our new life in Yemen.

In April 2001 I flew into Sana'a again. It felt strangely like I belonged there. What had been an assault on the senses on my first visit was now pleasantly familiar. The chaos of the streets was welcoming rather than overwhelming; I was excited to catch up with my acquaintances there and spend long evenings on roof terraces talking about faith and the world. And I felt a real affinity for this poor corner of the Arabian Peninsula. This was where the struggle for the soul of my religion was being waged.

The neighbourhood of Sana'a where I settled seemed much more spontaneous than the bland, well-ordered suburbs of Denmark. I smiled to see the battered carts of fruit and vegetables being hauled through the streets by thin young men, the tiny kiosks selling gum and cigarettes, the old men gathered on corners with their prayer beads.

Yemen's bureaucracy meant it would be several months before Karima could join me in Sana'a. That same bureaucracy was also having trouble keeping up with my former Salafist comrades, who had become even more active and radical in my absence. And it was by now beyond doubt that al-Qaeda saw Yemen as a 'space' in which to attack Western interests. A few months before my return, terrorists aboard a skiff had approached the visiting USS *Cole* in Aden harbour. They saluted the sailors on board before detonating hundreds of pounds of C4 explosives against the *Cole*'s hull. Seventeen US sailors lost their lives and the ship nearly sank.

Young Abdul, a skinny teenager when I had left, was now a confident young man with a growing jihadist network and much-improved English. He often visited the house I had rented and we fell back into long conversations about religion. He urged me not to read books by Salafis who did not support jihad and we devoured websites that reported on the conflicts in Indonesia and Chechnya.

One evening I went to visit him at his mother's home – a plain breeze-block house on an unpaved street in Sana'a. Emaciated cats wandered among the piles of garbage as children played football or ran with hoops. Hussein al-Masri, the Egyptian jihadi who had previously offered to get me to bin Laden's camps, was there when I arrived.

As we sat on the floor, drinking tea, it became clear Abdul had been busy while I'd been in London. He told me in hushed tones but with unmistakable pride that he had travelled to Afghanistan, spent time in al-Qaeda's camps and even – he claimed – met Osama bin Laden.

'He is doing Allah's work,' Abdul said. 'The attack on the American warship and on the embassies is just the beginning,' he continued, referring to al-Qaeda's bombing of US embassies in Nairobi and Dar es Salaam in 1998. 'There are good Muslims from all over the world who are now in Kandahar and Jalalabad.' He and al-Masri told me they could get me to Afghanistan to help build the promised land. I sometimes wondered whether Abdul was embellishing his exploits and encounters, but he certainly displayed first-hand knowledge of Afghanistan and none of the al-Qaeda members I subsequently met contradicted his account.

I was tempted to go myself. My religious views were certainly no longer an obstacle. Once back in Yemen, encouraged by Abdul, I had devoured books by pro-jihadist Islamic scholars – even translating some into Danish. I had forsaken my Salafi purism to view preparation for jihad as a necessity.

It was not religious fervour alone that tempted me to head to Afghanistan. One of my circle in London – a half-Barbadian, half-Englishman – had told stories of training in Afghanistan, stimulating the sense of adventure that always itched within me. He spoke of roaming the majestic mountains, weapons training and an intense fellowship among the fighters.

'I might be going back soon,' Abdul said. 'The Sheikh said that people like you should come,' he added, referring to bin Laden. He showed me a video from Afghanistan with scenes of al-Qaeda recruits training on monkey bars and firing rockets, footage which later became iconic.

'I would like to go,' I said. I could not restrain my excitement about being with the mujahideen in the mountains of Afghanistan. My new wife was soon to join me in Sana'a, but training for jihad was all I could think about.

'We can arrange a plane ticket to Karachi, from where you'll be picked up and driven over to Afghanistan,' Abdul said.

Karima arrived in the height of summer, but I was now in a quandary. I felt I could not just leave her in Sana'a while I disappeared to the Hindu Kush – even though she accepted it was my religious duty to prepare for jihad. She knew nobody in Sana'a.

I sought an audience with Mohammed al-Hazmi, one of the radical clerics I had encountered during my previous stay in Sana'a.

'I want to train with the mujahideen in Afghanistan,' I told him.

'*Masha'Allah*, this is good. According to Sharia you can't leave your wife unless she is with a responsible family member: a father, brother or uncle. But for jihad there is an exception. Your wife can stay in your residence in Sana'a and the landlord can take her as family.'

There seemed a lot of flexibility in the rules as applied to Holy War.

Abdul, just back from Afghanistan, had different advice, telling me that if I travelled there I should take my wife with me, so that we could make *hijra* – emigrate to a Muslim land. He was relaying Osama bin Laden's appeal for jihadis to bring their families. Many did: when al-Qaeda's last redoubt at Tora Bora was cleared later that year, women and children were among those killed or put to flight.

I decided against taking Karima, a decision that seemed all the more realistic when she told me she was pregnant in August. Despite this, she still agreed to my imminent departure.

One morning after returning from prayers, I caught a glimpse of her as she struggled down the stairs. She was suffering in the heat – debilitated with morning sickness and back pain. She looked pale and tired and my instinct to protect her – and my unborn child – smothered my dream of becoming a trained warrior for Allah, at least for the time being.

'I am staying here with you,' I told her. 'You can't remain alone here – pregnant and penniless in a strange city, supposedly under the protection of a landlord.'

She began to weep. I felt less than chivalrous for even contemplating leaving her. And the prospect of fatherhood dulled the disappointment of not being able to travel to Afghanistan.

Instead of going there I returned to Dammaj for a short visit. Sheikh Muqbil, the great Salafi religious guide, had passed away in July while receiving treatment for liver disease in Saudi Arabia. His funeral took place in Mecca, but the seminary was holding a memorial. Hundreds of his former pupils gathered from around the Arab world, many of them weeping during prayers. There seemed to be a vacuum without him. My friend the American convert Clifford Newman and his son, Abdullah, were among the mourners. Clifford showed me an Uzi machine gun he had acquired for their protection from the Shia tribes in the area.

My drift towards full-blooded militancy was brought into focus on 11 September 2001. Late in the afternoon I went to a barber's shop in Sana'a. The Arabic news channel, Al Jazeera, was blaring in the corner. Soon after I arrived, it began airing live footage from New York. Smoke was drifting from the upper storeys of the World Trade Center. The breathless commentary soon made clear that a terrorist attack had occurred.

I rushed home and turned on the radio as further details of the attacks came in. Until that day, the name Osama bin Laden had meant little to the average Salafi. He was respected for giving up the trappings of wealth and fighting in Afghanistan to establish an Islamic state there. But of al-Qaeda's growing capabilities and ambitions little was known. Despite the attacks on the US embassies in East Africa and the USS *Cole*, no one I knew had expected al-Qaeda to take its war to the US homeland. Some regarded it as misguided, others as wrong because it targeted civilians. But among most of my acquaintances in Sana'a – especially those who flocked to Sheikh Mohammed al-Hazmi's mosque that evening – euphoria drowned out any more sober perspective on the attacks.

Al-Hazmi was popular among young militant Muslims in Sana'a. Addressing an overflowing congregation in the stifling heat that evening, he was unequivocal.

'What has happened is just retribution for American oppression of Muslims and the occupation of Muslim lands,' he said – a reference to the continuing presence of US forces in Saudi Arabia and elsewhere in the Gulf.

The congregation prostrated themselves in gratitude to Allah. At that point I was unsure who had committed the attacks and had heard that as many as 20,000 people might have died. I had seen few pictures and was unsure how to respond to such an act – even if it had been carried out by fellow Muslims as an act of jihad. I had so many questions. Did Islam permit a suicide attack? Was targeting civilians in a far-off country justifiable?

Many Salafis, even in Sana'a, were critical of the 9/11 attacks – saying they had no justification in Islam. But for me the theological answer came a few days later and helped cement a sense of obligation to make jihad. A Saudi cleric, Sheikh Humud bin Uqla, published a long fatwa in support of 9/11, saying it was permissible to kill civilians when they were 'mixed up' with fighters and drawing a comparison with a US military strike in 1998 on an alleged al-Qaeda facility in the Sudanese capital, Khartoum.

'When America attacked a pharmaceutical firm in Sudan, using its planes and bombs, destroying it and killing everybody in it, staff and labourers, what was this called? Shouldn't the action of America in the Sudanese firm be considered as an act of terrorism?' the Sheikh asked.

I devoured the fatwa, even as Sheikh bin Uqla was condemned by other clerics. A prominent supporter of the Taliban before 9/11, he was constantly under attack by the Saudi religious establishment. But his arguments, in those feverish days after 9/11, were what I wanted to hear.

Ultimately I accepted that in this clash of civilizations I was a Muslim. Weeks after 9/11, as the United States embarked on its invasion of Afghanistan, President George W. Bush would say, 'You are either with us or with the terrorists.' That left me no option; I could not side with the *kuffar*. Osama bin Laden was pure; he was a hero. President Bush did not believe in Allah or accept Mohammed as His messenger. His was a crusade against Islam; he had even used the word – and that pushed many doubters into the camp of the mujahideen.

In the debate over how Muslims should respond I lost a lot of friends who were Salafis. To me they were cowards; they had turned their backs on fellow Muslims. But I gained many other friends and they were jihadis. Many of them left for Afghanistan. Some militants I knew expected a US invasion of Yemen any day; I even told Karima that she would be safer back in Morocco.

Abdul and I had many discussions about the way forward.

'I have something to tell you, Murad,' he said one evening. 'I have been travelling around for Sheikh Osama. I've been delivering messages for him. You know the training video I showed you? I myself smuggled that out of Afghanistan.'

'*Masha'Allah!*' I replied. It was frowned upon to praise someone directly. Everything had to come from God.

'You can see one of the hijackers in the video – he's the guy filmed from behind firing the anti-aircraft gun. I met him while I was over there. But nobody told me what was being planned.'

I was impressed. Abdul, scarcely out of his teens, was moving in rarefied jihadist circles.

On 7 October – the day US cruise missiles were launched against Afghanistan, I was with friends at a house in Sana'a. We saw the battle for Afghanistan in very distinct colours. On one side the Taliban, who for all their faults represented Islam; on the other an unholy alliance of America, communists, Tajik warlords and Shi'ites.

I hated the Salafi scholars who refrained from depicting the conflict with the US as a Holy War of defensive jihad. One of the *hadith* became popular in our circle at the time: 'When you see that black flags have appeared from Khorasan [Afghanistan] then join them.' It was as if the Prophet had predicted Operation Enduring Freedom as a war for the future of Islam.

Clifford Newman, my American Salafi friend, felt the same way. In early December he came to my house in an excited state.

'Murad – have you seen the news?' he blurted out. 'The American they captured in Afghanistan who's all over TV. I was the guy who sent him.'

He was referring to John Walker Lindh, the so-called 'American Taliban' who had just been interviewed by CNN in Afghanistan after being captured. Lindh had studied at the CALES language institute in Sana'a the previous year, and flown from there to Pakistan, before travelling into Afghanistan. Newman told me he'd helped Lindh travel.

As far as I was concerned the attack on our Muslim brothers meant that jihad was now obligatory for every Muslim. To play my part I had begun collecting money for the Taliban and fighters hoping to join them, which attracted the attention of the Yemeni intelligence services. I was summoned to meet the committee that ran the mosque I usually attended in Sana'a.

'Murad,' said a frail, elderly man, 'this is a mosque that welcomes all Muslims, and we have a duty to all our congregation. Some are concerned, as we are, that this holy place is receiving the wrong sort of attention. You may have noticed that there are men standing across the street, watching. And they are watching you. We cannot have members of the congregation using this place to raise money for foreign wars.'

He paused and glanced at the rest of the committee.

'We have been told it would not be good for you to come here any more, for our sake and for your own sake. I hope you understand.'

I began to glance over my shoulder when walking through the streets. More than once I was sure a man had stopped to study a shop window or turned in a different direction. I even started checking my car, in case someone had tampered with the brakes or planted a device. I imagined strange clicks or interference on my phone. Things were becoming unpleasant. It was time to get out of the capital, so in the dying days of 2001 I took Karima south.

The city of Taiz is one of the most historic in Yemen – sitting amid towering mountain ranges halfway between Sana'a and Aden. In the rainy season electric storms illuminate the peaks. Its inhabitants see Sana'a as lazy and backward, and there is certainly a greater sense of industry in Taiz – none of it very picturesque. The outskirts are scarred with hideous cement plants and ramshackle factories that would be condemned in an instant if sited in the West. But its mosques are glorious. Not a few of its young men had embraced the militancy that I had also seen in Sana'a. I attended a mosque that welcomed combat veterans of Bosnia and Chechnya as well as several who had trained in bin Laden's Afghan camps. When they learned that I was being watched by the Yemeni security services they embraced me straight away. Soon I was criss-crossing the city, meeting at the homes of bright-eyed young militants, many of whom were looking for ways to join in the new war.

Among the young men I knew in Taiz were several who would be involved in a suicide attack in October 2002 on a French tanker, the MV *Limburg*, in the Gulf of Aden.

Karima gave birth a few months after we arrived, in the first week of May 2002; we called our son Osama. When I told my mother of the name she yelled down the phone.

'No, you cannot give him that name. Are you mad?'

'Mum,' I replied, 'if that's the case no Western families can call their sons George or Tony. They are the ones who have declared war on Islam.'

We were talking different languages.

CHAPTER SEVEN

FAMILY FEUDS

Summer 2002–Spring 2005

Even if my first-born was called Osama, his grandmother had a right to meet him. It was also a good moment to leave Yemen for a while. The security services, no doubt encouraged by the Americans, seemed much more intent on monitoring foreign 'activists'.

On a balmy late-summer's day in 2002, a neat suburban house near my home-town of Korsør was decked out incongruously in Moroccan and Danish flags. It was the welcome that my family had prepared for an unlikely couple: the Danish jihadi and his Moroccan bride. Aunts, uncles and new great-grandparents – all were there to greet the first of a new generation, a three-month-old boy with a shock of black hair named Osama.

My stepfather brooded in the background; he had not forgotten that I had put him in hospital. My mother tried to conceal her anger at the choice of Osama as her grandson's name, just as I tried to suppress my disdain for her as a non-Muslim. I tried (as was my duty) but inevitably failed to persuade her to convert to Islam, and she could never bring herself to call me Murad. But she found some solace in my faith – at least I was now not going to become a criminal. She may not have felt so confident had she known some of the people I counted as friends in Sana'a and Taiz. She had no idea how radical I had become. I think it was partly because she was in denial. She simply didn't want to know.

The atmosphere in Denmark after 9/11 hardened towards Muslims. Karima wore a niqab in the streets, so only her eyes could be seen. She wore gloves even on a summer's day. I wore a traditional, long, flowing *thawb*. Between us we drew plenty of suspicious glances.

After a couple of months my mother's welcome began to wear out and I found the primness of our surroundings too much to bear. In the wake of the attack on the MV *Limburg*, I had been advised by contacts in Taiz not to return to Yemen yet; the 'brothers' were being rounded up in dozens. If I had to stay in Denmark I would rather it be among 'my own' – among the grey apartment buildings of the Odense suburb of Vollsmose, where Muslims outnumbered native Danes. Many were Somali, Bosnian and Palestinian immigrants. Stories were beginning to appear in the Danish media about the crime rate in Vollsmose, stories that were meat and drink to the far-right parties.

We moved into a bare three-bedroom apartment. While Karima felt more comfortable to hear Arabic on the streets and see other veiled women, she did not appreciate our modest surroundings, nor my preference for debating jihad rather than clocking on for some menial job. Vollsmose had plenty of gang-related trouble and occasionally we would be woken by the sound of gunfire.

I soon reconnected with old associates such as Mohammad Zaher, my fishing partner from a couple of years previously. I noticed Zaher had become more militant and now had a recent convert to Islam trailing around as his sidekick.

Abdallah Andersen, who worked as a teaching assistant, was clean-shaven with a mop of dark hair and a fleshy round face. He was insecure and timid, easily led, and looked up to Zaher.

Nothing suggested they would soon plan to bring terror to the streets of Denmark.

In September 2006 Zaher, Andersen and several others would be arrested in Vollsmose after a sting operation by the Danish intelligence agency, PET, involving an informant. Angered by the publication of controversial cartoons in Denmark that lampooned the Prophet, the group had discussed attacking the Danish parliament, Copenhagen town hall square and the Danish newspaper *Jyllands-Posten*. Police found fifty grams of detonating explosive in a glass flask in Zaher's bathroom. He was convicted and sentenced to eleven years. Andersen received a four-year sentence.

I found that I was something of a celebrity among the more radical in Vollsmose thanks to an interview I had done with a Danish newspaper in which I refused to condemn the 9/11 attacks so long as people in the West declined to condemn the sanctions that had caused the premature deaths of so many Iraqi children. It was a glib comparison, but one that made me plenty of friends in the more radical mosques.[1]

I had no work but was still receiving an allowance from the Danish government for studying in Yemen, even though I was now in my midtwenties, living in Denmark and not even attending college courses. The income allowed me to spend my days in prayer. I posted on Islamist chat forums and watched the growing archive of jihadist videos. I began to adopt a *takfiri* viewpoint, seeing some other Muslims as *kuffar* – no better than disbelievers because of their views. One of them was Naser Khader, a Syrian-born immigrant and Denmark's first Muslim MP, who took to the airwaves to argue that Islam and democracy were compatible. Then he began criticizing Sharia law. Seething with anger I wrote on an online Islamic forum: 'He is a murtad [apostate]. You don't need a fatwa to kill him.'

My commitment to the cause went beyond words. I joined other would-be jihadis, including Zaher and my Pakistani friend Shiraz Tariq, for training at paintball sites. To us it was not a game; we declined protective gear so that when we were hit by a pellet it hurt. One drill involved a team member charging out in a suicide-style attack to draw fire from the other team. Although I did not know it at the time, my activities, especially online, were being monitored by Danish intelligence. My situation was faintly ridiculous – funded by one Danish ministry, housed by another, watched by a third.

---

1 Among my circle was a Moroccan called Said Mansour who had married a Danish woman. He often came to my home and spent much of his time producing CDs and DVDs of sermons and speeches by al-Qaeda figures. He was also alleged to have been in contact with Omar Abdel Rahman, the blind Egyptian cleric convicted of conspiracy in the first attack on the World Trade Center in 1993. After three police raids on his home, Mansour would eventually become the first person in Denmark to be prosecuted and convicted under new legislation that criminalized incitement to terrorism. But by 2009 he was freed and disappeared underground. After spending time in jail he was arrested again for 'incitement' in February 2014.

Everywhere I went, militant groups were growing and coalescing – and the intelligence services were struggling to identify those who would cross the line from talk to terrorism.

Karima did not like Odense, nor Denmark, and by early 2003 was pregnant with our second child. I hoped that she might settle better in Britain. For the second time I set off for England to find work and a place to live so that the woman in my life could follow me. And for the second time, the woman had other ideas. When I called home, day after day, there was no answer. I called hospitals, the police, my family; no one had seen Karima. Eventually I found out by calling her brother in Rabat that she had returned to Morocco with Osama.

Our relationship had been struggling. She was still pious but she also seemed to hanker after a life of comfort in Europe. A rundown apartment did not match her expectations, and she had begun berating me for not providing sufficiently. I began to think that her humility and deference years earlier in Rabat had been a well-acted play.

Angry and frustrated, I flew to Morocco. It took a month and a good deal of money to be allowed to see Osama, and Karima also insisted on a private hospital to give birth. With help from friends, I scraped the money together. Our daughter, Sarah, was born in early August.

It was a time of upheaval. The US invasion of Iraq – its 'shock and awe' resembling some Hollywood script – had begun in March. I watched videos of US soldiers crossing into Iraq carrying bibles as if to bait Muslims. Neither I nor anyone I knew had any sympathy for a tyrant such as Saddam Hussein, whom we regarded as an atheist. But none of us believed the claims made by President Bush that Saddam's regime had worked with al-Qaeda or was hiding weapons of mass destruction. We saw the invasion as another declaration of war against Muslims and another reason to embrace jihad.

The humiliation of another Muslim country seemed complete. It had taken days for US tanks to advance on Baghdad. The Iraqi army had crumbled; its leadership surrendered or fled. The Stars and Stripes fluttered across the country. There was an arrogance to the Americans' war aims. They would make Iraq a beacon of democracy and the rest of the Arab world would follow gratefully. Islam could take a running jump.

For now I had more immediate and personal issues to deal with. If I wanted to repair my marriage, I needed to find work and improve our standard of living. In Denmark my criminal record stalked me, preventing me from getting a job. In England I had a better chance of finding work and someone to stay with – the former prison inmate Suleiman with whom I had arrived on the ferry six years earlier. Karima and I made a pact: if I could find a job in England she would bring the children over.

Suleiman had moved from Milton Keynes to a small ground floor flat in Luton, just north of London. On my return there from Morocco I got work driving a forklift truck in a warehouse in nearby Hemel Hempstead. It was hardly the goal of an aspiring jihadi. But if I wanted to see my children again, it would have to do.

If Vollsmose had been simmering with militancy, Luton was ready to boil over. It had a high concentration of Kashmiri immigrants from Pakistan, and unemployment and discrimination were pervasive. Many of their children had grown disaffected with mainstream British society and rejected their parents' efforts at assimilation. They had turned to radical Islam and the war in Iraq had added fuel to the fire.

I saved enough cash to begin renting a nondescript terraced house; by the end of 2003 my rare bout of self-discipline had paid off. Karima, Osama and Sarah arrived and settled into an anonymous existence on Connaught Road among the backstreets of Luton. It was a tightly packed street of post-war homes crammed with cars and vans. None had any sort of front garden; just a few paving slabs decorated with dustbins. Karima, to start with, was happier. Dressed in the full veil she was like hundreds of women in Luton. But, for that very reason, the town was also beginning to attract far-right parties, and racial assaults were not uncommon.

In Luton I quickly fell in with like-minded brothers. We would hang out, eat chicken and chips and talk jihad. I developed a following because I had met some of the best-known radical figures in the Arab world. The Islamist insurgency in Iraq had emboldened us and provided a platform for a radical preacher called Omar Bakri Mohammed – a man who could whip up a crowd.

I first heard him speak in the spring of 2004 at a small community centre on Woodland Avenue, where some of the most militant Muslims in Luton congregated.

It was packed for the occasion – rows of young bearded men wearing Taliban-style salwar kameez. Women shrouded completely in black stood in a segregated section at the back of the hall.

A hush went around the room when the cleric, a large and portly figure, climbed up on stage, supporting his girth with a walking stick. He had oversized spectacles and a thick beard.

'Brothers, I carry important news. The mujahideen in Iraq are fighting back and they are winning. They are striking fear into the Americans,' he roared in an accent that was a cross between his native Syria and East London.

The resistance of one city had given jihadis cause for hope. Fallujah, fifty miles west of Baghdad, was a Sunni stronghold whose people had never welcomed the Americans. Within days of their arriving and commandeering a school there were protests which turned violent. US forces opened fire on rioters, killing several. The Americans had just launched an offensive in the city after the charred bodies of four US. security contractors were strung up on a bridge by insurgents. But the Americans had run into stiff resistance, and around the world jihadis were looking to Fallujah as the defining battle to save Iraq from the apostates. Emboldened by the failure of the Americans to capture the city, the jihadists had declared an Islamic emirate, and started implementing Sharia law.

'*Subhan'Allah, Allahu Akbar* [Glory be to God, God is Great]!' Bakri Mohammed bellowed. 'I just received greetings from brothers in Iraq from Fallujah saying the fight is going well. They ask us to keep on working for our Deen. Sheikh Abu Musab al-Zarqawi himself gives us his greetings,' he thundered.

Zarqawi, a Jordanian building a new al-Qaeda franchise, was winning growing fame in extremist circles as the standard bearer for resistance against the American occupation.

The audience lapped up Omar Bakri's remarks. He was not a man wracked by self-doubt. While his Arabic rendition of the Koran left something to be desired, he had charisma and answers to the questions of the day and remarkable contacts. What particularly appealed to me was the way he marshalled the Koran, *Hadith* and centuries-old Islamic law to justify bin Laden's war.

Omar Bakri led the group al-Muhajiroun, a radical UK outfit that was the cheerleader for al-Qaeda, and walked a thin line between freedom of speech and incitement to terrorism. He had called the 9/11 hijackers the 'magnificent nineteen' and his online sermons – followed by hundreds of young militants – justified jihad against those he called the 'crusaders' in Iraq and Afghanistan.

At the next few lectures I attended his message was inflammatory. Omar Bakri said the United States was massacring Muslims and it was the duty of all Muslims to fight back. He was fond of quoting one verse from the Koran:

'The punishment of those who wage war against Allah and His Prophet and strive to make mischief in the land is only this: that they should be murdered or crucified or their hands and their feet should be cut off on opposite sides, or they should be imprisoned.'

His acolytes would sometimes set up a projector, flashing images of Iraqis allegedly killed by the Americans. There were also photos of the prisoner abuse at Abu Ghraib prison near Baghdad, which had just been made public. Such humiliation of Muslims made me seethe with anger.

Omar Bakri also told us that in this war there was no distinction between civilians and non-civilians, innocents and non-innocents. The only real distinction was between Muslims and disbelievers and the life of a disbeliever was worthless. Bakri had formed al-Muhajiroun in Britain in 1996 and had steadily become more radical, especially after 9/11. Though he was dismissed by many as a loudmouth, his followers, many of whom only had a superficial knowledge of Islam, hung on his every word and sometimes gravitated towards violence. Several of his acolytes had become involved in terrorist plots – including one sponsored by al-Qaeda to set off large fertilizer-based bombs in crowded spaces, such as the Ministry of Sound nightclub in London. He had a remarkable record of mentoring and teaching young militants who subsequently plotted violence – but of never being involved in, nor aware of, their plans.

After two British men carried out a suicide attack against a bar in Tel Aviv, he boasted that one of them had taken a course he had run on

Islamic law, but insisted he was unaware of their plot. He also spoke of a 'Covenant of Security' – which held that Muslims living in Britain should not commit acts of jihad there, but could wage jihad overseas. He told a story about the companions of the Prophet Mohammed who were given protection and hospitality in Christian-ruled Abyssinia. This had brought about the concept in the Koran of a covenant, whereby Muslims are not allowed to attack the inhabitants of a country where they find refuge. It was a cunning way to avoid getting into trouble with the UK's tough terrorism legislation.

At Omar Bakri's lectures a quiet British-Pakistani called Abdul Waheed Majeed sat at the back, taking the official minutes of the proceedings. He lived in Crawley, a sleepy market town south of London, but drove up for the talks. He had been one of a group of young men mentored by Omar Bakri in Crawley, several of whom had planned to blow up the Ministry of Sound nightclub in London. Majeed was not implicated in the plot but years later would himself make the ultimate sacrifice for al-Qaeda.

Soon I was attending Omar Bakri's 'VIP' lectures, which were open to only a few of his closest followers like Abdul Majeed. Omar Bakri was impressed by the fact I had spent time in Yemen and by the name I had given my son. He liked to call me Abu Osama (the father of Osama).

These sessions were held at least once a week in followers' houses in Luton with six to ten of us. They were followed by a large dinner of lamb or chicken offered by the host. Omar Bakri liked his food.

Behind closed doors his message was very different. On one occasion he said he was issuing a fatwa that allowed for the killing of the disbelievers – the *kuffar* – in England because in his view they were part of a larger conflict. Asked by one of the group – a red-bearded optician of Pakistani origin from Birmingham – whether it was permissible to stab *kuffar* on the street, he confirmed that it was.

Omar Bakri had come to the UK to escape prosecution in Saudi Arabia, but was quietly giving his blessing to followers to kill people on the streets of the country he now called home.

I was among a small group of his followers who tore down advertising posters showing scantily clad women and maintained a stall in

Luton town centre to distribute leaflets and proselytize with megaphones. For me, it was belonging to another gang. But the fractious atmosphere – including a growing number of assaults on Muslim women – gave us a real sense of purpose in defending our community. It was not Fallujah, but it was a much smaller part of the same struggle.

We would beat up drunkards who were harassing veiled women. On one occasion a fellow al-Muhajiroun member and I chased two men through the Arndale Shopping Centre after they had abused Muslim women. I caught up with one in a Boots chemist's store and dragged him to the ground among the shelves of cosmetics, punching him repeatedly before escaping as the police arrived. When Luton Town football club played home matches, which attracted groups of neo-Nazi skinheads, I would carry a baseball bat or hammer with me. And my little circle rejected attempts by other Muslims to engage politically in England, regarding such efforts as useless and against Islam.

I felt Islamophobia at first hand, especially when subjected to 'additional screening' at airports on a regular basis. On one trip from Denmark, I was held up for two hours at customs at Luton airport while they checked through my luggage and asked me the usual questions.

'Are you doing this because you hate Muslims? That's the reason, isn't it?' I asked accusingly. They looked offended. One went to fetch a colleague, a British-Pakistani woman wearing a hijab.

'I'm a Muslim too and I can assure you this is nothing to do with our religion,' she said.

'You're not a Muslim. You're just pretending to be one. What you actually are is a hypocrite,' I snapped.

Jihadi-Salafism was not exactly an inclusive creed.

Omar Bakri designated me the 'Emir of training' for the group because of my boxing background. I instructed a small group of al-Muhajiroun in boxing in the gym. And I began leading expeditions of young British extremists to Barton Hills, a nature reserve north of Luton, where we conducted paramilitary exercises without weapons.

I made the drills up as I went along, using al-Qaeda training videos I had seen online as inspiration. Getting my trainees to crawl through an icy stream and then run up a steep bank was a staple. I loved being outdoors and so did my students. They got to play at being mujahideen for the day; shouts of *'Allahu Akbar!'* resounded through the forested hills.

Soon there was so much demand for the training that I was leading groups of a dozen into the hills twice a week. They came from as far away as Birmingham to join in.

Among those I encountered in Luton was Taimour Abdulwahab al-Abdaly, a young man of Iraqi descent who had spent much of his childhood in Sweden. We bumped into each other in the men's clothing department at a large store where he worked. Al-Abdaly had deep-brown eyes and luxuriant black hair; he could have been a matinee idol. But he was in Luton, a place that did not scream opportunity. We played football and went to the gym together, and met at Friday prayers.

Occasionally Taimour came along to al-Muhajiroun's open meetings, more out of curiosity than conviction. He was a quiet character who rarely expressed any views. From time to time we did get into theological debates, and he would gently challenge me on my uncompromising embrace of the *takfiri* position. Like my Danish friends in Vollsmose, he seemed an unlikely candidate for terrorism. His wife did not wear the full veil, or *niqab*, but a modern loose hijab. Years later Taimour would be another to confound my expectations.

For extremists like me, the imprisonment without trial of alleged al-Qaeda members at Guantanamo Bay and the scandal at Abu Ghraib infuriated us. My Luton fraternity would mockingly describe the US President as Sheikh Bush because the Saudi religious establishment was so deferential to the Americans, condemning terrorist attacks in Iraq but never mentioning the deaths of ordinary Iraqis at the hands of US forces.

On 7 May 2004 the American civilian Nick Berg was executed in Iraq by Abu Musab al-Zarqawi, the Jordanian jihadi for whom no level of violence or brutality seemed excessive. Zarqawi ensured that Berg's beheading was filmed.

At that time Zarqawi was something of a hero to us; he was on the frontline and not cowed by vastly superior forces. He was ready to use the sword himself and was developing even more of a following than Osama bin Laden among my Luton circle.

The video of Berg's killing, and others of attacks on US forces in Iraq, became popular among jihadis in Luton and elsewhere in the UK, turning up on DVDs distributed by al-Muhajiroun.

I too watched the video of Berg's murder, but had no idea until later that the man to his right, restraining him as Zarqawi prepared for the fatal blow, was Mustapha Darwich Ramadan, whom I had spoken with in a Danish prison in 1997. After his release Ramadan had got into more trouble and fled to Lebanon and then Iraq, where he had adopted a *nom de guerre*, Abu Mohammed Lubnani, and joined the militant Islamist group Ansar al-Islam.

Lubnani and his sixteen-year-old son were killed in Fallujah, fighting with al-Qaeda against US forces.

I was not alienated by the brutality of the videos emerging from Iraq because they represented justifiable retribution for the invasion of Muslim lands. They would instil terror in the enemy. Allah had told Mohammed that in war slaughter was preferable to taking many captives. In the words of the Koran: 'It is not for any prophet to have captives until he has made slaughter in the land. You desire the lure of this world and Allah desires (for you) the Hereafter, and Allah is Mighty, Wise.'

I could separate these remote acts of war from my everyday surroundings in a way that many of Omar Bakri's followers could not. To young men like the optician who attended his private lectures, the enemy was everywhere, in uniform and out of uniform, in Baghdad and Birmingham. They had bought into a very simple distinction: it was the disciples of Allah against the disbelievers.

I found it difficult to accept that simplistic formula. Perhaps my basic humanity held me back from seeing the world as a struggle between good and evil, where the evil included ordinary people trying to raise families and hold down jobs. Despite the fatwas that justified the 9/11 attacks, I had begun to feel nagging doubts about the targeting of civilians. Jihad to me was still a defensive action to protect the faith. And on a personal level, I simply liked to be liked – by Muslims and non-Muslims. Whether it was a brief chat with a supermarket cashier

or a bus driver, a conversation about football at the warehouse or helping someone struggling with their shopping, I saw non-Muslims I
knew as fellow human beings, albeit misguided ones.

I became adept at distinguishing between my commitment to the
cause – and to al-Muhajiroun – and the rapport I developed with ordinary people I encountered.

I was proving less adept at keeping my marriage alive. I had given up
my job as a forklift driver and was working as an occasional nightclub
bouncer. I certainly had the build to qualify, and made more money
than when I had a regular job. Being paid in cash at the clubs and pubs
of Luton and nearby towns had one additional benefit: tax on my
income would not directly go into the British government's coffers for
its war against Muslims overseas.

But Karima was unhappy, prone to mood swings, intolerant of my
lifestyle as the 'Muslim bouncer'. She felt alone and struggled to cope
with the children. Osama had become a boisterous toddler. At one
point – during a row about my lengthy absences from Connaught
Road – she spat in my face.

On a grim evening of drizzle in the autumn of 2004 she came to me
with a simple request.

'Can you leave?' she asked. 'I don't want you here any more.'

Karima asked me for a 'divorce in Islam' and even wanted me to
help find her a new husband. Rather than allow a man I did not know
to move into the house where my young children lived, I went as far as
introducing her to a Turkish friend of mine. He became her new
husband – at least in Islam if not according to the law of the land – and
moved in with Karima. But three days later he moved out again.

'I couldn't take her,' he sighed. We laughed.

With nowhere to live and a sense of failure, I hit a low that recalled
my trip to jail in Denmark. Then my response had been very different:
no more crime, find discipline and self-respect through becoming a
good Muslim. As 2005 began, turmoil produced the opposite effect: it
was like a relapse to my Bandido days. There was nothing in the Koran
to guide the conduct of a nightclub bouncer. When I found club-goers
with cocaine, I gave them the option of handing it to me or handing it
to the police. Soon I had a lot of cocaine and began using it again after

seven years of self-denial. I also had a wild partner, a blonde called Cindy[2] who worked for a car dealership and filled the rest of her waking hours with hardcore partying.

Within about three minutes of meeting her and a friend outside one of the clubs where I was working, Cindy had leered at me.

'I love spanking,' she said.

'What do you want me to spank you with?' I shot back.

She named a certain whip apparently well known in S&M circles and gave me her phone number.

Whether I was still technically married to Karima or not, the Koran promised severe punishment for sex outside marriage.

'The woman and the man who fornicate scourge each of them a hundred whips; and in the matter of God's religion, let no tenderness for them seize you if you believe in God and the Last Day.'

It was the sort of punishment that Cindy might appreciate. But I spent the next few months living a life of contradictions, giving in to every sort of temptation but then trying to repent through prayer. I was hopelessly adrift, in a maelstrom of sex, drugs and brawls, interrupted by occasional reconnections to the faith.

One of the clubs where I worked was in the town of Leighton Buzzard. Shades was a pitiful place: a scar on what had once been a pretty street in a country town. It saw plenty of fights and I earned my keep. Tony, the head doorman, was an affable guy in his early forties and smarter than your average bouncer. He could be thoughtful and inquisitive, unlike the louts that we threw out of Shades most nights. I was the first Muslim convert he had worked with and he was curious about why I had chosen Islam.

On a bitterly cold evening in February 2005 Tony picked me up at Leighton Buzzard station in his ageing Honda Accord. Normally we would talk about boxing, work or the weather. But on that evening, as we sat at traffic lights, he turned to me and asked simply:

'Why does Allah want people to kill other people? Don't you think, Murad, Allah would prefer you to teach people to read?'

I stumbled, before offering up stock answers about the need for

---

2 Cindy is not her real name. I have used a pseudonym.

jihad to protect my religion in the face of Western oppression. But the nakedness of Tony's question troubled me. Since becoming a Muslim seven years before, I had learned to cultivate or imagine enemies – Shi'ites, the Muslim Brotherhood, racists in Luton, more recently the US government. Somehow I had become identified by whom or what I loathed; enemies provided an outlet for my anger. But they also camouflaged the real reasons for embracing hatred. Anger and frustration had been part of me since childhood; how much easier it was to hate than to reconcile.

My reflex reaction when confronted with painful questions was to blame the Devil for trying to undermine my faith. Since becoming a Muslim I had been constantly reminded by imams and scholars that Satan was always looking to sow doubt. As it was written in the Koran: 'Satan said: "O my Lord! Because You misled me, I shall indeed adorn the path of error for mankind on earth, and I shall mislead them all. Except Your chosen slaves among them." '

Amid the hedonism of life with Cindy, I felt weak – as if slipping back towards my clubbing days in Korsør. I had to escape before the quicksand enveloped me. And it was my estranged wife who would – at least for a while – rescue me.

'Would you come back?' was Karima's simple question when I picked up the phone. It was the early spring of 2005. She sounded exhausted rather than desperate for my company. Even so I was elated at the chance to be reunited with my children. I would miss the sex with Cindy but not the unhinged lifestyle – nor the lack of any purpose.

Repentance is a formidable force, and helped me to put the wild interlude behind me. Walking through the backstreets of Luton, I would recite to myself the words of Allah.

'Those are the true believers who, when they commit an evil deed, or wrong their souls, remember Allah, and seek forgiveness for their sins – and who but Allah forgives sins?'

CHAPTER EIGHT

MI5 COMES
TO LUTON

Spring–Autumn 2005

On 30 April 2005, *Newsweek* went to print with an incendiary story. US military personnel at Guantanamo Bay had defiled the Koran and humiliated prisoners.

The magazine reported that 'Interrogators, in an attempt to rattle suspects, flushed a Qur'an down a toilet and led a detainee around with a collar and dog leash. An army spokesman confirms that 10 Gitmo interrogators have already been disciplined for mistreating prisoners, including one woman who took off her top, rubbed her finger through a detainee's hair and sat on the detainee's lap.'

Newsweek retracted part of the story, but by then Muslims around the world were outraged. There were deadly riots in Afghanistan, and in Pakistan the opposition politician Imran Khan used the story to undermine the country's military leader, General Pervez Musharraf. Jihadist communities everywhere thirsted for revenge, among them our band of brothers in Luton.

Omar Bakri helped organize a protest outside the US embassy in London on Grosvenor Square in mid-May, and I drove down from Luton in a convoy of his followers.[1]

---

1 Omar Bakri announced the dissolution of al-Muhajiroun in October 2004, citing the need for Muslims to 'merge together as one global sect against the crusaders and occupiers of Muslim land', but in practice the disbandment was a ruse to confuse

A video of the event is still available online, and among the Pakistani and Arab men yelling abuse there is a tall, broad-shouldered Dane, stamping on the Stars and Stripes as it smouldered on the London pavement, smiling and chanting.

'Bomb, bomb USA.' 'Remember, remember, eleventh September.' The chants were as provocative as possible. Then we knelt to pray, before, to my astonishment, the 200 or so protesters drifted away, as if a few slogans had restored Islam's self-respect and caused the diplomats of the Big Satan to quiver behind the bullet-proof glass of their embassy.

I was furious. Just as my adrenalin was beginning to run, the protest was over. These so-called militants were pussies. Surely we had a duty to take on the police cordon and try to enter the embassy. So we would most likely be hurt and arrested, but that would be a pin-prick compared to the injury done to our faith. I was frustrated, disappointed by Omar Bakri. He had delivered a fiery speech and then retired to his comfortable car. It was all talk. I also began to doubt whether he really had contacts in Iraq and other jihadist battlegrounds.

I returned to Luton that evening determined to expose the blowhards who proclaimed jihad but did not want to miss lunch. With the passion of a man recently redeemed from straying into the wilderness, I threw myself into research on Salafism and jihad. As an ordinary Muslim I could not pretend that I could compose a fatwa, but I planned to publish a booklet, 'Exposing the Fake Salafis'.

Over the next few weeks, working day and night, I wrote a pamphlet that became a paper and then a treatise – more than 140 pages of closely argued rhetoric, crammed with quotations from the Koran and the ancient scholars. The fake Salafis liked to talk but were secretly in league with the *kuffar* who had invaded Muslim lands.

'The Fake Salafis in our time use thousand and one excuses to deny the obligation of Jihad Fard Ayn in Iraq and other Muslim lands, also denying that those who assist the Kuffar (disbelievers) in this crusade against Islam are apostates,' I wrote.

---

those investigating his activities. The group's operations continued and have done ever since. Al-Muhajiroun has periodically changed its name to avoid being banned. For example, recently it operated under the name 'Shariah4UK'.

My conclusion was a call to arms:

'Your duty as a true Muslim, is to support your Muslim brothers and sisters, who right now are being killed by the neo-crusaders and Jews, I ask you kindly to at least make Dua [prayers] for them, collect finance for them, and try your best to reach the frontline where your brothers are striving or at least help someone to go there.'

Intellectually at least I was already on the battlefield.

My studying was interrupted one morning in June 2005 when there was a knock on the door at our semi-detached house. (By then, we had moved to Pomfret Avenue, another nondescript street in Luton.) I looked through the bedroom window and saw a policeman. There was another knock. I whispered to Karima to tell them I was not home.

From the landing I listened.

'What do you want?' Karima asked.

'It's the police. We'd like to speak to Mr Storm.'

'He's not here.'

'Yes, he's here – we know he's here.'

I put on my clothes and went down to the door.

The officer was soft-spoken but did not give me his name.

'Can you come with me, Mr Storm? We have some questions we'd like to ask you.'

It seemed like this was a routine he had performed a hundred times before.

'No,' I replied. 'I can't come with you but if you want you can come into my house.'

He declined, and I asked what the problem was.

'Your car has been seen filling up at a petrol station. Thirty pounds of fuel and then whoever was driving left without paying.'

I knew it was a fabrication. Surely they could do better than this.

'Here, take the key. Go look at the gauge. No one put thirty pounds of fuel in.'

I accompanied him outside and unlocked the car. As soon as I turned on the ignition, the police officer melted away. In his place, opening the passenger door, was a dapper young man in a suit.

'Mr Storm – my name is Robert. I'm with British intelligence.'

His words went straight to the pit of my stomach.

'All right,' I said weakly, getting out of the car. 'What do you want to speak to me about?'

'This is dangerous,' Robert said, 'very, very dangerous. It's very important that we speak.'

It was far from clear to me what was dangerous. I invited him to come inside, but insisted I had nothing to tell him.

He declined and we stood beside the car. As I began to recover my composure I was struck by how young he was. He must have just graduated. This was probably one of his first jobs in the field.

Perhaps, I thought, the security services were aware of my relapse into drugs and believed it might make me vulnerable.

'Can I ask you a few questions?' he resumed. Across the street I noticed glances from neighbours leaving for work.

'Morten,' he said, trying to be familiar and informal, 'there's a very dangerous situation in the UK with terrorism.'

'First, my name is Murad,' I replied. 'Second, you don't have any-thing to fear from Muslims. There have been IRA attacks, by Catholics, so why don't you go to search for Catholics, or the Spanish ETA? Why are you harassing Muslims? There's never been a terrorist attack by Muslims in the UK.'

Warming to my theme, I raised Iraq. 'How many hundreds of thou-sands of children have you killed? You don't expect Muslims to be angry? You expect to be able to hit people but for them not to retaliate? I am not scared of you. If you want I will pack a bag of clothes and you can take me to prison.'

Robert smiled and shook his head.

'We don't want to arrest you. We just want to ask you some things.'

Here we were – the Danish Muslim and the man from MI5 – engaged in debate on Pomfret Avenue, just around the corner from Treetop Close, in Luton.

Then the generalities ended.

'What do you think of Abu Hamza?' he asked.

Abu Hamza al-Masri was a militant Egyptian cleric known in the racy English tabloids as 'Captain Hook' because of his prosthetic hand. He claimed he had sustained the injury while on a de-mining project in Afghanistan. He had been the imam of the Finsbury Park mosque in North London.[2]

'I don't know much about him,' I replied, which was the truth. Our paths had never crossed and I had never read his lectures. 'And I am not going to backbite him just to please you. You are a non-believer and he is a brother Muslim.'

We talked for about two hours, standing by the car outside my house. All the time, I asked myself whether I would be charged with one of the many anti-terrorism charges already on the books. Perhaps MI5 were somehow aware of the diatribe I had drafted to justify jihad, or had identified me from the protest at the US embassy. Or perhaps I had been grassed up by the Islamic Centre in Luton, which saw me and my friends as dangerously radical.

Robert took his leave. We shook hands, both aware that I was now part of the game. What I did not know is that two officers from Danish intelligence had seen everything from a car parked nearby. MI5 and their friends clearly thought I was worth spending time with and were angling for me to share my contacts.

Just three weeks after that conversation, on 6 July 2005, the world's leaders converged on a Scottish golf resort for the G8 summit, hosted by Tony Blair. After nearly eight years in office, Blair seemed unassailable. He had tied Britain closely to Bush by his support for the wars in Afghanistan and Iraq, where a large chunk of the UK's armed forces were now deployed. But at home public opinion had turned decisively against the war. The rationale for the invasion had been undermined by allegations that evidence of Saddam Hussein's weapons of mass destruction had – at the very least – been embellished.

The wars had also enraged many British Muslims. A few had travelled to Pakistan with the aim of joining al-Qaeda, the Taliban and

---

2 Abu Hamza had been charged in 2004 with encouraging the murder of non-Muslims and incitement to racial hatred. At the time of my meeting with Robert the beginning of Hamza's trial was just days away. After being convicted and serving jail time he was extradited in 2012 to face trial on terrorism charges in the US.

other groups. Some had stayed and been killed – or disappeared into the tribal territories, their fate unknown. A few had come home.

On the morning of 7 July Blair and his senior ministers were presenting an ambitious agenda to the summit. An aide passed the British Prime Minister a note. Three suicide bombers had attacked the London Underground system; there were casualties and the capital was paralysed. Shortly afterwards a fourth suicide bomber blew up a London bus.

Blair emerged from the conference looking shaken.

'It is reasonably clear that there have been a series of terrorist attacks in London,' he said, before hurrying to a helicopter.

That morning I was oblivious to the carnage some thirty miles to the south; and I had no idea that the bombers had caught a train from Luton on their way to the capital. But my insistence to the MI5 man Robert weeks earlier – that Britain had nothing to worry about from Muslims – was suddenly null and void. And as news spread of the bombings and speculation spiked, I got hostile stares as I walked through Luton in my Muslim garb, still unaware of events in London.

A friend called me to tell me of the attacks and we all hurried to meet at the Woodland Avenue community centre. Everyone was wary of a backlash. By now we knew that some fifty people had been killed and several hundred injured.

Despite the casualties, all of them civilians, I found a way to justify the attack. Brothers in Islam had struck fear into the hearts of the *kuffar* and a blow at the financial heart of a state committed to war against Muslims. The attack would surely cost the British economy tens of millions, money that could not be spent on war.

My adrenalin was pumping. We had all talked about jihad; we had cheered on the brothers in Iraq. Now it was on our doorstep. Was England the next frontline in this war of religions? Anything seemed possible.

As we travelled to London the following day for a Muslim wedding, the tension was palpable. A young white man on the pavement saw us pass and raised his hand as if to take aim with a pistol. I stopped the car and called him over. He saw I was white and may have thought he had an ally in his provocation.

I spat at him and he ran to his car to grab a crowbar. I jumped out, ready for a fight, but others held me back. The last thing this wedding party needed was a brawl on a London street.

There was a spate of assaults on Muslims in Luton; Karima was harassed. Community meetings brought together Muslim sects that usually avoided each other, to discuss a common threat.

Omar Bakri Mohammed saw a dividend out of the 7/7 bombings. He summoned close followers to a meeting in Leyton in East London days later. The situation had changed, he said. The 'Covenant of Security' – that British jihadis should not consider attacking targets in Britain – was dead.

'Now,' he told us, 'jihad has come to the UK. You can do whatever you wish.'

Perhaps he knew he was on safe ground. Most of his acolytes were not ready to follow the path of the 7/7 bombers. But it was not for want of permission.

Had it not been for an old Danish associate and a mislaid mobile phone, I would probably have continued listening to Omar Bakri's bombast and training in the English countryside for the day that jihad would inevitably call.

I had met Nagieb in 2000 – he was a Danish journalism graduate of Afghan descent. He knew of my time in Yemen and wanted to make a film about the mujahideen there. And he wanted me to go with him to open doors.

I was excited by the prospect; my spirit was beginning to stir again and I still wanted to return to a truly Muslim land as Allah had ordained. I felt more in common with my friends there than with the radical blowhards in the UK. The rush that immediately followed the London bombings had worn off and I was worried that MI5 might come calling again as they stepped up their efforts to discover more about UK-based jihadist cells in the wake of the London attack.

I even began to indoctrinate my son, Osama, who was now three. We would play a game of call and response.

'What do you want to be?'

'I want to be mujahid.'

'What do you want to do?'

'I want to kill *kuffar*.'

I argued to myself that if Western children could kill dark-skinned turbaned figures in computer games, I could teach my son about retribution. Hatred again.

My relationship with Karima had never really recovered. When Karima asked me back, Cindy had come looking for me in my family home in Luton, not realizing Karima would be there. It was the second time I witnessed the full force of Karima's volcanic temper, as she shouted abuse – angered not so much by the fact that Cindy had slept with me but because she represented the decadence and permissiveness of Western women.

When I told Karima of my plans to return to Yemen, she shrugged and turned away. There was no discussion, just resignation. She felt abandoned, unwanted.

So perhaps it should not have come as a surprise when one afternoon I picked up her mobile phone as it buzzed – Karima had gone out – and read the following text: 'Meet me in the hotel. I love you.'

It was not the fact that she had found someone else that bothered me. We had long ceased to love each other; our relationship was more a pact for the sake of the children. It was the fact that she still sheltered in the house I was paying for, still used my name to keep her European residency, and while happy to take another man in Islamic law would not divorce me in civil law.

When she returned home, she was nervous. Had I seen her phone? I lied. It was in my pocket.

'I want you out of the house while I look for it.'

She was not very good at keeping her nerve.

I called the number from which the suggestive text had come. A man answered. I found out later that he was a Palestinian living in Luton, whose Moroccan wife was Karima's best friend. He and Karima had had a secret Islamic wedding.

I went back inside and confronted her.

'I know exactly what you are up to,' I told her quietly. 'I know where you are going and everything. I am just asking you to give me my children.'

She looked at me with spite.

'You will never see your children again,' she said. 'Never.'

She grabbed Osama and Sarah and made for the front door. I held her back and she swung round and hit me in the face. She pulled Osama by the hood of his jacket, nearly throttling him. He was crying.

'Osama is staying with me,' I told Karima as he cowered on the floor.

Shortly afterwards I left the house with my three-year-old son, only to find out the following day that the police were looking for me. Karima had told them that I had abducted him. I felt as if I were on the run for a crime I had never committed.

Before any sort of mediation could begin, Karima left for Morocco with Sarah – without telling me or seeing Osama.

Eventually the police tracked me down to a friend's house in Luton. His mother had been caring for Osama while I was out. Her eyes were red and swollen when I returned.

'They took Osama,' she sobbed. 'They said they were taking him to the police station.'

I summoned fellow militants and nearly a dozen of us converged on the police station. The waiting room was full of beards and robes.

I was blind with anger.

'Where is my son?' I demanded loudly. 'Give me my son back.'

By then Osama was in the care of the social services department and I was redirected to an adjacent building while the rest of the unlikely delegation sat in the police waiting room.

I looked out of a featureless waiting room at a thousand shades of grey. Luton in the approaching British winter was not cheering. There was a knock and a woman brought Osama in.

To my relief, he didn't say, 'Kill Bush and the *kuffar*, victory to the mujahideen.' I might have lost custody of him there and then. Instead he ran to me and wrapped his arms tightly around my neck.

'Why did you take him?' I asked the woman.

'We were told you had kidnapped him,' she replied.

'Where is his mum?' I asked.

'We don't know.'

'Exactly,' I replied – unable to hide my sense of triumph. 'That's because she is in Morocco, with my daughter. I should report her for kidnapping.'

I walked out of the building, clutching my son's hand tightly and leading a group of bearded Salafis with angry faces who had come to rescue a child called Osama from Bedfordshire Social Services.

The drizzle began to seep into our clothes.

CHAPTER NINE

MEETING THE SHEIKH

Late 2005–Late Summer 2006

There is a popular joke in the Arab world. There are different versions but its essence is this. Millennia after creating the earth, God returns to see how things have changed. First He looks down at Egypt. 'Ah, the industry, the cities, the beautiful buildings; I would never have recognized it,' He marvels. Then He surveys Syria. 'The architectural splendour, the sophistication of society,' He says. Moving south, He then sees something more familiar. 'Ah, Yemen – same as ever.'

I had that same feeling in the dying days of 2005, when I arrived at Sana'a airport. Yemen was a country that kept drawing me back – despite its poverty, its almost medieval treatment of women and the growing dossier held by the Yemeni security services on one Murad Storm.

I had good reasons for returning – to help Nagieb make his film and reconnect with old friends, or those who were not languishing at the pleasure of the Yemeni state. I felt like a different person this time. I was about to turn thirty and I had my son, Osama, with me. Now he would grow up to be a God-fearing Muslim.

A fresh start: I seemed to need one every eighteen months. Was it boredom? The hope of one day finding the perfect wife? A compulsion to be on the road?

I was still serious about Islam. I enrolled at the al-Iman Islamic

University in Sana'a, which was still being run by Sheikh Abdul Majid al-Zindani. Since our previous encounter seven years before, when I had insolently questioned his Salafist credentials, the Sheikh had attracted the attention of the US government. He was now designated a 'global terrorist' for fundraising on behalf of al-Qaeda. Despite that dubious honour, he was still a public presence at al-Iman. And he welcomed me back, assigning me a special room to study in at the university. Al-Zindani became particularly fond of Osama, who used to tag along with me.

I also caught up with Abdul, the young Yemeni courier who was so proud of his association with Osama bin Laden. His English was more polished and he had recently married. He now had a much bigger home in Sana'a and a relatively new car parked in front of it. Being an al-Qaeda courier clearly had not prevented him from embarking on some promising business ventures.

It was refreshing to be away from the endless circular chatter of *faux*-jihadis in England, and instead in a place where imprisonment and even death were daily risks, a place at the centre of a web that spread to Pakistan and Indonesia in the east, and Somalia to the south. I found out that the jihadist presence had become more intense in my absence, despite the growing scrutiny of the security services.

Word spread that the big European was back in Sana'a, the one with the red hair and tattoos. And one man was intrigued to meet me. He had heard that I had spent time in Taiz back in 2002 and knew that I had attended Dammaj.

His name was Anwar al-Awlaki. He taught at al-Iman University, and he too had recently returned to Yemen.

Awlaki's father was an eminent member of Yemen's establishment and a grandee of the Awalik tribe. He had studied in the United States, where Anwar had been born, and been Minister for Agriculture in his home country. Early in 2006 I was invited to a banquet at the Awlaki family home.

Awlaki had asked an Australian-Polish convert studying at the Sana'a Institute of Languages who called himself Abdul Malik to gather together some of the young foreign Muslims living in Sana'a and bring them to dinner. Malik's real name was Marek Samulski. In his mid-thirties, he was tall and well-built, and like so many Western Salafists had been radicalized by the events that followed 9/11. He had been persuaded by his South African wife to come to Yemen so their sons could be brought up as good Muslims.

Awlaki by then had developed quite a reputation as a preacher in militant circles in the West. I was only dimly aware of his English-language sermons because I had preferred listening to Arabic clerics, but I knew he was a rising star in Salafi circles.

The Awlakis' home was an imposing three-floor building of grey stone not far from Sana'a's old university – a house that was laid out in traditional Yemeni style, with large windows. The younger Awlaki occupied the middle floor, which he shared with his first wife, a woman from a well-connected Sana'a family, who had lived with him in the United States.

I took my son with me to the dinner. It was a cool evening in January, one of the few months of the year in Sana'a when the weather is familiar to a north European. I made sure Osama looked his best, and bought a new *thawb* for the occasion.

We were ushered into Awlaki's apartment, which was furnished with impeccable but not ostentatious taste. Books lined the walls, most of them Islamic texts. Samulski introduced me to the preacher, and I warmed to him immediately. He was urbane and well-informed, with a scholarly air and an undeniable presence. He exuded self-assurance without coming across as arrogant. But he also had a sly sense of humour. Awlaki was well-groomed, with a neat beard and gentle brown eyes behind wire-rimmed glasses. Like most Yemenis, he was slight; unlike them he was very nearly six feet tall. He conversed easily in English and Arabic and was a generous host.

'How did you like Dammaj?' he asked me.

'It opened my eyes. And Sheikh Muqbil had such deep knowledge and understanding. I just wish my Arabic had been better then.'

'And now?'

'Oh, it's much better. But my religious Arabic is stronger than my street Arabic.'

Awlaki was interested in finding out more about my contacts – in Sana'a and Taiz. He asked me about the other foreigners in my circle and some of the Yemenis – like Abdul – that I had got to know. It seemed that he was looking to tap into a wider pool of radicals in the Yemeni capital and beyond.

I asked Awlaki how long he had been back in Yemen.

'On and off about three years. Sometimes I find it a little dull, but life in the West was not easy after 9/11.'

'It wasn't very easy here either,' I laughed.

Our exchanges were little more than pleasantries, but afterwards I thought he had been gently trying to get the measure of me, find out the depth of my commitment and the circles in which I moved.

At one point Awlaki's son, Abdulrahman, came in to show him some homework. He was about ten, tall for his age, with his father's eyes. There was clearly a close bond between them. Abdulrahman seemed to be in awe of his father, who in turn was much more affectionate and attentive than many Yemeni fathers I had met. A gentle and polite boy, Abdulrahman helped entertain Osama despite the difference in their ages.

Samulski, probably by prior arrangement with Awlaki, suggested we start a study circle to learn more about Islam – a weekly occasion for an honoured group of students to discuss the issues of the day and their implications for Islam. Awlaki agreed and I offered to host some of the meetings.

Awlaki started coming to my home to give his lectures to our small group of English-speaking militants. It was a beautiful old house with whitewashed walls and I had decked it out with dark-blue Arabic furniture and a thick Yemeni carpet. It was a privilege for me, but he clearly enjoyed our company. We were more worldly than most of his students, and he loved being our mentor, seeing his every word absorbed. Sitting cross-legged on the floor with notes in front of him, poised and eloquent, he liked to show off his intellect and learning, peering occasionally over his glasses at us.

He focused a great deal on Islamic jurisprudence related to jihad, marshalling verses from the Koran and *Hadith* to make his case. One of his most popular online tracts, '44 Ways of Supporting Jihad', grew out of these lectures on my carpet.

He reserved much of his ire for the Yemeni government for its cooperation with the United States. A favourite phrase of his was: 'We should clean the dirt in front of our doorsteps.'

After the study sessions he never lingered for lunch or dinner with the rest of us, perhaps because he wanted his relationship with the group to remain formal. He'd politely accept a biscuit and take his leave. If Omar Bakri was the gourmand, he was the ascetic.

But as I got to know him our relationship became more informal. He had a good sense of humour and liked a candid discussion. Some of the attendees at his lectures were deferential to the point of fawning. There was no danger of that with me, and he probably warmed to me because I could be his intellectual foil.

Awlaki had a rare ability to combine his learning with a talent to communicate and a broad understanding of the world. So many Islamic scholars I had met could talk endlessly about the nuances of the Koran but were unable to connect with a wider audience, and especially a younger audience.

I began to do some background reading on him and asked him about his time overseas, to get beyond the reputation that preceded him and to try to discover what made him tick. He was five years older than me. He had been born in New Mexico in 1971 while his father was studying there and had returned to Yemen when he was seven. He had clearly been a brilliant student across the board and had won a full scholarship to study in the United States.

He had chosen to attend Colorado State University at Fort Collins to study civil engineering and told me he enjoyed fishing in the nearby Rockies. Then he had come home for a short period to get married, before returning to the US. A popular preacher at Denver-area mosques, he came to feel that education and propagating Islam were his vocation. One of the reasons, he later told me, was the US-led campaign to oust Saddam Hussein's forces from Kuwait in 1991, which had prompted him to take his religion 'more seriously'.[1]

---

1 Awlaki later claimed to have made a trip to Afghanistan to wage jihad in this period, but said he abandoned attempts to fight after the Mujahideen 'opened' Kabul. While there is little evidence that he had already become radicalized in the mid-1990s, Awlaki even then had connections that were unusual and unexplained. In 1999 the FBI had

In 1996 – at the age of just twenty-five – he was appointed as an imam at the Rabat mosque in San Diego, a small bungalow squeezed among ranch homes in La Mesa. He said he liked the climate in southern California, and stayed there nearly five years. Awlaki was justifiably proud of his academic record in the US. After leaving the west coast, he began preaching at the al-Hijrah Islamic Center in north Virginia and attended graduate school at George Washington University, intending to complete a doctorate in Human Resource Development. In his first term, he scored a 3.85 GPA (Grade Point Average).

The young cleric appeared to have a glittering future: he was bright, well-connected and very well-educated. The University of Sana'a expected him to return home and head a newly created Faculty of Education to help raise the standard of education in his poor and largely illiterate homeland.

And then, after 9/11, everything changed.

Among a large number of articles I found that featured him, I was drawn to one published the day after the 9/11 attacks. A *Washington Post* photographer, Andrea Bruce Woodall, went to the al-Hijrah Center, which had called an interfaith prayer meeting. One photograph was of Awlaki from above, showing his cap and clasped hands. 'It shows the grief that Muslims felt but also their fear that people might think they were responsible for this tragedy,' wrote Woodall.

Soon after the attack Awlaki gave an interview to *National Geographic*.

'There is no way that the people who did this could be Muslim, and if they claim to be Muslim, then they have perverted their religion,' he said. 'I would also add that we have been pushed to the forefront because of these events. There has been huge media attention towards us, in addition to FBI scrutiny.'

But there was also this warning:

'Osama bin Laden, who was considered to be an extremist, radical in his views, could end up becoming mainstream. That's a very

---

opened but not pursued an investigation into Awlaki's association with one of the men in the entourage of Omar Abdel Rahman, the so-called Blind Sheikh convicted of conspiracy in the 1993 bombing of the World Trade Center.

frightening thing, so the US needs to be very careful and not have itself perceived as an enemy of Islam.'

Vast resources – money, agents, technical surveillance – were poured into the 9/11 investigation and thousands of leads followed. In the immediate aftermath of such an outrage, civil liberties took a back seat to the need to know. Who had helped the hijackers? Who had they met? Were other attacks planned?

Awlaki was just one of those caught in the dragnet and was interviewed four times in the weeks after the attacks.[2] By early 2002 he felt intimidated and harassed. He always insisted he had nothing to hide, and in conversations we had in Sana'a he made no attempt to conceal his feeling that the Muslim community in America had been targeted by a deeply intrusive investigation.

2 Handwritten notes by Special Agents – released in 2013 under the Freedom of Information Act and posted by Judicial Watch – show Awlaki was frequently under surveillance between November 2001 and January 2002. Comings and goings at his suburban Falls Church home were noted, as were his travels in his white Dodge Caravan, the times of his mobile-phone calls, and his visits to the mosque and the Islamic Society at Woodlawn, Maryland.

On 15 November 2001 he was tailed on his way to National Public Radio in Washington DC, where he took part in a panel discussion for the show *Talk of the Nation*.

The surveillance of Awlaki revealed no contacts that might have had consequences for US national security, but did uncover an almost compulsive appetite for sex. Agents found that Awlaki was making visits to area hotels but staying just an hour or so, and they began contacting escorts known to have worked out of those hotels.

On 9 November an escort met FBI officers at the Loews Hotel in Washington. She showed them notes about a customer who had paid her $400 in cash four days previously for oral sex. The listed name was Anwar Aulaqi, with an address in Falls Church. Another escort working out of the Washington Suites Hotel told agents that on 23 November she had met a client who 'was tall and thin with a full beard, and polite. He claimed to be from India and employed as a computer engineer', according to the agents' notes of an interview with the woman. She recognized Awlaki from a photograph and said he had paid $400 for an hour with her.

The documents show that Awlaki had several more encounters with different escorts at a number of Washington-area hotels in the winter of 2001. He paid between $220 and $400 for a variety of acts. One escort who met him at the Melrose Hotel told agents that he looked very much like Osama bin Laden. Altogether, the FBI interviewed seven women about their appointments with Awlaki, but he was never charged.

Awlaki decided to quit his doctoral programme and return to Yemen, and by March 2002 he was gone, his wife and child following a month later. He returned only briefly in October to settle his affairs in the US. He was detained when he arrived at New York's JFK because a warrant for his arrest on suspicion of passport fraud had been signed by a Denver judge. But the US attorney in Denver had cancelled it the day before he arrived.

The manner of his departure from the US, the premature end to his studies, the aura of suspicion, still rankled with him when we got to know each other four years later. And the sense of grievance had been deepened by the publication of the 9/11 Commission's report in 2004.

I found the Commission's report online and devoured it, reading great chunks late into the night.

Tracing the hijackers' movements in the United States, the Commission had noted that two of them had known Awlaki while staying in San Diego, and one of them had visited his mosque after he had moved to Virginia early in 2001, which the Commission said 'may have not been coincidental'.

One of the Commission's staff reports had said: 'There is reporting that [Awlaki] has extremist ties, and the circumstances surrounding his relationship with the hijackers remain suspicious. However, we have not uncovered evidence that he associated with the hijackers knowing that they were terrorists.'

To Awlaki, this was accusation by innuendo. The Commission noted several times it had been unable to interview the cleric, suggesting he was on the run.

There was more in the footnotes of the report. 'The FBI investigated Aulaqi in 1999 and 2000 after learning that he may have been contacted by a possible procurement agent for Osama bin Laden. During this investigation, the FBI learned that Aulaqi knew individuals from the Holy Land Foundation and others involved in raising money for the Palestinian terrorist group Hamas.'

Worse still for a Muslim preacher were leaks to the media about his arrests in San Diego in 1996 and 1997 for soliciting prostitutes – and allegations of similar misconduct after he moved to the Washington DC area. One article written around the same time as the 9/11

Commission report was published said: 'FBI sources say agents observed the imam allegedly taking Washington-area prostitutes into Virginia and contemplated using a federal statute usually reserved for nabbing pimps who transport prostitutes across state lines.'

It was all, in Awlaki's view, the dark art of character assassination.

'They did everything they could to humiliate me, to make me a laughing stock among Muslims,' he told me.

I also began to watch some of his online sermons, which had been viewed by tens of thousands on YouTube. Awlaki had begun recording video sermons in English after leaving the US, refining and sharpening a narrative that depicted the West as hostile to Islam. His gift was breaking down the complexity of the Koran into language readily understood by young English-speaking Muslims. His eloquent and authoritative tone was pitch-perfect; and he made the radical sound reasonable.

He made several visits to the UK between 2002 and 2004, staying for the most part in East London. His celebrity meant that when he gave sermons, the rooms were packed. Sales of box sets of his CDs and later DVDs did brisk business. Among the avid consumers were some of the suicide bombers who attacked London in July 2005.

While he whipped up anger against the oppression of Muslims, Awlaki was careful not to be too specific lest he attract the attention of British security services. Even so, Muslim community leaders became concerned that he was luring at least some of his audience towards what they called 'rejectionism'. As one East London imam later put it, 'he left the congregations all revved up with nowhere to go.'

Behind closed doors, as with Omar Bakri, it was a different story. In small study circles Awlaki spoke out in favour of suicide bombings in the West. One such meeting was attended by undercover MI5 informants, prompting the British authorities to ban him from travelling to the UK.

In 2005 Awlaki recorded 'Constants on the Path of Jihad', a six-hour online audio lecture series. Building on the work of a Saudi al-Qaeda ideologue, Awlaki argued that Muslims needed to fight continually against their enemies until the Day of Judgement. It was an intricate yet eloquent exposition that drew on Islamic texts, history and current events. Gently, without hectoring, he dwelt on the plight of Muslims in the West, identifying their situation with that of the Prophet and his followers.

'[The Prophet Mohammed] did not customize Islam based on his location . . . he customized the location based on Islam,' Awlaki said.

Efforts by moderate Muslim groups in the West to interpret jihad as a non-violent struggle were just one element of the drive to destroy Islam, he said. Muslims should reject non-Muslim practices and avoid relationships with disbelievers.

The lecture was a tour de force – widely disseminated online, expanding his following in extremist circles in the West.

I got to know Awlaki in Sana'a shortly after the lecture began to get traction online. During long, all-encompassing conversations we talked about Salafism, al-Qaeda, the legitimacy of jihad and the civilian casualties it so often caused. And we talked about bin Laden.

One evening in the late spring of 2006, after we had met about half a dozen times in the study group, he lingered after the others left.

He fixed me with those dark eyes and said simply: '9/11 was justified.'

To his mind, a global struggle between Muslims and disbelievers was underway, and the 9/11 attacks – despite the civilian victims – were a legitimate episode in that battle. Soon after we spoke, he recorded a lecture entitled 'Allah is Preparing Us for Victory', in which he said America had declared war on Muslims.

It is impossible to be sure whether his outlook stemmed from his treatment in the US, and was now fed by a vendetta because of the leaks about his visits to escorts, or whether like me he saw the waging of jihad as the logical and obligatory response to the Muslim predicament. It was probably both. He may also have been swayed by the fact that as his sermons became more militant and as his criticism of the US grew more strident, so his online following around the world grew.

While the cleric was openly sympathetic to al-Qaeda, I did not detect any ambition in him to join the group – nor signs that he had any influence over the rising numbers of al-Qaeda fighters in Yemen. But within days of our first meeting al-Qaeda became a much more potent force.

At morning prayers one cool day in early February, the congregation was abuzz at the news of a major prison break in Sana'a. Two dozen of al-Qaeda's most dangerous men had crawled through a tunnel they had dug from a basement in a political prison to an adjoining mosque. Among the escapees were a number of those involved in the attack on the MV *Limburg* in the Gulf of Aden, and a slight man in his late twenties called Nasir al-Wuhayshi, who had been bin Laden's private secretary in Afghanistan.

The prison escape breathed fresh life into al-Qaeda in Yemen. In the years after 9/11 US and Yemeni counter-terrorism operations had arrested and killed dozens of operatives, bringing the group to the brink of defeat. Wuhayshi would spend the next several years building a new and highly effective al-Qaeda franchise in Yemen.

The sessions with Awlaki soon became a weekly fixture. Anwar's study group, as we began to call ourselves, was a diverse collection of about a dozen English-speakers from the four corners of the earth, including from as far afield as Mexico and Mauritius. I would cook huge meals, and some of the group would stay over in the several spare bedrooms I had. Most of the circle were in Sana'a to learn Arabic or study Islam, but some had other agendas. My neighbour – a Yemeni general who prayed at the same mosque I attended – saw the comings and goings and warned me about some of my visitors. I was being watched, he told me.

One of those visitors was Jehad Serwan Mostafa, a lanky, bearded young man from San Diego with distant blue eyes. His lips seemed perpetually curled into a scowl of disdain, the only exception being when he listened spellbound to Awlaki. His father was Kurdish and his mother an American convert. Once upon a time he had worked in a car repair shop on El Cajon Boulevard. Now he was studying at al-Iman – and applying for a Somali visa. The Somali embassy had told him to go to the US embassy to collect the right paperwork to apply to enter Somalia. I was amazed to find out that the US embassy had given him the necessary documents, no questions asked. Within three years, Mostafa would graduate to the FBI's Rewards for Justice list, accused of aiding and fighting with the Somali terror group al-Shabaab.

Another regular at the study sessions was a Danish convert with auburn hair I knew from extremist circles in Copenhagen. He came from a wealthy family and even I was unnerved by his wild-eyed radicalism. He called himself Ali.[3]

Through the circle I got to know many other militants in Sana'a.[4] One of them – Abdullah Misri, a dark-skinned tribesman from Marib with a neatly trimmed beard – was already al-Qaeda in Yemen's senior money man. He would buy cars in Dubai and smuggle them into Yemen, using the proceeds to bankroll the group's growing capabilities. It occurred to me I was probably by now under surveillance by Western counter-terrorism agencies. After all, I knew a lot of interesting people.

In Sana'a I was also reunited with a Danish convert called Kenneth Sorensen. He had gravitated to Sana'a partly because of what I had told him about my time in Yemen when we met in 2002 in Odense. He had read about me in the Danish newspapers and had sought me out.

Sorensen was younger than me, broad-shouldered and burly, the product of a harsh upbringing. His mother, he told me, was a drug addict, he had little education, and in Denmark he had scraped by as a part-time dustman.

Sorensen had arrived in Sana'a ostensibly to study Arabic, but craved action on the frontline. Awlaki had not invited him to his study sessions because he had a reputation as a loudmouth and loose cannon, dressing up as a jihadi and brandishing guns on the streets of Sana'a.

But I enjoyed his company. He was one of several friends who accompanied me to a rally in Tahrir Square in the centre of Sana'a early in 2006 to protest against cartoons published in Denmark and other European countries which we saw as insulting the Prophet Mohammed. The cartoons had originally been published the previous year by a Danish newspaper, setting off a firestorm across the Muslim world, because of

3 Ali's last name is omitted for legal reasons.

4 Another member of the study circle was Abdullah Mustafa Ayub, an Australian militant whose father was allegedly a leading figure in the terrorist group Jamaat al-Islamiyya. Ayub's convert mother – Rabiah Hutchison, an ex-surfer girl, dubbed the 'the matriarch of radical Islam' in Australia – was even more notorious; rumour had it Osama bin Laden had once courted her in Afghanistan.

a taboo in Islam against the physical representation of the Prophet. One by the Danish cartoonist Kurt Westergaard depicted the Prophet Mohammed with a bomb in his turban, and a Norwegian newspaper had just poured fuel on that fire by republishing them.

'Death to Denmark!' I shouted with the others till I was hoarse. Unlike the feeble crew that had protested in Grosvenor Square the previous year I felt those around me had the courage of their convictions, and that felt intoxicating.

The film-maker Nagieb and I had not given up on his project to make a documentary about the mujahideen, and Abdul said he would try to introduce us to one of the al-Qaeda figures who had escaped from jail in Sana'a. His name was Sheikh Adil al-Abab; Abdul said he had spent time with him in Afghanistan. He would later become the religious Emir of al-Qaeda in the Arabian Peninsula and among the top half-dozen in its leadership.

Abdul drove us to a residence in a rough part of town. He stopped the car but kept the engine running. Within minutes the cleric jumped into the car. He was a young but portly figure with a handlebar moustache.

I became friendly with al-Abab and fascinated by his command of religious texts and his views on jihad. Getting to know him would pay a significant dividend in years to come.

It never ceased to amaze me that the Yemeni security services failed to arrest al-Abab. We met several times without great secrecy in Sana'a. Al-Abab was clearly on the same journey as Awlaki, moving towards a declaration of war against the US and bitterly critical of the Yemeni government for its submissive attitude towards the US.

I had no doubts about the loyalty and principles of the militants I knew. So I was disturbed by what Awlaki told me in the spring of 2006 about Abdul, by then my closest friend in Sana'a.

'Abdul lost $25,000 while on a mission for the brothers in Djibouti,' he said, with more than a hint of disbelief about 'lost'. 'He disappeared off the map for six months and the money has never been recovered, but, as you know, Abdul now has a new house here which seems to be beyond his means. Just be careful,' Awlaki said. 'I don't think Abdul is trustworthy.'

I was taken aback, but also intrigued that Awlaki had spoken about 'the brothers'. He could only mean al-Qaeda; perhaps he was closer to the group than I had imagined.

Without naming my source, I broached the subject with Abdul.

'I swear by Allah that I did not steal the money and what they accuse me of is unjust,' he said. He said he had been arrested in Djibouti, and the intelligence services had confiscated the cash. He showed me passport entry and exit stamps that were some six months apart.

'That's how long I was detained,' he said.

'What were you doing there?'

'I was a courier. I was working for Abu Talha al-Sudani.'

He watched closely for my reaction.

I was taken aback. Abdul, if he was speaking the truth, was clearly moving in rarified and perilous circles. Abu Talha was one of al-Qaeda's leading operatives in East Africa and near the top of the US most-wanted list.[5]

'*Masha'Allah.* That's amazing,' I blurted out. I wondered, did Awlaki know this? Or did he not believe it?

By now I had managed to get my son into a local school and he was beginning to learn Arabic. But both of us missed female company; Awlaki had told me I should find a new wife to look after Osama, and even offered – with a wry laugh – to set me up. But his matchmaking services were not required. After picking Osama up from school one afternoon, I had told him to run ahead and find me a sweet woman to marry. Never a shy boy, he ran into the offices of a driving school for women and when I caught up with him he was talking to a young Yemeni woman. Petite, very pretty and with a winning smile and infectious laugh, she won me over within minutes.

I asked her where she had gone to school and what she did – the usual introductions. Within minutes I told her that I was divorced and living in Sana'a alone with my son. I tried to sound helpless and a little lost; it must have seemed an obvious ploy.

---

5 Abu Talha al-Sudani was suspected of involvement in al-Qaeda's bombing of US embassies in Nairobi and Dar es Salaam in 1998. In 2003 he ordered the casing of a US military base in Djibouti. He was killed in an air strike in Somalia in 2007.

A week later I returned to the driving school in the hope of seeing her again. I sent Osama in.

'My dad wants to speak with you,' he told her in Arabic.

Her co-workers looked on with a mixture of curiosity and amusement. This was not how introductions between the sexes were usually handled in Yemen. We agreed to meet at the Libyan Centre in Sana'a, a place where many foreigners gathered.

I turned up with Osama. She said her name was Fadia and she peppered me with questions, about my divorce, why I was staying in Yemen, what I wanted from a wife.

'I want someone who doesn't pretend to be something she isn't,' I said. 'I was married to a woman who pretended to be a pious Muslim but she wasn't.'

I followed up with an unusual question for what might be described as a first date, Yemeni-style.

'What do you think about Sheikh Osama bin Laden?'

Fadia looked taken aback and hesitated. But then she surprised me.

'I think he has given honour to the Muslims,' she said. 'But I don't like that he killed innocent civilians. If he had attacked the military it would have been better.'

I was delighted and impressed: a Yemeni woman who was not only attractive but spoke English, and was thoughtful. But I also had the arrogance of a true Salafi and believed I could mould her to become a better Muslim. I gave her a CD, embossed with a heart. She probably expected it to be full of romantic music, but it contained nothing but jihadist chants.

I had other questions, most of them to do with religion. As a genuine Salafi, that was what mattered, not her tastes in music or family background. How much of the Koran had she memorized? (My first wife, Karima, knew the entire Koran by heart in two dialects.)

Fadia's parents were both dead, so within a few days she asked her uncle, with whom she was very close, to meet me and to find out whether I was the genuine article or some chancer. The interview was held in Sana'a's only Pizza Hut, which looked exactly like its US counterparts and could have been dropped into the Yemeni capital from Arizona. Apparently I performed adequately. The uncle reported back that I was very likeable and had a sense of humour, but had some dangerous ideas.

'He also has a temper,' the uncle told her, 'but I believe any woman can change her husband.'

Others in her family, a well-respected Sana'a household, were less enthusiastic. Some even checked with contacts in the intelligence services, who said that I should be avoided at all costs because I associated with militants.

That changed the uncle's outlook.

'You can marry him,' he said, 'but we want to see all his papers: residency, health, everything.'

The confident expectation was that I would be unable to trawl Yemen's byzantine bureaucracy for the documents. Then she could be steered towards another suitor preferred by her family, a wealthy surgeon who did not have my baggage of divorce, a young son and the wrong friends.

Somehow I gathered all the papers, even one from the Ministry of the Interior that granted me residency. I could sense the animosity among some of the officials; I was an unwelcome guest.

The new love of my life chose me rather than the wealthy surgeon. One Friday in the late spring of 2006, our marriage contract was sealed at her uncle's house. While he had grudgingly accepted the match, other family members had not. Her brother refused to attend the wedding.

I didn't tell any of them that the paperwork for my divorce to Karima had not been completed: as far as I was concerned the man-made laws of the UK had no jurisdiction over such matters.

I went to the tailor to order a sumptuous new *thawb* for the ceremony and asked a Yemeni friend to lend me the equivalent of $2,000, as a dowry to the bride's family. The only hitch was that my friend forgot to bring the cash – and Fadia's uncle had to intervene and find the money, to give to himself.

Her family looked askance at some of the guests – most of whom were from my immediate circle. Abdul, Jehad Mostafa, Samulski and Ali – the red-haired Danish convert – were there; so was Rasheed Laskar, a British convert from Aylesbury, with a long thick beard and glasses, who went by the name Abu Mu'aadh and often stayed at my house.

And then, as is customary in Yemen and much of the Muslim world, the party divided into men and women. My new wife wanted me to join her so photographs could be taken. To me that was wholly un-Islamic, a form of idolatry. She also insisted on music at the post-wedding celebrations. Mindful of the Odense fight, I ensured my jihadist friends were gone by then.

At the end of a long day, my bride was brought to my large rented home by her female relatives. So many women dressed in black and wearing the full niqab descended on the house that I had no idea who among them I had married.

When the rest of the party were gone, I realized Fadia was anxious to the point of panic. She stood with all her possessions in a suitcase, in a large house she didn't know, with a hulking north European who was a militant jihadi – and now her husband. Like me when I was on the road to Dammaj, she must have wondered what she was doing.

I recited a few words from the Koran and said a prayer and then carefully lifted the veil from her face. In true Yemeni tradition, she had been caked in heavy Arabic make-up and henna tattoos for the ceremony.

'Darling,' I said, 'why don't you go and wash your face?'

Fadia looked crestfallen, thinking that the hours of beautification would bring me to my knees. But to me she was beautiful without make-up, with her caramel skin and dark almond eyes.

I helped her take off her elaborate wedding dress. It was astonishingly weighty.

'I can't believe it,' I said. 'How did you manage to carry this all day and not die of heat exhaustion?'

What she did not expect was a European sense of romance and seduction. I had prepared her a bath with candles, rose petals and herbs – even a hardcore jihadi can turn on the charm.

Unfortunately, after bathing, she applied a liberal dose of a heavy sweet Yemeni perfume that I could not abide. I asked her to take another shower.

She soon realized she had married a man for whom Islam was ever-present and whose interpretation of the Koran was unyielding. My home had no television; the computer was overflowing with jihadist videos; a cassette recorder played and replayed Islamic lectures. She was surprised to be woken at 4 a.m. on her first day of married life. For me it was a routine occurrence to prepare for *fajr* – the first prayers of the new day. I immediately rose to wash and walk in the pre-dawn cool to the mosque, while my drowsy wife eventually rose from her slumbers to pray at home.

I asked after our first breakfast together whether she would help me read the Koran in Arabic, just as Karima had. I also showed her several of the more gory jihadist videos on my computer. This was completely natural as I was so immersed in this holy battle. She winced and gently reminded me that as this was our first full day of married life, we should treat it as a honeymoon and try to relax together. So we took Osama to Fun City, Sana'a's answer to Disney World. Its gates were a feeble multicoloured reproduction of a castle's turrets, and inside girls clad in black niqabs rode merry-go-rounds, like witches flying through the air.

Fadia was not very religiously observant; I thought it would take me a few weeks to educate her to the path of the true Muslim. She had other ideas and was reluctant to wear the niqab, while also harbouring designs to loosen my religious straitjacket.

Before we had been married a week, I asked her to sit with me one afternoon so I could tell her something very serious. She looked apprehensive: perhaps I was HIV-positive or had some disease.

'I have to go to jihad and I have to go to Somalia,' I told her. 'So you have to prepare yourself.'

Plenty of would-be jihadis – in the West and from Arab countries – were excited by events in Somalia. A militia called the Islamic Courts Union had put an end to years of warlordism and anarchy across much of that benighted country. It had brought calm to Mogadishu, a city that had turned into a quagmire for international peacekeepers. For militant Islamists like me, Somalia was a rare victory to be celebrated, where authentic Islamic principles had brought stability.

'You have to be proud of me and support me,' I told her.

Fadia was taken aback, but said nothing. It was not customary for a young Yemeni wife to challenge her husband on such issues.

'Jihad in these times is obligatory. Islam is not only about peace, and if they suggested that when you went to school they were wrong.'

My determination to travel to Somalia grew when Ethiopia – with the encouragement of the Bush administration – sent troops into Somalia in July 2006 to prop up the feeble transitional government, which was at risk of being overrun by the Islamic Courts. To any self-respecting jihadi, the invasion of a Muslim country by Christian soldiers was the ultimate provocation. If I wanted to be the true jihadi I would have to return home to Denmark to raise the necessary cash – thousands of dollars – so that I could help expel the Ethiopians.

As I was preparing to leave Yemen, Anwar al-Awlaki disappeared. On a boiling day that summer, he failed to turn up at my house to continue his lecture series. I was irritated: they were a highlight of my week.

A few days later I learned from al-Qaeda's money man in Yemen, Abdullah Misri, that Awlaki had been arrested. He faced a vague and almost certainly fabricated charge of being involved in plots to kidnap a Shi'ite and a US official. The case never went to trial and his followers were convinced the charges were the result of pressure on Yemeni authorities from the Americans.[6]

---

6 Documents obtained by the group Judicial Watch under the US Freedom of Information Act – and posted in July 2013 – showed that the FBI's interest in Awlaki had certainly grown in the years since he had left America. A memo marked 'Secret' and written by the Bureau's San Diego office on 1 December 2006 requested access to Awlaki while in jail.

'Aulaqi left the United States in the early part of 2002. Significant information regarding Aulaqi has developed since this time and since the time he was interviewed in September 2001,' it said. 'It is unknown at this time whether the interview will take one or two days or if a polygraph will be conducted. Specific requests from San Diego will be made after approval for access to Aulaqi from Yemen officials,' the memo continued.

The same document recalled an FBI interview with a man called Eyad al-Rarabah, who had helped some of the 9/11 hijackers find accommodation in Virginia as well as

The FBI would get its way and obtain access to Awlaki while he was held in a Sana'a jail, most of the time in solitary confinement. His family's prominence meant that he was not mistreated, nor were his conditions as deplorable as those of most inmates. But he was not allowed any contact with the outside world and his study circle evaporated, none of us knowing if or when we would see our mentor again.

It was time to leave Yemen for a while. With the words of Awlaki and al-Abab still fresh in my mind, I wanted to start preparing to make my own contribution to the cause of global jihad – and my heart was set on Somalia.

---

illegal driving licences. Al-Rababah 'later stated that he met [9/11 hijackers] Hani Hanjour and Nawaf Alhamzi [sic] at the Dar al-Hijrah mosque with Anwar Aulaqi'.

There were a host of other topics the Bureau wanted to discuss with Awlaki, including 'his overseas travel in 2000 and 2001; his association with San Diego individuals believed to be involved with international terrorism; his involvement in fund raising in the United States for known terrorist organizations; and his involvement in criminal activity in an effort to support terrorist organizations'.

CHAPTER TEN
THE FALL

Late Summer 2006–Spring 2007

My plan was to return to Denmark and work for a building company run by a Muslim friend so I could save money to go to Somalia. I had initially wanted to help the Islamic Courts Union by starting a dairy farm in southern Somalia, using the skills I had gained during a few months at an agricultural college in Denmark. But as Ethiopian forces advanced towards the capital, Mogadishu, I knew I would be drawn into the battle for the future of Somalia. Even if it brought martyrdom I had no option but to fight for my religion. Only then would my son grow up being proud of his father.

Fadia, however, persuaded me that she and Osama should follow me to Denmark. On arrival she would need to apply for an EU 'Schengen visa' rather than come in as my spouse – because I was not technically yet divorced from Karima.

Fadia had never flown before and was more than a little anxious. When she passed through Frankfurt airport, a security officer demanded she take off her long jacket. She refused, saying it was traditional dress, and was nearly detained. All the same, when she arrived in Copenhagen, I was less than happy to see she was wearing nothing more than a scarf on her head, far less the niqab I had bought her in Sana'a.

'It doesn't matter that you are in Europe; you have to dress like a Muslim woman,' I told her. 'Did you marry me just so you could come to Europe and get a passport here?' I asked bitterly. Perhaps I was haunted by previous relationships. Within days she found a Yemeni woman who supplied her with all the garments she needed to appear respectable.

We moved into a rented apartment in a neighbourhood of Aarhus heavily populated by immigrant families. My network of extremist contacts continued to grow. My strident views and exotic travel had made me something of a celebrity in Danish Islamist circles.

I was happy with Fadia. She was gentle, intelligent and kind to Osama, who adored her. But I knew that at some point my son had to be with his mother and so I came to an agreement with Karima. She had left Morocco to resettle in Birmingham and said that if I brought Osama home I could have regular access to both children.

The arrangement meant that I would be shuttling between Denmark and Birmingham, but I was overjoyed to be reconnected with my daughter, Sarah, and was capable of keeping the peace with Karima. I wanted to see as much of my children as I could before the next chapter of my march towards jihad.

Commuting between Aarhus and Birmingham also extended my contacts with supporters of the Islamic Courts in Somalia, of whom there were a surprising number in the English Midlands. They had a significant presence at a large mosque in the rundown Small Heath district of Birmingham. The Ethiopian incursion had enraged the Somali community and dramatically boosted the popularity of the Islamic Courts, fusing their cause with Somali nationalism.

I went to a crowded event at the mosque with a Danish-Somali friend, who had travelled with me from Aarhus. He also had family in Birmingham – a cousin called Ahmed Abdulkadir Warsame.

Warsame was a wiry teenager, with drooping eyelids that gave him the appearance of being half asleep. He had protruding front teeth.

He had evidently been inspired by the speeches from representatives of the Islamic courts.

'I'm going. I'm definitely going.'

'*Masha'Allah*. That makes two of us,' I replied. It would be the beginning of a long and momentous relationship. I was keener to get to Somalia than ever. I was being regaled with stories via email about the killing of 'disbelievers'; mainly Ethiopian troops. Two of my Sana'a study circle had already travelled to fight in Somalia – Ali, the Danish convert, and the American, Jehad Serwan Mostafa. Mostafa had emailed me, urging me to join the fight. 'We are winning!' he had exclaimed.

Warsame invited me to a dinner at a Somali-Yemeni restaurant for the Islamic Courts representatives who had attended the conference. He had come to the UK three years before as a refugee and was desperate to return home to fight the Ethiopians but lacked the funds to travel.

I quickly befriended this kid. His ardour for the cause impressed me. I would drop by his small council flat near the Small Heath mosque. An ancient leather sofa, piled high with lecture notes, dominated the room. He was taking a course in electronic engineering. But all he could talk about was confronting the Ethiopians and liberating his country. In October 2006 the Ethiopians began to push eastwards from the town where they had been protecting Somalia's hapless government. As we followed news reports and received messages from friends it seemed obvious the troops were intent on attacking the capital.

At the same time, authorities in Yemen, a short journey by sea across the Gulf of Aden, moved against militants they suspected of helping the Islamic Courts.

Early on the morning of 17 October I had a frantic call from the wife of Kenneth Sorensen, one of my Sana'a study circle. He had been arrested along with Samulski, two young Australians and my British friend, Rasheed Laskar. They were allegedly involved in a plot to smuggle weapons from tribes in lawless eastern Yemen to the Islamic Courts Union, a transaction organized on the Yemeni side by Abdullah Misri, the car-dealer and al-Qaeda financier.

I knew the reputation of the Yemeni security services and worried that Sorensen and the others would be tortured in jail. I told Sorensen's wife I would try to publicize the case in Denmark. I asked my friend Nagieb to put me in touch with a television station and the next day recorded an interview with Denmark's TV2.

The crew met me in a shopping arcade in Aarhus. I knew the interview would be heavily edited so tried to get across my appeal as succinctly as possible. Sorensen was innocent, I insisted. He was a friend who was studying Arabic and had no involvement with militants.

The Danish government should be working for his release or at least ensuring it had consular access to him.

In reality, I suspected he was involved in the scheme, though I had no idea how far it had evolved. My suspicions were deepened by the arrest in Yemen of another associate of mine from radical circles in Denmark, Abu Musab al-Somali. He had come to Denmark as a refugee when he was a child, but returned to Somalia and joined with foreign fighters affiliated with the Islamic Courts Union – shuttling between Mogadishu and Yemen. He received a two-year jail sentence for his part in the weapons plot.

Sorensen and the others were luckier – they were released and deported in December. But my television interview had made me an even greater 'person of interest' to the Danish authorities.

On a grim afternoon of drizzle and mist, I received a call at my apartment in Aarhus.

'This is Martin Jensen. I am with PET,' a voice said flatly.[1]

PET is the Danish security and intelligence service, and in the state apparatus a branch of the police.

'We need to speak with you. Can we arrange a meeting?'

'No,' I said. 'There's nothing to talk about. You are fighting against Islam and we are protecting ourselves. In any case, you could be Mossad, the CIA. I could be just "rendered" somewhere. It's all the fashion.'

I tried to sound relaxed but my mind was racing. Were my travel plans known? Were my phone and internet monitored? Had one of the Sana'a group identified me as some sort of ringleader? Had the Yemenis given MI6 or the CIA access to their new crop of detainees?

In the end we agreed that I would come to a local police station. But first I called my mother. I had to tell somebody and I didn't want to alarm my wife.

'Mum, I can't go into this on the phone but PET have asked me to go and meet them. I just want to let you know in case anything happens to me.'

She let out a sigh. I imagined her raising her eyebrows and gently

---

1 He was not using his real name.

shaking her head, resigned to yet another twist in her wayward son's life. 'Okay. Be careful,' she said.

There were two agents waiting for me in a conference room, including a tall well-built man who introduced himself as Jensen. The other, a paunchy bald guy, was looking out of the window and smoking. Barely forty, he moved with difficulty.

Jensen pushed an open Coke bottle towards me.

'I don't drink anything you give me that's already open. You could have put anything in it,' I said, being deliberately melodramatic.

He shrugged and went to fetch me a sealed bottle.

So what did I know about Sorensen and the rest of the group detained in Sana'a? I repeated what I had said on television.

Then they turned the screw. Jensen leaned forward across the table. He was handsome, in his late thirties with a carefully maintained suntan and perfectly groomed hair. He could have passed for a Danish George Clooney. And he had the self-assurance of a man who knew he looked the part.

'We know your wife has outstayed her visa. But that's fine. We just want to be sure that neither you nor your friends have any violent intentions towards Denmark. Perhaps you could even help us.'

'I would never help you,' I shot back. 'To help the *kuffar* against a Muslim brother is apostasy.'

'By the way,' I added as I got up to leave, 'I want to go to Somalia. Can you check if that is against Danish law?'

They looked taken aback by my chutzpah. In fact it was perfectly legal for me to travel there as the Islamic Courts Union had not been declared a terrorist organization by Denmark or other Western governments.

My connections in Yemen had clearly placed me under suspicion. One of the Sana'a group who had been arrested told me later that he'd been questioned by a Western intelligence agent while he was in prison.

'They were trying to find out more about you,' he told me. 'They said, "We know Storm is behind this."'

As I left the police station it dawned on me I was a marked man. I realized that very soon I would have to make a choice – to go to

Somalia and invite even greater scrutiny or to retreat from wearing my commitment so plainly on my sleeve. But if anything my encounter with the agents had made me more determined to leave. They knew they were making no progress. Jensen left me his number just in case. For some reason I did not tear up his card in front of him, but tucked it in my pocket as I left.

Soon my mission had a godfather – Abdelghani, a Somali friend from Denmark who had already travelled to join the Islamic Courts militia. On 19 December he emailed me formal permission from the Islamic Courts' 'Foreign Affairs Office' to enter the country.

I felt a surge of adrenalin. It was a religious duty beyond debate – the sort of decisive action that the pitiful preachers in Denmark, the blathering Omar Bakri Mohammed, would talk about endlessly but never carry out.

I bought a plane ticket – one-way to Mogadishu. I would be travelling solo. My Birmingham sidekick Warsame still did not have the funds to travel. I emailed him to tell him I hoped he could join me soon.

A new chapter was about to begin with new comrades, on the newest frontline of a global conflict. But my wife would burst into tears whenever the subject arose.

'What's going to happen to me? I will be left here alone in a country I don't know, with no rights, no money.'

'Allah will provide and take care of you. And when we've pushed out the Ethiopians you'll be able to join me,' I told her. It was not exactly reassuring, and at the time less than convincing even for me. But that was the answer for everything.

She told me she would return to Yemen if I was gone for long.

As the first snowflakes of an early winter storm drifted down, I drove to a military surplus store in Copenhagen to buy the supplies Abdelghani had requested: camouflage gear, water bottles and Swiss army knives. Hardly lethal weapons, and easy enough to take without raising suspicion.

Getting to the frontline in Somalia seemed more necessary than ever. Ethiopian forces were closing in on Mogadishu. Some of my friends had already retreated with other fighters south towards Kismayo, a port city south of Mogadishu. In a few days I was due to leave.

As I went around the shop, I had a call from Somalia. It was from Ali, the Danish member of the Sana'a study circle. He told me excitedly that he had just beheaded a Somali spy the group had discovered near Kismayo.

Setting aside his naivety in calling me on a mobile phone, I congratulated him loudly in Arabic. The shopkeeper looked at me with a hint of suspicion.

On the drive back from the store Abdelghani called. I started telling him about all the supplies I had bought, but he cut me off.

'You must not fly down here now. It's too dangerous. Ethiopians have surrounded the airport and are arresting all holy warriors who have come to the country to fight alongside the Islamic Courts. Stay away!'

I was stunned, and infuriated by Abdelghani's defeatism.

A question started ringing in my ears, one directed to Allah: 'Why won't You let me go? Why am I being prevented from serving You?'

It was – after all – His decision. Allah was all-knowing; as mere mortals we had no influence over our destinies.

And then another question: 'Why have You let the mujahideen lose – yet again?'

My wife was waiting for me when I returned home.

'They lost,' I mumbled, my eyes averting her gaze. 'They lost the fight.'

I dragged the equipment up the stairs and discarded it in the bedroom. I was quiet, brooding, defeated – and reminded of the time I sat in the police car on my way to prison in Denmark, vowing somehow to change course. I needed answers.

Dejection soon became anger, and anger began to ask some difficult questions. At every turn I had been stopped; every plan had disintegrated. I had spent a decade – what should have been the best years of my life – devoted to a cause, sacrificing my relationships and any potential I might have had as a boxer. And that cause now seemed so distant.

I sat in the darkened bedroom, the silence interrupted only by the purr of cars passing through the snow. I was days away from my thirty-first birthday, but my future seemed empty. My children were in a different country, my friends in Sana'a scattered, my wife baffled by my mood swings. I had spent the last of what I had earned working at the construction site on supplies that now sat unopened beside me, mocking my failure.

I had been driven on in my quest to fight for the underdog. Years earlier I had come to the aid of my Muslim friends on the streets of Korsør when they were picked on by bullies. I had sat in the library, transfixed by the story of the Prophet's battles against far greater forces in Mecca. I had dreamt of going to Afghanistan to join the mujahideen, and of helping build a beacon of true Islam in Somalia. Everything had turned to dust.

I thought of the bluster of Omar Bakri Mohammed, of the mealy-mouthed preachers in Brixton, the fair-weather protesters outside the US embassy, the cowardice of the Sheikhs all too ready to send ignorant, gullible men to their deaths. Perhaps my devotion to the cause had stifled all sorts of unresolved questions. Perhaps my embrace of Islam was only a way of lashing out at the world and my real inspiration – even if I did not fully understand it – was not doctrinaire Salafism but to fight injustice.

And then the unthinkable began to seep into my mind. Was my understanding of Islam flawed? Was the faith being distorted by men like Awlaki? Or was Islam itself riddled with inconsistencies to which I had been blind?

I had already begun questioning the concept of predestination – *Qadar* – one of the articles of the faith. I had been taught that it held that Allah had decided everything, both in the past and in the future.

In the words of the Koran, 'Allah is the Creator of all things, and He is the Guardian over all things . . . He has created everything, and has measured it exactly according to its due measurements.'

So what was the place of free will, where was the capacity to make a difference? It seemed that none of the scholars I had talked to could explain how *Qadar* fitted with the obligation of jihad, nor why Allah would create a man He had already condemned to hellfire. Even Anwar al-Awlaki had skirted around the subject.

One *hadith* seemed to me to render the individual as a helpless puppet: 'Allah, the Exalted and Glorious, has ordained for every servant amongst His creation five things: his death, his action, his abode, the places of his moving about and his means of sustenance.'

Eventually I roused myself and went downstairs to the kitchen. Fadia looked worried.

'What has happened to you?' she asked.

'I don't know. I just feel that there is no point to anything any more.'

I made myself a coffee and sat down in front of my laptop at the kitchen table. Impulsively my fingers typed: 'Contradictions in the Koran.'

There were more than a million hits. Plenty of entries were just anti-Islamic diatribes, frequently on Christian Evangelical websites that were less than coherent. But in other places I read commentaries that revived long-held but suppressed questions in my head. The words I had once shouted in Hyde Park came back to me: 'Had it issued from any but God, they would surely have found in it many a contradiction.'

The whole construction of my faith was a house of cards built one layer upon the next. Remove one, and all the others would collapse. It had relied on a sense of momentum – a journey from finding Islam to becoming a Salafi to taking up jihad in spirit and action. My reading of the holy texts had been clear. Waging jihad to protect the faith was ordained. But somehow I had been prevented from carrying out my religious duty, while other Muslims evaded or denied it.

I also began to reconsider some of the justifications made for the murder and maiming of civilians. I had accepted such prescriptions in my obedience to the Salafist creed. I had lapped up the words of scholars who had found vindication for the events of 9/11 in scripture. But now I thought of the Twin Towers, the Bali bombings, Madrid in 2004, London in 2005. These were acts of violence targeting ordinary people. If they were part of Allah's preordained plan, I now wanted no part of it.

The words of my bouncer friend Tony replayed in my mind: 'Why does Allah want people to kill other people? Don't you think, Murad, Allah would prefer you to teach people to read?'

My loss of faith was as frightening as it was sudden. I was staring into a void, and knew that should I desert the faith I would soon be a target for many of my former 'brothers'. I knew so much about them and their plans. At least half the Sana'a circle alone had joined terror groups. To them I would be the worst of all: the convert who had given up and become an atheist, the foulest of hypocrites. Just as the convert had been promised a double reward in paradise, so the convert who recanted must be doubly punished.

The questions that crowded in on me made me withdrawn at home and prone to anger. My wife seemed worried that I was slipping away from her. Her EU entry visa had expired and, now living in Denmark illegally, she was afraid of being marooned. The atmosphere at home was toxic.

I had to get out, to find time and space to think. On a bitter March morning, I set out to do some fishing in Braband Lake on the outskirts of Aarhus. Winter was clinging on. The reeds along the fringe of the lake were brown and crackled in the breeze, and there were still patches of ice in inlets. The path around the lake was deserted.

I sat down and cast my line, but my mind was elsewhere. For nearly three months, I had prayed without conviction. I had read the Koran again but kept seeing new inconsistencies and contradictions. I had listened to preachers in Aarhus mosques but none had revived my spirits. And all the while the drumbeat of jihadism was intensifying, moving on from the defence of Muslim lands towards a declaration of war against all disbelievers, the meek as well as the mighty.

Out of nowhere, the volcano inside me erupted. Throwing my fishing rod into the lake, I shouted into the water.

'Fuck Allah, and fuck the Prophet Mohammed. Why should my family go to hellfire just because they are not Muslims?'

I thought of my mother and grandparents. We had had our issues but they were decent people who had no malice.

'What if Zaher and Andersen had not been uncovered and my mum or Vibeke had been in the way when they detonated their bomb?'

There were more men in Denmark with their mindset – perhaps dozens within 100 miles of where I lived. Some of them had the potential to bring terror to my country; but how could I help prevent them from taking the lives of innocents?

I reached the car.

'I wasted ten years of my life,' I said, as I gripped the steering wheel and stared through the mist at the outline of pine trees. 'I gave myself to Allah. I believed in the justice of the struggle. But I deceived myself, and I allowed others to deceive me. I could have been a sportsman, I could have enjoyed life, kept my children, made something of myself.'

The rebel in me had rekindled my free will, but I knew how dangerous that would be. Suddenly I was walking in the shadow of Kurt Westergaard, the cartoonist who had drawn the Prophet Mohammed and had his life threatened for doing so. Not so long ago, I had wanted him dead.

Now, I am my friends' enemy, I thought one night as I lay in bed, restless. My wife lay peacefully at my side. What danger might she be in if I abandoned my 'brothers'? For now, the less she knew the better.

The next morning I tried to busy myself with chores, washing-up and laundry. As I threw a shirt into the washing machine, a card fell out. I picked it up. Frayed and crumpled, it was still legible. It was the business card of the so-called Martin Jensen at PET.

The card had a phone number. I tucked it in my pocket and left the house, wandering the streets of suburban Aarhus. If I called him there would be no turning back, no middle ground. I would have to lead a double life, one in which a single mistake could cost me my life. But the alternative seemed worse. Would I stand by as people I knew, people I could stop, brought carnage to my homeland and the rest of Europe?

That same evening I called the number.

Not for a moment did I think his real name was Martin Jensen, and I was doubtful he would even answer. But he did.

'This is Murad Storm. I need to meet you, soon,' I said. 'I have something I want to tell you.'

I could sense him struggling to stay calm.

'Okay, how about the Radisson Hotel in Aarhus?'

CHAPTER ELEVEN
SWITCHING SIDES

Spring 2007

The Radisson looks like a slab of ice, eight storeys high, with glass that reflects the clouds drifting above. The view from the Presidential Suite took in the canals and old cobbled streets of Aarhus, a spacious room of leather sofas, cool Scandinavian fixtures in birch and ash.

The same PET officers who had been at the police station late the previous year were there.

'Martin Jensen', the Clooney lookalike, clearly had a penchant for designer clothes: that day he was sporting a Hugo Boss shirt, expensive loafers and an even more expensive watch.

'Murad, it's good to see you again,' he said, shaking my hand. He had a crisp Copenhagen accent and exuded confidence. This was his show.

'You remember my colleague?' he said, introducing the bald over-weight smoker. 'We call him Buddha,' he said with a smile. 'And you can call me Klang.' He gave no explanation for the code name.

I sat down opposite the two agents on the leather sofas. They perched on the edge of their seats, attentively. This could be a career-defining moment for them – they knew I would be a treasure trove of information about jihadis. Buddha thrust a menu into my hand. 'Should it be halal? Chicken? Fish? Something vegetarian?' he asked, sensitive to my Muslim diet. 'Some bottled water? Coffee?'

His politeness amused me. It was time to make a statement.

'No, I will have a bacon sandwich, and a beer, a Carlsberg Classic,' I replied.

There was a stunned silence.

'That's what I want, guys.' It was my way of saying: 'I'm on your side.' I felt like a weight had been lifted from me.

'I've decided I'm no longer a Muslim,' I said. 'I am ready to help you in the fight against terrorism. For me, the religion that became my life has lost its meaning.'

'This is going to be the biggest,' Klang said, barely able to contain himself. They had a high estimation of my jihadist Rolodex.

The food arrived.

'Skol,' I said – raising my glass and savouring my first taste of alcohol in years. And then I set about a substantial bacon roll. I was a Dane again.

'Let's get started,' I said, and I began to tell my story.

I was the convert unconverted; the scales fell from my eyes. Having been so rigid, I had swung to the other end of the pendulum. While I could do nothing to change the past, my embrace of 9/11, my delusions about jihad and my admiration for Awlaki, I could atone for it. I knew the murderous world-view of al-Qaeda and I wanted to play a part in stopping them.

The agents could hardly take notes fast enough. They kept stopping me – staring in disbelief that I could know so many militants in so many places. The meeting went on for three hours, but it was no more than a prologue.

To share my story was liberating, and the more I told the more I felt myself distanced from my former life. When I walked out of the lobby into the late-afternoon sunshine, I felt at peace. This was the right thing to do.

Klang and Buddha asked me to meet them again in a few days.

'This work is going to take up a lot of your time so we can pay you 10,000 kroner a month,' Klang said after we exchanged greetings in the follow-up meeting.

It was $1,800 – hardly a sum to make me blush but I had not expected to be paid anything at all. Given how cash-strapped I was it would be welcome. 'That sounds good.' Klang handed me a Nokia mobile phone.

'You'll need this to contact us. We'll pay the bill,' he said.

'And it'll make it easier for you to keep tabs on me,' I replied. It was meant as a joke.

'No, no – we wouldn't do that. We trust you,' Buddha replied, protesting too much.

They had my first homework assignment. From a manila folder, Buddha produced two photographs and sheets with short biographies of two of my Islamist contacts in Aarhus.

'We want to know if we need to worry about them,' Klang explained.

The first was Abu Hamza, an overweight Moroccan cleric who liked to preach the merits of jihad, but whom I had always thought to be a blowhard. As I sipped tea in the sitting room of his mosque, listening to him sound off on the oppression of Muslims overseas while he devoured biscuit after biscuit, a suspicion that I had felt for some time hardened. Maybe Hamza was an informant on the payroll of PET. Was I testing him or was he testing me?

While I wasn't sure where he stood, I felt increasingly confident about the decision I had made. It felt surreal but empowering. As I listened to the cleric rant on I nodded my head occasionally. But it was as if I was listening with a different part of the brain. No longer was I seeking religious truth, guidance on what Allah demanded. Instead I was filing away every last detail to take back to my handlers.

The second target was Ibrahim, an Algerian I knew from the mosque in Aarhus. I knew I would meet him at Friday prayers. Afterwards Ibrahim offered me some tea and I walked with him to his shabby apartment nearby.

'Murad, I've found where Kurt Westergaard lives and I know where we can get weapons,' he blurted out once we were inside.

I looked into his excited eyes. Why was he telling me this now? Was he working for PET too? Was this another test? Or did he mean every word?

'Will you join me?' he asked.

'Let me think about it,' I replied.

As soon as I left I punched Klang's number into the mobile phone he had given me.

'We need to meet as soon as possible,' I said.

That evening I met him and Buddha in a hotel room in the city centre and relayed everything I had been told. They didn't seem that alarmed, which made me think my instincts had been right all along: these first targets had been a test. PET had needed to know if they could trust me.

Just to be sure, I went to see Ibrahim again. We met outside the mosque.

'So is it on?' I asked. He looked startled.

'I'm not interested any more,' he replied, cutting off the conversation and walking away quickly.

In the weeks that followed I had frequent meetings with Klang and Buddha. Soon I seemed to know every hotel in Aarhus. We also spoke often on the phone, sometimes several times a day. I was being developed into a regular informant.

I warmed to Klang, who had become my main point of contact. Despite acting as the dandy, he came from a modest background like me. He had worked in the drugs squad before being redeployed to counter-terrorism after 9/11. He knew how life on the streets worked – even if he had little interest in the religious side of jihadism or the places that were breeding militancy. I gradually laid out my web of connections in Denmark. I came up with a colour-coding system: green for harmless, orange for those with potential for violence, and red for dangerous. There were some 150 names.

My task was to keep my eyes and ears open, and report back to my handlers on any potential threat.

'Follow where your nose takes you but keep us informed each step of the way,' Klang said.

The agents told me that occasionally they would ask me to visit radicals on their radar screen. They also gave me a USB stick specially configured to quickly suck out the contents of a hard drive when inserted into a target's computer.

My cash flow steadily improved. The PET agents gave me a further 15,000 DKK so that I could pay the deposit on a new apartment. The payments were masked – either arriving as Western Union cash trans-fers or deposits to my bank account via a PET front company called 'Mola Consult'. PET would use the company to pay expenses relating to my work, including hotel bookings. To process invoices the com-pany had a registered address in Lyngby, a Copenhagen suburb just a couple of miles from PET headquarters.

Fadia had no idea of my new source of income, nor of my contacts with PET. I told her I had received a bonus from the building firm. As a young Muslim woman in a foreign country she asked few questions about her husband's activities. I also did my best to put on a show of recovering my religious faith. It was a necessary deceit – to protect us both. If she knew about my real work and let it slip, her life could be in danger, as could her family back in Yemen. Instead I tried to make her believe my sudden collapse in December had been an aberration brought on by depression.

Every Friday I left the house as usual to go to *Jumma* (Friday prayers). More often than not I did go to the mosque, but not to pray. The gath-erings of 'like-minded' young men in fast-food joints or tea shops afterwards were always rich sources of information.

While my wife was safer knowing nothing, I needed to share the sea-change in my life with someone. And there was only one person in the world who could begin to fathom what had happened and would tell no one.

'Mum, you can't tell anybody this. And you're the only person in the world who knows. I'm not a Muslim any more and I've started to work for Danish intelligence.'

There was silence for a few moments.

'There's never a dull moment with you,' she finally replied.

I wasn't even sure that she believed me but telling her was a relief. For the first time my work as a PET agent felt real. On the few occa-sions we met in the following years she never brought it up.

The first few months of 2007 had been traumatic for Fadia. I had not been a predictable companion and she seemed to expect that at any moment I would announce my departure for some foreign battlefield. She missed her family and had overstayed her visitor's visa. PET told me that if she returned to Yemen they could enrol her in a Danish university and then arrange a student visa, so she could quickly return to Europe.

But leaving Denmark would prove another trial for her. The immigration officer at Copenhagen airport noticed her lapsed status and began berating her. Fearful that she might be arrested, she called me – and I called my new friends at PET. Within a few minutes, the officer's demeanour changed. He saluted my wife smartly and wished her *bon voyage*. She had no idea why.

I remembered my hostile encounter with officers at Luton airport a couple of years before. Being on the side of the 'disbelievers' had its advantages.

Now on my own, I found myself in great demand with Klang and Buddha. One of the Islamists I had coded red was Ali, the Danish convert who had called me up from Somalia to boast that he had beheaded a Somali spy. He had fled advancing Ethiopian troops but was captured shortly afterwards in Kismayo and held for two months before being deported to Denmark.

PET wanted to build a criminal case against Ali so enlisted my help in a sting operation.

'Invite him to your home and get him talking,' Klang instructed me.

He handed me a small black battery-operated electronic recording device, disguised to look like a pager, and showed me how to activate it. A couple of days later, I called Ali. I had carefully rehearsed what I wanted to say.

'Ali, it's Murad. I'm still in Denmark. I heard you came back. What happened? Can you come and see me in Aarhus? I want to hear everything about Somalia. I still want to go, *Insha'Allah* [God willing].'

Ali came to my apartment with several friends from Copenhagen. As they knocked at the door, I turned on the recording device and slipped it into my pocket.

I greeted them with Islamic salutations. It was like being in a film or a play. I had simply reverted to being Murad Storm. I could assume the role as easily as flicking on a light switch.

Ali looked thinner than when I had last seen him in Sana'a, but had that same fierce intensity in his eyes. After we prayed I made them glasses of tea and we sat down cross-legged on the carpet to talk.

'Tell me about the fighting,' I said. 'I can't believe what happened to you.'

This was gathering intelligence, in its purest form.

As he began describing his time in Somalia I looked around the room. His friends were listening with rapt attention. So was I, for rather different reasons. Ali clearly loved the attention. He needed little encouragement to describe the beheading of the Somali spy.

'He had been pretending to be one of the mujahideen. But there was something about him that made us suspicious, and when he was interrogated he admitted he had been sent by the Ethiopians to find out our plans.

'He begged for mercy and said he would join us as a fighter but he was sentenced to death by the Islamic Courts. I volunteered to carry out the sentence. Praise be to Allah for letting me serve Him,' he said.

'*Alhamdulillah* [praise be to God],' I replied. He had just told me everything I needed. I decided not to wash the tea glasses. If the courts needed proof he had been in my apartment they could match his fingerprints.

Klang had disappointing news for me the next time I saw him.

'The recording didn't work.'

'I did everything exactly as you told me.'

'Don't worry about it. It was a glitch. We'll find another way.'

The Danish authorities never charged Ali. I began to suspect that the recording had worked but that PET did not want to compromise me as a source by handing it over to prosecutors. When I later asked Klang whether a case was being prepared against Ali he claimed that as the Somali spy had not been identified there was as a matter of law no victim. Ali remains free to this day and still lives in Denmark.

There were plenty of equally dangerous targets to pursue, and I was given great latitude to follow my instincts. On a breezy spring day in 2007, I was wandering through an immigrant neighbourhood in Copenhagen, hoping I might come across an old associate. I did. His name was Abdelghani Tokhi, a Danish resident of Afghan descent. His appearance made me suspicious. Gone was the long beard – he was now clean-shaven. It was a telltale sign. Jihadis in Western societies frequently shave off their beards to blend in better as they prepare to go operational.

I told PET it might be a good idea to take a closer look at him. It transpired Tokhi was an associate of a Danish-born Pakistani called Hammad Khurshid who had just returned from Pakistan's tribal areas. At that time, before the drone campaign ravaged jihadist ranks in Pakistan, the mountainous tribal areas were still the wellspring of international jihad. Khurshid had received bomb-making training from a senior Egyptian al-Qaeda operative who had supervised the explosives training of the bombers involved in the 2005 London attacks.

Unbeknown to him, Khurshid's notes on how to make explosives were discovered in his luggage by security at Copenhagen airport. PET had subsequently used a front company to offer a cheap apartment for rent close to where Khurshid lived. The apartment was equipped with secret cameras and bugs. The agency turned away several prospective renters, before Khurshid and Abdelghani came calling. A short while later they would film Khurshid making ten grams of the powerful detonating explosive TATP in the apartment, and in September 2007 Danish police would arrest Khurshid and Abdelghani. They were convicted of terrorism offences and remain in prison.

My bona fides – and value as an informant – were growing with every tip. And PET wanted to show me off to their allies in the intelligence world.

CHAPTER TWELVE

LONDON CALLING

Spring 2007

My Luton mentor, Omar Bakri Mohammed, had left Britain in 2005, weeks after the London attacks, amid hostility from the media and growing scrutiny from the security services. 'Send him Bak!' screamed the front page of the tabloid *Sun*.

Omar Bakri insisted he was going to see his mother in Lebanon for a holiday and planned to return to the UK. Britain's Deputy Prime Minister had commented: 'Enjoy your holiday – make it a long one.'

The preacher had taken refuge in the city of Tripoli on the coast of northern Lebanon and soon developed ties to Salafist militants. PET were interested that my former comrade and fellow Danish citizen Kenneth Sorensen was also there.

'How about a visit to Lebanon?' Klang had asked me. 'See what Omar Bakri might be planning, who he's hanging out with.'

I couldn't wait.

Staring out at the twinkling lights on the hills as the plane began its final descent into Beirut on 25 April 2007, I felt a rush. The city had not so long ago been torn apart by religious conflict. How appropriate that this place of sectarian rivalry should be the first destination in my new mission.

The Danes planned to share my findings with the British intelligence agencies MI5 and MI6, part of the back-and-forth trade that is the lifeblood of intelligence services the world over. The Danes had nothing like the resources of the CIA or the British, but they were keen to show they could punch above their weight. They also calculated that reconnecting with the preacher would further enhance my reputation in radical circles in the UK, something that one day might be useful to their British friends.

Omar Bakri and a couple of men with long beards and the look of enforcers were waiting for me in the Beirut airport arrivals hall. The preacher locked me in a bear hug.

'How are you, Murad, my brother – it is good to see you,' he exclaimed. I could not help but notice that his girth had expanded further.

We stepped out into the balmy April night and climbed into his gleaming black four-wheel-drive GMC. As he collapsed into the seat, the vehicle shook. He was clearly getting money from somewhere, probably from those young extremists that I'd sat with in Luton, listening to his bluster. We drove through the Christian suburbs of north Beirut and two hours later were in Tripoli.

On my first day in Tripoli, Omar Bakri took me to the mosque packed with worshippers by the old market. After prayers he bellowed out, 'This is brother Abu Osama al-Denmarki – he studied in Yemen and knows all the brothers there and he would like to say a few words.'

That caught me by surprise. It seemed the cleric wanted to bathe in the reflected light of my jihadist connections. I managed to wing it – recycling all the old lines on the religious obligation of jihad – and it seemed to do the trick because many of the eager-eyed young men came up to embrace me afterwards. It was a moment I would have relished if I had still been on their side.

After a week in the cleric's company, I tired of Omar Bakri's outlandish claims. The preacher may have radicalized a generation of young British Muslims, but he was clearly out of his depth among the hardened militants of Tripoli. They had had to survive real war in the streets. Omar Bakri by comparison was a vacuous windbag.

Keen to impress my handlers, I decided to go after bigger prey. I would not have long to wait. One day when I was in Omar Bakri's company, I met a young man with an impressive beard at a tailor's in the old market in Tripoli. My Nordic complexion clearly took him aback.

'*Masha'Allah!* Where are you from, brother?' he asked me in Arabic.

'Denmark,' I replied.

'Me too,' he said, in Danish, laughing, introducing himself as Abu Arab. He was a Palestinian who had moved to Denmark as a young refugee; his real name was Ali al-Hajdib.

Abu Arab invited me to his house a few days later. Soon after I arrived he received a telephone call. 'Come with me!' Abu Arab said.

He led me down an alley. A black BMW with its engine running was waiting for us.

'Get in!' Abu Arab said, his eyes flashing.

We clambered into the back of the car. In the front were two fighters wearing military fatigues and headscarves. A Kalashnikov assault rifle was thrust into my hands and I was offered a pistol. After I declined, the man riding shotgun held up a hand grenade.

'Perhaps you would like this?' he asked. He seemed to be a commander.

'Or maybe one of these?' he said, opening his camouflage jacket to reveal an explosive belt around his waist. As the car accelerated down the narrow streets, the commander confided that if they were stopped by the security forces or a rival militia it was better to die than suffer the horrors of interrogation.

I tried not to wince whenever the car hit a pothole; explosive belts have an awkward tendency to detonate when jolted.

I did not immediately realize it but I had just been given a backstage pass to Fatah al-Islam, a hardline Sunni group with ties to al-Qaeda which was then sprouting in the Palestinian refugee camps of northern Lebanon.

The commander in the car was Abu Arab's younger brother, Saddam al-Hajdib, a senior member of the group and one of several al-Hajdib brothers in a budding terror dynasty. Saddam was in his late twenties, had fought with al-Qaeda in Iraq and knew its top leadership.[1] Another brother, Youssef, had been arrested in Germany the previous year – at

1 Saddam al-Hajdib knew al-Qaeda in Iraq's then newly installed Egyptian operations' chief, Abu Hamza al-Muhajir, who, along with an Iraqi, took over after Abu Musab al-Zarqawi's death in a US strike in June 2006. Al-Hajdib had recently brought

the age of just twenty-one – after leaving two suitcases full of explosives on trains near Cologne in a failed attack.[2]

Over the next several weeks I was given a tour of the Tripoli refugee camps, where preparations seemed to be afoot for the 'next war' in Lebanon. Abu Arab told me they would stop at nothing in their quest to bring Sharia law to the camps, then to the north of Lebanon, and one day to the whole country. Given the resources of the rival Shi'ite militia Hezbollah, and Lebanon's raw sectarian divides, that seemed a pipedream. But their ambition was irrepressible, they had powerful allies that saw Fatah as a useful counterweight to Hezbollah – and their willingness to make common cause with international terrorism was unquestionable.

I left Lebanon early in May and flew to London, to be debriefed by Klang and Buddha. This time, their immediate boss, whose given name was Soren, was also present. He was in his late thirties and in good shape – his athletic appearance let down by his regular fumbling for cigarettes. Like Klang, he had switched to counter-terrorism after working in the drugs squad, a unit I once had particular reason to hate during my days with the Bandidos. Now he and Klang were partners in the fight against terrorism. The Danes ordered beers for the debriefing. They seemed to want to make me as relaxed as possible.

Soren told me with a smile that half a decade previously he had once been part of the team that had me under surveillance, following my communications with fellow radicals as far apart as Odense and Indonesia. It was Soren and Klang who had witnessed my pavement meeting with Robert from MI5 in the UK.

'He looked like a schoolboy trying to scare you,' Soren laughed. As we swapped stories Klang revealed to me that he and Buddha had worked on the Vollsmose terrorism case – the investigation that led to the arrest and conviction of Mohammad Zaher and Abdallah Andersen – once my friends – for a bomb plot the previous year.

---

funds back from Iraq to Lebanon with him and had killed a Syrian soldier on his return across the border.

2 Youssef al-Hajdib – caught as he tried to escape to Denmark – would receive a life sentence without parole, a punishment he would greet in court by raising both middle fingers in defiance.

'The informant we used testified in the trial. And we then had to arrange for him to change his identity and leave Denmark – it's been pretty tough for him because he rarely sees his kids.'

His words weighed on me for a while. Would that be my fate?

The Danes seemed impressed with the information I had gathered about the convoluted alliances and shadowy leaders behind the Tripoli violence. Would I care to meet their British colleagues?

The Churchill Hotel – close to Hyde Park – is one of London's finest. Behind the elegant facade, the lobby boasted marble floors and columns and mellow walnut furniture. If this was the typical venue for intelligence debriefings, then I was in the right business. The further I travelled from the spartan demands of Salafism the more I was seduced by the trappings of the espionage business.

As I crossed the threshold of the Churchill with my Danish handlers on a glorious spring evening, I had to restrain myself; it was just too easy to replay the Bond theme in my head. It became even more tempting when I set eyes on the MI6 officer who was waiting for us in the hotel suite.

He introduced himself as Matt. He knew how to wear a suit, had a cut-glass accent and impeccable manners, and was ruggedly handsome. He was the epitome of the British intelligence officer, with his oversize, fleshy ears the only part that seemed incongruous.

I imagined his background: one of England's finest boarding schools, where he no doubt excelled at both rugby and Latin, followed by Oxford or Cambridge. And then perhaps someone at the careers department had casually inquired whether intelligence work for Her Majesty's Government would be of any interest.

While I had developed a laddish repartee with my Danish handlers, Matt was all business and polish. In contrast to the sometimes crude Danes and the demanding Americans, the British spies I dealt with were polite and formal, almost to the point of being apologetic.

Even so, Matt laughed out loud when I called room service for some pork scratchings. It was not what he expected from a former jihadi.

I told him that Fatah al-Islam would try to ignite a war inside Lebanon, but he seemed more interested in what I had to say about Omar

Bakri, who had developed a network of supporters in the UK and was probably using them as a source of revenue.

Since the July 2005 bombings, MI5 was intensely focused on uncovering jihadist networks in places like Luton and Birmingham, networks and places I knew well. Since Karima had moved to Birmingham I had spent plenty of time there, renting temporary accommodation so that I could see my children whenever possible.

Not long after my meeting with MI6 my warning about events in Lebanon was borne out. Saddam al-Hajdib, the Fatah al-Islam commander I had met, robbed a bank near Tripoli and made off with $125,000. Lebanese security forces tracked him to an apartment block in the city. Al-Hajdib was true to his pledge: he blew himself up as the security services stormed the building. But the raid triggered days of clashes between Fatah and the security forces around the Nahr al-Barid refugee camp. More than twenty Lebanese soldiers and a similar number of Fatah fighters were killed.

Soon afterwards the Danes told me the British wanted to meet again. 'You impressed them on Lebanon: they didn't really see that coming,' Klang said.

At my second meeting with the British, Matt was accompanied by an MI5 officer called Andy. He was from the English Midlands, in his late forties and not wearing a suit. He seemed harder – more operational than a handler, someone used to being on the streets. I later found out he had previously been a police officer targeting drug traffickers. He and the patrician Matt made an odd couple, but Andy had a very specific mandate – the extremist scene in Birmingham.

'Can you keep your eyes open for us?' he asked.

The initial arrangement was for me to report to the Danes, who would pass on my information to the British, and for me to travel back to Denmark whenever needed. PET were happy with the arrangement because it improved their standing with the British. Soon, however, it was agreed I should also report directly to MI5.

At the behest of MI5 I moved into a modest terraced house in the Alum Rock area of Birmingham. They paid me £400 each month to cover the rent. Like Luton, Birmingham epitomized Britain's industrial decline, its poorer neighbourhoods of rundown terraces and drab tower blocks home to a large South Asian immigrant community, and a hotspot for Islamist radicals. Weather aside, Alum Rock could be mistaken for the rough-and-tumble streets of Karachi.

In the early summer of 2007, as a new season of cricket games began in Birmingham's parks, I immersed myself in the extremist scene. Most mornings I got up before dawn for the first prayer of the day at local mosques. As much as I was used to it, it was harder now that I was only a Muslim on the outside. Afterwards I'd often go to breakfast with 'like-minded' brothers at a halal restaurant. Then we might visit someone else's home to read the Koran together or discuss the latest news from Pakistan or Iraq. And so the sequence would continue: cheap meals on polystyrene plates in cafés with Formica tables, invariably followed by a talk from a radical preacher. One of the most popular was Anjem Choudary, a British-Pakistani lawyer who had been Omar Bakri's deputy in al-Muhajiroun and had taken over his mantle as the most controversial militant in the UK. I was not impressed by him, but noticed how many young men lapped up his every word.

Not all my time was spent in Birmingham. With Fadia away in Yemen and only occasional custody of my children, I had time on my hands. I returned periodically to Luton to keep tabs on the radical circle I had frequented two years before.

Getting 'fellow' extremists to open up was not difficult. Most loved nothing better than to talk. Sometimes I mentioned a new video sermon by Awlaki to get the conversation started. As in Denmark, I colour-coded UK-based radicals for MI5, according to the potential danger they posed. At the Small Heath mosque in Birmingham I rekindled my friendship with the young Somali, Ahmed Abdulkadir Warsame. He was still desperate to return home to fight the Ethiopians but had yet to raise the funds to travel.

If I could help him to Somalia, we could gain valuable intelligence from a region where there was precious little. Andy liked the idea and with his approval I began fundraising in mosques for Warsame's travel. A bureaucratic idiosyncrasy meant that MI5 rather than its sister service would run the operation because the intelligence would be collected through my email account.

The stories of rivalry between the domestic and overseas branches of the UK intelligence services are legendary. But I found that the MI5 and MI6 officers I dealt with cooperated and respected each other's needs. They were fighting different fronts of the same battle – MI6 in Somalia, Yemen and Pakistan, MI5 in Luton and Alum Rock. The suicide bomb attacks in London had given that collaboration new urgency.

It did not take me long to raise the money for Warsame's travel in the mosques and from my militant contacts in Birmingham. He was overcome with emotion when I handed him £600 in cash. 'May Allah reward you,' he said as he embraced me.

We agreed to keep in touch by leaving messages in the draft inbox of a shared email account. Warsame left the UK to join the fight in Somalia, and before very long had a shopping list for me and a request for funds.

One man impressed by my fundraising – and by my friendship with Anwar al-Awlaki – was a Syrian in his mid-thirties called Hassan Tabbakh. He also knew me by reputation from my days with al-Muhajiroun. And we found we had several mutual acquaintances, including Hamid Elasmar, a British-Moroccan, convicted in connection with a plot to behead a British Muslim soldier in Birmingham. It seemed I was not short of links to extremists across the UK.

Tabbakh was a balding chemistry graduate in his late thirties with a beard just beginning to show flecks of grey. I was struck by the sneer that seemed never to leave his lips and by his rather dispirited eyes. He was not a man that radiated enthusiasm. But we were among the few non-Somalis at the Small Heath mosque so it was inevitable that our paths would cross.

I had my son with me the first time we met. 'This is Osama,' I told him.

'*Masha'Allah*, this is a good name,' he replied unsmilingly. He told me he had been granted political asylum in the UK after fleeing for his life from Syria. He said he had been detained for possessing anti-government literature. His constant anxiety suggested that his interrogation by the secret police of the Assad regime had been vicious.

Tabbakh invited me to his home, a small dark ground-floor apartment in a decaying terraced house around the corner from the mosque.

It suited his morose temperament. But he was not short of ideas, and he was desperate to share them.

'I've been busy,' he said.

He had been learning how to build bombs and showed me sketches of targets in London. They included Oxford Street, packed every day with shoppers and tourists, and the area around Parliament.

On the sketches he showed me where exactly he planned to set off his bombs. I noticed his hands were trembling.

'Brother, what do you think? Will it work?' he asked. He wanted me to join the plot. I was stunned that he should share so many details with someone he hardly knew.

With his background as a physics and maths graduate, I had little doubt he would be able to build the bombs, but what was his timetable?

I looked him in the eye. *'Insha'Allah.'*

'You need to be careful, brother,' I added, trying to coax him into slowing down. Anything to buy time.

I alerted MI5. Tabbakh had until then not been on their radar. He was the archetypal 'lone-wolf terrorist', the sort that are most difficult to detect for their lack of contact – by any means – with others. And I had stumbled into his plans.

'We need you to stick very close to him in the coming weeks,' Andy told me.

At another meeting soon afterwards, Andy asked me about the keys Tabbakh used to open his door.

'Big keys, small keys, double keys?' he asked. They were clearly planning to break in. I was told later that in the course of a break-in agents had found the sketches, photographed and carefully replaced them. They would be prima facie evidence of Tabbakh's plans.

As part of the operation MI5 even staged detaining me at Gatwick airport to bolster Tabbakh's trust in me. To set this up I asked Idriss, a well-connected British-Pakistani extremist from Walsall, to drive me to the airport to catch a flight to Yemen. When I tried to pass through security, a police officer made a big show of detaining me, knowing that my driver would tell all and sundry.

I was frogmarched to a small room near the security screening area where an MI5 officer was awaiting me. The police officer was – to say the least – surprised when the agent jumped up and gave me a bear hug. We chatted for a while and then I was escorted back to the departure lounge, where I made a plaintive call to Idriss, complaining about the brutal British security service and asking him to come back to Gatwick to collect me. The incident burnished my credentials among the militants in Birmingham.

Tabbakh hadn't settled on a date to launch his attack but sketched out a diagram of the electronics of the bomb design and told me which chemical ingredients he planned to mix. He said he would use large soda bottles to hold the charge. I wished I had paid more attention during science classes at school, but I told MI5 he seemed to know what he was doing.

The police did not move in immediately because MI5 was wary of blowing my cover. After all, I was the only one in whom Tabbakh had confided. In the following weeks, MI5 took elaborate steps to mask my role by shifting suspicion on to one of his radical associates.

Tabbakh was arrested in December 2007 and later convicted of making bombs to launch a terrorist attack. Police found bottles containing acetone and nitrocellulose in his dingy flat and instructions for converting the ingredients into bombs. They would have been crude and basic, but the judge at his trial said they had 'great potential for destruction, injury and death'.

My street-by-street knowledge of the militant scene in the UK and my Rolodex of jihadis abroad were generating results. Islamist terrorism posed a multitude of problems for agencies which not so long ago had concentrated the lion's share of their resources on the Soviet bloc. It was young, difficult to penetrate and spreading quickly. Inside information was hard to come by; a Dane with good Arabic and nearly a decade of militancy behind him was the ideal informant.

No wonder the Americans came calling.

CHAPTER THIRTEEN

FROM LANGLEY WITH LOVE

Summer 2007–Early 2008

My handlers at PET always talked of the British as 'the cousins'. The CIA were 'Big Brother'. Klang and Buddha found it difficult to contain their excitement when word reached them that the Americans would like to meet Mr Storm.

The Danes set up a meeting at the Scandic Hotel on the waterfront in Copenhagen. Eighteen storeys of steel and glass, it looked like a functional American office building from the outside. But inside it was all pale woods, minimalist Scandinavian furniture and peculiar white perspex trees climbing through the lobby.

Klang and Buddha fussed over me when I arrived. Even Klang's familiar mask was slipping with the Americans sitting upstairs.

'Joshua' and 'Amanda' must have been in their early thirties, both neatly attired in business suits. Joshua was tall with dark hair, good-looking in that preppy, north-eastern way. He had clearly never done a day's manual labour in his life. Amanda made an altogether different impression. I was drawn to her eyes. They were cornflower blue and had a searching, almost beseeching aspect. She had full lips and high cheekbones; honey-coloured hair fell from her shoulders.

For the CIA, the Scandic meeting was a fishing expedition. How much had I learned about Fatah al-Islam, al-Qaeda, and the militants I had met in Yemen? They were especially interested in two topics: Anwar al-Awlaki – still held in solitary confinement in a Sana'a prison but not charged – and the Yemeni connection to Somalia. At that time, the militant Islamist group al-Shabaab, a spinoff of the Islamic Courts Union, was emerging to challenge the Ethiopian troops that had intervened to save the Somali government, and it was beginning to attract fighters from the Somali diaspora in Europe and North America.

Amanda had a way of asking questions which was disarming. Perhaps it was her enthusiasm, her ability to find the same wavelength, or those eyes. For several hours I held court, laying out a spider diagram of my jihadist militant contacts on three continents.

Amanda said the CIA might be interested in having me travel to Somalia, whose anarchy had haunted US policymakers since the disastrous intervention of 1992–4 and 'Blackhawk Down'. Should militants seize large tracts of the coastline or bog down the Ethiopians in urban warfare, it could become much more dangerous than Yemen.

Throughout the meeting Joshua and Amanda took notes. I watched Amanda's manicured hand moving gracefully across the pages of her notebook, her neat script soon filling twenty pages. At the end they had a simple question: 'How would you feel about working for us?'

'I would feel very good about that.'

'We'll be in touch,' Amanda said, that smile finally escaping the corners of her mouth. I could only hope so.

I wanted to keep my options open. I could probably keep both the British and the Americans happy with some agile footwork, but their methods and priorities were different. The British seemed methodical to the point of pedestrian, cautious but well-informed. They had an almost academic approach to developing expertise overseas, relishing discussion of tribal rivalries and geographic oddities. But they were preoccupied by an enemy at home whose strength and determination they could not gauge.

The Americans by contrast wanted to use their formidable technical resources to take the battle overseas – to Yemen, Somalia and Pakistan. The homeland had been hit once; never again. They would prove impatient for results – ready to throw money at problems. They had been seared by 9/11 and were prepared to pursue targets with little consideration for legal niceties. The British could not countenance assassination. Their resources, I fast discovered, were very different too. PET and now MI6 flew economy, even on long-haul flights. So much for the James Bond lifestyle. CIA agents still turned left when they boarded. The Danes used to joke with their CIA counterparts that if they ever flew together, the Americans ought to send their leftovers back to them.

I was also fast discovering that PET wanted everyone to share the adventures I might provide, just so long as they were taken along on the magic carpet. And the next stop would be exotic enough. Klang at PET had a strange request.

'Send me a draft email requesting a meeting in Bangkok.' We had a practice of leaving draft emails in an account to which we both had access, the same trick that al-Qaeda used. The fewer emails that actually travelled the better.

For my PET handlers I was the passport to places they would otherwise never see on their government salaries. They appeared to be able to justify top-class hotels for meetings with Morten (aka Murad) Storm.

A three-day visit to Bangkok at the beginning of December to plan a mission to Kenya seemed ludicrous, but I soon found out why Klang was so enthusiastic about the Orient. Within hours of touching down he was in the red-light district with the rest of the Danish team, including team leader Soren, drinking beer after beer and negotiating terms for the services of a shy teenage girl.

And so it was that the taxpayers of Denmark subsidized the varied appetites of a government servant. Once he had found a girl, I left. The next few days would be arduous and I did not need to start with a monstrous hangover.

'I guess I'll see you later,' he said with a leer.

At least one of Klang's escapades ended in his humiliation. After he had spent some hours canoodling with another woman at a lap-dancing club, he brought her along to a restaurant. The waitress whispered that the woman was not all she seemed; in fact she was a very well-made-up 'lady-boy'. As Klang's face turned pale, the rest of us were bent double with laughter.

The Danes were taking a risk going out drinking with me. American and British agents never socialized with me in this way. But the Danes were more cavalier. There was always the possibility that I might be recognized by someone, blowing my cover and endangering my life. But I was happy to let my hair down. I needed the release and assumed it was unlikely that any of my extremist acquaintances would be frequenting Bangkok nightclubs.

The weakness of several of my Danish handlers for escorts, exotic locales and expensive booze may have begun when they were working in the drugs squad, which had a reputation for hard partying and sampling the powder they confiscated. Now equipped with diplomatic passports, my squad were reaching horizons they had only dreamt about. As we logged more and more 'debriefings' in foreign fleshpots it would become all too easy to forget the PET agents were meant to be my professional partners.

Matt was as usual much more restrained, his only concession to this unusual field trip being an unbuttoned business shirt and neatly pressed jeans.

'Hello, Morten. Beats damp, grey old London, doesn't it?' he said with a glint in his eye when we met in my luxurious hotel suite high above the thronging city.

'We want you to go to Kenya; we have some presents for your Somali friends,' he said to me.

By now, in the dying days of 2007, al-Shabaab was winning territory in large swathes of Somalia. The Transitional Government was confined to a few blocks of Mogadishu, propped up by the Ethiopian troops that had brought down the Islamic Courts Union and an African Union peacekeeping force.

Among al-Shabaab's youthful ranks there were a growing number of foreign fighters. Within weeks, the US State Department would designate the group as a foreign terrorist organization. Somalia – once just written off as a failed state – was a source of increasing alarm in Western capitals.

One young man climbing the ranks of al-Shabaab was Ahmed Abdulkadir Warsame, whom I had helped to travel to Somalia earlier that year. Since then, he had left several messages in our shared draft email folder asking me to find and deliver equipment such as a laptop, camcorder and portable water filtration equipment.

For MI6 such a mission would open the door to the group's inner workings and senior personnel. A laptop – suitably fitted out – could convey valuable information when connected to the internet or when seeking a WiFi connection, and Matt had made arrangements to provide one. He introduced me to an earnest young man in thick-rimmed glasses who looked like he had not seen sunshine for weeks.

'You look a bit young to be Q,' I said, referencing the boffin made famous in the Bond films.

He carefully placed the laptop into a sports bag containing the other supplies: a camcorder, portable filtration equipment, a PowerMonkey solar mobile-phone charger, a Suunto GPS watch (useful for tracking a terrorist if suitably adulterated), run-of-the-mill night-vision goggles and a few hundred dollars in cash.

I wrote a draft email in the account I shared with Warsame to let him know I had what he needed.

As I left Bangkok for Nairobi, I was sharply focused. I rehearsed scenarios exhaustively, devised answers for any questions. I needed to rest but could not sleep, instead gazing out of the window at huge formations of clouds below. This was my first mission for MI6 and I felt I was at the centre of a global battle. Both they and Danish intelligence were assembling teams in Nairobi to support the mission.

I landed in Nairobi on 7 December 2007. I couldn't stay at a luxury hotel. I was in jihadist mode, and that meant the modest Pan Afrique Hotel. At a nearby internet café, I logged on to the shared email account and found Warsame had left me a Nairobi phone number to arrange the drop.

In my room, I inserted a local SIM card into my mobile phone and called.

The voice that answered had a thick Kenyan accent. He was expecting to hear from me.

'I have the equipment,' I told him. 'I'll meet you tomorrow in the car park at the Intercontinental Hotel – three o'clock.'

The Danes had set the location and time of the pick-up; they and the British wanted to monitor it. To my surprise the contact did not argue.

My first field operation was going too smoothly. I kicked back in my room and watched Floyd Mayweather slug it out with Ricky Hatton for the world light welterweight title. It took me back a decade to the

Tyson–Holyfield bout, when I was bundled into that police car in Korsør. A lot had happened in the intervening years, but the Pan Afrique Hotel was surely better than a Danish prison cell.

I was early for the handover. A lanky Somali with large ears loped into the car park and spotted me. There were times when being a large Dane with flame-red hair could be useful. I felt my heartbeat accelerate as he walked towards me. Without a word, he took the bag and was gone. We had an audience – MI6 and a Danish agent had been watching.

There was another quick dividend to getting inside al-Shabaab. Kenyan intelligence trailed the man who collected the equipment to a Shabaab safe house in the Eastleigh neighbourhood of Nairobi. Several days later – on 13 December – the police raided the house, seizing a large quantity of weapons and fake identity papers, and arresting more than twenty men alleged to have been planning attacks on Western targets in Kenya.[1]

By the time those arrests had been made, I had been debriefed by the triad of PET, CIA and MI6 in faraway Amsterdam. It would be my last encounter with the elegant Amanda. As always she took copious notes about my travels, though I left out some of the interludes in Bangkok.

As we said goodbye, I expected we would see each other again. But Amanda was soon back at CIA headquarters, being trained for a mission to Afghanistan. It would be her last overseas assignment. She was killed with six of her colleagues in a suicide bombing at a CIA base in Khost, Afghanistan, in December 2009. It was a tragic day for the Agency, later brought to the screen in the film *Zero Dark Thirty*. I recognized her from pictures published in newspapers; her real name was Elizabeth Hanson. She was from suburban Chicago and was widely regarded as one of the CIA's most talented young analysts.

Exhausted but elated that I had completed my first real overseas mission, I left Amsterdam to return to Yemen. The Americans and Danes wanted me back in Sana'a to work the Yemeni and Somali networks, and the British, who I sensed would have preferred me to

---

1 One of the Danish agents subsequently told me my operation led to the arrests.

continue countering terrorist plots in the UK, had agreed. And I badly needed to be reunited with Fadia; we had not seen each other for months. She had no idea that in the last few days alone I had been on three continents working with three intelligence agencies. She thought I had been living off UK benefits in Birmingham.

As I presented my boarding pass at Amsterdam airport, I suddenly realized it was almost exactly a year since I had trawled through a camping store collecting supplies for the Islamic Courts in Somalia. Now I had finally delivered supplies to the group that had risen from its ashes, but how different were the circumstances. I shuddered to think what might have been.

The arrivals hall at Sana'a airport was the usual mixture of shouting, half-formed queues and surly immigration officers. It was so familiar, but now I observed it from the opposite end of the spectrum. I had first passed through this building as a wide-eyed convert. Now my work was to find, track and inform on people whose beliefs were those I had shared not so long ago.

Fadia was much more buoyant than during my crisis of faith in Denmark, happy to be around her family and showing greater self-assurance and maturity. She had rented and furnished a home on 40th Street, a pleasant area of the city, and her family was impressed that she seemed prosperous, though of course neither they nor she had any idea that Danish intelligence was the source of much of our income.

Days after I returned, Anwar al-Awlaki was released after more than eighteen months in detention. He had never been brought to trial. A week or so later, I visited him at his home, the same place where he had entertained a group of us nearly two years earlier. He looked pale and thin.

'I was in solitary confinement for the first nine months,' he told me. 'The only contact I had with humanity was my guards, and the cell was three metres long. It was underground. There were times when I thought the isolation and the claustrophobia would drive me insane . . . I had no paper to write on. I got no exercise.'

Awlaki was bitter and angry, but also thankful.

'I survived thanks to the will of Allah and the suffering has deepened my faith. And although it was very difficult to get books, I was able to read Qutb again.'

The Egyptian religious scholar Sayyid Qutb was widely regarded by many as having provided the intellectual cornerstone of al-Qaeda's global jihad. One of his devoted students was Ayman al-Zawahiri, Osama bin Laden's second-in-command.

'Because of the flowing style of Sayyid I would read between 100 and 150 pages a day,' Awlaki wrote later of his time in jail. 'I would be so immersed with the author I would feel Sayyid was with me in my cell speaking to me directly.'

I knew my handlers would be interested in information on Awlaki's state of mind. Prison had hardened him. I could see it in his eyes. They'd danced before; now there was steel. There was also a hint of paranoia. He saw spies everywhere.

He recounted being visited by FBI agents wanting to know more about his meetings with two of the 9/11 hijackers. He said that he had refused to speak English to them, insisting on communicating through a translator. At one point he said he had pushed a CIA officer down into a chair in protest at being questioned by the Americans. He said his only consolation was that unlike other prisoners he had never been harmed in jail. The guards were well aware that his father knew President Saleh.

His anger was directed as much towards the government that had imprisoned him as the Americans. He told me that jihad was necessary to overthrow President Saleh, who he said paid lip service to Islam but was a puppet of the Americans.

'The mujahideen need to establish an Islamic State in Abyan, as the *hadith* have foretold,' he told me. The *hadith* said, 'An army of twelve thousand will come out of Aden-Abyan. They will give victory to Allah and His messenger; they are the best between myself and them.'

Awlaki believed God had given him a mission to carry the banner of jihad, and to start in southern Yemen.

By the time Anwar left prison, al-Qaeda was regenerating itself in ungoverned tribal areas east and south of Sana'a.

Wuhayshi, the bin Laden protégé who had broken out of prison in 2006, was leading a newly formed group: al-Qaeda in the Land of

Yemen. Suicide bombers in cars packed with explosives had recently attacked two oil facilities in Marib and Hadramaut provinces. Attacks on Yemeni security forces and Westerners followed. For Wuhayshi it was the first chapter in a rapid ascent towards the upper echelons of al-Qaeda.

The group built up a network of safe houses, including in the capital, Sana'a. But its main haven was in the mountains and rugged terrain of the southern and eastern provinces of the country – Marib, Abyan and Shabwa, where Awlaki's family was influential. These areas were still dominated by local tribes who were suspicious of the central government in Sana'a. Keen to keep their autonomy, some tribal factions provided sanctuary and support to al-Qaeda fighters.

This was the militant environment into which Awlaki emerged, even if he was not yet an active figure in al-Qaeda.

In late January 2008, Awlaki came to lunch at our home on 40th Street. A few other friends from the lecture days (those not arrested or deported) came along too.[2] Sana'a was quite the jihadist melting pot. My wife cooked a huge array of dishes – including chicken, rice and a pot of *selta* – a traditional Yemeni dish of ground beef, eggs, okra and fenugreek. The food was laid on the floor, which was protected by a large plastic sheet as the assembled company ate.

After the plates had been cleared away, I lit a *bakhoor*, an incense smoke pile which filled the room with its herbal scent. We reclined on cushions against the walls and talked about the state of jihad, including al-Qaeda's progress in the south of Yemen and how best to topple the Saleh regime. It was treasonable talk.

The conversation then turned to Somalia, and progress made by al-Shabaab in extending its reach across the country.

I had a mischievous idea.

---

2 Among the other guests was a young black South African and a nineteen-year-old Somali called Issa Hussein Barre. The latter would soon take advantage of my connection to Warsame to join the struggle in Somalia. The usually cautious MI5 even approved cash transfers to him to finance his wedding so that I could nourish my connection for information. Unfortunately he was killed while fighting for al-Shabaab – a young husband sacrificed in an ever more brutal cause.

'Sheikh, why don't we call up the brothers in Somalia and ask them how it's going?' I asked with a provocative grin.

They were sceptical: how could I just place a call like that?

The reason was Ahmed Warsame, now rising through the ranks of al-Shabaab.

'*Masha'Allah*, it's Murad, how are you? I have someone here who wants to talk to you,' I said, handing the phone to Awlaki.

When Warsame recovered from the surprise of speaking to the famous cleric, he told him how the fight was going. Awlaki seemed elated, pleased to be talking to the mujahideen in Somalia. The two exchanged email addresses and mobile-phone numbers.

I had just brokered a connection between Somali and Yemeni militants. As Awlaki gravitated towards al-Qaeda's inner circle in Yemen, his connection to Warsame would prove useful to both sides, but even more useful to Western intelligence services, now furnished with email addresses and phone numbers.

Before Awlaki took his leave that evening, we agreed on a new mode of communication, the tested technique of writing draft emails in a shared email account. I explained to him how it worked. In the wake of his incarceration, and amid the persistent attention of Yemen's security services, he was more cautious about his links to the outside world.

A few weeks later, he abruptly left Sana'a – perhaps under pressure from his family, as his father had pleaded with him to soft-pedal his fundamentalist views. But equally he may have felt that he could not relaunch himself as a spiritual guide under the eye of Yemen's intelligence services.

The city of Ataq sits on the fringe of the Empty Quarter, the endless expanse of desert that straddles the Yemeni–Saudi border. Some 200 miles south-east of Sana'a, Ataq is overlooked by dun-coloured mountains on three sides. Its skyline is dominated by functional government buildings, but several medieval jewels in and around the town have survived, elaborate mud-brick buildings baked into towering rock-faces. Ataq is also the provincial capital of Shabwa, where Awlaki's family has influence. And so it was in Ataq that Anwar resettled and was spending time with his second, very young, wife.

Awlaki's first wife had shared his life in the United States. She was from a prominent family in the Yemeni capital, was well-educated and spoke good English. She also had a strong personality, driving herself around Sana'a and frequently putting Anwar in his place. So she had not reacted positively when he had told her in 2006 that he planned to take a second wife, especially when she found out that the new bride was a teenager.

Awlaki had been offered the girl in marriage by her two brothers (this was, after all, Yemen), who were great admirers of his. Instead of declining this generous gesture, Awlaki had accepted enthusiastically. The wedding ceremony was not a triumph. The family of the first wife were offended by this young *arriviste* and felt her social standing was inferior.

At first Anwar had installed his new teenage bride in an apartment near the Air Force Academy in Sana'a. Now she had accompanied him – apparently with little enthusiasm – to the wilds of Shabwa.

In Ataq, Awlaki spent much of his time online. The cleric's incarceration had seen his fame in Islamist circles in the West grow. Weeks after emerging from prison, Anwar created a website – anwar-alawlaki. com – and a Facebook page. From the town's internet cafés with their crawling connection speeds, he began railing against the United States and its allies, including the Saleh government, for 'waging a war on Islam'. He started exchanging messages with dozens among his legion of followers through more than sixty email accounts he registered.

My wife and I made the journey from Sana'a to Ataq in February 2008 to catch up with Awlaki. It was the first time we ventured into Yemen's deep interior to seek out the cleric, but would not be the last. The trip was on my own initiative but approved by both PET and the CIA. To begin with, the security forces blocked us from the route because of tribal fighting in Marib (no unusual occurrence) – forcing us to try again the following day. For my wife, it was a social visit; she had no idea of my real intent in seeing Anwar again.

The nine-hour road trip passed along the fringes of the Ramlat al-Saba'tayn, where the wind had corrugated the sand into immense dunes. Once in a while, an adobe house of three or four storeys would emerge from the haze, defying the ages, the winds and the swirling sands. The edge of the desert was defined by black granite domes – like giant loaves of pumpkin bread – rising hundreds of feet above the desert.

It was important that I stayed in character, even in the privacy of the car. I played CDs of *nashids* – Islamic songs – and my wife remained fully veiled. When we finally reached Ataq at sunset, Anwar was waiting for us in a new Toyota Land Cruiser. He was not short of cash. He wore tribal dress and the Yemeni sword, or *janbiya*, on his hip.

We found a curious domestic arrangement for the emerging star of Islamic fundamentalism. Awlaki and his young wife had rented a modest third-floor apartment in the middle of the town. I was struck by the simple furnishings – a far cry from the grand living quarters of clerics like Sheikh Abdul Majid al-Zindani. Awlaki lived almost ascetically, his only luxury being the best honey available, which he insisted on every morning.[3]

A ceiling fan whirred above – it was already warm outside, even in February. The street below sent up the muffled sound of cars and the shouts of traders.

I never interacted with his new wife because of strict segregation of the sexes in conservative Yemeni circles. But my wife spent a lot of time with her, and soon found out she was hardly the obvious partner for a scholar of Anwar's standing. By this time, she was nineteen – petite, very pretty and still with the bubby personality of a teenager. Anwar had been out of prison just three months but she was already pregnant – and prone to bouts of morning sickness.

She found Ataq tedious and hot, a remote and conservative corner of a remote and conservative country. She told my wife that the early days with Anwar had been tough. The wedding had felt like a funeral because of the first wife's hostility. The two did not speak for months, but eventually they reached an accommodation. Now they took turns spending time with their husband in Ataq.

The younger wife could not wait to escape the stifling apartment and return to Sana'a to see her family. She seemed to love Anwar but

---

3 Perhaps it wasn't just the taste. Control of stores selling top-grade Yemeni honey had once been used by Osama bin Laden to fund al-Qaeda.

told my wife that all he did was read. His study was crammed with books from floor to ceiling, on Koranic law and Islamic jurisprudence.

He studied Islamic teachings compulsively. But he was selective about how he applied them at home. He had installed a TV in the bedroom so that his wife could watch Turkish soaps dubbed into Arabic – to which she was addicted. It was a surprising concession: many militants within al-Qaeda considered television *haram* – strictly forbidden by Islamic law. Her viewing schedule also appeared to have taken priority over housework. The maids had taken care of that in Sana'a, but not in this backwater. More than once Anwar indulged her and went into the kitchen to prepare a meal for the two of us.

The teenage wife had little education and not much to say – it seemed to my wife that she was little more than a plaything for Anwar. But even as she carried his child, Anwar broached with me the possibility of finding him yet another wife – a convert from the West.

Most of the time we talked about Islam. He was an ocean of knowledge and a tower of authority. But he also talked about his days in America and told me more about his fishing trips in Colorado.

Then he paused and went back to 9/11. 'The Americans had it coming. We need to drive them out of Muslim lands!' His rhetoric was sharper than before.

Word had reached him that he should not return to Sana'a if he wanted to avoid another spell in detention. The message from Yemen's intelligence services was blunt: 'Don't call for jihad and don't meet with foreigners, or you'll be in more trouble.' At this I felt a pang of anxiety. If he was being watched constantly, I might find myself back on the authorities' radar, and that would be awkward for both me and my handlers.

I was careful not to probe too far with Anwar. His words were deliberate; I had the sense he was being more cautious than before and was not ready to trust me with his plans. But I suspected those plans would be fed by the visceral hostility he now felt towards America and its client in the Presidential Palace in Sana'a.

CHAPTER FOURTEEN

COCAINE
AND ALLAH

Early 2008

The traffic thundered down London's Euston Road. It was a sunny afternoon in March 2008 – one of those days that dare hint spring is not too far away. Carpets of purple-blue and golden crocus illuminated the city's squares and parks. Overhead the airliners drifted towards Heathrow. I had just flown in after four months in Yemen.

As I crossed the road, I glanced towards King's Cross, the station that had been at the heart of the carnage in 2005 when suicide bombers struck London. Nearly three years later the British security services were still under pressure over intelligence failures in the run-up to the attacks. They did not want to be caught out again and were keen to exploit my familiarity with the jihadis of Luton, Birmingham and Manchester. But the CIA wanted to use my knowledge of the militant fraternity in Yemen and Somalia.

At an anonymous hotel near Euston station, the three agencies had gathered to debrief me and I gave them a detailed account of my recent stay with Awlaki in Ataq.

The CIA team was now headed by an officer in his late thirties whom I guessed to be the Agency's number two in Copenhagen. Jed was balding with ginger stubble on his chin, a man whose plain looks were at odds with his iceberg-blue eyes. And he used them to great effect, impaling me with an intense stare. He spoke with precision and took detailed notes. Jed was all business, with the occasional flair of laconic humour. He was ambitious and wanted results. On the rare occasions that he lost his temper, his left eye would begin to twitch as if sending Morse code.

Jed clearly had the authority to make a pitch for my services, once he was persuaded that I had a direct path to Awlaki.

The rest of the meeting focused on gathering more intelligence on al-Shabaab in Somalia. PET was interested in developing a line to Shabaab by sending equipment to them: water purifiers, tents, sleeping mats, but nothing combat-related. Curiously the British drew the line at hammocks, perhaps on the grounds that no terrorist should get a good night's sleep. I witnessed the strange spectacle of three intelligence services arguing about hammocks – the first obvious dissent among them.

Matt from MI6 was at the Euston meeting, and it was clear that Her Majesty's Government was worried that a valuable source who had made his home in England was about to be coaxed away by all the Americans' baubles. So the British met and raised the Americans' offer with a series of team-building exercises which were smartly calculated to appeal to my love of the outdoors but were also a serious bid for my services.

The first card they played was a day of fly-fishing in north Wales. As always there was also a Danish presence. I was first and foremost their man, and they weren't about to let me spend time alone with MI6, to be dispatched to far-flung corners of the world.

Klang, my Danish handler, turned up looking like a mail-order catalogue model in a Barbour jacket, hunting trousers and a tartan cap. He was in love with the idea of playing the country gentleman for a day, even if he was in the wrong part of Britain for tartan. It took all Matt's self-restraint not to laugh.

Klang was accompanied by a PET agent I called Trailer because he had grown up on a farm. He had replaced Buddha, who had been incapacitated with a bad back. There was nothing designer about Trailer's grimy jacket. He was as unpretentious as Klang was sophisticated – very tall, from rural Jutland, and once an accomplished handball player. He had been the agent who observed the handover of equipment to the al-Shabaab courier at the Intercontinental in Nairobi.

It was a cloudless spring day. As the Danish pair tried unsuccessfully to hook a trout out of the River Dee with the help of an instructor, Matt sidled up to me on the bank, out of their hearing.

'We don't want you to go to Somalia for the Americans,' he said. 'I think you should stay here a little bit more: we need you.' The British wanted me to develop leads in England's inner cities as well as focus on the Somali contacts I had established.

Not long afterwards there was another exercise at an imposing country house near Aviemore in Scotland. MI6 had sent a car to pick me up at Inverness airport and the forty-minute drive took us past Loch Ness to the property, nestled in hilly woodland.

Matt was waiting for me on the steps, standing next to a striking brunette who was about thirty years old. Emma would be my new MI6 handler as Matt was being moved to other duties. Tall and athletic with high cheekbones and an immaculate complexion, she spoke in an unforced upper-class tone and seemed imperturbable. Her chiselled features and wide smile reminded me of Julia Roberts.

'It's good to finally meet you,' she said, flashing me a smile.

During the retreat, Emma revealed that her grandmother was Swedish and she could speak the language. I tried out some Danish on her, and she laughed, answering back in Swedish, which Danes can more or less understand. It helped break the ice.

Again the Danes came along; and Andy was there from MI5, but the Americans were not invited. They must have resented that. The two-day course featured training by a UK Special Forces (SAS) specialist in mountain navigation, abseiling and survival skills. His name was Rob and he had just come back from undisclosed duties in Iraq.

There was also a psychologist on hand, who introduced himself as Luke. A dapper, well-educated Scot in his mid-forties, he was softly spoken and had grey-blue eyes. He had a neatly trimmed beard that made him look older than he probably was. His mission was to see how resilient and suitable I was for life as an informant on the front-line. I felt I was being fast-tracked by the British.

Luke presented me with some difficult hypothetical choices.

'What would you do if you were with al-Qaeda and ordered to execute a prisoner?' he asked.

As I pondered, he leaned forward and said quietly: 'You'd execute him to avoid attracting any suspicion or provoking any doubts among your comrades.'

We talked through the burden of living a double life, and my break-up with Karima. He understood better than I could imagine the pressure I was going to face.

The evening was more light-hearted. We played bingo, and the Danes cheated. They also thought it hysterical to point the beam of a laser pointer on to the faces of my British handlers as we tried to talk business, focusing on Matt's outsize ears. At times their antics were embarrassing and I felt they had become much too familiar with me.

To add to my discomfort, Klang made a none too subtle play for the attention of Emma. Matt, it seemed, had more luck. I noticed, as they cooked a Scottish breakfast for the house guests, that there seemed to be a special chemistry between the two.

The British were subtle about their entreaties, but quietly insistent. I would be better off working with them; it would be a genuine commitment on both sides. I would be properly trained and supported. The unspoken implication was that at some point the CIA would hang me out to dry.

As the tension between the British and American agencies grew more palpable I sought the advice of my PET handlers. It was the wrong thing to do. They smelt money and opportunity with the CIA.

'You'll get to do more with the Yanks,' Klang told me, 'and they pay more.'

I was conflicted. Matt, Andy, Emma and the others from the two UK agencies had been good companions, straightforward and intelligent. They were trapped by bureaucracy and regulation, but they were professionals.

The American riposte to the special treatment by the British took place in the Danish coastal resort of Helsingør, sometimes called the capital of the Danish riviera. Its most famous landmark was Kronberg Castle, a Renaissance pile that Shakespeare used in inventing Elsinore for *Hamlet*. It was an appropriate place to plot against Awlaki, the future prince of jihad.

At the end of our meeting, Jed took me aside.

'You never took your wife on a honeymoon, right?' he asked, the iceberg eyes melting just for an instant.

'No. I've not exactly had much time over the last two years.'

'Well, consider it a gift from us. Just let us know where you'd like to go and we can make the arrangements,' Jed said.

I was flattered. They were taking me seriously. Perhaps it was standard practice to win the loyalty of an impressionable source. And given the treats showered on me by the British it was a well-timed gesture. I began to make plans for another visit to Thailand, hopefully one that would be more relaxing.

My work for PET and the British was becoming more demanding, and more perilous. I needed cover stories. My cover, or 'legend', in Denmark came courtesy of a garrulous, dim-witted Danish Bosnian called Adnan Avdic, whom I knew from my extremist days. He had been held in jail before being acquitted in a terrorism case.[1]

One afternoon I picked him up on the outskirts of Copenhagen in a brand-new Toyota. It was rented by PET as part of the ruse but Adnan thought it was mine.

'Nice wheels, Murad! That must have cost you a packet,' he said. As we drove, our conversation soon turned to jihad.

'I have to drop something off so need to take a bit of a detour.'

His curiosity got the better of him, as I knew it would.

'What?'

'It's to help the cause. Don't tell anybody this.'

I paused and made a show of looking in every direction furtively.

'Open the glove compartment, but don't touch what you see because you'll leave fingerprints.'

He stared in amazement at a small bag of white powder.

'Wow – Murad – are you sure this is permissible?'

'I have a fatwa,' I replied.

Little did he know that it was a mixture of flour and crumbled candle wax.

I pulled up just before the meeting point.

'You need to get out and wait for me here,' I told him.

---

1 Avdic was arrested in 2005 in connection with a terror plot uncovered in Bosnia. A jury ruled there was sufficient evidence to convict him, but he was acquitted a few days later by a three-judge panel who disagreed.

A man in a brown bomber jacket was standing at the street corner. I handed him the bag and walked back to the car, knowing that Adnan would have seen the deal go down.

There was the glint of a smile on my senior handler Soren's face as he walked off in the other direction with the bag. He had apparently enjoyed his brief cameo as a street dealer.

In England MI5 also arranged a cover for me to allay any suspicions about the cash I was receiving: fully licensed Birmingham cab driver. Her Majesty's Government even bought me a Mercedes minivan with leather-trim seats.

I started work for an Alum Rock cab company owned by a Pakistani businessman. His son, Salim, whom I had first met in al-Muhajiroun meetings in Luton, was on MI5's radar screen. They hoped that if we worked together I would gain greater access to his British-Pakistani extremist contacts in the city. The security service was especially concerned about this demographic because several plots in the UK had involved young men of Pakistani descent, some of whom had received bomb-making training in al-Qaeda camps in their ancestral country.

But radicalized British-Pakistanis were proving hard for me to infiltrate. They tended to be wary of Muslims from other ethnic and national groups and were especially distrustful of converts. After trekking across the deserts of Yemen, driving my cab around Birmingham was exceptionally dull. Eventually I told MI5 taxi driving was not for me.

I did not adapt well to domestic life in Birmingham. Fadia had returned with me and we had moved into a council house on Watson Road, a drab street in Alum Rock. Our new digs could not have been more depressing, but it was the price of living my cover. Discarded needles and trash littered the street. Young gangs of British-Pakistanis roamed the area, sometimes getting into knife fights. Fadia complained that the rats were bigger than the cats. I was desperate to tell her that she deserved better and I could provide it; our diminished circumstances had put up a wall between us. But, for her safety and mine, I couldn't let her know the real reason why we were living there.

Fadia had no idea her return to Europe had been engineered by the intelligence services. PET had been true to their promise by providing her with a student visa to return to Denmark and she had then been provided with a five-year European residence permit at the British embassy in Copenhagen, courtesy of Her Majesty's Secret Service.

My lifeline was the mobile phone with which I communicated with my handlers. They alone knew my secret purpose. Klang and I spoke several times each day, running information and ideas past each other but always being careful with our language. My MI5 handlers called several times a week, usually to arrange meetings.

Even when things were slow I found it difficult to switch off. Often Fadia would have to ask the same question several times before I responded. My mind was elsewhere, thinking of the next email I needed to write or plotting ways I could enhance my jihadist network. I found it difficult even to fully focus on my kids on the weekends I had custody. The espionage business was all-consuming.

One evening Fadia and I sat down to watch the George Clooney movie *Syriana*, a thriller set in the Middle East. I was soon absorbed in the film, recognizing both the implausible parts and the efforts to re-create the tradecraft of espionage. But the sense of mistrust among some of its characters resonated. I was desperate to tell Fadia, to point to the screen and say, 'That's how I feel.' But I knew it was impossible.

Occasionally I took long drives deep into the British countryside. I'd put on a Metallica CD, turn up the volume and breathe deeply. Sometimes after a walk I would drop into a country pub for a pint of bitter and a chat with the regulars. It was unlikely that Muslims would hang out in such places. For a few precious minutes I just needed to drop the mask.

Not all the extremists in Birmingham were blowhards. I soon encountered one of the most volatile figures in the city, a British-Pakistani I knew only as Saheer. He was in his late twenties, muscular and always wearing a tracksuit. He was clean-shaven and good-looking with a buzz-cut hairstyle, but his eyes seemed to be on the lookout for trouble and his hands itching for a fight. He already had a criminal record, having gone inside for armed robbery while still a teenager, and had only recently been released.

I met Saheer through one of the most active extremists in Birmingham at a Moroccan cake shop in Alum Rock. Like a growing number of young Muslims, Saheer had been radicalized while in prison. Perhaps like others he also sought redemption. Saheer was a man of few words but had a craving for action. When I revealed I knew Awlaki and told him of my recent meeting with him in Yemen, he started opening up.

'Brother, we need to fight back against the *kuffar*,' he said, as we shared *meskouta*, a Moroccan yoghurt cake.

As we walked out into the evening drizzle, Saheer looked at me with intense almond eyes.

'Murad, I'd like to do a martyrdom operation, *Insha'Allah*.'

His words hung in the air. Had he really just said that? Was he testing me? I told myself to go slowly, let this play out. I would be neither dismissive nor overly eager to help. I tried to remember the advice of MI5's psychologist, Luke.

'Do you have any ideas? You know the Danish newspaper that drew the pictures of the Prophet Mohammed, peace be upon him. Do you know anything about its security?' he asked me.[2]

'I can try to find out,' I replied.

'Do you know how to get weapons in Denmark?' he asked.

'Oh, that can be done,' I said. I dropped in my background with the Bandidos.

'You must understand that what I want is to die in this attack. I want to get shot and I want to be killed *"fee sabeel Allah* [for the sake of Allah]",' he said.

Time to call Sunshine, I thought.

Sunshine worked with my senior MI5 handler, Andy, and had become my principal point of contact in the agency. Klang and the Danes had given her that name because she was irrepressibly cheerful. She was in her mid- to late twenties, clearly learning the trade but with an instinct that would carry her a long way. She also had a no-nonsense attitude.

---

2 The Danish newspaper in question was *Jyllands-Posten*, which had published controversial cartoons of the Prophet Mohammed in September 2005.

Klang had placed his hand on her leg once during an after-hours drink and she'd shouted so loudly that he recoiled like a scalded cat.

Sunshine might not be able to recite Latin poetry like Matt, but she was good at reading faces. She dyed her hair blonde and was pretty in a girl-next-door kind of way. Perhaps, I thought, she cultivated ordinariness because it set people at ease and led them to drop their guard.

'I need to set up a meeting,' I told her on the phone later that night. 'Roger that – eleven a.m.,' she said, hanging up the phone. She liked the military clichés.

The next morning I waited in the car park of a Sainsbury's supermarket on the outskirts of Birmingham, our rendezvous. I sat in my car and watched harried mothers deal with carts of shopping and rebellious kids.

My phone started buzzing.

'Walk to the far end of the car park. You'll see a red Volvo. Keep going. We'll pick you up.'

On cue a white van with a ventilation unit on its roof skidded to a stop beside me. Sunshine was there, with the trademark smile.

'Jump in the back.'

There were no windows in the back so I had no idea where we were going. Forty minutes later we arrived. It could have been round the corner for all I knew.

I heard a chain and then a mechanical grind – perhaps a garage door being raised. The driver, hidden from me, gunned the engine and we drove in. The door rattled down behind us.

'Clear!' I heard Sunshine say on her walkie-talkie up front. A man opened the door. It was Kevin, another of Andy's MI5 team. Kevin looked like he was in his twenties and might have been a presenter on one of those outdoor adventure shows, building fires out of dung and coaxing deadly snakes out of holes in trees. I would not have messed with him.

We seemed to be in a large warehouse – one of MI5's operations centres.

It looked like a printing press that had been turned into an architect's office. There were posters on the wall and rows of workshop tables lit by lamps hanging from the high ceiling. It was hardly high tech. There was an internet connection, and a few PCs, and that was about it.

In the corner was a small glass-walled office with chairs set around a table. Andy was waiting for me. Sunshine and Kevin let him take the lead. I told him about my encounter with Saheer.

'You need to keep talking to him,' Andy said, after hearing me out. It was the first of several debriefing sessions as Saheer's intent became clearer.

Saheer was extremely security-conscious. In many ways he was MI5's worst nightmare: a savvy career criminal who was morphing into a jihadi with a death wish. He only spoke to me about his plans when we were alone and outdoors. We used to take long walks in a park in Alum Rock. He insisted that I not carry my mobile, and each time we went out he patted me down for any devices.

'Just a precaution, brother,' he said.

'He's really dangerous, a total psycho,' I told Andy at my next debriefing. 'What the hell am I supposed to do? I'm the only one he's telling this stuff to.'

'Just keep talking to him,' Andy replied, with concern in his voice.

Given Saheer's intended target, I was not surprised to see my Danish handlers make an appearance.

'The Minister has been briefed on this,' Klang told me. 'The bosses really appreciate what you are doing.'

For once, Klang was being serious.

But as I saw it we still had a problem. There was no evidence beyond Saheer's less than coherent plan to take out the Danish newspaper, a plan that he had confided only to me and of which there was no record. There was certainly nothing to warrant his arrest or charges. It was all hearsay and I might be accused of entrapment. So I improvised, taking advantage of his doubts about raising money for the guns and planning.

'You know Sheikh Anwar agrees to the selling of drugs as long as we support the brothers for jihad,' I said to him during our next walk in the park. 'First of all you're destroying the *kuffar*, you're ruining their society. Secondly you're getting money you can send to the mujahideen.'

Saheer looked interested.

'And you get to keep a fifth of the proceeds yourself as war booty, *Inshallah.*'

'Murad, are you sure about this?' he said, his eyes widening.

'Yes. He gave me a fatwa,' I replied, knowing a similar story was now most likely circulating in extremist Danish circles if he should ever check.

My attempt to have Saheer return to the world of crime was not well received by Andy at MI5.

'We can't encourage people to commit crimes. What the hell were you thinking? You can't just do this sort of thing without checking with us,' he said.

'I was improvising – how else are we going to arrest this guy?' I replied.

Andy disappeared into the glass office with Kevin and Sunshine and made several phone calls.

When he came out his mood had brightened. He was still irritated, but seemed to recognize the opportunity.

'All right, all right, you said it so it's too late now. There's not much we can do about it.'

Not long afterwards, Saheer came calling – in a silver Lexus. Drugs money, I thought: he must be wanting to enjoy his last days on earth.

We reached the park. As we walked in the rain towards the duck pond, I realized that we must make for a strange sight.

'I've got hold of the money – can you make sure about the weapons,' he said.

I looked around as casually as I could to see if we were being followed. I knew MI5 were now trying to monitor his every step, but it just seemed to be me and him. The ducks were quacking urgently. It was surreal.

'Brother, let's go, just me and you, and do this mission. I need you to be there with me in Denmark.'

'I'm with you, brother,' I replied, feeling the words sounded less than convincing.

He embraced me. 'This is the best, Murad, the best. We get to be *shuhada* [martyrs]. There's nothing better than this, remember that.'

If anyone was looking at us at that moment, they might get the wrong impression.

'I know. This is paradise. We are mujahideen and this is what we fight for,' I replied, summoning all the conviction I could manage.

He wants me to die with him, I thought. How am I going to get out of this?

Klang was at the next debrief. He made clear the Danes wanted the plot stopped well before Saheer could get to Denmark.

'We'll kill him if he comes to Denmark. We'll shoot him.'

It was bravado. Danish law would not permit a summary execution.

'We've been following him,' Kevin from MI5 told me. 'He's selling drugs all right. But he isn't touching the stuff himself.'

'This is where you're going to have to trust us,' Andy said.

'I want to go to Denmark in two weeks,' Saheer told me at our next meeting. He asked me to reconnect with my underworld contacts there so that we could buy guns and ammunition.

The day of our departure loomed, but my handlers kept me in the dark.

I had travelled through the wilder reaches of Yemen and driven around with heavily armed fighters in Lebanon, but the idea of travelling to my homeland with this psychopath was giving me sleepless nights.

British police arrested Saheer a week before we were meant to travel, as he sold drugs on the streets of Birmingham. It was not his first offence so he received a lengthy prison sentence. The beauty of the operation was that even after he was jailed he never suspected I was working for intelligence. But even inside he appeared to exercise a chilling effect on other jihadis in Birmingham; none would dare talk about the mysterious Saheer, and I never found out his real name.

With Saheer safely behind bars, my handlers and I could plot my next trip to see Awlaki.

CHAPTER FIFTEEN

CLERICAL TERROR

Spring–Autumn 2008

In April 2008, I wrote an email to Anwar al-Awlaki, telling him I'd presently be making a short trip to Yemen.

The cleric soon replied and had a special request.

'Cheese and chocolates please:)'

I knew he liked pralines but I needed to get some guidance first: 'Sheikh, regarding the chocolate, is it permissible to eat it when it has got like alcohol flavour in it[?]'

The answer came back. 'No it is not allowed because even though all of the alchohol evaporates it is najasah [impure] and that najasah has mixed with the chocolate.'

The Holy Book had an answer for liqueur chocolates.

I assured him I would bring the non-alcoholic variety and added a little flattery.

'Went into a shop yesterday in Birmingham, the owner was listening to one of your lectures . . . he told me, that he only listen to your lectures, as he couldn't trust anyone else anymore hahahahaha Masha'Allah, I was laughing and so happy, the people here in uk and denmark, really loves you sheikh, you have done a great job and won their hearts, masha'Allah, may Allah reward you.'

On 13 May 2008 Fadia and I landed in Sana'a. Leaving the plane, I inhaled the warm moist air, happy to have escaped the chill dullness of Birmingham. Fadia too was pleased to be away from Alum Rock and looking forward to seeing her beloved uncle. She also knew I was an admirer of Awlaki and perhaps saw my relationship with him as a stabilizing influence after witnessing my crisis of conscience in Denmark.

Awlaki told us to come down to Aden to meet him. He had decamped to the southern port city from Ataq for a few weeks with his pregnant wife. We met them for lunch in a restaurant near the fish market. I embraced him at the entrance and handed him the chocolates.

He thanked me profusely.

'Our wives can eat separately. We'll order for them,' he said. It was standard procedure.

Fadia and Awlaki's wife disappeared into the 'family section'. She was six months pregnant by now.

Anwar and I were digging into grilled white fish when I almost choked. His wife had wandered brazenly into the men's section.

'Where's my fish?' she demanded, through her niqab.

Awlaki smiled knowingly at me.

Throughout lunch I kept the conversation away from his plans. I saw the encounter as a confidence-building measure. He seemed more relaxed than when he had emerged from prison. He was careful to be discreet, but not exactly in hiding. It seemed typical of the way Yemen worked: there were understandings, coded warnings, limits. In Aden, Anwar was being protected and housed by a wealthy businessman.

'Brother, I have been doing a lot of writing, a lot of thinking,' he offered, leaning back and looking across the very harbour where the USS *Cole* had been attacked.

That writing and thinking were coming to fruition. As the boiling summer approached, Awlaki recorded a brace of lectures for followers in the West.

In one, 'Battle of the Hearts and Minds', he railed against attempts by the US government to empower 'moderate' Islam.

The other, 'The Dust Will Never Settle Down', was given live over Paltalk, an online voice chat forum, and directly addressed the continuing cartoons controversy. Awlaki challenged Muslims the world over:

'How concerned are you? How concerned are we when it comes to the honor of the Rasool [the messenger], when it comes to the honor of Islam, when it comes to the book of Allah? How seriously do we take it?' he asked.

'We are not followers of Gandhi . . . [as] Ibn Taymiyah says it is mandatory to kill the one who curses the Messenger of Allah,' he said.

The cleric could not have chosen a more hot-button issue. A Swedish artist had poured fuel on the fire by depicting the Prophet as a dog. Awlaki's calmly articulated outrage struck a deep chord with extremists in the West. The talk was widely circulated online.

Anwar al-Awlaki had reached the Islamist stratosphere. And Western intelligence services were beginning to notice just how often his lectures were cropping up in terrorism trials in Europe and North America.[1]

For those seeking to contribute financially to the cause, looking for moral justification for their actions or the terrorists' equivalent of a changing-room pep-talk, Awlaki's online output had become essential reading. Awlaki could harness the power of ideas. But it was soon apparent that he wanted to do more to restore the honour of the Rasool.

In the early autumn of 2008, I was back in Birmingham, helping MI5 keep tabs on the burgeoning militant scene in England's second city, when Awlaki left a draft email in our shared account. After the customary greetings and praise to Allah, he got down to business. He wanted supplies for the mujahideen: solar panels, night-vision goggles, water purification equipment and more. And he wanted money. He suggested I collect funds from mosques in Europe and said $20,000 would be greatly appreciated. Awlaki was smart enough not to ask for anything that could be obviously used in combat, but was evidently aware of what al-Qaeda lacked in infrastructure. I wondered who had helped compile the shopping list. My handlers were surprised and alarmed by the request. Awlaki was then regarded by the more

---

1 Avid consumers of Awlaki's videos included the so-called Toronto 18, who plotted to launch attacks across Canada in 2006, and the British al-Qaeda cell that plotted to blow up transatlantic airliners the same year. Several of those who conspired to attack the Fort Dix military base in New Jersey in 2007 were also devotees of the cleric's sermons.

complacent analysts as a blowhard, and few if any of the intelligence officers I knew imagined him becoming more than a rhetorical outlet for jihad.

'Didn't I warn you he was dangerous?' I reminded Jed when we met to discuss the request.

Jed was clear about what needed to be done. Deliver some $5,000 in cash and several items of the equipment requested. My Danish handlers told me this had caused further friction between Big Brother and the British. Senior UK intelligence officials had baulked at such a large cash handover, nervous they would later be accused of funding terrorism should the media find out. Solar panels were all very well; cash (and hammocks) were not. MI6 made clear their limit would be £500.

Jed was intolerant of such finer points. At a meeting in Copenhagen which the British did not attend, he handed me the money in $100 notes.

'Just take it.'

Once the supplies were organized I contacted Awlaki by writing a draft email.

'I have gifts.'

On 23 October 2008 Fadia and I waited in line at customs and immigration at Sana'a airport. I was apprehensive. Inside my large suitcase, which was sealed with a rigid, heavy-duty plastic strap, was a sports bag. And inside the bag were the small solar panels, night-vision goggles, portable water purification units and a laptop.

Try to sound confident, I thought, as I approached the customs desk and a weathered middle-aged man perspiring through his worn uniform. He looked listless in the stifling heat, dealing with another plane-load of Yemenis returning with whatever goods they could afford to bring back from wealthier places.

Yemeni customs officials are not renowned for their dedication or perceptiveness. We had hoped that even if the equipment was discovered it would not be regarded as suspicious. I was about to find out.

'Open it,' the official said – pointing at the plastic belt.

'I'm going to need a knife or something,' I told him in Arabic.

Annoyed to have to get off his chair he shuffled off to a side room. I tried hard to remain nonchalant.

The protocol was for me to stonewall. Jed's orders were simple.

'On no account tell them you are working for Western intelligence. If that makes you look like you're working for the bad guys then so be it. Leave it to us to sort out through diplomatic channels.'

The customs man returned empty-handed.

'Go,' he said.

It was a lucky break and, I hoped, an omen for the mission.

The Nairobi operation the previous year had shown that al-Qaeda affiliates always wanted more equipment, things that were difficult to obtain locally and expensive. My supplying that equipment was a promising way to find out more about their members and plans. By now, AQAP had become the most effective of all al-Qaeda's franchises. The month before we arrived with supplies for Awlaki, it had carried out a coordinated gun and car attack on the US embassy in Sana'a. Ten Yemenis had been killed. The attack had induced a state of high anxiety among Yemen's security services.

I decided to lie low for a few days before contacting Awlaki. I would have to take Fadia with me. Driving down solo into Yemen's southern badlands alone as a white European was not an option. I had told her I was taking supplies to Anwar and left her with the impression that they were to help his pastoral work.

'And then on the way back, why don't we see your relatives in Taiz?' I said.

She was quietly pleased that I wanted to see her family.

Less than a week after we arrived, I received a text message from Awlaki. He told me to set out south towards Aden and to text him once we got to the port city so that he could provide further directions. He was more conscious of security than before and would only specify the meeting place once I was through the final checkpoint. And he didn't want to use the phone because he was concerned that American voice recognition software might identify him. He clearly saw himself as more of a target than the Americans did.

We set off shortly after dawn. As we navigated the checkpoints on the road out of Sana'a I was nervous about the equipment hidden in the trunk. Now we were heading towards areas where al-Qaeda was active, the discovery of night-vision goggles by some over-zealous police officer would require some explaining.

The journey south towards Taiz is dramatic. The road descends from the Sana'a plateau for a while until the Yemeni Highlands come into view. October marks the end of the rainy season in Taiz, and the mountains were shrouded in morning mist.

We found lodgings that evening in Aden, and I texted Awlaki again. He told me to take the road up the coast. We were essentially driving an exaggerated U-shaped route to avoid the more serious checkpoints. Fadia accepted the convoluted journey as a typically Yemeni inconvenience. If we were stopped and questioned, she would explain that we were going to see friends in Ataq. But for some reason – perhaps because Aden was more secular than Sana'a – vehicles tended to get less scrutiny along the coast road.

The next morning we passed through lush oases close to the ocean. Camels loped beside the road, telegraph poles bent by the onshore wind stood like matchsticks against the emptiness of the coastal plain. My final instructions were to leave the coast and climb towards the mountains. Just one look at the impenetrable ranges ahead was evidence enough of why al-Qaeda had made this area home.

The rendezvous point was near an isolated hamlet in Shabwa province. Seas of boulder-strewn shale stretched towards the horizon, to be met by steep, craggy mountains. Even at the end of October, the midday heat would generate a rippling haze. I marvelled at the survival of the few plants and bushes that dotted the lunar landscape.

I was especially nervous around a town called Lawdar, which had seen tribal violence and abductions, and was – even by Yemeni standards – an area where the word of the central government had little impact.

After several hours in the car, Fadia and I finally approached the rendezvous point in a flat, parched valley surrounded by mountains. There was an eerie beauty in the desolate landscape.

I was relieved to see the concrete structure that Anwar had told me to look for. A dusty vehicle with a canvas roof was parked a short distance away. Inside was Anwar with a young bodyguard who had a thick pitch-black beard and was clutching a Kalashnikov. I parked the car, leaving Fadia inside, and walked up to them. The cleric got out and embraced me.

'*As salaam aleikum akhi* [brother], finally!' he said. 'This is my nephew, Saddam,' he added.

Anwar was wearing a green military camouflage jacket, bin Laden style, over his robe. He had a Yemeni ceremonial dagger and a revolver in his belt and a Kalashnikov was slung over his shoulder.

I tried not to look surprised. The preacher had become a fighter.

I fetched the sports bag with the supplies: the laptop, night-vision goggles, headlamps, matches, sandals for the mujahideen and solar panels, and we walked to the shade of a solitary tree beside the road. It was the first tree I had seen for many miles. But it provided more than shade. Al-Qaeda leaders had begun instructing fighters to use the shelter of trees in case drones, now being used by the US in Pakistan's tribal areas, should also be deployed to Yemen.

British agents had asked me to purchase the solar panels at a Maplin's electronics store and had shown me how they worked. The laptop had a backstory to it. At the MI5 warehouse in Birmingham a technician had provided me with the computer and told me that some of the components had been switched for identical but 'modified' parts. Even experts would not find the programs they had installed. I assumed their modifications were designed to locate Awlaki through the laptop's WiFi signal as well as upload data if he ever connected to the internet.

But at the final meeting before the mission, my Danish handlers told me they were exchanging the British laptop for one supplied by the Americans. Now that I had told the CIA of Awlaki's 'operational status' tracking him down had become a priority for the Americans. Big Brother was pulling rank.

I handed Awlaki the laptop and the other equipment and explained how the solar panels functioned. I also gave him the $5,000.

He put it in his breast pocket without uttering a word. He looked disappointed I had not brought more. But it somehow seemed judicious not to provide his every need all at once. After all, I was a struggling jihadi.

'*Alhamdulillah*, that's all I could raise so far, brother,' I told him.

After fifteen minutes sitting under the shade of the tree by the roadside, I returned to the car.

'Anwar says we should eat,' I told Fadia. 'Come, follow us.' We walked towards the building nearby. It was a restaurant, but only half built, and I wondered how it stayed upright.

Two men in the doorway looked suspiciously at my red hair and beard. This was bandit territory. Even Yemenis not from the area were kidnapped for ransom. But we were under Awlaki's protection and therefore safe. Or so I hoped.

The owner greeted Awlaki warmly and asked his wife to escort Fadia to the women's section. He then took the cleric and me up to the roof, where we sat on the concrete and ate platters of lamb and rice on tin plates. A merciful breeze had begun to drift through the valley. When Awlaki finished eating he tapped on the wad of dollars in his breast pocket, and looked me straight in the eye.

'The money from the brothers – can it be used to buy weapons?' he asked.

For a fraction of a second, I considered how to reply.

'You can buy anything you like with this money.'

We did not stay long. I wanted to reach the coast again before dusk. Even then we would have a long, arduous trek to Taiz and Fadia's relatives. So immediately after we finished eating, I told Awlaki we had to go. He seemed disappointed. Although we would stay in touch, I would not see him again for nearly a year.

As the restaurant disappeared in a haze of dust and heat behind us, I handed Fadia my phone.

'Could you shoot some video of the scenery? It's so spectacular and I doubt we will ever see this part of Yemen again.'

But I had other reasons for wanting the footage. I knew Jed would be interested to see the area where I had met the Sheikh. It might also give him and his colleagues pause, I thought. Winning a war in this sort of territory would not come easily.

We weaved through the ravines, the hairpin bends apparently never-ending. At the top of the climb a vast barren panorama opened up below us, like a lunar sea, and we began driving downhill towards the sea.[2]

---

2 I have a saved copy of this video and dozens of pictures during the journey.

Two weeks later I was in a luxurious Bangkok hotel suite being debriefed by my intelligence handlers. Fadia and I had flown in for our CIA-sponsored honeymoon, although I led her to believe that I'd been saving some money from construction and driving jobs to pay for the trip.

I had slipped away to meet my handlers on the pretence that I wanted to do some shopping.

I recounted every detail of the meeting in Shabwa and our conversation about the money.

'You just passed the test, brother,' Jed told me. 'He was testing you to see if you were genuine. If you were working for an intelligence agency, you'd have to say no, this is for food or something like that.'

Jed handed me an envelope with a $6,000 bonus in cash after the meeting. 'This is for a helluva good job – enjoy your honeymoon,' he told me. He was not so subtly delivering a message: when it came down to choosing between the CIA and the British, it literally paid to be their guy.

Awlaki never tested me again.

CHAPTER SIXTEEN
KILLING
MR JOHN

Autumn 2008–Spring 2009

Through 2008 I kept in contact via draft emails with Ahmed Abdulkadir Warsame, the stringy Somali youth I had first met in Birmingham. What he lacked in ability he had made up for in dedication. He was now one of al-Shabaab's senior operatives, his CV no doubt burnished by my connecting him with Awlaki.

To keep the communications going MI5 authorized my sending the first in a series of cash transfers to Warsame via Dahabshiil, an African money transfer company with a branch in Birmingham.[1] In another email he requested I supply him with chemical suits and rubber gloves so al-Shabaab could experiment with explosives. I purchased this equipment with funds from the British but was never greenlighted to deliver it.

During the second week of November – just before my delayed honeymoon in Thailand – I returned to Nairobi to deliver new supplies Warsame had requested. He wanted another laptop and some cash. My Western intelligence handlers had welcomed the opportunity for me to enhance my credentials with the group, and had no doubt planted another tracking device in the laptop they supplied me.

1 I have receipts for the Dahabshiil transfers made to Warsame: $100 in March 2008, $200 in July 2008, $400 in September 2008, $138 in January 2009 and $500 in January 2010.

Warsame sent a Kenyan al-Shabaab operative who had lived in Norway to meet me. He called himself Ikrimah al-Muhajir.[2]

'You'll recognize him because of his long hair,' Warsame had told me.

We met at a Somali restaurant in Nairobi. He walked in with a confident stride and sat down at the corner booth I had chosen. Ikrimah did indeed have long, flowing locks and from that day my nickname for him was 'Long Hair'. Trailing behind him was his driver, Mohammed, a Kenyan of Somali ethnicity.

Ikrimah was built like one of Kenya's long-distance runners, and had a trimmed beard and gleaming white teeth. He was of Somali and Yemeni descent – on his father's side he belonged to the Ansi tribe in Yemen. He would later start changing his appearance to evade detection, at one point wearing a thick Saddam Hussein-style moustache.

We bonded over our shared Scandinavian background. He spoke Norwegian, as well as English, French, Arabic, Somali and Swahili. He had been brought up in Kenya and his family were middle class. Ikrimah spent his early years in Mombasa on the Indian Ocean coast, before the family moved to Nairobi. He told me he had moved to Norway four years previously to look for work and had sought refugee status.

'They never let me settle there,' he said. 'I never really felt accepted. I began to spend more time in the mosque.'

I found Ikrimah cheerful and sharp – smarter than Warsame, who had sent him. There was an intense ambition about him and an unshakable commitment to Holy War. Over goat meat and *canjeero* – a Somali-style pancake bread – he revealed he had been in Mogadishu, fighting for the Islamic Courts Union, when Ethiopian troops invaded in 2006.

'Do you know a Danish convert called Ali?' he asked me.

'Of course!' I exclaimed. 'He called me during the fighting. He cut the head off one of the Somali *kuffar*.'

'*Subhan'Allah*,' Ikrimah replied, incredulous. 'I was with him: I filmed this blessed act on my phone.' He went on to cheerfully describe

2 Al-Muhajir means 'the foreigner' in Arabic. His real name was Mohamed Abdikadir Mohamed.

the execution: how Ali had kicked the spy's legs from under him, and then pinned him down as he struggled for life, and slowly sawn off his head.

After Ethiopian forces finally expelled the Islamic Courts Union from the capital and much of central Somalia, Ikrimah said he had returned to Norway but failed to gain political asylum. He had spent about a year in London and then in 2008 returned to East Africa. Now he was working as a messenger for Warsame and other Shabaab leaders, splitting his time between Somalia and Kenya.

I feared he might mention the arrests in Nairobi that had followed the handover at the Intercontinental Hotel the previous year. But he didn't and it seemed no one in al-Shabaab had made the link. I had to remind myself to be careful, to be sure my handlers never put me in a situation where someone might begin to turn apparent coincidences into related events.

After dinner Ikrimah picked up the laptop for Warsame from my hotel room.

For the next several days I travelled around Nairobi with Ikrimah in Mohammed's white Toyota estate. Mohammed was irrepressibly cheerful and spoke Swahili and a decent smattering of English. He lived in the Eastleigh district of Nairobi and like me moonlighted as a taxi driver, but much of his time was spent helping al-Shabaab with their logistics. If you needed someone to drive you to a secret rendez-vous in Nairobi, or into Somalia, Mohammed was your man. He also housed Shabaab operatives.

As we hurtled through the chaotic traffic of Nairobi, Mohammed made elaborate manoeuvres to make sure we were not being fol-lowed. He'd accelerate quickly when the traffic light went green, then a mile later screech to a halt, and take a random turn. Some-times he ran red lights to put distance between him and the cars behind.

We stopped off at some of Ikrimah's favourite haunts in Nairobi, including some of its shopping malls. It was a city he knew very well; I could see how useful he would be to al-Shabaab.

My time with Ikrimah fascinated and alarmed my handlers during my debriefing in Bangkok. He was not on their radar, but was evidence of al-Shabaab's growing reach and support network in Kenya. Western intelligence was already stretched trying to deal with al-Qaeda as it metastasized, as well as home-grown radical cells. Now al-Shabaab and its legion of foreign followers had joined the club.

In the spring of 2009, Warsame, now in command of hundreds of Shabaab fighters, asked for more equipment, but made the mistake of telling me – via a saved draft email – that the equipment was for a Kenyan called 'Mr John'. He said once I sent word I was in Nairobi he would arrange for me to be smuggled across the border into Somalia to deliver the equipment and meet 'Mr John'.

'Mr John', it transpired, was Saleh Ali Nabhan – an individual of great interest to Western intelligence. Even though he was only in his late twenties, Nabhan was suspected of involvement in the bombing of the US embassy in Nairobi in 1998, as well as a bomb attack on a resort in Mombasa in 2002, and on the same day a failed missile attack on an Israeli airliner taking off from Mombasa's airport. He was now regarded as al-Qaeda's most dangerous operative in East Africa – and Warsame and Ikrimah were his protégés.

Al-Shabaab might espouse a medieval view of the world and oppose television and sport, but Nabhan apparently needed a BlackBerry and a laptop. (It is a strange fact of Somali life that amid all the anarchy it had a viable mobile-phone network.)

Jed, now my chief point of contact in the CIA, asked me to come to the Hotel Ascot in Copenhagen to discuss the mission they had in mind.

Among the Danes at the meeting was a new agent, Anders. Ginger-haired, tall and burly, Anders was as informal as his colleagues, but his intelligence and background set him apart. He had studied Arabic in Syria and Lebanon, and understood the mindset of the region. He had served in the military and then studied the rise of Islamist militancy. I took to him immediately, because alone among my handlers he had worked hard to understand what made al-Qaeda and its sympathizers tick. He was principally an analyst, which led the others to tease him as a bookish nerd. They also called him 'the puppy' because of his relative youth. But he did his homework and provided me with invaluable details about al-Shabaab's structure and leading lights.

Jed was even more intense than usual. He scented blood: the chance to take out one of al-Qaeda's most dangerous. He slid a BlackBerry and laptop to me across the conference table in the penthouse suite. 'This is for Mr Nahban with our compliments,' he said.

I had no doubt the CIA had played around with the hardware. I was learning that mobile phones and laptops have a unique digital signature that allows their location to be pinpointed. Even a phone not being used to make calls can be located, because – when connected to a power source – it continuously transmits a weak signal to seek out the nearest base station. The same principle applies to WiFi-enabled laptops, which seek an internet connection.

By the time Nabhan came into our sights, advances in technology were already making it easier for security services. Manufacturers had started rolling out GPS-enabled phones, making it possible for security services to track targets even more precisely. The beauty for the agencies was that even if a phone was turned on in an area completely off the grid, or a laptop was powered up hundreds of miles from the nearest WiFi-hotspot, spy satellites could still lock on to the signal.

Jed said he would fly to Nairobi and link up with CIA agents there to manage the operation. He explained the protocol for getting in touch with him.

'You'll need to take a bunch of jabs for Somalia,' he said with his laconic drawl.

'Malaria will be the least of my worries,' I laughed.

Before I departed, PET ran some weapons training at the military firing range in Jægerspris on the northern shore of Zealand. A short, stocky former special-forces soldier taught me to fire a Kalashnikov. Klang and Trailer looked on as I learned to fire at fixed and moving targets. The power of the weapon was overwhelming, but gradually my accuracy improved. I had carried a handgun during my Bandidos days, done target practice at Dammaj and had a Kalashnikov thrust into my hands in Tripoli, but this was my first real training in handling and firing a weapon. It was a humbling but invaluable experience.

It was pouring with rain when I flew into Nairobi on 12 May 2009.

'It's been like this for a week now,' the cab driver told me on the drive from the airport. I booked into the Jamia Hotel, a modest travellers' hostel squeezed into a shabby shopping mall near Nairobi's largest mosque. It was just the sort of place that an international jihadi might pick to stay under the radar.

The rains persisted, sheets of steamy tropical water cascading from the sky.

I sent an email to Warsame to tell him I had arrived. A day later he replied: 'Bad news: border closed because of flooding: working on new plan.' The few roads across the Kenya–Somali border were not in the best repair.

My handlers were across town at the Holiday Inn. We met in a private room on the ground floor overlooking a lush tropical garden. Only a lazy ceiling fan provided relief from the steamy humidity. Jed was clearly not enjoying the monsoon conditions, and even the ever cool Klang looked overheated. Perspiration glistened on his brow and he dabbed his forehead with a monogrammed handkerchief. Despite his discomfort Klang could not help but steal furtive glances at his MI6 counterpart. Emma seemed unaffected by the heat. She was wearing a green safari shirt and beige shorts which showed off her long tanned legs.

She turned to me.

'Morten: as you seem to have a bit of spare time on your hands, we'd like you to do something for us. There's somebody in the Eastleigh district that we'd rather like you to meet.'

She started explaining the mission.

Jed exploded. 'You Brits always fucking do this,' he shouted. His eyes were bulging. He threw his papers and stormed out, slamming the door. The room went silent. Klang and I exchanged looks.

Through the window I could see Jed light a cigarette and pace around in his cowboy boots.

After he finished he came back into the room.

'All right, let's continue,' he said.

Emma said nothing – I had to admire her cool. I guessed Jed was furious because the CIA had funded this mission and he felt the British were trying to take advantage. An intelligence coup that could advance his career seemed to be slipping from his grasp.

The next day another email came in from Warsame. 'New Plan: Longhair will come to you tomorrow.'

It was a risky enterprise for Ikrimah, who may by now have felt that the Kenyan security services were aware of him. When he came to my room at the Jamia, it was clear we would not be having dinner together again.

'I can't hang around, brother,' he told me. I handed over the phone and computer; he checked them out and looked pleased. This Murad delivers, he seemed to be thinking.

Before he left, he mentioned other equipment al-Shabaab wanted: model aeroplanes with live transmission cameras for surveillance and remote-controlled model cars to which they could attach explosives to attack government checkpoints. I resisted the temptation to raise an eyebrow and promised to look into the possibilities. He hurried away.

A week later I received a coded email from Warsame, which said very simply: 'Mr John says thanks.'

On 14 September, about three months after the equipment was delivered, Nabhan was travelling along the coastal road that linked Mogadishu with al-Shabaab's heartland in the south of Somalia. Four dots appeared on the horizon. They were US assault helicopters. Unnoticed by Nabhan, they raced towards the coast above the waters of the Indian Ocean. As they crossed the sandy coastline, a volley of rockets destroyed the two-car convoy. US Navy SEALs descended from the helicopters and dragged the bodies out of the cars to try to identify them. They later positively identified Nabhan. President Obama, who had authorized the kill mission, was immediately notified. The Americans buried Nabhan's body at sea.

The Danes later told me my equipment had allowed the SEALs to zero in on their target.[3]

---

3 Klang, Trailer and Soren were later honoured at a ceremony in Washington DC for their role in the mission that led to the successful targeting of Nabhan. Klang told me each of them had received gold coins from the Americans. He said the equipment had indeed allowed the Navy SEALs to zero in on their target. I neither requested nor was offered any reward for helping track down Nabhan.

A week later, I received an email from Ikrimah. 'Mr John was killed in a US helicopter attack,' it said flatly. My other al-Shabaab contact, Ahmed Abdulkadir Warsame, told me that Nabhan's entourage suspected the Americans had located him by tracking the BlackBerry and computer. He said the group blamed a Somali courier used by Ikrimah to deliver them. Al-Shabaab believed the courier was in Kenya and was trying to track him down and eliminate him.

My connection to Awlaki seemed to put me beyond suspicion.

CHAPTER SEVENTEEN
MUJAHIDEEN SECRETS

Autumn 2009

As Saleh Ali Nabhan's body was being lowered into the Indian Ocean, I was preparing to reconnect with Awlaki – a man the Americans had been less successful in tracking. Nearly a year had passed since I had taken him supplies deep in Shabwa province. We had remained in regular touch via our shared draft email folder, but he wanted to meet, and Western intelligence very much wanted me to meet him.

Once again I had to follow his drip-by-drip directions into Shabwa, for the encounter in the compound of the tribal leader Abdullah Mehdar which begins this story. Not only had I found Awlaki (when the CIA seemed to have no idea where he was) but I gained a much clearer idea of his evolution from intellectual guide to organizational brain. Western intelligence agencies were struggling to get a handle on the strength and intentions of AQAP (al-Qaeda in Yemen's new name after an influx of Saudi fighters) – and on what specific role Awlaki might be playing. Drones could show pick-ups moving, camps and compounds – but not who was in them. 'Humint' – raw, first-hand reporting from ground level – was precious.

My meeting with Awlaki that September night provided me with not only a window into his evolution from thinker into planner, but also some hard evidence of that transition.

'I need to show you something,' he said – reaching for his laptop and a thumb drive as we sat together after dinner. 'This is how we need to communicate from now on.'

The thumb drive had encryption software called – appropriately – 'Mujahideen Secrets 2.0'. Awlaki had already begun using it in his contacts with followers in the West and it was based on a 256-bit key 'advanced encryption standard' algorithm. He believed our draft inbox method was no longer secure.[1]

I was fascinated as he demonstrated the software. The programmers had created a few flourishes – an image of an AK-47 flashed up with a muzzle in the shape of a key as the software loaded.

I began taking notes.

'You can find the software online. Never download the program to your hard drive and never load it when you are connected to the internet,' he told me. He explained that authentic copies of the software had a particular digital fingerprint displayed in a pixilated pattern on the screen which I would need to check.

'To communicate with me you need to create a private key,' he said, showing me how to generate it. The private key was in essence a unique secret digital code which I could use to lock and unlock messages sent to me, protected by a personal password and saved inside the program on the thumb drive. It seemed that Awlaki had delivered this tutorial before.

'Now you need to create a public key,' he said, showing me how to navigate the program. 'We can exchange our public keys through email and then start sending each other encrypted communications. When you receive an encrypted email click on the text and copy it, then open up the program. The software will prompt you to enter both our public keys and the password for your private key. Then paste the text into the program and hit decrypt.'

---

1 Awlaki reiterated his concern over the draft message technique in a February 2010 encrypted email to me: 'some brs have advised me that the draft system is suspicious because the enemy know that the brs use it.' In the same email he also revealed that he was not now opening emails himself. He had presumably switched to using a courier to open and send emails for him.

I was amazed how a random assortment of letters, numbers and symbols turned within fifteen seconds into clear prose. To encrypt messages I would carry out the same steps in reverse. It was possible to encode just about any file using this method, including images and video. Anwar told me to send the actual scrambled message via an anonymous email account, but I found out later that an encoded message could equally be copied on to a thumb drive.

'We believe this method to be secure but obviously be cautious what you say on it all the same,' he said.

Awlaki had become very aware of security. As I was about to retire, exhausted at the end of a nerve-wracking day, he stopped me.

'There's one other thing. You know Mohammed Usman?'

'Yes,' I said. 'He stayed with us in Sana'a for a while.'

'He came down here – he said he was suspicious of you.'

'Really?'

I was stunned, and anxious.

'Yes, he said he suspected you were working for British intelligence. Of course, he had nothing to back up such a ridiculous accusation. I thought he was a strange guy.'

'When was he here?' I asked.

'A few days ago. I don't know where he went.'

'Well, he won't be staying with us again,' I laughed – trying to make light of an awkward moment. Awlaki seemed to be studying my expression intently.

I had met Usman by accident, or so I had thought. On my way to Yemen from Europe, I had been politely but firmly detained by two security officers at Dubai airport and taken to a detention room. My retinas were scanned, I was fingerprinted and held for eight hours. There were few questions, and only a cursory check of my documents and belongings. Before dawn the following morning, bleary-eyed and irritable, I was escorted to the gate of the Yemenia flight to Sana'a. It was half empty, but I was given a seat next to a man in his thirties who looked as if he were Pakistani.

Halfway through the flight he introduced himself as Mohammed Usman; he was from Leyton in East London. He knew some of the 'brothers' in Luton and wanted to meet some like-minded radicals in Yemen. But he had no entrance visa. Would that be a problem?

I suggested that he tell the Yemenis that he had come for a wedding. It had worked before – and it worked for him. I offered him a place to stay for a few nights and he began asking about Awlaki; he wanted to meet him. I had not even told him that I knew the cleric, but replied cautiously that it might be possible.

'But how do I know you are not a spy?' Usman asked.

He was smiling but there was an intent in his question that I found troubling.

'I could ask the same about you,' I retorted.

Despite my misgivings I had connected him with some jihadist contacts and through them he had reached Shabwa – and Awlaki, only to repay my hospitality with scurrilous allegations.

I replayed in my mind time and again the way Awlaki had raised the issue and then dismissed it. I was as sure as I could be that he gave Usman's claims no credence, and on the drive back to Sana'a I began to think more optimistically about what the trip had achieved, and especially about how the CIA would salivate over the Mujahideen Secrets software.

As Fadia dozed beside me, I sent the briefest text message to Klang. 'Fucking good,' it read.

As soon as I landed in London the following day, I was summoned to a debriefing. Andy and Kevin were there from MI5, Jed from the CIA, and two Danish agents. The British Foreign Intelligence Service, MI6, was represented by Emma.

I recounted every detail of the journey and meeting – the roads, the terrain, Anwar's demeanour and security. And I showed them the encryption software as an encore.

As a thank you for my efforts, the British had arranged for me to go on a bushcraft outdoors course in East Sussex. It was run by Woodlore, the company owned by Ray Mears, a survival expert who had turned bushcraft into a television series and a successful business.[2]

---

2 I later met Mears on a course that I signed up for in the Arctic Circle. He never knew of my work for the intelligence services.

As we sat around the campfire, exchanging introductions, I found out that the dozen or so participants were bankers, lawyers and accountants from high-profile firms in London. They described their day jobs with smug satisfaction.

'So what line of work are you in?' the instructor asked me when it was my turn.

'I'm a taxi driver in Birmingham,' I replied.

I caught some condescending glances. If only they knew that earlier that week I had been in a remote corner of Yemen on behalf of Western intelligence.

No sooner had I left the Sussex countryside than I was asked to a meeting in Copenhagen. Jed showed me satellite images of the village where I had met Anwar and Abdullah Mehdar. He asked me to pinpoint the compound where I had stayed. There were more images from a different angle and then a third.

I could clearly make out the compound and its high walls and was quietly astonished that a satellite photograph could provide such fine resolution.

'That is definitely the place,' I said.

'Thank you,' said Jed – his glacial eyes betraying no satisfaction but the smirk at the corner of his mouth directed at the British contingent.

I detected a growing tension between the Americans and the British, who had very different priorities for me. I began to wonder whether Usman had been an MI6 plant. Perhaps they wanted to sow confusion among Awlaki and the AQAP leadership. Perhaps they were testing my loyalties; perhaps they wanted their own man close to the action – rather than acquiesce to Jed and all his money as ringmaster? The spy business was all about 'perhaps'.

At the end of the meeting I took Emma aside and told her about the mysterious Usman.

'That's very interesting,' she said and asked a few more questions about him.

I tried to read her expression. She had been well trained.

'Come on – I know he's working for you. Don't play this game with me,' I said.

'No – you're mistaken, Morten. He's not.'

Perhaps it was fatigue or a budding paranoia that inevitably fed off this double life. I would never know for sure because Usman never resurfaced. But the incident made me edgy. I had always enjoyed a good relationship with my British handlers, but was apprehensive that they might be using me to develop their own exclusive sources.

My anxiety was fed by another episode when I returned home to Birmingham. As I climbed into my venerable Jaguar one morning, I noticed that the panels above the glove compartment had come loose. I thought they'd been tampered with and a bug had been hidden. I furiously ripped out the panels but found nothing.

I told Sunshine that I needed a meeting with the MI5 station chief in Birmingham. We met at a rundown local hotel, in a room which reeked of stale cigarette smoke. He looked like a middle-aged football hooligan.

He lit up a cigarette while he heard me out, and then took a long drag before responding.

'Morten, we trust you – we wouldn't do something like that.'

'Do you think I'm stupid?' I replied.

'I swear on my son's life.'

I doubted he even had a son, but didn't press the point further. From that point on I presumed my car, my phone and my home were bugged by MI5.

Perhaps the pressures were beginning to get to me. By now I realized that loyalty and trust were not exactly overflowing in this business; no one got results by fair play. I might be discarded or betrayed at any moment as priorities shifted and competition intensified. For my handlers, the first rule of the game seemed ruthlessly simple: the ends always justified the means.

Even if they were not playing me, maybe one of the agencies would get careless, or I would slip up – and be unmasked by the groups I had infiltrated. The first Nairobi mission had made it all seem so easy.

I had no one to confide in, no one to test my suspicions. Fadia still knew nothing, and as the deceit went on it became impossible to introduce her to this dark world. My mother knew vaguely what I was doing but had never been a sympathetic shoulder. The loneliness that came with being an agent began to gnaw at me.

In the autumn of 2009, the CIA was concerned by Awlaki's evolving role, but it was an event in Texas that transformed a figure of growing interest into a target of urgent necessity.

At 1.30 p.m. on 5 November, a 39-year-old US army major named Nidal Hasan entered the sprawling Fort Hood base, some sixty miles from Austin. A psychiatrist, Hasan was assigned to the Soldier Readiness Processing Center, where troops received medical evaluation before and after deployment.

Hasan was armed with an FN Five-seven pistol, a powerful handgun which he had fitted with two laser sights. In the space of a few minutes he shot dead thirteen people and injured thirty more. Some witnesses said they heard him exclaim: '*Allahu Akbar*' as he began shooting. There was so much blood at the scene that the first responders kept slipping as they tried to attend the wounded.

In Birmingham it was late evening when the news networks began reporting the story. I was at home with Fadia when I stumbled across the breathless breaking coverage. To begin with I had no idea there was some terrorist motive. When I heard the name of the suspect late that night, I sat up.

Hasan apparently picked out personnel in uniform during his brief rampage, which ended when he was shot and wounded outside the centre. As he was taken into military custody, an urgent investigation began into his background and contacts. But even before the horrendous carnage of that day, the FBI knew Hasan had been exchanging emails with Anwar al-Awlaki.

Between December 2008 and June 2009, Hasan had written some twenty emails to Awlaki – focusing on whether it was permissible for a Muslim to serve in a foreign army and the conditions for jihad. He had been troubled and radicalized by the accounts of combat he heard from soldiers who had returned from Iraq and Afghanistan. He was clearly in awe of the cleric, whom he had heard preach at the mosque in Falls Church, Virginia, in 2001.

In one email he said he could not wait to join Awlaki in the afterlife, where they could talk over non-alcoholic wine. Two FBI Task Forces had reviewed the intercepted emails and concluded there were no grounds for action against Hasan, because the communications were seen as within the scope of an army psychiatrist's legitimate area of interest and research.

By the morning of 6 November 2009, those communications were seen in a very different light. Federal agencies began a rushed review of communications that other Americans might have had with Awlaki, trawling through databases of intercepts.

I was not surprised that eventually someone in direct contact with Awlaki had committed an act of terror. That likelihood had increased as the cleric's views had become more incendiary. And Awlaki was quick to celebrate Hasan's attack. Within four days of Fort Hood, the cleric wrote on his website: 'Nidal Hasan is a hero. He is a man of conscience who could not bear living the contradiction of being a Muslim and serving in an army that is fighting against his own people.

'The US is leading the war against terrorism, which in reality is a war against Islam. Its army is directly invading two Muslim countries and indirectly occupying the rest through its stooges,' Awlaki added. And he encouraged other Muslims in America to follow Hasan's example.

'The heroic act of brother Nidal also shows the dilemma of the Muslim-American community. Increasingly they are being cornered into taking stances that would either make them betray Islam or betray their nation.'

It was an uncompromising clarion call to Muslims living in the West, urging them to violence.

I had seen at first hand Awlaki's hold over his followers in the West. In March that year I had organized a secret fundraising call via Skype with a group of British-Pakistani supporters in Rochdale. Among them were several doctors eager to contribute to jihad. They listened spellbound to Awlaki's assured answers on a variety of religious topics. MI5 had given its blessing to the event to bolster my credentials in militant circles, on the condition no funds raised reached the cleric.

I still have a recording of the event. Awlaki was as adept at fundraising as any American politician:

'The enemy is oppressing the Muslims. It becomes important for every brother and sister who knows the *Haq* [truth] to act upon it . . . if Allah has blessed you with wealth then you should support the Islamic causes, whether we are talking about Somalia, Afghanistan or Iraq . . . and not just sit on the sidelines and watch.

'When it comes to Yemen because it's not on the news, it's being forgotten and therefore I would encourage every brother who has the capability to assist.'

But now – in lionizing Nidal Hasan – Awlaki must have known that he was crossing a Rubicon. I suspected it would be a matter of hours before I was called to another meeting. I was looking forward to a weekend with my children, but would have to bow to the inevitable.

I told Fadia I might need to go to Denmark.

'My mum's not so well,' I said, at a loss for something more original.

Jed was a bundle of nervous energy when I arrived at the designated Copenhagen hotel.

'It's time to take Awlaki out,' he said bluntly.

'You mean to arrest him?' I asked, knowing otherwise.

'Nah, I don't think so.'

The CIA wanted to use the information I had gleaned to target the man who had both sanctioned and glorified an act of terrorism against American citizens. The gloves had come off.

I was not the only route to the cleric; other intelligence sources were being developed, and the Yemeni government was being heavily pressured into cooperating with a new drive against the militants. But no one had the sort of relationship with Awlaki that I did. As he realized that Western intelligence was stepping up its search for him, his trusted circle would shrink. I would most likely be one of the few on the inside.

Just six weeks after Fort Hood, US Navy warships in the Gulf of Aden fired cruise missiles at suspected al-Qaeda training camps in Yemen. The mission was claimed by the Yemeni government in an effort to mitigate a public backlash against American military action on Yemeni territory. It said that thirty-four al-Qaeda fighters had been killed, including some mid-level commanders.

But the intelligence behind that strike was flawed – again demonstrating the difficulty of accurate targeting where there were few informants on the ground. The cruise missiles destroyed a Bedouin hamlet where an al-Qaeda operative and around a dozen other militants were staying. Local officials said many women and children were among the nearly sixty killed in one strike.

'The Americans just scored a big own goal,' Awlaki wrote to me shortly after the attack.

That strike took place on 17 December, and exactly one week later came the first attempt to take out Awlaki, in another cruise missile strike.

He was presumed to be attending a meeting of senior al-Qaeda figures who had been discussing a response to the previous attack.[3]

First reports indicated Awlaki had been killed. I was watching the news the next day – Christmas Day, 2009 – while on a short vacation in Scotland when I received a text from Abdullah Mehdar, the tribal fighter close to Awlaki whom I had befriended three months earlier. 'The tall guy is fine,' it read.

On 28 December Awlaki himself confirmed his survival in an encrypted email. 'Phew. Maaaaaan – that was close,' he said. He also warned me not to get in touch with Mehdar, because he was a 'hot potato'.

At the very moment I was told 'the tall guy is fine', Northwest Airlines flight 253 to Detroit from Amsterdam was approaching the eastern seaboard of the United States. A young Nigerian – Umar Farouk Abdulmutallab – was in seat 19A, above the wing and close to the fuel tanks. As the flight descended through slate-grey skies to its destination he retired to the toilet for twenty minutes.

When he came back, he covered himself with a blanket and tried to detonate an explosive device hidden in his underwear. The main charge failed to explode and he was left with smoking underpants as several passengers – perhaps recalling Richard Reid or the heroics of the passengers on board United flight 93 on 9/11 – rushed at him.[4]

---

3 A statement from the Yemeni embassy in Washington said Awlaki was 'presumed' to have been at the site of an al-Qaeda meeting south of the capital city of Sana'a.
4 Bomb experts later theorized that the only reason the device didn't work was that Abdulmutallab's perspiration had desensitized the main charge: the result of wearing

The young Nigerian's mission had begun in Yemen four months earlier. He had been drawn there from his studies in Dubai, enticed by the velvet tones of Awlaki and the contemplation of martyrdom. In summer 2009 he had trawled the mosques of Sana'a, looking for someone who could put him in touch with the preacher. Eventually someone had taken his mobile-phone number and a few days later he received a text with a phone number. Abdulmutallab was surprised when the voice at the other end was that of his hero, who instructed him to make his case for joining jihad – in writing.

His essay written and his plea for guidance sent, Abdulmutallab was collected and driven to Shabwa to meet Awlaki – just a few days after I had left the cleric to travel in the opposite direction.

Abdulmutallab told the preacher that he was ready for any mission, including one that would take his own life. Awlaki arranged for and helped write a martyrdom video for Abdulmutallab to record. He told him not to fly directly from Yemen to Europe, aware that might provoke suspicion. And his final words, according to the young Nigerian, were chilling: be sure to wait until the plane was over the United States, and then bring it down.

In the hours after his arrest a badly burned Abdulmutallab began detailing these instructions to FBI agents by his hospital bedside. I would only discover the full extent of what he had confessed later, but my handlers made it clear that Awlaki had been both aware of and involved in the plot. Americans had only just been spared another attack on the homeland, and Awlaki was becoming almost as influential as Osama bin Laden himself.[5]

More disturbing still was Abdulmutallab's claim that Awlaki had consulted directly with the man emerging as AQAP's master bomb-maker – a young Saudi called Ibrahim al-Asiri. Al-Asiri had built the

---

the explosive underwear for three weeks as he travelled from Yemen through Africa to Nigeria. But all agreed he had come terrifyingly close to bringing down a US airliner over a major city.

5 Within weeks, lawyers at the US Department of Justice took the unprecedented step of writing up a short memorandum justifying the targeted killing of an American citizen overseas.

underwear device. Just months earlier he had built a bomb to be inserted into the rectum of his younger brother, Abdullah. The device contained around 100 grams of the high-explosive PETN, a difficult-to-detect white powder, also later used in the underwear device. Abdullah's target was Prince Mohammed bin Nayef, the head of Saudi counter-terrorism, whose security services had driven the brothers out of Saudi Arabia two years earlier.

Abdullah told the Saudis he wanted to become an informant and was granted an audience with bin Nayef. He went through security checks at the airport, but nothing was found. When he detonated the explosive, the force of the explosion was directed upwards. Abdullah's body parts were scraped from the ceiling of bin Nayef's office – but the Prince himself was only slightly injured. Despite the failure of the mission, al-Asiri's brother and comrades had been emboldened. Never had al-Qaeda come so close to killing a member of the Saudi royal family.

As the FBI's intense questioning of Abdulmutallab continued in Detroit, a few hundred miles to the south in Washington DC intelligence officials turned their attention to those satellite images of the compound that I had visited.

On 12 January 2010 Yemeni counter-terrorism commandos descended quietly on the compound in the al-Hota area of Shabwa, where the previous September I had been housed by the tribal leader Abdullah Mehdar. Their main target was undoubtedly Anwar al-Awlaki, whom I had identified as a frequent house guest. But the terrorist cleric was not there that day. Mehdar refused to surrender and fought to the bitter end, despite being urged by other fighters to flee.

I received the news a few days later from Awlaki himself, in an encrypted email:

'Remember the guy you stayed with? Its confirmed. He was killed. I had spoken to him a while back and requested from him if the gov attacks to retreat to the mountains. He said that he will fight until he is killed and will not retreat and that is what he did. There were 20 of them and they fought against the gov and killed over 6 soldiers and then they retreated in front of overwhelming forces. He refused and fought from his house until they killed him. May Allah curse them.' He added in a follow-up email that he had been with Mehdar just 'a few days' before he was killed.[6]

Later that day, Anders – the PET analyst who had recently joined the team – told me that the Americans had confirmed my information had led to the operation against Mehdar's compound.[7]

The news deeply unsettled me. My role in targeting Nabhan had not disturbed me in the slightest; he was a ruthless terrorist involved in the murder of dozens of civilians. Mehdar was different: an apparently honourable man prepared to fight for his beliefs and in defence of his territory. He had no dreams of global jihad, of bringing carnage to the streets of Europe or the skies above America.

Never before in my work as a double agent had I brought about the death of someone I knew. I recalled the last time we had met, when the tearful Sheikh had told me as he helped change the tyre on my hired car: 'If we don't meet again, we will see each other in paradise.'

For days I stayed at home in Birmingham, paralysed with guilt. Fadia must have thought I was having one of my dark moods. I found myself incapable of running even basic errands like going to the supermarket. A grim realization haunted me, and I cursed my naivety in not expecting and preparing for it. My work as an informant – to put it coldly – was killing people. And I had no say in who should be a target. The Americans, helped by the Yemeni government, had cast a wide net – and no distinction was drawn between men like Mehdar and men like Nabhan.

But the stakes were now too high and the urgency too great for me to wallow for long. I remembered that one of the fighters who had

---

6 On 29 January 2010 Awlaki sent me this follow-up email: 'a few days [before] Shaykh Abdullah [Mehdar] died (btw he was the chief of his tribe) I was talking to him about you and remembering your visit to his house. He was a brave and sincere brother. A few weeks before his death I was advising him that if the government attacks him he should retreat to the mountains. He refused and said if they come to me I will not retreat but will fight until I am killed, and that is what he did. Alhamdulillah his family is doing well.'

7 Several weeks later AQAP released a short video eulogy claiming the raid on Mehdar's compound was a joint US–Yemeni operation. US officials have not publicly acknowledged US special forces were involved.

attached himself to Mehdar had gone on to carry out a suicide bombing against South Korean tourists in Yemen. I never found out if Mehdar had had any role in the attack, but it gave me some solace.

Several weeks after the death of Mehdar, Awlaki declared war on the United States in a recorded audio message. 'We are not against Americans for just being American, we are against evil. And America as a whole has turned into a nation of evil,' he said calmly and deliberately.

'Jihad against America is binding upon myself, just as it is binding on every other able Muslim.'

Me aged seven.

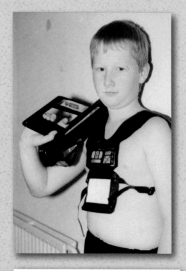

The 'king' of laser tag.

Vibeke and me in the summer
of 1993. I was seventeen.

Vikings do housework too.

The Korsør Library in Denmark,
in which I found a book about Islam
and began reading.

Returning to the bookshelf many
years later.

A meal with my mother in 1999.

In Yemen, 2006.

Holding my son, Osama, in Denmark during my radical years. (Credit: Politiken)

In 2006 after arrest of Kenneth Sorensen. (Credit: TV2 Denmark)

Protesting outside the US embassy in London in 2005.

Omar Bakri Mohammed led the protests outside the embassy.

Taimour Abdulwahab al-Abdaly, my friend from Luton who carried out a suicide bombing in Stockholm in 2010.

Zacarias Moussaoui, my one-time friend in Brixton and the so-called 'twentieth hijacker' of 9/11.

Sana'a, Yemen.
(Credit: Cityskylines.org)

Dammaj, Yemen. (Credit: Wikipedia)

Taiz, Yemeni highlands.
(Credit: Supportyemen.org)

On the misty mountain
road to deliver
supplies to Awlaki,
October 2008.

Shabwa province.

Ataq, Yemen. (Credit: Panoramio.com)

Yemen visa stamp, 2001.

Yemen driving licence.

Awlaki while living in the US. (Credit: *Washington Post*)

Re: From Viking land   Tue, 8 Apr 2008 at 12:06

From   Anwar Awlaki

To   Murad Storm

No it is not allowed because even though all of the alchohol evaporates it is najasah (impure) and that najasah has mixed with the chocolate.

Murad Storm wrote:
> Waleikum Salaam Warahmatullah
> Sheikh, regarding the chocolate, is it permissible to eat it when it has got like alcohol flavour in it. I asked one who makes it, and they use real wine or wisky, however they burn up the alcohol before using it for the chocolate, otherwise the chocolate would melt, so only they wisky flavour stays.
> What is the ruling regarding this?
> May Allah reward you
> Assalamu Aleikum Warahmatullah
> Abu Osama
>
> "/Anwar Awlaki <al_aulaqi@yahoo.com>/" wrote:
>
> Asslamu alaykum Murad,
> Jazaki Allahu khairan. I use xl in shirts. Forget about shoes since I
> only use sandles.
> Cheese and chocolates please:)
> AA
> Anwar

Email chain with Awlaki in the weeks before I met him in Aden in May 2008. The cleric had requested cheese and chocolate.

Shaykh Anwar with the mujahideen's leader
in the Arabian Peninsula, Shaykh Abu Baseer al-Wuhaishi.

SAVE 25%

NOORPRO

- DIGITALLY REMASTERED
- OVER 20 HRS LECTURE

- 9 DVD'S BOX SET
- INCLUDES Q & A

IMAM ANWAR AL-AWLAQI'S
UMAR IBN AL-KHATTAAB

Irena Horak, who changed her name to Aminah (from her public social media page).

Awlaki's video proposal to Aminah.

Aminah Muslimah Fisabilillah

I would go with him anywhere, I am 32 years old and I am ready for dangerous things, I am not afraid of death or to die in the sake of Allah subhane we te'alla. I didn't know he has 2 wife already. But I do not mind at all. I want to help him in his work and make dawa to other non-muslims or Muslims. I am good in housekeeping jobs. As he already have 2 wifes and kids I am sure it would be a problem to have a wife with him all the time, without kids, inshaalllah.

I do not know what I will see but I am willing to be a very hardworking and active wife, J support wife and if it is requires I can go inshaallah.

Aminah's Facebook message affirming her desire to marry Awlaki.

The hotel receipt from my first trip to Vienna to meet Aminah, March 2010.

Before Irena became Aminah (from her public social media page).

Aminah's veiled video recording for Awlaki.

Aminah's unveiled recording.

The $250,000 CIA reward for the Aminah mission —
the combination for the lock was 007.

Kenneth Sorensen in Syria, from a jihadist video.

Hassan Tabbakh.
(Credit: Press Association)

Ikrimah in Norway. (Credit: TV2 Norway)

Ahmed Abdulkadir Warsame in court.

Abdullah Mehdar.

Commiseration of Shaykh: Anwer Al-Awlaki
May Allah have mercy on him

The voice of Shaykh: Ibrahim Al-Rubaish - May Allah preserve him

we ask Allah to make him
among the chiefs of martyrs

AQAP claimed this was what was left of Awlaki's vehicle after it was hit by a drone.

My tour guide in Jaar, AQAP emir and al-Qaeda global #2 Nasir al-Wuhayshi, taken from *Inspire* Magazine.

SEEKING
INFORMATION
Saleh Ali Saleh Nabhan

The FBI's most-wanted poster for Saleh Ali Nabhan, who masterminded the bombing of the US embassy in Nairobi in August 1998.

At the Masinga Dam.

Storm Bushcraft
in Kenya.

Bathing in a geothermal spa in
Reykjavik with my Danish handlers
in early 2010.

My CIA recruiter, Elizabeth Hanson.
(Credit: colby.edu)

Dog sledding with Western intelligence in northern Sweden, March 2010.

My Ice Hotel bedroom on trip organized by British intelligence.

Skiing in the Arctic Circle.

My Kenya visa stamp for mission to deliver supplies to Nabhan in May 2009.

On my way to deliver equipment to Awlaki in October 2008 ...

... I recorded the drive.

On the road in Shabwa, just after meeting Awlaki, in September 2009.

Yemen visa stamps during mission targeting Awlaki in the summer of 2011. On 28 June I left Yemen for a debriefing in Malaga and returned on 27 July.

3 things: If you email me please write down the date on all your messages. Second, keep in mind that it takes a few days for emails to get to me so if you are setting an appointment then give me advance notice. Third: you do not need to write "to the sheikh" when you email inspire. Anything from your email will be delivered to me.

Please respond to this message with what you want to say and give it to the brother. We cannot have our brother travel with a laptop plus it is suspicious for you guys to type out a message in a public place.

This brother may be the messenger between us for now. One IMPORTANT note: The brother does not know that he is delivering messages for me and he doesn't know where I am so do not mention that this message is for me. Just give it to him and he will deliver it where it needs to be delivered and will get to me insha Allah.

For future correspondence I believe it would be better if your wife delivers the flash to the brother. It's up to you but I believe that you would definitely be watched and that might put you and the brother in jeopardy. Agree with the brother on the place of meeting. Also we need to keep the meetings to a minimum. The brother says it is not safe for him to enter sanaa frequently. So please mention all what you need to say in the message you send me. Please let me know what your program is and the latest news from the west. Also please send the emails of ikrimah and this other brother with your message.

My wife needs some stuff from sanaa so can your wife buy it for her? We have sent other people before and nothing really suited her taste.

Soren used Klang's phone to forward a message to me from the CIA after I returned their equipment in a Sana'a car park in May 2012.

Awlaki's first thumb drive message to me.

The KFC in Sana'a where I met one of Awlaki's couriers, summer 2011. (Credit: Panoramio.com)

Set-up/start

Key generator

1. Key manager 2. Type user name and code
3. Close Key generator.
4. Go back key manager/import.
5. Opens window with public/private key
6. Type password for my user Id/click ok
7. Go to import key - click public key -/close

8 Create connection. Click on "friend" and the my Pub/Priv.

Decrypt a message

1. Click on friend user key.
2. Click on my own key
3. Messages - copy message and paste in message
4. Type your password in order to decrypt click "decrypt" - Read and close.

My notes from Awlaki's tutorial on Mujahideen Secrets when I visited him in Shabwa in September 2009.

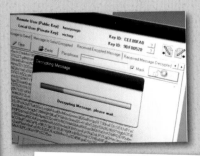

Decrypting an email from Awlaki, received on 5 March 2010, using Mujahideen Secrets.

My picture and others pinned up against a wall in Syria.

Al-Qaeda-linked fighters fired at our photographs.

After I went public my story was picked up around the world.

Drawing by my daughter Sarah showing me apologizing to former Danish politician Naser Khader.

On a recent trip to Korsør.

CHAPTER EIGHTEEN
ANWAR'S BLONDE

Spring–Summer 2010

On 9 March 2010 I stood outside the international bus terminal on Erd-
bergstraße in Vienna, waiting for the 11 a.m. bus from Zagreb to arrive.
It was cold and breezy, typical of March in the Austrian capital. A
steady stream of tourists emerged from the buses and headed to see
the palaces of the Habsburgs.

Jed had told me there would be a CIA team shadowing me. I looked
at a man in a cowboy hat on the street corner checking his watch.
Surely they would not be that obvious.

Then I saw her. She wore a long black skirt as I had anticipated, but
instead of being fully veiled, she was wearing a simple headscarf. A few
stray strands of blonde hair fluttered in the breeze.

'*As salaam aleikum.* I'm Aminah,' she said in soft-accented English,
fixing me with her blue-green eyes.

Despite the fact that Awlaki had instructed me to wear Western
clothes to avoid suspicion, I had to keep my distance from a woman
who was not related to me. I didn't even shake her hand. But I was
impressed; the photos had not done her justice. Aminah was strikingly
pretty, with full lips, high cheekbones and an angular nose. She looked
several years younger than her age, thirty-two. Gwyneth Paltrow, I
thought – Anwar will love this girl.

I had come across her on a Facebook fan page for Awlaki in November 2009 – two months after he had repeated his request that I find him

a wife in the West. I had left a message on the site requesting support and Aminah had replied.

'What kind of support and are you in direct contact with Shaikh?' she wrote in her first message on 28 November 2009.

Two days later, after we exchanged several messages, she wrote this: 'I have one question tho. Do you know personally AAA? And if it is so, may I be so liberal to ask you something?' AAA was our code for Anwar al-Awlaki.

'Yes I do know him. Feel free to ask,' I replied immediately. She had written back:

'I sent Shaikh a letter by mail, I am not sure if I had his correct email address, but actually I was wondering will he search for a second wife, I proposed him a marriage, and I do not know how silly it is. But I tried. Now, as I am in contact with you there is a possibility for you to get know me better in a way you can recommended me.

'I seek a way how to get out of this country, and I search a husband who will teach me and whom I can help a lot. I deeply respect him and the all things he do for this Ummah and I want to help him in any way.'

I wrote back:

'You will be wife number 3, as he already got two wives, however he don't stay with them because they are in the capital, and only see him now and then. But you will stay with him all the time, as you don't have a family there. You should expect hardship, and moving from place to place once in a while. Taking care of your duties in house as a wife. Be patience with all what you will see and face, as AAA may be expose to danger etc. and Allah is our protector. Can you accept this?'

She replied within ten minutes:

'I would go with him anywhere, I am 32 years old and I am ready for dangerous things, I am not afraid of death or to die in the sake of Allah. I didn't know he has 2 wife already. But I do not mind at all. I want to help him in his work . . . I am good in housekeeping job [and] I'm willing to be a very hardworking and active wife.'

Aminah's real name was Irena Horak. I would get to know her well. Dozens of emails and Facebook exchanges would follow. She sent many long notes about her life for me to pass on to Awlaki.

Irena came from Bjelovar, a small town surrounded by farmland east of Croatia's capital, Zagreb. In one of her subsequent messages for Awlaki, Aminah described coming from a loving home and being brought up, like most Croats, as a Catholic with 'family values and high moral standards'. She was particularly close to her twin sister, Helena, her only sibling.

As a teenager Irena excelled in athletics. Such was her dedication that she became a champion junior 100-metre sprinter. There were pictures of her in the local newspaper ducking at the finishing line, her arms flung out in victory. She was driven, throwing herself headlong into her sprinting in the hope she might one day represent Croatia in the Olympics.

The twin sisters both enrolled at the Faculty of Education and Rehabilitation Sciences at Zagreb University. Irena wanted to work with people with special needs. By then her dreams of athletic glory had faded. She devoted herself to her studies. By night, like many of her fellow students, she hit Zagreb's nightclubs, drinking and dancing till the early hours.

Much later I discovered that during this time she posted photos on social media showing herself in a variety of uninhibited poses in which she sported various figure-hugging outfits, low tops, knee-high lace-up boots, and even a sleeveless black-leather catsuit.

After graduating, Irena found work at a residential centre for children without parental care. The centre housed around fifty kids between the ages of seven and eighteen, many of them with behavioural problems.

Later, Aminah recognized the diffident streak in her own character. In one of her messages for Awlaki she wrote:

'People say about me I am strong character but actually this is my shield, I am strong but I am very emotional, sensitive and I hate injustice. I like to work, I am not lazy, people describe me as a empathic, kind, open to new people.'

She had found Islam by accident, at a wedding ceremony in Zagreb. One of the guests was Sage, a handsome lawyer with long dreadlocks and a broad smile. He was a Muslim and worked in London. A few days later she was on a plane to London, having unceremoniously dumped her boyfriend. The two started a long-distance relationship.

Sage saw himself as a believer and spoke to her fondly about Islam, but he wore his religion lightly. He enjoyed going out for drinks, and by all accounts she was thrilled to be on his arm in the bars of London and Zagreb. She told a friend she hoped they would get married.

Later, she would write to Awlaki about Sage:

'He talked about Islam so nicely and peacefully and he discovers to me a lot of different thing I didn't know before. I was curious . . . so I start to explore by myself.'

She connected with a group of Muslim women in Bosnia who in turn introduced her to others in Zagreb. She began to spend time with them in the mosque.

'When I saw description of God – Allah in Quran I said to myself – this is a God I always thought it should be,' she would tell Awlaki in one message.

'It was always a nonsense to me that God have a son, everything I discover in Islam was logical and simple, but yet very frustrated and hard to accept, in that period of my searching.'

I was reminded of my own sense of discovery in the library at Korsør.

After six months her relationship with Sage soured. It seemed Islam had become more important to Irena than the relationship. She began sending him hostile emails, criticizing him for not praying five times a day and for drinking alcohol.

Irena's faith may have been reinforced by a bout with cancer. She said she had treatment and made a recovery, but it ended her dream of having children. She threw herself into Islam, began learning Arabic, and changed her habits, the way she dressed – wrapping herself in long skirts and a headscarf. She lost touch with her former friends. Irena became Aminah.

She told Awlaki about this turbulent time in her life:

'After a period of ang[er] and frustration I find peace in my heart I never felt before . . . I was so happy for learning new things about Islam . . . I was very emotional about everything due to Islam, I crying during prayers, I cried when I heard Azan [the call to prayer].'

And just like me, she felt a surge of energy, a liberation, when she formally converted to Islam in May 2009 by saying the *Shahada* – the profession of faith.

One of Aminah's longtime friends would later describe how she was consumed by her new faith. All she could talk about was Islam and she tried repeatedly to get her friends to convert.

It was around this time that Aminah came across Awlaki's English-language sermons – by now all over the internet. His call for followers to live the simple life of the Prophet, uncorrupted by Western modernity, seduced her. He might not have movie-star good looks, but she came to admire his sincerity and intellect and his quiet charisma. And she began to daydream about being his wife; he could teach her a lot about Islam.

By the time we connected on Facebook, Aminah told me she was being ostracized in Zagreb. At work, her manager complained about the way she dressed. She felt cut off from society and even from Croatia's mainstream Muslim community.

'I live in a country of kuffar. I really want to get out of this place,' she later told Awlaki in one of her messages. Again I was able to recognize the sentiment, recalling that grim day I had washed the lifeless body of the old man who had collapsed outside Regent's Park's mosque.

'I was rejected a lot of proposal cause brothers weren't serious about marriage or they are not on the same ideology.'

Aminah could not bring herself to tell her father about her conversion, but her mother had reluctantly accepted it. By the time that first Facebook message reached me, she seemed shrouded in sadness. She felt she had few meaningful relationships beside her family. How familiar it was.

But I realized that in this lost, impressionable woman I had an opportunity.

'Aminah can lead us to Awlaki,' I told my MI5 handlers – Sunshine, Andy and Kevin – soon after our conversations started on Facebook.

'We understand your logic but we'll have to take this up the chain of command,' Andy said.

The British shared my concern that sending Aminah to the wilder parts of a volatile country might put her at risk. The Americans, sup-ported by the Danes, were more enthusiastic.

'We like the idea,' Jed said when we met in Copenhagen. There was excitement in his eyes as he contemplated the mother of all honeytraps. The gloves had come off in the days since Fort Hood, and in Washing-ton discussions had already begun on whether Awlaki – as an American citizen – could legally be targeted for assassination. Jed realized Aminah represented a golden opportunity to target the terrorist cleric.

The CIA was officially entering the matchmaking business.

At their bidding I sent word to Awlaki that I had found him a pos-sible wife, and on 11 December 2009 he got in touch, asking that she write a brief description of herself.

She sent me this reply for the cleric:

'I am 32 years old, never married, no kids. I am tall (1,73cm) slim-athletic build, I am not sure is it permissible for me to describe my hair. Anyway, ppl say I am good looking, atractive, I look much younger, everybody giving me 23–25 year.'

On 15 December, Awlaki sent me another encrypted message to pass on to her:

'There are two things that I would like to stress. The first is that I do not live in a fixed location. Therefore my living conditions vary widely. Sometimes I even live in a tent. Second, because of my security situ-ation I sometimes have to seclude myself which means me and my family would not meet with any persons for extended periods. If you can live in difficult conditions, do not mind loneliness and can live with restrictions on your communications with others then alhamdulillah that is great. I have no problems with both of my wives and we get along well. Nevertheless they both chose to live in a city because they could not handle village life with me. I do not want this to happen again with another wife. What I need is someone who could bear with me the difficulties of this path.

'One more thing. Can you please send me a photo of yours? Please send it as an attachment.'

With the 'underwear plot' in the pipeline, Anwar must have sus-pected he was about to shoot up the US wanted list; perhaps that is why he emphasized the hardships of life in hiding for any future Mrs Awlaki.

In mid-December Aminah asked me to pass a new message to Awlaki, laying down some ground rules.

'I do not want a husband just on paper, I want to be with him and live in Islam cause I can't do it here. I am not housewife type, I can cook and do all other house duties but this is not all with what I will be pleased. I started to translate your lectures on my native language so I can help brothers and sisters on this part of the world.'

She also asked Awlaki whether she would be able to travel in and out of Yemen. 'My biggest concern are my parents, I know it will be a great shock to them if I say I will go there,' she wrote. 'If I can't see them ever again I am afraid I can't accept that condition.'

Her naivety at times was worrying.

I encrypted her message through the Mujahideen Secrets software and sent it to Awlaki. He replied on 18 December:

'I forsee that if you come in the country you come in for good and if you leave the country you also leave for good . . . the country is heading towards war. Only Allah knows what implications that would bring,' he wrote.

And then he responded to her request for more personal details.

'I am a quiet person. I do not interfere alot in the affairs of my family but when i do it must go my way. I do not tolerate disobedience from my wives. With my kids its the opposite especially my girls. I am very flexible with them so it is the mother who needs to dicipline them because I don't. I love reading. I spend some time with my family when they are with me but my committments pull me away . . . My work takes priority over family therefore I would love to have a wife that is lightweight and part of my work. Having lived most of my life in the West I would like to be in company of a Muslim from the West.'

Awlaki asked for Aminah's email address so he could ask her some 'private questions' directly. Given his obsession with operational security, and the fact the 'underwear plot' was only days away, it was a remarkable risk to take. Lust had again got the better of him.

On Christmas Eve, after the missile strike against al-Qaeda in Shabwa province, Aminah again got in touch with me.

'Do you have news from brother, there is a rumour he is dead or prisoned? Is it true?' she asked.

As soon as I found out that Awlaki was unharmed, I wrote to her, using our agreed name of Sami for Awlaki.

'Sami is fine and well Alhamdolillah . . . just have some patience sister, he is under huge pressure, are you sure you can handle this huge test?'

Despite his brush with death, Anwar was still thinking of the Croatian blonde when he wrote to me just four days after his brush with mortality. I let her know this:

'Sami sends u his greetings, and cannot contact u directly again, however I will pass on his message to u and u can reply to him via me. he is fine and well. He is still interested and ask when we can arrange the travel etc.'

After the Christmas Eve missile strike, the disquiet of British intelligence became outright opposition. They wanted nothing to do with a plan that could send an innocent European woman to her death. I sympathized with their position. I wanted to be sure that Aminah would not be seen as expendable, 'collateral damage' in the pursuit of Awlaki.

The British bid to prise me away from the Americans began a few weeks earlier at a secret facility straight out of 007's playbook.

Fort Monckton had been built to protect the naval harbour of Portsmouth towards the end of the eighteenth century and retains its bastions, casemates and drawbridge. It also boasts high razor-wire fences, floodlighting and CCTV cameras and is nowadays referred to by the army as the No. 1 Training Establishment.

It is in fact the main field-training centre for the Secret Intelligence Services. For close to a century Britain's top agents have been trained there.

Emma, my MI6 handler, picked me up in London for the drive down to Fort Monckton. She was dressed all in black with her brunette hair tied tightly in a bun. As she weaved through traffic on the motorway she opened up about her background. She had attended Oxford

University but afterwards needed some quick cash and had become what might politely be described as an exotic dancer.

I was pleased that she felt she could confide in me. But later I wondered whether it was part of a routine, a confidence-building measure to make me feel closer to my British team.

When we neared the gates, Emma handed me a scarf.

'Put this on your head – we don't want the guards on the outer perimeter to see you,' she said.

Fort Monckton was old school in every sense. At dinner, elderly butlers in formal attire waited on the MI6 officers assembled in the wood-panelled banqueting hall. I stayed in the private quarters of Sir Mansfield Cumming, the legendary early-twentieth-century British intelligence chief who in signing his letters 'C' provided the inspiration for Ian Fleming's spymaster, 'M'.

'Who on earth are you?' I was asked by Steve, a veteran instructor. He was in his fifties and had led MI6 attempts to hunt down Uday Hussein, the sadistic son of the Iraqi dictator Saddam Hussein after the invasion of Iraq in 2003.

'They don't let civilians into this facility, period. And I've never been allowed to sleep in the Colonel's bedroom,' he added.

'Well, my name's Morten Storm . . .' I replied, immediately realizing my mistake. Emma had told me not to talk about myself during my stay.

'It's okay, don't worry,' she said.

During the day MI6 agents and I did role-playing games. I would be handed a scenario and given fifteen minutes to prepare. Cameras fed my responses to a team in another room. In the debrief Steve told me I was a natural problem-solver and had passed the tests. I couldn't be sure whether he was being serious or if it was part of a charm offensive.

The special treatment continued into the New Year.

I was invited to a course in counter-surveillance in Edinburgh run by Andy and Kevin from MI5.

In the morning, in my hotel room, they explained how I could detect that I was being followed and ways to shake a tail. One method involved finding an excuse to stop while walking and discreetly look around. Another way involved taking an apparently random zigzag route to see if the tail followed. But if your route was too random, professionals would know you were on to them. They said the same principles applied if I was driving. It made me recall my helter-skelter ride through the streets of Nairobi courtesy of Ikrimah's driver, Mohammed. Andy and Kevin also told me how to check whether a contact was being followed. I should tell them to pass through various locations and discreetly observe them.

My MI5 handlers told me that several agents I had never met had been assigned to follow me through the streets of Edinburgh. The first drill was for me to spot any pursuers and then shake them off. I set off up the hill from my hotel near the train station, admiring the turrets of Edinburgh Castle high above, gleaming in the winter sunshine. When I reached the castle I took a left and started walking down the Royal Mile. Despite a cold wind, the street was packed with tourists. It would be difficult to know who, if anyone, was on my tail.

I abruptly stopped at a cashmere store and checked the prices in the window. In the reflection I noticed a man in a black-and-blue jacket walk past me. When I set off again down the street he had stopped, and was looking at postcards on an outdoor stall. After I passed him I didn't look round. Instead I ducked into an alley. When I peered back from behind a wall I noticed he had taken the same route.

I increased my pace, taking as random a path as possible through the cobbled side streets. This was proving a very enjoyable exercise. Soon I had no idea where I was, but my tail had disappeared. When I recovered my bearings and got back to the hotel, I was told I'd passed the first test.

That evening, after several more drills, Kevin and Andy took me to a small shop specializing in haggis on the Royal Mile. I had no idea what it was.

'You need to taste this. It's a Scottish tradition,' Andy said.

As my face broke into a puzzled frown, they both began laughing. And then they told me exactly how haggis was made. But the fun was over. British intelligence were not investing so much valuable time in me for my own pleasure.

As we sat down in a quiet corner of a local restaurant, Kevin looked me in the eye and addressed me in a serious tone.

'We're not comfortable with what the Americans want to do with Aminah. Our job is to gather information. We don't participate in assassinations. We don't believe we should help get Aminah to Yemen. We fear she may get killed.'

But there was another element to Kevin's message which didn't exactly speak to the famous 'special relationship' between the British and US intelligence communities.

'Morten, we can't offer you anything like the money they can but one thing we can promise you is this. We won't fuck you over. You know we don't lie. We don't like this plan with Aminah and we don't want you to get fucked over.'

I turned over my options. The British seemed willing to invest in me for the long term. I liked my handlers and I too was concerned for Aminah's safety. But I had not so long ago harboured doubts about their endgame, and had suspected they were trying to manoeuvre their own informant into Awlaki's inner circle.

In the next few days both the Danes and the Americans pressed the mission hard, despite the fact that Danish law explicitly forbade PET from taking part in any assassination operation overseas.

Soon after my Edinburgh training, Klang called.

'We're going to Iceland – just us Danes, and Big Brother is paying.'

A few days later we were relaxing in the thermal waters of the blue lagoon in Reykjavik. There was a new addition to the team – an officer in his late forties called Jesper. He was Klang's opposite. Klang was a peacock, showing off his physique. There was nothing of the show-off in Jesper, who had a restrained dry wit. He had a receding hairline and plain features, and was thin to the point of looking frail. While Klang had cut his teeth in the hurly-burly of the drugs squad, Jesper was something of a desk jockey. Before joining PET he'd worked in banking and the financial crimes division of the police. I asked a fellow bather to take a picture of me and the PET agents. Surprisingly my handlers did not object.

Later in my suite in the five-star Radisson Blu hotel in Reykjavik I relayed to them what the British had told me.

'Morten, our view is that we should proceed with the Americans. It'll be more fun. And they have more money,' Klang said.

The money was a factor. They were offering to double my retainer. It was hardly a CEO's salary – some $4,000 a month. But to someone who had frequently been reduced to gathering the loose change trapped in the sofa, it felt like serious money.

I also felt I had an opportunity to influence the way the Aminah mission unfolded. Perhaps there was a way to cage Awlaki – rather than kill him.

In the first weeks of 2010 Awlaki and I continued to exchange emails, despite the intense pressure on him. He wanted Aminah to travel as soon as possible.

'Since things are getting stricter for foreigners over here with new laws . . . if you could try to speed up her travel into Yemen before she gets on the radar or is prevented from entering the country,' he wrote.

On the last day of January he strongly advised me against travelling to meet Aminah, concerned it might jeoparadize her chances of reaching Yemen.

'If you go there or inquire about her you may get her in trouble or yourself in trouble because the eyes are on you.

'There are millions of people around the world that listen to me but in the end it is a handful whom I can count upon. It's like looking for needles in a haystack. And since you are one of those brs that I can count on, I care about you, and your security, and your wellness, but I also care about your ideas and manhaj [methodology].'

For a few moments I was touched by his words. There was still a streak of humanity about him – he was a marked man but looking out for people he felt he could rely upon. I began to think how I might reel him in quietly and present him to the Yemeni authorities. He would no longer be free, but he would be alive.

Just two weeks later the CIA fast-tracked the Aminah mission. I was summoned to a meeting in Helsingør. Klang and Jesper picked me up at the railway station, a magnificent neo-Renaissance building with a towering triangular roof and an impressive array of turrets and spires.

'We've negotiated with the Americans,' Klang said as we drove out from the station. 'They are prepared to offer you $250,000. The deal is the moment Aminah lands in Sana'a and leaves the airport the money is yours.'

Jesper chimed in: 'But obviously you didn't hear this from us. One of the "masters of the universe" is here from Washington DC to make the offer in person.'

His delivery was acidic. The Danes might want to share a bed with the Americans, but they could be a jealous partner.

To our right the waters of the Øresund, the channel separating Sweden and Denmark, sparkled in the winter sunshine. After a few miles we reached Hornbaek, a holiday hamlet. Danish intelligence had rented a villa on the banks of a tree-lined lake, a setting of tranquillity in which to plot the elimination of one of America's enemies.

The third-highest-ranking official in Danish intelligence was in the reception room waiting for me in chinos and a blue open-neck shirt. He was tall and had cobalt-blue eyes and straw-coloured hair, which he combed neatly in a parting. Soren, the team leader, introduced him as 'Tommy' and from then on my handlers always referred to him as Tommy Chef because of his natural authority and his rank as PET's most senior covert officer. I was told he reported directly to PET's powerful director, Jakob Scharf. He gave me a firm handshake and thanked me for my efforts.

The remaining members of my PET team were assembled around a white dining table, on their best behaviour. The American delegation arrived a short time later. There was Jed in jeans and cowboy boots followed by a tall man with carefully parted salt-and-pepper hair. For a moment I thought he must be the man with the chequebook, but he was the CIA's Copenhagen station chief, 'George'. He held the door open for a short balding man. This was 'Alex', one of the masters of the universe, and one with a Napoleon complex.

Tommy Chef greeted him with a formal handshake, and then the American turned to me.

'We are really pleased with your results so far and thank you for them,' he said. His voice seemed to bounce off the walls.

'We see this as a big opportunity to stop Awlaki, which as you know is a high priority for my government. President Obama himself has been briefed on this. I know that because I report up to the White

House,' he said, unnecessarily. His two subordinates put on a show of being suitably impressed.

'So let's cut to the chase: my government is prepared to remunerate you a quarter-million dollars for your matchmaking services. Get Aminah to Yemen and we will transfer the money.'

Remunerate, I thought: how these guys love to play with the big words.

'You've got yourself a deal,' I replied.

'That's very good,' he said. 'I want to make one thing clear: you'll be mainly reporting to us now, not our British friends.'

The Danish agents brought in a collection of *smørrebrød* – sandwiches with smoked salmon, pickled herring and salami sausage.

Alex sat forward earnestly. 'We need a pretext for you to meet Aminah.'

Despite Awlaki's reservations about me travelling to meet her in Vienna, the Americans weren't about to let Aminah travel to Yemen without checking her out first.

I pulled out my laptop and began drafting an email to the cleric, writing:

'Regarding the sister, she insist me to meet her in Wienna, Austria, as she got questions which cannot be asked over the phone.'

Alex insisted on changing some of the language, no doubt so he could claim credit for its authorship.

I then opened up the Mujahideen Secrets software on my computer, entered my personal key and Awlaki's public key and hit 'encrypt'. I copied and pasted the resulting encoded text into my email browser, selected an anonymous email address Awlaki used, and hit 'send'.

Alex observed the process, fascinated.

'You know you're literally making hundreds of agents busy back Stateside,' he said.

Awlaki replied five days later.

'If you visit her I may upload for you a short clip from myself as an encrypted file and you can have her hear it to make sure it is myself.'

In offering up a video recording Awlaki was responding to Aminah's request for a private message on camera so she could be reassured that it really was Awlaki at the other end.

I told PET of Awlaki's email via the Norwegian email service provider Telenor. We used Telenor because it had better encryption safeguards than most providers. The Danes shared a great deal with the Americans, but like any intelligence service PET wanted the information first. It was a way of reminding the Americans that I was after all a Danish asset. But using Telenor's encryption safeguards was also symptomatic of the suspicions that every agency had about its communications being intercepted. MI5 had told me not to say anything of importance over the phone – in case the Russians or Mossad were listening in. And MI6 simply refused to use the phone at all.

Days later Awlaki wrote again, saying he was now living in a house rather than a tent.

'I personally prefer this arrangement over the tent in the mountains because it gives me a better setup for reading, writing and doing research.'

He attached a long private note for Aminah and asked me to instruct her how to use the Mujahideen Secrets software, adding: 'Most importantly she needs to setup a clean email that is not opened from home.'

Jed accompanied me to Vienna for the rendezvous, and over a beer the night before Aminah's arrival I was taken aback to find out we shared an appreciation of Metallica. I still knew so little about him. He was married and had several kids and a Dobermann dog. Where he was from, where he lived and worked – that was not my business and not my place to ask. But I did appreciate his determination to get results.

Alex's plan required me to bring Aminah past the way station of a designated bakery shop to the Lounge Gersthof, a nearby bar and restaurant where they had a surveillance team waiting. But at the last minute it dawned on me that it would be absurd to take her to a place that served alcohol. Instead I suggested a nearby McDonald's.

We slid into a booth. I showed her the note from Awlaki on my laptop.

'Sister the step you are about to make is a great one and I pray you are ready for it. However, let me share this with you from my personal experience . . .' his message stated.

'Overall for a while I had a very easy and comfortable life. On the other hand, I have lived in a tent with no running water and [been] stripped from my freedom of movement.

'But let me tell you that the pleasure Allah put in my heart and the tranquillity and peace that I felt going through difficulty for His sake made me despise going back to my former life. I would not exchange it for the world.

'[The months in prison] were the best days of my life. I never thought that I could handle that . . . but I did. Why? Because Allah helped me to . . .

'The problem [you'll face] is limitations on freedom of movement and communicating with others. Also being in a foreign country with no friends and the language barrier is an issue . . .'

Aminah read the letter slowly and without expression. She turned away from the screen and looked at me.

'Do you know the consequences?' I asked her.

'Yes, I'm ready, *Inshallah*,' Aminah replied. 'I want to devote myself to Islam and I want Sheikh Anwar to be my teacher.'

She asked me many questions about Yemen; her lack of overseas travel (her only visit to the Arab world had been to a resort in Tunisia) meant she had little idea about the life she would face. But there seemed little doubt about her devotion.

As Awlaki had requested, I showed her how to send encrypted email using the Mujahideen Secrets encryption software.

'Does this mean I'm part of the mujahideen?' she asked me with an intense look.

'Yes, sister, it does,' I replied.

She had tears in her eyes. 'I'm a mujahida,' she whispered, trembling.

I relayed details of the encounter that same evening in a hotel suite in Copenhagen.

George, the local CIA station chief, was delighted.

'We'll pass on the information to Washington and see what the next step will be.'

The British had still not given up hope of diverting me from the mission. In the second half of March I was invited to join my British contacts at the Ice Hotel in the far north of Sweden: a palace of wonders carved entirely out of ice and snow.

Several of my handlers came along: my MI5 handlers Andy and

Kevin, and Emma in her element, decked out in a chic ski outfit and moon boots. Klang, never one to miss a party, also came along. But no Americans were invited.

We went dog sledding through the powdery snow, zoomed around on the ice on four-wheel-drive cars and raced snowmobiles.

The British didn't discuss Aminah with me during the trip. Perhaps they thought it would have been too obvious and vulgar, perhaps they were wary of Klang. They knew Danish intelligence and the Americans had invested in the Aminah gambit. I think they hoped that after bonding with them in the northern snows I would reconsider.

But the Aminah mission had too much momentum now.

On a spring day in 2010 I was queuing at the check-in at Birmingham airport to catch a flight to Copenhagen for another Aminah planning mission, when I received a call.

It was Kevin, my MI5 handler. He knew where I was.

'Morten, if you travel now, you have to realize we are not going to see each other again,' he said.

I stepped away from the check-in counter. To the British, I had chosen the wrong side, and it was a terminal decision.

'I just want to say we had a fantastic time together,' Kevin continued with obvious sincerity. 'We've done such good work. It's really sad to see this happening but you know it's a bureaucracy and we can't do anything about it.'

MI5 and MI6 were cutting their ties to me.

I was restless on the flight to Copenhagen. I had grown close to Kevin, Andy, Emma, Sunshine and my other British handlers. The UK was my adopted homeland; and they seemed to understand me better than the Danes. But the break was complete. The Danes told me the Brits had mandated I could no longer open any emails from Awlaki on British soil. From then on I was forced to travel to Copenhagen to check for messages from the cleric.

I had little time to dwell on my divorce from MI5 and MI6. After reaching Copenhagen I was driven to a holiday villa on the southern shore of the Roskilde Fjord, some twenty-five miles west of Copenhagen.

Jed told me that I would need to purchase a suitcase for Aminah.

'Isn't that a bit risky – isn't she just going to think that's weird?' I asked.

I came up with an alternative. I would ask Awlaki what Aminah should bring. If she saw the request had come from him there was no way she would be suspicious.

Jed also showed me a wooden cosmetic case they wanted me to give Aminah. He didn't need to say there was a tracking device embedded somewhere. But it seemed to be inviting trouble.

Klang thought so too.

'There's no way we're going to let you hand her this; if someone drops it and discovers the transponder you'll be fucked,' he said. 'Sometimes I can't believe the Americans. They just don't think.'

On 21 April, just before flying to Vienna, I received a reply from Awlaki.

'She shouldn't have more than a medium-sized suitcase and a carry-on bag. She should also have on her some cash just in case . . . She should have with her at least $3k. Also the ticket needs to be round trip just in case she runs into any unexpected problems at the airport.'

Awlaki was expecting me to raise the money through mosques in the UK.

Awlaki's attention to the smallest detail was extraordinary, especially as just three weeks earlier it had been widely reported the Obama administration had designated him for what was known as 'targeted killing'. The *New York Times* had reported that the White House had taken 'the extremely rare if not unprecedented' step of approving the assassination of Awlaki despite his being an American citizen because he was now regarded as actively involved in terror plots.

Jed and George were pleased with Awlaki's reply. Another hurdle had been overcome, and their project might be the first to put the cleric in the crosshairs. They emailed me, using an encryption tool and referring to Awlaki as 'Hook' – one of his nicknames among jihadis.

'Our conversations about what the Hook might advise for her travel appears to have paid off! . . . We suggest you can use the Hook's guidance as a reason to give the sister the suitcase . . . pls tell the sister that the hook wants her to have 3000 dollars . . . this is perfect cover for your next trip to see her. have a safe trip and good luck, your brothers.'

It was one of the very few occasions the CIA left a paper trail, however coded the language.

On a breezy spring afternoon I met Aminah in a park in Vienna and strolled with her to a Turkish restaurant. I told her about Awlaki's suitcase requirements and that he had entrusted me with securing funds for her trip.

Alex flew in from Washington for the debriefing in Roskilde the next day. Apart from Soren, who sat with us, the Danish agents mostly hovered nearby, bringing us coffee and snacks from the kitchen: that said it all about the pecking order.

'It's time for the love messages,' Alex said. Awlaki had sent me a recording for Aminah several weeks previously and had requested Aminah record a video of herself before travelling. Jed fished out a camcorder from his bag and slid it across the table.

It was also time to buy a suitcase.

'We need to know the exact type, colour, everything,' Jed said. He suggested a Samsonite model. No doubt it would be substituted for an identical one with a tracking device at the airport when she left for Yemen.

There was a tension in the air. Gone were the attempts at camaraderie, the flashes of humour. There was a lot riding on this. Occasionally, Alex would slip out of the villa and down to the jetty – out of earshot. I could see him gesticulating as he barked into his mobile phone. Orders to be obeyed, no doubt. Jed seemed to be smoking more frequently. But I was worried that in their rush to see this mission through, the CIA would miss crucial details.

The Americans had been unhappy that – on my own initiative – on my previous trip to Vienna I had taken Aminah to a McDonald's rather than the bar/restaurant they had carefully staked out.

'This time when we ask you to do something we expect you to do it,' Alex snapped.

'I didn't think it was logical,' I retorted, annoyed by his arrogance. But I refused to get drawn into an argument.

I sat down to draft Awlaki an email, referring to the *New York Times* article about the approval of targeted killing.

'May Allah curse the Americans for this – the filthy Kuffar pigs,' I wrote, as a true jihadi might.

As Alex read the draft, a frown hardened on his oversized forehead.

'You can't say that – it's just not acceptable,' he said.

To my amazement, it was Anders who spoke next.

'You know what? That's the way we have always done it. We Danes like to do it our own way,' he said acidly.

Alex turned round to face the young Dane but Anders stared back. Without a word Alex got up and walked through the open French windows into the garden.

Later Klàng beckoned me into the kitchen: 'Don't worry about it, Morten – we'll just change back the language when our friend leaves.'

But I had another dilemma – one that my handlers in their blissful ignorance of Salafist necessities had overlooked. I could not invite Aminah into some hotel room in Vienna and film her without a veil. It would seriously call into question my religious credentials. There was, however, one possibility.

By now, Fadia and I had moved from Birmingham to the nearby city of Coventry. Raleigh Road was considerably more appealing than Alum Rock in Birmingham, a street of neat pre-war terraced houses. I arrived home from Roskilde with money in my pocket, courtesy of another fictional stint on a Danish construction site, and began laying the foundations of my plan as we prepared dinner one evening.

'Darling, you remember Sheikh Anwar told me he was looking for a Western wife? Well, I found him one, on Facebook. She's from Croatia.'

She was surprised.

'A Western woman who wants to go to Shabwa? How would she survive?'

'She's really serious; she's mad about the Sheikh. So I need to tell you something. I had to go to Vienna to meet her. He asked me to.'

'Why didn't you tell me before?' Fadia asked. She was both hurt by the deceit and suspicious about my meeting a young Croatian woman in a far-off city.

'I didn't want you involved. Some Western governments think Anwar is a terrorist. And it happened very suddenly.'

Luckily, Fadia rarely followed the news and had no idea that Awlaki was now targeted for assassination by the US.

I looked at her. Those dark almond eyes were glistening with tears.

'Sometimes I feel I don't know you,' she said.

'I am sorry. But here's an idea. Anwar wants me to go back again to record a video of her, so he can see her. I can't go alone. You know it is forbidden by our religion that I should see a woman who is not related to me on my own in a private place. As the Prophet said: "Never is a man alone with a woman except that Satan is the third party with them."'

Fadia seemed relieved that my Salafist code excluded the possibility of extramarital misbehaviour.

'So,' I continued after a long pause, 'would you come with me? I would feel my honour preserved and you could help set her at ease. It would be a huge favour for Anwar. And then we can have some time in Vienna together.'

The sales pitch worked.

On 27 April we flew to Vienna. I had calculated that even with Awlaki's new profile, being involved in sending him a video of a prospective wife did not amount to 'material support for terrorism'. In any case, Fadia would – unwittingly – be assisting in tracking down a wanted man. We took a room in a modest hotel in central Vienna. Aminah arrived wearing large trendy sunglasses and a black hijab. I introduced her to Fadia and said that as a good Muslim I could not have met her alone in a private place. Thankfully they warmed to each other very quickly. Aminah even seemed reassured by Fadia's presence.

I asked her again whether she was sure she wanted to marry Awlaki. I needed this to be her call.

The promise of a quarter of a million dollars to act as matchmaker had given me qualms. What was my real motive now – to prevent terror or make money? I sensed the plan was to target Awlaki in a missile strike once he was united with his new wife, and it made me feel uneasy.

On my laptop I showed her the fifty-second video clip Awlaki had recorded. The cleric was dressed in a white tunic and wore around his head a copper-coloured scarf layered like a bandana over a traditional white *ghuthra*. He was sitting in front of a pink background with a floral motif. The trouble he had gone to was almost touching. He occasionally reached up to adjust his spectacles as he spoke. His tone was a seductive version of his video sermons.

'This recording is done specifically for Sister Aminah at her request and the brother who is carrying this recording is a trustworthy brother, the brother that is communicating with you.

'I pray that Allah guides you to that which is best for you . . . and guides you to choose what is better for you regarding this proposal.'

He also asked her to send him a recorded message.

At first Aminah smiled at these words, and then her eyes began to shine. She was overwhelmed by such familiarity with a man she revered.

Fadia stood behind the camera and told her gently to try to relax. Aminah, with only her face visible, addressed the cleric in a soft halting voice, swallowing her words nervously like a teenager with stagefright.

'I just want to tell you that right now I feel nervous and this is very awkward for me so I will just tape this just so you can see how I look and just to know I'm okay. I will accept everything what is needed to do now this way that I have chosen . . . I will send you another message, a private, private message – *Insha'Allah*.'

That was my cue to leave them and leave the room. On the second recording Aminah was a woman transformed. She took off her veil and her blonde hair tumbled down over her black blouse. A clip held back shorter layers – making her seem, not accidentally, much younger. She had coquettishly applied a little mascara and lip gloss. It was seduction by video.

'Brother, this is me without the headscarf so you can see my hair. I described it to you before. So now you've seen me without it and I hope you will be pleased with it – *Insha'Allah*,' she said, tilting her head to one side.

She ended with a halting Arabic salutation that she must have practised for days.

When she had finished recording the private message with Fadia, I handed Aminah the suitcase – a grey hard-top Samsonite. 'This is the one Sheikh Anwar recommended,' I said. She was trembling.

Fadia embraced her and said she should contact her through me if she needed anything or advice on being a wife in Yemen.

Three weeks later, I met Aminah in a McDonald's near the Yemeni embassy in Vienna. I gave her the $3,000 in cash which supposedly came from 'the brothers' in England but in fact was from the US Treasury.

I had shown her how to apply for a course at the Sana'a Institute for Arabic Language. At some point Awlaki's intermediaries would come to fetch his new bride. 'The Sheikh says you should take off your hijab before entering the embassy,' I told her.

Awlaki's instructions were for her to go to the embassy unveiled so as not to create suspicion. He also wanted her to put on Western clothing for her journey to Yemen. He had even issued a fatwa for me to pass on granting her permission. The need not to arouse suspicion trumped religious rules.

The embassy apparently thought there was nothing out of the ordinary in a Croatian blonde going to Yemen to learn Arabic and told her a visa would be ready the next day. Aminah was elated but nervous. She was leaving behind everything she knew and heading towards the unknown.

My CIA handlers had instructed me that Aminah should not take a direct flight to Yemen. I took her to the Turkish Airlines office in Vienna. I also gave her a new pair of all-weather sandals for Awlaki and an electronic Arabic pocket dictionary the CIA had provided me with, tracking device inserted.

We found a café that didn't serve alcohol and sat down outside. Every detail of her journey had been considered. Now, as we prepared to part, I realized that I was unlikely to see her again and suddenly felt tender towards her, a yearning to protect her from her own gullibility.

'I don't know how I will ever pay you back,' she said as I left. 'You've done so much for me. May Allah reward you.'

Her parting words lodged in my mind. She was so grateful but I knew I might be sending her into great danger. I could not know whether the American ploy would work, nor what would follow. I glanced back as I walked away. Her blonde hair was cocooned inside her hijab. She looked slight and vulnerable as she sipped her coffee and watched the elegant Viennese stroll by.

Allah wouldn't reward me, but Uncle Sam might.

The day of her flight I got together with my Danish and American handlers at the Hornbaek villa. It was the beginning of June and one of those endless Scandinavian summer evenings when dusk descends after 11 p.m.

Before Jed and George would let me open a beer they requested I draft Awlaki an encrypted email about Aminah's travels to send once we got confirmation she had arrived. He had indicated it could take one or two months before his couriers could organize her travel from Sana'a to wherever he happened to be. That had made the CIA jumpy.

I wrote the following:

'She is all by herself in Yemen, and a month or even two weeks is a very long time for her to wait, as she cannot be as a normal muslim, she constantly have to hide her reality . . . Try to arrange that she get picked up sooner, she will need support as she is alone.'

The entire Danish squad was present – Soren, Klang, Trailer, Jesper and the analyst Anders along with the spymaster, Tommy Chef. Buddha's back was better and he had been invited to join the party. He had gone on a diet; we inevitably called him 'Buddha-lite'. Jed was manning the barbecue, grilling steaks, and the atmosphere was better for Alex's absence.

Jed got text updates on his phone as Aminah took connecting flights: Zagreb, Vienna and Istanbul. Finally word came that she had landed in Sana'a. There were bear hugs and high-fives.

The next day Aminah sent me an encrypted message from Sana'a to tell me she had arrived. As planned she had bought a Yemeni SIM card for her phone and she provided me with the number. I emailed it to Awlaki later that day.

'Congratulations brother, you just got rich, very rich,' Klang texted me.

My reward followed a few days later at a suite in the Crowne Plaza Hotel near Copenhagen. Klang strode in with the CIA station chief, George, and beckoned me to follow them to the elevator. He looked self-important, holding a slim black briefcase tightly in his right hand.

When we reached the room, I discovered that the briefcase was handcuffed to Klang's wrist, and with good reason.

'Guess the code,' George said with a smile on his face.

I looked puzzled.

'Try 007,' George said with a smile on the corner of his lips. With a satisfying metallic click the case popped open. It was filled with thick bundles of $100 bills. Each of the twenty-five bundles contained $10,000.

'How am I going to exchange all this money?' I asked.

'That's your problem, not ours,' George replied, laughing.

My train ride home to my mother's house on Korsør was a strange experience. If only my fellow commuters had known what was inside the briefcase, wedged tightly between my knees.

'My goodness – is this from drugs?' my mother asked, laughing. In reality, she knew that I was now working for PET, but had no idea what I was doing – and no clue of the Aminah mission that had led to the jackpot. I took a photograph of the bill-filled briefcase. The kid from Korsør, outlawed, jailed, exiled – now standing in his mother's kitchen with $250,000 from the US government.

After what seemed like an endless wait in late June I received encrypted messages from Awlaki and Aminah. She had managed to join him in the tribal areas:

'Alhamdidullah I am fine and well,' she wrote. 'Everything went good and according to a plan.'

Then the bombshell.

'I couldn't take my suitcase from institute, so I need almost everything I left there.'

I stared at the screen, willing the words to change. No tracking device had made the journey with her into the tribal areas. Al-Qaeda had told her to repack her belongings in a plastic bag and leave behind all her electronics. The Americans verified this by sending an informant to her lodgings in Sana'a. They were furious that their carefully laid trap had been evaded by some conscientious al-Qaeda operative.

If the Americans were disappointed with the outcome of the Aminah mission, Anwar al-Awlaki was not.

'Alhamdulillah we got married. May Allah reward you for all what you have done. However, according to your description of her I expected something different. I am not saying you tricked me or anything. . . . I do not blame you or your wife because I believe you were sincere and you were doing your best . . .,' he wrote to me. 'So she turned out to be different then what you described. Masha'Allah she turned out to be better than I expected and better than you described:)'

While Awlaki was re-energized by my matchmaking, the CIA and especially the ambitions of Alex and Jed were frustrated that the investment in Aminah had come to naught.

Danish intelligence seemed less worried and planned a trip to Barcelona for what they described as a 'debriefing'. Soren, Klang and Jesper picked me up from Barcelona airport in a BMW hire car and drove me to a penthouse apartment overlooking the city's main avenue.

'I've organized some entertainment for the evening,' Soren announced with a glint in his eye as we sipped champagne. After a dinner at one of the city's best restaurants we drove through the automatic gates of a secluded villa. Soren handed over a thick wad of euros to a hostess and we were ushered into a low-lit bar. Girls in shimmering chiffon dresses and stilettos lounged on leather sofas. They bore no comparison with the escorts who had hung out at Underground in Korsør, but they had the same vacant look in their eyes.

This was clearly a different sort of debriefing to the one I anticipated.

As the others paired off, I was awoken from my reverie by a petite woman who announced she was 'Olea from Moldova'. But when I looked up in the gloom all I saw was Aminah. Unease came over me as I thought about how the blonde Croatian was now deep behind al-Qaeda lines, sleeping beside one of the world's most wanted men.

Olea took me by the hand and led me towards one of the bedrooms down the corridor. I told her that I couldn't sleep with her because I was married.

'So you want to talk?' she said with a sigh. She looked relieved when I asked if there was any way to get high instead. I needed to blow away my guilt about Aminah. Olea walked across the room and took down one of the oil paintings. From behind its frame she procured a vial of white powder.

I had started using cocaine again at the beginning of the year after learning that my work had resulted in the killing of the tribal leader Abdullah Mehdar. For a while his death had been all that I could think about; the guilt had paralysed me. But the first blinding high in my home in Birmingham had made it all go away for a few hours.

I was bending down next to Olea to snort a line when someone burst into the room. It was Klang.

'What the hell are you doing?' he protested. 'You can't do that!'

'Why not?'

'You can't do that with us.'

'Why the hell not?' I snapped back. 'First of all I'm only abusing myself. You are abusing women who are probably victims of human trafficking. And it's not like you're a police officer on duty here in Spain.'

The Barcelona visit increased the distance I felt from my Danish handlers. I asked myself whether their superiors had any idea of what was going on in far-off places, whether this was a rogue team, or whether PET was rotten.

The next few months would offer some answers.

CHAPTER NINETEEN
A NEW COVER

Summer–Winter 2010

The Americans froze contact with me after the failure of the Aminah mission.

'They aren't happy with you,' Klang told me. 'You got a quarter-million dollars, Awlaki got a beautiful blonde, and Big Brother got your charming letter,' he laughed.

I had written an angry email to Alex, criticizing the American way of doing things and reminding them that we Danes had invented my double life long before he knew of my existence.

For a time it seemed that double life would again be a solely Danish enterprise. The British had vanished; the Americans were smarting over an expensive failure. But I was undeterred. I knew the contacts I had in jihadist groups would soon have the agencies calling again.

I poured much of my energy into a new venture – Storm Bushcraft – an adventure travel company I had registered in the UK. A couple of Birmingham militants had begun questioning how I could travel back and forth to Yemen and East Africa with such ease. I had insinuated that I was making good money from selling drugs for the cause, but I badly needed a watertight cover story.[1]

---

1 Storm Bushcraft was not the only cover company I set up to justify my travel overseas. In October 2009 MI5 helped me register a company called 'HelpHandtoHand', which we described as an NGO providing aid for the needy in Africa and the Middle East. I even opened up a Twitter account to advertise the new venture. But I was eventually forced to abandon it after MI5 cut ties with me in April 2010.

Adventure travel was in my blood. I had always loved being out-doors and had made camps as a kid in the woods around Korsør. My endurance training with the British in Aviemore had rekindled my enthusiasm. And after my trip with British intelligence to the Ice Hotel in northern Sweden in March 2010, I had gone further north for an Arctic expedition course. The cold was so intense that it was difficult to breathe. But I was in my element – learning how to survive in the Arc-tic by hunting, tracking and lighting fires.

The course was led by Toby Cowern, a member of the Royal Marines Reserves. He was well regarded among fellow explorers, hav-ing trained the winning team for the 2006 Polar Challenge, a race to the North Pole. Toby was one of life's enthusiasts and had extraordi-nary powers of endurance. While the rest of us lay exhausted in our snow shelters at the end of each day he would be reading by torchlight.

I sensed Toby yearned to do more than teach Arctic survival. He had been frustrated that a back injury had prevented him from deploying overseas when so many of the Royal Marines were sent to Afghanistan.

I felt he was exactly the sort of person Western intelligence needed to infiltrate jihadist circles overseas. He certainly knew how to deal with extreme situations and his dark complexion meant he could be mistaken for a Middle Easterner.

'Would you like to do something that makes a difference?' I asked him as we trudged side by side through the snow.

'What do you mean?'

'Would you consider something related to intelligence?'

'Why? What do you do?'

I laid out the contours of my work without revealing any specifics.

'I think you could be a huge asset. Would you be interested in meet-ing some of my friends in the intelligence business?'

'Why not?' he replied.

In the midst of the Aminah mission I introduced Toby to Klang, Soren and Anders, at the holiday villa on Roskilde Fjord. We made sure the Americans were long gone. I was told I couldn't stay in the house while my handlers spoke to him, so took a walk along the shore.

'We like this guy,' Klang said to me when I returned.

Soon Toby was working with me on Storm Bushcraft as I tried to build it into a vehicle for my intelligence work. I could persuade jihadis that it was a front to hide my work for the cause. In reality it would help me more deeply infiltrate their ranks.

I was meticulous in setting up the company, purchasing a camping vehicle and outdoor gear. I even approached Marek Samulski, the Australian-Polish convert I had met in militant circles in Sana'a, to design a website and Facebook page. After being deported from Yemen he had moved to South Africa, where he had found work as a web designer, but Danish intelligence still suspected he had ties to radicals. Salmulski agreed to design the site for $5,000, and so unwittingly helped me build the platform for my future work against al-Qaeda.

In order to get photographs and testimonials for the website I advertised expeditions in nature spots in northern Europe at below market rate, and employed two assistants.

My outdoor expeditions had the added benefit of attracting the attention of militants dreaming of jihad.

Earlier that year – before MI5 cut their ties to me – I had infiltrated a group of British-Pakistanis who used to work out at a gym in an immigrant area of Birmingham. As intended, word had spread like wildfire about the Awlaki call I had organized for the doctors in Rochdale, making it easier for me to gain the trust of young radicalized British-Pakistanis.

Tucked in an alleyway behind a fish and chip shop, the gym – known locally as 'Jimmy's' – was housed in a concrete and metal shed with a martial arts and boxing area on the ground floor and a weights room and prayer room above. The gym played Islamic chants on loudspeakers to pump up the young men working out. Fliers on the wall advertised paintballing trips. Many of the regulars looked like they were on steroids; some wore long Salafi beards.

'Jimmy' owned the gym. He was a British-Pakistani in his early forties with flecks of grey in his long beard. He saw it as his vocation to bring young British-Pakistanis who were deviating from their religion off the streets, away from drugs, and back to the true path. And there could not have been a better place than the gym for him to instil his world-view.

Jimmy and some of the young radicals who attended the gym were impressed that I knew Awlaki. After training sessions, we would sit and listen to his online sermons. Among their number were several radicals in their late twenties. Jewel Uddin was quietly spoken and collected money locally for 'religious' causes. By contrast Anzal Hussain could not have been more boisterous. He had been an overweight spiritual Sufi Muslim before a sudden and complete change in his beliefs turned him into a lean, intensely serious Salafi, with a suitably serious beard to match. He had heard about the training exercises I had run for al-Muhajiroun in Barton Hills, and implored me to do the same for his group.

So one weekend seven of us squeezed into a battered Mitsubishi Pagero to drive up to Wetherby in the Yorkshire countryside. For £2,000 a year I had rented a small patch of woodland among rolling fields from a local farmer.

It did not take long for me to find out that this group had watched too many YouTube videos. When we arrived at our destination, Anzal and two others jumped out of the car with walkie-talkies in their hands.

'*Allahu Akbar*,' they whispered urgently, glancing furtively around the woodland. I was dumbstruck.

Anzal then went into a frenzy and started hacking at saplings wildly with a machete. Another joined in with an axe.

'You can't cut trees like that – they are Allah's creation,' I shouted.

Anzal stopped, machete in mid-air. 'You got a point, bruv – *Subhan'Allah*, brother,' he said in his thick Birmingham accent.

Anzal and another of the party kept us all awake that night by exchanging jihadist supplications every few minutes by walkie-talkie from their hammocks. '*As salaam aleikum Allah all Mujahideen!*'

The following morning after dawn prayers Anzal grabbed an air-gun. He began moving stealthily about the woodland.

'I'm going to kill some rabbits,' he announced. I felt embarrassed for him.

Then Anzal froze and went pale. A man and a black dog were walking towards us through the trees. It was the farmer, Dr Mike, who lived just next to the woodland, coming to say hello. The dog was an amiable creature called Billy, wagging his tail at the prospect of meeting some new people. Dr Mike was rather surprised to see a gaggle of wild-eyed young men with long beards and put Billy on a leash. Anzal retreated like he had seen a demon: in some fundamentalist circles black dogs are synonymous with the Devil.

When I saw the movie *Four Lions* later that year I felt I had already witnessed one of its scenes.

Dr Mike ended up reporting what he'd seen to the local police. My MI5 handler Andy was furious the next time I saw him.

'What the fuck were you thinking – doing this without our prior approval?' he said. The last thing British intelligence needed was the newspapers finding out an MI5 agent was training would-be terrorists.

Despite all the information I provided on the group, MI5 dropped the ball. On 30 June 2012 – just days before the start of the London Olympic Games – several of them would head to Yorkshire once again.

This time they were travelling with an arsenal of home-made weaponry – including machetes, kitchen knives, sawn-off shotguns, a partially built pipe-bomb and an improvised explosive device built out of fireworks and shrapnel – very similar to those later used by the Boston bombers. As in that later attack, the group had built it by downloading instructions from Awlaki's *Inspire* magazine.

Their target was a rally by the English Defence League – an extremist anti-Muslim group – in Dewsbury, West Yorkshire. Fortuitously for the EDL, the rally ended before the British-Pakistanis arrived. Although I had alerted MI5 to the cell several years previously, police only discovered the weapons and the plot because their car was stopped on the way back to Birmingham by a traffic patrol and found to have no insurance.

Police found a message in the car addressed to the EDL. 'Today is the day for retaliation (especially) for your blasphemy of Allah and His blessed messenger Mohammed. We love death more than you love life.'

It later emerged that Uddin had also been on the fringes of a terrorist cell arrested in Birmingham in September 2011 which had been plotting a suicide-bombing campaign in the UK. Several of the plotters were familiar to me from Jimmy's gym and the militant scene in Birmingham, including two of the ringleaders of the cell who received training with al-Qaeda in Pakistan in the spring of 2011. Security services suspected Uddin may have raised money for the cell but had not arrested him.

The EDL plot raised some disturbing questions. Uddin had been under observation by agents just five days before the men drove to Dewsbury, but without someone on the inside MI5 failed to detect the plot. Agents had seen him enter a shop where he purchased the knives but had not followed him inside.

In June 2013 Anzal Hussain, Jewel Uddin and three others I knew were sentenced to lengthy prison terms for the EDL plot.

But by the time they were planning to attack the EDL, I had long ceased working for MI5 because of British distaste for the Aminah mission.

Back in 2010 adulthood and paternity had unfortunately not made me any smarter about my resources. Rather than stow away the $250,000 reward, I poured much of it into Storm Bushcraft and travel. PET were delighted; they wanted local eyes and ears in East Africa because of the number of Scandinavian Somalis who had joined al-Shabaab, and they were getting them for free.

Despite the Ethiopian intervention and the presence of an African Union force to protect the government, al-Shabaab had taken over much of central and southern Somalia. And a lot of ethnic Somalis from Europe and North America were fighting for the group. Some had already returned to northern Europe, including a young militant called Mohammed Geele. Danish investigators established that Geele had close ties to al-Shabaab and senior al-Qaeda leaders in East Africa, and had emerged as an important player in the group during time he spent in Kenya in the 2000s.

In January 2010 Geele took a taxi to the street in Aarhus where the cartoonist Kurt Westergaard lived. Westergaard was hated by radical Islamists because he had drawn cartoons of the Prophet Mohammed for a Danish newspaper in 2005. Geele approached the front door armed with an axe and a knife and shattered the glass, setting off an alarm. Westergaard rushed to a safe room before the killer could reach him.

When the police arrived minutes later Geele lunged at them with his weapons. They fired into his left hand and right leg and took him into custody.

I had come across Geele in the months before the attack. PET had asked me to pay a visit to Kenneth Sorensen, my former associate in Sana'a, who was now back in Denmark. The two of us ran into Geele in a Somali mosque in Copenhagen, and Sorensen suggested we have lunch. Nothing about Geele at that time indicated he was planning an attack, but had I developed a relationship with him I might have picked it up.[2]

To me the growing terrorism in East Africa – in both Somalia and Kenya – was an invitation. I calculated that an outdoor adventure business there would allow Toby and myself cover to maintain contact with al-Shabaab. But first I needed to provide Toby with a 'legend' – credentials to make him a plausible partner.

Toby had grown his beard long. I taught him everything I knew about Islam and the circles I frequented, and shelled out thousands of dollars to send him on training courses for leading expeditions. We started peppering our emails to each other with Arabic and Islamic expressions to create a digital record of his conversion to Islamic fundamentalism.

2 PET was also worried by the influence of Abu Musab al-Somali, a Somali refugee I knew from my radical days, who had returned to Somalia. Phone intercepts indicated a number of Somali extremists in Denmark were contacting him. Al-Somali had come to Denmark as a refugee in his youth, then moved to Yemen, and had been arrested in 2006 along with several other members of my Sana'a circle for his part in the plan to smuggle guns from Yemen to militants in Somalia. But he had only received a two-year sentence and when freed had crossed the Gulf of Aden to Somalia. Danish intelligence were now concerned he might be plotting attacks in Denmark.

I then spread the word to some of my radical circle in the UK that I had joined forces with a member of the Royal Marines Reserves who had converted to Islam. I introduced Cowern to Rasheed Laskar, one of my Sana'a circle, who was now back in the UK, and to a number of radicals in Luton. I won the backing of Awlaki for my plans.

'I am happy to hear the news of your NGO and insha Allah you are the right person for the job. It is a good long term idea and could serve many needs in the future,' he wrote to me.

But the critical breakthrough came from al-Shabaab itself. In encrypted emails I outlined to Warsame and Ikrimah how the business would make it easier for me to get money and supplies to the group in Somalia: tents, hammocks, solar panels, water purification units and GPS locators.

'The NGO'S is really good cover for everything on Business,' Warsame wrote to me.

Ikrimah, by now a rising star among al-Shabaab operatives, was equally enthusiastic about Storm Bushcraft, writing to me: 'how is shompole, is it a good place? how is the regestration and paper word going on? . . . this wil b a very good project to all muslims.'

And he ended: 'May Allah bless this project and keep it away from the eyes and suspicions of the kufar.'

Shompole – a reserve in the Great Rift Valley in the south of Kenya – was one site I was considering for Storm Bushcraft. It had the major advantage of being very remote; there would be no prying eyes.

Ikrimah's endorsement of the project was critical. His credentials within al-Shabaab had been burnished by the money and equipment I had provided, and his time in Europe had given him deep contacts in extremist circles there. He now supervised foreign and Western recruits joining the group, most of whom transited through Nairobi.

Ikrimah's status in the group had also been bolstered by his ties to AQAP. And for that I and my Western intelligence handlers were entirely responsible. Awlaki had told me in the Shabwa compound the previous September that AQAP now had an arsenal of anti-tank rockets thanks to the ambush of several military convoys. I relayed the news to Ikrimah and it piqued his interest.

'The anti-tank mine that brothers got will they be willing to sell them to us and do they have weapons that can hit a tank frm far like the ones hisbullah used to destroy israel merkeva tank? or rpg 29 etc?' he asked.

Ikrimah asked to be put in direct contact with Awlaki, whom he called 'Hook'. In early 2010 they started exchanging encrypted messages and began working on a plan by which al-Shabaab recruits would travel to Yemen for training before being sent back to fight – or more ominously dispatched to the West to launch attacks.

'And as for going to hooks place . . . then i was told by hook that they want to train brothers and then send them back or to the west,' Ikrimah wrote to me later that year.

As my visits multiplied and I became established in Kenya I met with al-Shabaab envoys. The local intelligence services seemed overwhelmed by the group's growing presence and unable to stem the recruitment of young Kenyan Muslims. I would email Warsame or Ikrimah and they would pass on a number to call. Then I would use a Safaricom SIM card to make the call.

A favourite rendezvous was the Paris Hotel in Nairobi; it was there that I met a short bespectacled Kenyan sent by my two al-Shabaab contacts. He wanted to speak Arabic but I insisted we speak in English to avoid attracting attention. I handed him $3,000 to give to Warsame, which Danish intelligence had given me to keep me in favour. Before he took his leave he asked me to hand over the mobile phone I had used to contact him.

'We need to check it out,' he said. Realizing I had used the same phone to contact Danish agents I had to think quickly.

'I never give my phone out – our mutual friend knows that,' I replied.

Anders in Danish intelligence later told me I was lucky; there were indications al-Shabaab had penetrated Safaricom, the East African mobile-phone company. If they'd obtained my SIM card they could have pulled up my phone records.

A few days after that meeting, suicide bombers affiliated with al-Shabaab blew themselves up at a restaurant and rugby club in Kampala, Uganda, where sports fans were watching the World Cup Final – killing more than seventy people. Many of those involved in the plot were

Kenyan. Ikrimah later told me his envoy was among those arrested in Kenya for helping plan the attack; the crackdown in Kenya meant it was no longer safe for him to travel from Somalia to meet me in Nairobi. I never found out whether he was involved in the Kampala attack but I got the sense he was taking on a greater operational role for the group. He had developed deep connections to Kenyan militants affiliated with al-Shabaab and told me of his regular trips to Uganda.

I had begun negotiating with the Kenyan authorities and the Masai tribe to establish an adventure camp. Beside Shompole, I was trying to lease a rundown resort at the Masinga Dam, built to harness hydroelectric power from the Tana River.

However, my expenses were beginning to overwhelm me. Money had a habit of running through my hands quickly, and I had not done much bookkeeping after my windfall from the CIA. I had ploughed more than a quarter of the proceeds into the Kenyan venture but it was like throwing money into a sinkhole. I still had no base from which to launch the next stage of my intelligence work. And while the Danes offered moral support, the British were less than delighted to find out that a UK national was involved in my scheme. If word leaked that a Royal Marine reservist had become a jihadist facilitator there would be explaining to do.

In late 2010 Toby Cowern was planning to relocate to Kenya from his Arctic Circle base in Sweden when he received a summons from the British embassy in Stockholm. An MI5 agent led him to a back room and told him it would be 'in his interest' to drop all plans involving me. The agent never spelled out why Toby should abandon the project; perhaps he didn't need to. The idea of a Royal Marine reservist consorting with al-Shabaab was just too much of a risk. Toby had no choice but to comply and my Kenyan venture began to unravel.

My confidence in my handlers was not enhanced when they asked me to take part in a sting operation that would have probably blown my cover.

Danish intelligence had learned that a group of radicals had bought a Kalashnikov from a Copenhagen drug dealer. The buyers were Swedes of Arab origin, and several of them had already travelled to jihadist battlegrounds.

A Tunisian in his mid-forties was the group's leader. He had recently returned from Pakistan, where he was suspected of having links with senior al-Qaeda operatives.

Klang asked me if I could travel to Copenhagen, where several of the group were staying.

'We believe they are doing target reconnaissance. We'd like you to befriend them and find out their plans,' he said.

The implication that I could sidle up to members of this group as they plotted a terrorist attack in Copenhagen was another disturbing sign of Klang's lack of tradecraft, or even basic common sense.

'Are you out of your mind?' I said. 'I don't know these guys from Adam – don't you think they're going to be just slightly suspicious?'

As it turned out the surveillance of both Swedish and Danish intelligence would be enough to thwart their plans. Several weeks later in the early morning of 29 December the four men crossed the Øresund bridge from Malmö to Copenhagen. They had a machine gun, ammunition, a silencer and dozens of plastic wrist straps. Wiretaps suggested that within days they planned to storm the offices of *Jyllands-Posten* in Copenhagen, the newspaper that had first published controversial cartoons of the Prophet Mohammed.[3]

All four were arrested later that day. The suspected Swedish-Yemeni mastermind of the plot went to ground and evaded capture. He soon headed to Yemen.

On a heavily overcast day early in December I arrived at Heathrow airport from Kenya to reassess my future. The skies matched my mood. Perhaps it was time to quit the spy game; I seemed to be running into opposition at every turn and was spending my own money to help the Danish government.

---

3 The men travelled to Denmark on 28 December 2010 and were arrested the next day. Mounir Dhahri was the Tunisian cell leader. Another member of the cell – Munir Awad, a Swede of Lebanese descent, whose curly, well-maintained long hair fell over his shoulders – had fought with the Islamic Courts Union in Somalia.

Western intelligence believed the plan was part of a wider conspiracy by al-Qaeda to launch 'Mumbai-style' attacks across Europe, which had triggered an unprecedented US State Department warning for Americans in Europe that October.

On the other hand I had moved in jihadist circles for more than ten years. I knew the networks and relationships among the groups, even though it was still difficult to predict who among the would-be jihadis would go operational.

I was reminded of just how difficult on 11 December 2010. A man plotting carnage on a huge scale drove into the centre of Stockholm with home-made explosive devices. Parking on a busy street amid hundreds of Christmas shoppers, he sent emails to Swedish intelligence and news outlets, saying his actions were in revenge for cartoons of the Prophet Mohammed published in the Swedish press and for the Swedish presence in Afghanistan. He then set fire to his car and walked away.

His plan was to wait until crowds converged on the burning vehicle, then set off a pressure-cooker device on the passenger seat by walkie-talkie. He had positioned himself so that those fleeing the scene would run towards him. He would then trigger devices in a backpack and waist belt.

The explosives in the car did not detonate. CCTV video showed that in a nearby street the man was trying to blow himself up. For ten minutes he walked through the area, trying to make the device attached to his stomach work. Finally part of the bomb exploded, killing the man instantly. No one else was hurt.

Later that day I discovered that the lone bomber was my former Luton friend Taimour Abdulwahab al-Abdaly. I had met him in a department store in the town and played football with him. Of all my circle in Luton I thought him the least likely to carry out an attack. In our discussions he had actually criticized me for my radical views. But that was more than five years ago.

Taimour had been operating on his own after training in Iraq. It seems no one else among the Luton set had any idea that he was preparing an act of terrorism, with the exception of Nasserdine Menni, an asylum seeker from Algeria who was subsequently convicted of sending funds to Taimour for the attack. It was possible that had I kept up my contacts in England I might at least have heard of Taimour's travel to Iraq, which in itself would have been warning enough. But after the falling-out of the intelligence services I was not allowed to work sources in the UK. So I laughed when Klang called me from Copenhagen.

'The Brits have asked us to get in touch with you about Taimour. Do you know his friends in Luton?'

'I don't think he was radicalized here, or at least if he was it was after I last saw him – and that was more than five years ago.'

The idea that the British could turn me on and off as a source was ridiculous. But I was soon to discover that they were not the only ones who wanted to reactivate me when it suited them.

CHAPTER TWENTY
TARGET AWLAKI

Early 2011–Summer 2011

There was a lull in my intelligence work in early 2011. The Danes were still paying my retainer but had no overseas missions. Instead I focused on developing Storm Bushcraft. I had begun to see the venture as a real business rather than as just a cover. After all I was sinking my own funds into it. I started thinking about a new life. My negotiations to buy the resort near the Masinga Dam in Kenya were finally coming to a head. Despite my dwindling bank balance, I had paid $20,000 for the option to buy the property outright within a year.

Most of the winter was spent brooding in my house in Coventry. Everyday life seemed so mundane. The gloomy skies and early darkness only added to my sense of restlessness. Although the British had cut ties to me, I was still on PET's books and had to keep up the pretence that I was Murad Storm, the zealous extremist. Living that lie had begun to gnaw at me. Was it really still worth it? From time to time the anxiety I felt about Abdullah Mehdar and Aminah would return, and I'd turn back to self-medicating with cocaine, snorting it joylessly alone at home.

In February I noticed on Facebook that my high school in Korsør was organizing a reunion. I signed up. I had lost contact with almost all the friends I had in Korsør as a teenager and it would be good to spend a weekend with them. But at the last minute I decided not to go – afraid that photographs of the occasion might appear online, showing me mixing with the *kuffar*. I was living in a prison of my own making.

Perhaps the most difficult aspect of that life was the constant need to deceive Fadia. I had managed to keep the cocaine a secret from her. But I had to explain my frequent absences overseas, where the money had come from for my investment in Storm Bushcraft, the negotiations in Kenya. I created a fiction that she seemed to believe. I told her that after I had recovered my faith, I had met some devout Muslims in Sana'a – from Yemen and Saudi Arabia – who wanted to build a retreat in the Kenyan bush for pious young men to attend. I claimed they knew of my Bushcraft experience and had raised the money to contract me to research the possibilities. It was a chance to build something valuable, I told her, and one that might open up other opportunities. There were one or two elements of truth in what I told her, but a big lie was at the heart of the story. Fadia had no idea that I had received $250,000 from the US Treasury – in cash – and no idea that it was quickly vanishing.

On the weekends that I had custody of my kids I longed to tell them that my Islamic robes, my beard, my prayers were all a sham, and I was secretly working against terrorists. But I never did. Such knowledge would only have put them in danger. And in any case even my eldest, Osama, was only turning nine.

It depressed me that the only people who knew my role, my real purpose, were my Danish handlers, but our contacts had become limited to phone calls. I felt redundant. The last thing I was expecting was another approach from the CIA. But, one morning in April, I received a text from PET. Big Brother had lost track of Anwar al-Awlaki and needed my help.

Klang said a 'very significant sum' was on the table from the Americans if I could lead them to the cleric. Perhaps the US government budget crisis was not as grave as I had thought, or perhaps they were that desperate. They had good reason to be.

Awlaki was rapidly becoming the face of al-Qaeda. Six months previously he had been involved in an ingenious AQAP plot to blow up US-bound cargo planes with explosives concealed in printer cartridges. Two bombs designed by master bomb-maker Ibrahim al-Asiri and inserted into laser printers had been dropped off at FedEx and UPS offices in Sana'a. They passed through airport security undetected and were then loaded on to the first leg of their journey towards the United States. Only an intelligence tip to Saudi authorities allowed authorities in Dubai and the UK to eventually intercept the deadly cargo.

Hours later President Obama addressed the American public, telling them that a dangerous plot had been averted.[1]

Al-Asiri had concealed the explosives so well that bomb disposal teams at both locations initially believed the printers were not bombs – even after examining them. It was the most sophisticated al-Qaeda device that Western counter-terrorism officials had ever seen and they said it had the potential to bring down a plane.

Awlaki had himself played a role in preparations for the attack. He had asked Rajib Karim, a British Airways employee in the UK, to provide technical details about X-ray scanning equipment deployed at airports and whether it was possible to get packages on board planes to the United States without their being scanned.

'Our highest priority is the US. Anything there, even on a smaller scale compared to what we may do in the UK, would be our choice,' he wrote in an encrypted email to Karim.

According to the US government, Awlaki 'not only helped plan and oversee the plot but was also directly involved in the details of its execution – to the point that he took part in the development and testing of the explosive devices that were placed on the planes'.

US officials spoke of Awlaki's involvement in 'numerous other plots against the US and Western interests'. And even when not involved, he inspired. Awlaki seemed the common denominator in almost every plot being uncovered in the West. Potentially the most dangerous was the plan by three young men in the US, including a naturalized Afghan called Najibullah Zazi, to blow up New York subway trains at rush hour in September 2009. Prior to connecting with al-Qaeda on a trip to Pakistan the trio had been radicalized by listening to Awlaki's sermons on their iPods. Another devotee was an American-Pakistani who tried to set off a car bomb in Times Square in May 2010.

---

1 Later British authorities revealed that one of the devices had been set to blow up over the eastern seaboard of the United States.

AQAP was also becoming the most sophisticated of the group's franchises in using the internet to rally supporters. In June 2010 it released the first issue of the online magazine *Inspire*. Awlaki was the driving force behind the magazine, which was edited by his protégé Samir Khan, an American Saudi-born extremist.

The first issue included a recipe 'Make a bomb in the kitchen of your Mom', which detailed how to make crude pressure-cooker bombs from gunpowder and shrapnel.[2]

So there were plenty of reasons for silencing Awlaki. And the Arab Spring that erupted in the first few months of 2011 would provide another. The unrest that had come to Yemen had provided jihadis with operational oxygen. And in the southern and eastern tribal areas, al-Qaeda began to take advantage of President Saleh's myopic focus on political survival and his growing unpopularity by recruiting fighters from sympathetic tribes.

Awlaki had an ever larger area in which to operate and growing resources with which to plot the next attack on the American homeland. In its publications AQAP promised it would only be a matter of time.

My Danish handlers knew me well enough by now to know that I would agree to rejoin the hunt for Awlaki – even as Yemen seemed to be imploding. They were aware of how frustrating the last several months had been for me.

At the beginning of May I was invited to a follow-up meeting in Copenhagen with them and my former CIA handler Jed. As I waited at Birmingham airport, the TV screens showed one face time and again: that of Osama bin Laden. Just a few hours earlier a team of US Navy SEALs had swooped on bin Laden's compound in Abbottabad, Pakistan. The leader of al-Qaeda had been killed, his body whisked away by helicopter to an ignominious burial at sea. Normally, few travellers bother to watch the news channels at airports; on this day there were clusters of people gazing at the screens. The great bogeyman of the West had been vanquished.

---

2 In the following years the recipe would be downloaded and used by militants in multiple terrorism plots on both sides of the Atlantic, including the Boston bombing.

I thought of all the fighters bin Laden had encouraged to embrace martyrdom while he cowered behind the high walls of a comfortable house. He may have risen to fame in jihadist circles as a fighter, but I felt that the way he had lived his last few years and the way he died in a house full of women and children might cost him some of his lustre.

Even so, the man who had been an inspirational figure to a generation of jihadis was gone. The torch had been passed, but who would grasp it? Plenty of observers – within al-Qaeda and the intelligence agencies that were trying to eradicate it – regarded Anwar al-Awlaki as a candidate.

From Copenhagen I was driven to the holiday villa at Hornbaek where we had plotted the Aminah mission with the Americans. The mood this time was even more intense.

To my surprise Jed gave me a bear hug when I arrived. He seemed slightly embarrassed that I had been so unceremoniously put out to pasture after the Aminah mission.

'Congratulations on getting bin Laden,' I said.

'Thanks, man – this is a huge day for us.'

Klang interjected: 'You know what this means? Awlaki has just become US public enemy number one.'

It seemed to be the cue Jed was waiting for.

'We want you to find him. This has become a huge priority for my government.'

'Don't worry. I'll find him,' I replied. I was thrilled to be back in the game.

We agreed I would return to Sana'a to try to reconnect with Awlaki. Within days of our meeting, he showed yet again how difficult he would be to eliminate, even after suddenly appearing in the cross-hairs.

On 5 May 2011, less than a week after bin Laden's death, US military drones over Yemen locked on to a pick-up truck leaving a trail of dust as it sped along a desert track some twenty miles from Ataq, the town where I had visited Awlaki three years previously. This was still his home turf.

US intelligence believed the cleric and several al-Qaeda associates were in the truck. But unlike the US Navy SEAL raid in Abbottabad, the Yemen operation had been hurriedly put together. Just a day previously, Yemeni intelligence had told US officials they had information indicating Awlaki was staying in a nearby village.

As US officials watched the satellite feed in real time three missiles were unleashed. Seconds later they slammed into the ground, sending up a cloud of debris and smoke. None scored a direct hit.

'We felt the wave of explosion near the car that shattered the windows,' Awlaki told a comrade the next day. 'We even saw a flash of light, so we thought that we were ambushed and under fire. We thought a rocket was fired on us.'

The car had accelerated away from the danger zone, making a mad dash along desert tracks. Despite the devastation outside nobody in the car had been injured. According to villagers, two brothers known for sheltering al-Qaeda fighters rushed to the scene of the attack and caught up with Awlaki's vehicle. With US drones still circling overhead they switched vehicles with Awlaki's group.

The swap saved the cleric's life. Minutes later the pick-up truck from which Awlaki had just tumbled exploded in an amber fireball, killing the two brothers instantly.

Awlaki was running for cover when he saw the explosion. The cleric's driver had sped to a nearby valley, where a few trees offered cover from the drones. Awlaki and his comrades had jumped out and scattered in different directions.

'Air strikes continued in the different areas, but I was directed by one of the brothers to one of the numerous cliffs in the mountains,' Awlaki told a comrade afterwards. He slept outside that night and was picked up by al-Qaeda fighters the following day.

'Something of fear befalls you, but the Almighty Allah sends down tranquility,' he told the comrade later. 'This time eleven missiles missed their target but the next time the first rocket may hit it.'

Prophetic words.

The preparations for this mission were more demanding than any before. PET sent me on a refresher weapons course because of the growing dangers of travelling into the tribal areas.

My instructors, Daniel and Frank, were men of few words, but put me through a punishing schedule of all-terrain driving and battlefield first aid. On the shooting range I fired live rounds from an MP-5 submachine gun, Magnum pump-action gun, a Kalashnikov assault rifle and a handgun. I was taught to shoot using left and right hands in case I was injured. I did drills where I raced towards a target, firing heavier weapons first before using the pistol at close range.

I was taught how to respond if my vehicle was ambushed – and how to shoot out of the windows while driving. If I came under sustained fire I should hide under the steering wheel because the engine block offered protection against incoming fire.

Daniel told me that if I felt my life was in danger at a checkpoint I should never wind down the window but shoot through the door with a handgun hidden in the folds of a newspaper. In one exercise I crouched on the tarmac beside the door and shot at a target on the other side of the car. The 9mm bullet pierced through both doors.

Finally I was taken into an abandoned complex, where I learned how to clear a building and respond to a hostage situation. I was given an MP-5 with ink bullets and each time I edged around a wall I had a split second to hit a target. As I cleared room after room my mind drifted back to the paintballing exercises I had joined with my militant 'brothers' in nearby Odense a decade previously. This felt rather more serious.

Frank laughed at the thought that he was training a former Bandido.

The Danes were teaching me these skills to protect me not only from al-Qaeda but from Yemeni government soldiers and tribal militias. In a volatile country where opening fire was a standard means of starting negotiations I could be the target of any number of well-armed groups. Klang told me that if my life was in danger it was permissible to shoot at Yemeni soldiers.

After the weapons training, a stern-looking psychologist working for PET conducted an evaluation on whether I was fit to proceed with the mission, asking me a battery of questions in a hotel suite north of Copenhagen.

'How do you feel about going back to Yemen?' he asked.

'I'm obviously a bit anxious.'

'It's good you feel that way. If you didn't I'd be worried,' he replied.

'I feel torn about going after Awlaki. He's been my friend, and I know he would give his life for me.' It felt good to talk.

'That's normal – it's only human to have a conscience,' he replied.

I told him that I'd been 'self-medicating' with cocaine to deal with the stress created by my intelligence work.

'That's just a temporary solution for a permanent problem,' he replied clinically.

The psychologist cleared me to return to Yemen. Nobody at PET ever suggested any treatment for my drug abuse. After the Barcelona trip I had told Klang that I was using cocaine to tackle bouts of anxiety but his only concern had been that I should not do it in his presence.

As preparations intensified agents were at my side every day – discussing travel arrangements, where I would live, the options for contacting Awlaki. Perhaps the best advice came from an outdoor specialist at PET whose name was Jacob. He looked at me earnestly as we discussed the mission ahead over coffee.

'You are the one doing the most dangerous job in the world and you shouldn't let them forget it,' he told me. 'Make sure you demand what you need. And when you are over there, don't sit with the terrorists because the Americans won't hesitate to kill you if you are with their target.'

I wasn't sure whether he spoke from experience or was exaggerating for effect. But it was chilling. I reminded myself that I was dispensable if a target of Awlaki's profile came into view.

Ultimately I could only rely on myself.

In mid-May I had a last pre-mission meeting with Jed and my Danish handlers, this time in a suite at the Marienlyst Hotel in Helsingør. From the windows there was a fabulous view of the Swedish coastline across the Øresund.

I opened up my laptop in front of Jed at the hotel and fired up the Mujahideen Secrets software. I typed out a message to the cleric, which I signed 'Polar Bear' – a private nickname Awlaki had given me. I then entered the public key supplied by *Inspire* magazine and hit 'encrypt' before sending it to an email address provided in *Inspire* magazine.

The Danes handed me an iPhone. It was configured so that everything I did was instantly uploaded to Danish intelligence. 'If you take a picture or video we'll see it in real time and we'll be alerted any time you send a message,' Klang explained. The phone had a Danish SIM card; I would end up running up a massive bill for the Danish taxpayer.

When Jed was gone the Danes also handed me an Acer notebook computer. They asked me to use the new computer when communicating with my al-Qaeda contacts instead of a Samsung laptop Jed had given me before the Aminah mission.

'We want to be one step ahead of the Americans,' Klang said. Danish intelligence were asserting their proprietorial rights.

On 23 May I flew into Sana'a. My cover story was that I was back in the country to set up a Yemeni branch of Storm Bushcraft. Fadia had travelled ahead of me. I had suggested to her she could reconnect with her family while I continued work on my Bushcraft venture. She was aware that I wanted to check on Awlaki's situation, but still had no idea why the cleric was so important to me.

The capital was in tumult with roiling protests, including a sit-in by students in the central square. The day I arrived clashes erupted between regime forces and an opposition faction after President Saleh backpedalled on a plan for peaceful transition. Al-Qaeda couldn't be happier, I thought.

I found a house on 50th Street. Its proximity to the Presidential Palace was problematic given Saleh's uncertain grip on power, but it was the most affluent neighbourhood in Sana'a. The Minister of Oil lived next door; almost all the properties had guards. It was – by Yemeni standards – an expensive rental. But I was hiding in plain sight. The Yemeni authorities would not expect a hardened jihadi to take up residence among cabinet ministers, and I could justify my extravagance to Awlaki and others on the same grounds – while boasting about the growth of my company Storm Bushcraft and my plans to bring it to Yemen one day.

I also thought there was a possibility that Awlaki might wilt under pressure and accept an offer to seek refuge with Aminah at our home, safe from drones and missile strikes. After all, bin Laden had done much the same – far from the killing grounds of Waziristan. Then I could turn the cleric over to the Yemeni authorities. He would live; Aminah would be free. And I would not have to glance anxiously at my withering bank balance every day.

Jed had said – grudgingly – that it was worth a try, but he really wanted to see Awlaki 'eliminated'.

When I returned to Sana'a the security situation was deteriorating. On the morning of Friday, 3 June, an explosion shook our building. My ears were ringing as I rushed to the roof. I trained my binoculars on a column of thick black smoke. It was coming from the Presidential Palace – and soon rumours swirled that President Saleh had been killed in a bomb attack. They were unfounded, but the ageing Yemeni leader was severely burned in the explosion, caused by a bomb that had been planted in a mosque in which he was praying.

As the President was flown to Saudi Arabia for emergency treatment, my mission took on extra urgency. Awlaki had not replied to my email to *Inspire* magazine and I feared he had gone into deep hiding after his recent close brush with US drones. If full-scale civil war erupted, I would not be able to stay in Yemen – let alone reach Awlaki. I turned to my old Yemeni jihadi contact, Abdul. He had a friend called Mujeeb who was a reliable go-between with al-Qaeda fighters in the southern tribal areas.

After reconnecting with Abdul, I bought thumb drives and set about writing a message to the cleric which I encrypted using Mujahideen Secrets. I asked Awlaki to send a messenger back with his reply. Polar Bear, I told him, would wait at a restaurant we both knew in Sana'a on three evenings I specified. I uploaded the message on to one of the thumb drives and gave it to Abdul.

'Tell Mujeeb to get this to Adil al-Abab,' I told him. Al-Abab, a Yemeni militant I had befriended in Sana'a in 2006, was now AQAP's religious emir in the tribal areas. I was confident he would be able to get the thumb drive to Awlaki.

'I'm using Abdul as a last resort because I don't totally trust him,' I wrote to Awlaki.

I was covering myself because of the doubts Awlaki had expressed about Abdul. At the same time I was taking a risk. If Abdul discovered the contents of my encrypted message, I would lose an intermediary at the very least and gain an enemy at worst.

The rendezvous restaurant was al-Shaibani, which served traditional meat dishes and was close to our home. I alerted my Danish handlers and they had in turn briefed the Americans. On the first of three designated evenings I waited at al-Shaibani, sipping tea. I had an eerie sensation that I was being watched. Two men dressed in Yemeni clothes were glancing my way a little too often. Perhaps I was worrying too much; after all I made an unusual sight in an Arab capital consumed by unrest. An hour ticked by and it was clear the courier was not coming. It was the same the second night, and I began to fear that Awlaki had not received my message.

On the third evening a slim, dark-skinned young man approached my table. He was wearing his scarf in the style of Marib, a province that was emerging as an al-Qaeda safe haven. He looked like he was in his late teens.

'Colour?' the young man asked me in Arabic. '*Akhdar*,' I replied, the Arabic word for green. It was the code word I had provided Awlaki. The messenger fished into his pocket and handed me a thumb drive, the same one I had given to Abdul. The young courier also handed me $300, gesturing at the thumb drive by way of explanation.

'Let me take a look at this. I'll meet you at the al-Hamra restaurant on al-Haddah Street in four hours, okay?' I told him.

Back in the house, my hands shaking, I inserted the thumb drive into my laptop, loaded the Mujahideen Secrets encryption software, and began reading.

'I did receive the flash you sent me,' he wrote, adding that it was 'fine if you don't want to use Abdul' for future messages.

Awlaki continued: '3 things: If you email me please write down the date on all your messages. Second, keep in mind that it takes a few days for emails to get to me so if you are setting an appointment then give me advance notice. Third: you do not need to write "to the sheikh" when you email Inspire. Anything from your email will be delivered to me.

'Please respond to this message with what you want to say and give it to the brother,' the cleric wrote.

'This brother may be the messenger between us for now. One IMPORTANT note: The brother does not know that he is delivering messages for me and he doesn't know where I am so do not mention that this message is for me. Just give it to him and he will deliver it where it needs to be delivered and will get to me insha Allah.'

Awlaki was employing a 'cut-out' to get his message to me. It was a classic technique. If the young Maribi were captured or followed he could not immediately lead the Americans to Awlaki. He was just one link in a chain and had no idea where the next courier would be going.

'For future correspondence I believe it would be better if your wife delivers the flash to the brother,' Awlaki wrote to me. 'It's up to you but I believe that you would definitely be watched and that might put you and the brother in jeopardy . . . The brother says it is not safe for him to enter sanaa frequently. So please mention all what you need to say in the message you send me.'

So much detailed guidance on security told me that Awlaki feared being betrayed and was aware just how important he had become. So he had insisted on several chains of custody.

'Please let me know what your program is and the latest news from the west,' he wrote. And he had this request: 'My wife needs some stuff from sanaa so can your wife buy it for her? We have sent other people before and nothing really suited her taste.'

The cleric had attached a message from Aminah for Fadia:

'I miss my family big time. Insha'Allah I hope one day I will see them. You probably wonder how I am doing here. I am fine alhamdid-ullah. Now after one year I did get used on condition we are living but restrictions we have just make our lives complicated . . . I am learning every day. I did learn to cook some Yemeni meals.'

Her shopping list had little to do with improving her Yemeni cooking.

'Please send us chocolate inside, Lindtt different flavor – 100g, Kinder Bueno 10 pc, Ferrero Roche. And I would like a parfume. It's Dolce&Gabbana – Light blue. Box is beautiful sky blue color.'

She really must miss home, I thought.

Then came a very different shopping list – one which must have been influenced by her husband. Taking Fadia to meet her in Vienna the previous year had turned out to be a useful move. Aminah had some detailed requests for her – clothes and other feminine requirements that I could not possibly have entertained as an upstanding Salafist. 'I give up of Yemeni clothes. All I have I don't like and it is too hot to wear it. Fabrics are not good, synthetic, it's just horrible.'

'Please if you can find some European clothes. I miss it so much,' she wrote. 'Dresses should be long, without sleeves . . . fabric should be light, non-transparent . . . and if you can find denim mini skirt – tight and very short.

'Next I need 10 packages of feminine pads . . .'

And so the list went on.

I pulled out my Danish iPhone and called up Klang, my PET handler, who was thousands of miles away in Denmark. 'The Agriculture Minister has replied, and he has a message for me,' I said.

'Whaaaat?' Klang replied, not remembering our code name for the cleric. (Awlaki's father had been Yemen's Minister for Agriculture.)

'Holy shit! This is big,' he exclaimed. We continued the conversation in a Danish dialect we were sure no one in Yemen – or even the US National Security Agency – could understand.

'Listen, we should meet soon in a warm place,' Klang said at the end of the call.

I wrote a short reply for Awlaki, shut down my laptop and hurried to the stores. I did not buy everything the cleric and his wife had asked for; in any case the 'luxury' stores in Sana'a were a pitiful sight. It was also important that they (especially Aminah) should need to stay in touch for other items. I then went to the al-Hamra restaurant to give the bags and the message to the courier.

When I got there he was outside, chewing khat, addictive leaves consumed by the large majority of Yemeni men which produces a 'high' not dissimilar to amphetamines or a quadruple espresso laced with tequila.

'I couldn't find everything but I'm going back to Europe soon and will buy the other stuff there,' I told him. I placed the $300 into his hands. 'I can't accept this. Please make sure it gets back to where it needs to,' I said.

'I will,' he replied. He rushed off into the evening.

The next day I sent Awlaki an encrypted email through *Inspire* as he had instructed, to re-establish online communication.

'Please find a new courier,' I wrote to him: 'The guy you sent was chewing khat and this is not something I appreciate.'

Awlaki had previously expressed to me his frustration that so many of his compatriots were addicted to khat. My disapproval would please him as well as show that I was serious about operational security.

Al-Qaeda in Yemen generally frowned on the narcotic but tolerated its consumption in areas they controlled because there was no specific injunction in Islam against it – and because they knew stamping it out would be a fast ticket to losing support. Some of their suicide bombers had even died with khat-filled cheeks.

Shortly afterwards an encrypted email came back with a new request: hexamine briquettes and a fridge (most likely for storing explosives), a Leatherman knife and all-terrain sandals. In the same message Aminah suggested that when things were a little calmer my wife and I should come to visit them. Despite a year in Yemen, Aminah still suffered from chronic naivety.

As usual I immediately pasted the message into a draft email account I shared with Danish intelligence so they could read it straight away.

It was time for me to file an interim report. On 28 June I left Sana'a for Malaga in Spain – the 'warm place' Klang had promised. I had a renewed sense of purpose. My old tradecraft had not deserted me. I had arrived in the midst of an uprising and still, within a month, had established contact with Awlaki and confirmed his trust in me.

Against all expectations we now had one of the world's most dangerous men firmly in our sights, and for all the billions the Americans poured into their intelligence services, our tiny Danish outfit was leading the way. But I told myself not to get carried away. The Aminah mission had failed; and arrogance begets mistakes.

True to form, Klang had picked Malaga more for his own pleasure than my comfort.

'Akhi – what have you done? This is great!' he exclaimed as I came out of the arrivals hall. Akhi, which means 'brother' in Arabic, was the nickname that PET had recently given me. Klang was sporting mirrored sunglasses, chinos and a polo shirt with a giant Ralph Lauren logo. In contrast Jesper, the frail former banker, had rather worn jeans and a cotton shirt.

In a Costa del Sol hotel I sat down with the Danes in a quiet, shady corner of the poolside restaurant. Soren and Anders looked tanned.

'You've made Big Brother very happy – this is a huge deal for them,' Klang told me, after we ordered club sandwiches. Apparently I had also made Danish intelligence happy – to the extent that they had sent no fewer than four representatives to Malaga to greet me.

I quickly found out why.

'The Americans are willing to give you five million dollars if you lead them to Awlaki,' Jesper said.

'I understand,' I replied, scarcely believing.

They had not been lying about the 'very significant sum' and were clearly desperate to find Awlaki. I imagined the White House was now taking an active interest in the pursuit of the man who had become arguably the biggest threat to the West. The sum involved matched that offered by the FBI for some of the most dangerous men in the world.

'There's just one thing Jed needs you to help him with,' Klang said. 'His bosses are upset you told Awlaki you didn't trust Abdul as a courier and want you to explain.'

'It was my judgement call; I knew Awlaki didn't fully trust him.'

'Okay,' said Klang. 'Just use that language with Jed and we'll be fine.'

I was puzzled by this sudden anxiety over Abdul's role.

'Why the big song and dance?' I replied. 'Do you think Abdul's working for them?'

'Who knows,' Klang replied with a shrug, avoiding eye contact and refilling his glass. Carlsberg, I noticed – you can take a Dane out of Denmark . . .

I was intrigued that Abdul, of all the people I knew in Yemen, might also be a double agent. I had known him for ten years and he had always seemed a committed jihadi, deeply involved with al-Qaeda and hostile to pro-Western Arab governments and the US. But there were perhaps clues. During my most recent stay in Yemen, Abdul seemed over-enthusiastic in wanting information about Awlaki. He had more cash than ever; and had a new car with no obvious source of earnings. He had also started chewing khat.

Most significant, I thought, was that he now had the same model of phone – a Nokia N900 with a flip keyboard – which Jed had given me. Had the CIA developed Abdul as an informer during my ten months in the wilderness?

For two full days I was debriefed in a suite. Even MI6 had rejoined the fray, sending a young agent to observe the meeting.

Jed asked his question about Abdul and I gave the response we had choreographed. He grunted 'okay' and jotted in his notebook.

We went through the list of supplies Awlaki wanted – hexamine briquettes and the fridge.

'We can't agree to the hexamine,' Klang said. It could be adapted to make explosives.

'So I should just go back empty-handed?' I shot back at him. 'Isn't that going to make me look amateurish? Or worse, make him suspect I'm a Western agent?'

There was an awkward silence. Klang did not appreciate being shot down in front of the CIA.

'Why don't I just provide them with wooden briquettes?'

The agents exchanged looks. 'You know what? You're not just a pretty face,' Jesper said with a smirk.

I gave Jed the USB stick Awlaki had used so that it could be sent for analysis, and also handed over the remaining thumb drives I had bought and intended to use for future messages. I thought the Americans might want to install some sort of tracking device on them.

'Do you think you might be able to travel out to see Awlaki?' Jed asked me.

'Possibly, but the security situation has got a lot worse,' I replied, 'especially in the south. Al-Qaeda is beginning to take control in some areas, and it's impossible to know which units to trust in the army.'

In the evening I took a stroll with the Danes and the deferential MI6 agent. In the streets around the hotel stood expensive villas with lush gardens. Sprinkler systems shot a golden mist into the evening sunshine. A lot of Russian money had made it to this part of Spain.

'You'll be able to afford one of these properties soon, Akhi,' Klang said. 'And you'd better let us come stay.'

We even discussed a joint business venture funded out of my 'winnings' – a restaurant or bar on the beach. For the first time I sensed my Danish handlers had more than a professional interest in my success. But I was still a long way from delivering Awlaki to the CIA. And even as we walked among the scent of jasmine and lemon trees, I could not relish the prospect of becoming rich by sending a man who had once been my friend to his death.

Jed had stayed in the hotel: CIA rules dictated he could not be seen in public with me. After we left I caught sight of him at Malaga airport. He walked past pretending not to know me but smiling out of the corner of his mouth.

Days after I left Malaga, I discovered that the US had made an important breakthrough – at the expense of my old Birmingham acquaintance, Ahmed Abdulkadir Warsame. After my telephone call connecting him with Awlaki, he had begun regular contact with AQAP. He shared details on some of these communications with me, which allowed Western intelligence to track his plans. In 2009 he emailed to tell me he wanted to travel to Yemen to meet with AQAP's leadership and later informed me that Awlaki had invited him to train in Yemen.

Warsame took the offer. In 2010 he travelled to Yemen to broker a weapons deal between AQAP and al-Shabaab. During that visit he met Awlaki and received explosives training. Not yet twenty-five, he had become the main point of liaison between the two groups, funnelling money and communications gear from Somalia to Yemen in exchange for weapons for Somali fighters.

In April 2011, Warsame had boarded a fishing dhow in a small Yemeni harbour to travel back across the Gulf of Aden to Somalia. But the Americans were waiting for him and took him into custody on the high seas. Warsame would spend two months on a US Navy amphibious assault ship, the USS *Boxer*, where he proved a rich source.[3]

---

3 He was transferred to a New York courtroom, where he pleaded guilty to nine terror charges, among them conspiracy and providing material support to al-Shabaab and AQAP.

So now I had helped take two of al-Shabaab's most important operatives out of circulation, men who had no qualms about murdering and maiming civilians, or creating a tide of helpless refugees, if it advanced the cause of their ideology. While the Islamic Courts had at least brought a measure of peace, al-Shabaab had brought little more than terror and suffering.

Awlaki later told me Warsame had acted against all advice – always talking on his mobile phone. I wondered whether a phone I had supplied to Warsame had helped the Americans track his movements.

The next phase of the Awlaki operation was discussed at the Marienlyst Hotel in Helsingør. When I walked into the room there was a new face.

'Let me introduce you to one of my colleagues in Sana'a. You'll understand if I don't introduce him by name,' Jed said.

About 5 foot 10 inches, he might have passed himself off as a Yemeni but told me he was an American of Indian descent. We exchanged a few words in Arabic.

With Jed looking on, I wrote a new email to Awlaki providing venues and times where a courier could pick up the briquettes and sandals from me in Sana'a.

I was not going to heed his advice to have my wife deliver the package. I encrypted the email and hit 'send'.

Then Jed and Klang went shopping for the supplies Aminah had requested. I could only imagine what an odd couple they would have made in the ladies' sections of Copenhagen's department stores – picking out skirts, tops, bras and underwear. Klang later joked that he at least knew his way around the lingerie section. They also bought the shampoo, conditioner and hair colouring. The expenses department at Langley must be used to unusual purchases in the name of keeping America safe.

The two agents neatly folded everything into a sports bag which Klang kept until I was ready to travel. Remembering the CIA plots to poison Fidel Castro, I made a mental note to keep the toiletries well away from my wife in Yemen.

I would not yet be bringing Awlaki his fridge. Klang said the CIA were 'customizing' one for the cleric and it would take several weeks to build. I had no doubt CIA technicians were busily at work figuring out the best way to hide a satellite transponder in the freezer compartment.

Before I left, Jed bought me a gift: a Viking horn with an inscription in gold. I was their warrior again – readying for another battle.

CHAPTER TWENTY-ONE

A LONG HOT SUMMER

July–September 2011

I flew back to Yemen on 27 July 2011 into blinding heat. The operation to neutralize Awlaki was moving into high gear, but the country was a failing state, with most of the south beyond government control and paralysis among competing factions in and around Sana'a.

I wondered whether the chaos had prevented Awlaki from organizing a courier, because none showed up on either day I had appointed. Had Awlaki got my message? Did he still trust me?

The next day I sent Awlaki an encrypted email:

'I am back in Sana'a and got your shoppinglist. I have waited for the brother to meet me on thursday and saturday, he did not show up. I ask Allah that he is safe and fine insha'Allah.'

I provided three new times and places for the courier to pick up the supplies, telling Awlaki I would only wait fifteen minutes.

'I do stick out and people notice my presence. I will try to come down and join you in mid Sept insha'Allah. Take care habibi,' I wrote.

Despite the considerable risk of such a trip, it would undoubtedly make it easier for the Americans to track him. I had just about given up on the idea of luring him to the capital.

On 9 August I received a reply. I copied the seemingly random string of letters, numbers and symbols in the body of the email and pasted them into the Mujahideen Secrets software on my laptop. Then I entered my personal cipher key and pressed 'decrypt'.

Nothing happened.

Perhaps I had entered the wrong values? Or had someone got to my computer? I had to calm down.

I started again. A few seconds later the random text turned into prose. I breathed deeply.

'Assalamu alaykum, sorry man communication is a bit slow with me. I will insha'Allah send someone to meet you at one of the 3 appointments you set. It will be a different brother from first time so we will use the same codes as before: he says lawn [colour] you say akhdar [green],' the cleric wrote.

'Try to write down everything in a letter to me because it is not safe sending someone to meet you to[o] many times. You should open up a new account to use when you email me from Yemen so that the enemies do not know that this guy was emailing from Europe and then from Yemen. This way they may be able to figure out who you are,' Awlaki added.

I copied the message into the draft folder of the Telenor email account I shared with Danish intelligence so they could pass the details on to the CIA and their Sana'a field operative.

I was impressed by Awlaki's awareness of operational security and his concern that I not be suspected by Western security services. It was an important detail. I remembered how he had once said to me: 'It is better to have an enemy close to you than having a stupid friend,' a judgement he might have reversed if he had known which side I was really on.

The first rendezvous was at 10.30 p.m. on 12 August in the car park outside a KFC restaurant in the centre of Sana'a.

The drive in my Suzuki pick-up truck from my home would normally have taken about fifteen minutes but that night I went a round-about way. As my instructors had taught me in Edinburgh I weaved through the narrow streets, taking turns at random.

I had weapons in the car which I had borrowed from Abdul, including a pistol in the glove compartment and a Kalashnikov under a blanket on the back seat. Guns are ubiquitous in Yemen; none of the locals would have batted an eyelid. I had told Abdul I wanted to be able to defend myself if the Yemeni security services came after me.

At the KFC I waited nervously. Given my size and skin colour I was easy to identify. There was no sign of the CIA field officer I had met in Copenhagen, but if he knew what he was doing that was the way it should be.

I took in the scene. Colonel Sanders in his apron stared down at me from a brightly lit hoarding. Soaring above the Colonel, and lit up in the night sky, were the six towering minarets and monumental white domes of the al-Saleh mosque complex. Built by the beleaguered President, the mosque had recently been completed at a cost of nearly $100m, in the Arab world's poorest country.

Gaggles of well-dressed young Yemeni men were coming in and out of the restaurant. KFC is considered an expensive treat for most Yemenis. It seemed to be a busy evening, no surprise because it was the middle of Ramadan and the night hours were a time of feasting.

Perhaps I ought to pop in for some fried chicken, I thought. But then I caught sight of him, walking towards me across the car park, silhouetted against the lights of the mosque. He was older than the other messenger – perhaps in his mid-twenties – and shorter. But he too was dark-skinned and wore the unmistakable Marib headgear. We exchanged the code word and I gave the courier the sports bag with the wooden briquettes and other supplies, including the clothes for Aminah.

I also passed him a thumb drive with a Word document I had written for the cleric. I wanted him to approve my creation of an 'Islamic Defence Force' to protect Muslims in the West from Islamophobic attacks by training them in shooting, martial arts and survival skills. The idea had come to me following the deadly terrorist bombing and shooting in Norway by the anti-Muslim extremist Anders Breivik the previous month. If I could get Awlaki engaged in the project I would have another pretext for continuing my communications with him. I also knew the outfit would be a draw for Islamist extremists across Europe, which might help me identify new targets.

'Is this for Samir Khan?' the courier asked.

That surprised me. It was terrible tradecraft.

The editor of AQAP's online *Inspire* magazine, Khan had been born in Saudi Arabia but had lived in the US for much of his life. He moved to Yemen in 2009, where he aligned himself with al-Qaeda and connected with Awlaki. Khan met with the Nigerian underwear bomber, Abdulmutallab, and helped Awlaki research the air cargo system for the printer bomb plot.

'No, my brother – this is secret,' I reprimanded him. With a crestfallen look he disappeared into the night.

I received an encrypted email from Awlaki three days later:

'Assalamu alaykum . . . I received all the stuff . . . except the flash! A brother who was delivering it got into a situation and had to destroy it. Things turned out to be fine but now I do not have the flash. The sandals are good. The tablets I was looking for are hexamine. The ones you sent are something else. If you are travelling again then see if you can get me hexamine tablets,' he wrote.

So they did want the tablets for detonating explosives.

Awlaki asked me for any new information on the arrest of Warsame. And he had a specific request: 'I heard on the news that the New York Times reported that al Qaeda in Yemen is buying a lot of castor beans to make ricin and attack the US. Find me what you can on that.'[1]

I found the *New York Times* article.

'For more than a year, according to classified intelligence reports, Al Qaeda's affiliate in Yemen has been making efforts to acquire large quantities of castor beans, which are required to produce ricin, a white, powdery toxin that is so deadly that just a speck can kill if it is inhaled or reaches the bloodstream. Intelligence officials say they have collected evidence that Qaeda operatives are trying to move castor beans and processing agents to a hideaway in Shabwa Province, in one of Yemen's rugged tribal areas controlled by insurgents.'

---

1 Although I did not know it at the time, Awlaki was then penning an Islamic justification for chemical and biological attacks on the United States and other Western countries. 'The use of poisons of chemical and biological weapons against population centers is allowed and strongly recommended due to its great effect on the enemy,' the cleric wrote in an article later that year in *Inspire* magazine.

I shuddered. It seemed like the cleric had something in the works and wanted to know what was being reported. For the first time, I thought that it did not matter any longer how he was stopped. He now seemed ready for any form of attack against the West, with civilians as the main target.

On 17 August I left Yemen again for Europe. Every summer my children spent a couple of weeks with me, camping, hiking, canoeing and fishing. That time was sacrosanct – even if it disrupted the mission to go after the most wanted terrorist in al-Qaeda. I also needed to get ready for a long-planned trip to the jungles of Borneo with a friend from the UK. I imagined my mission in Yemen might run many more months and I needed to recharge my batteries.

Just before leaving I sent an email to Awlaki that I would be overseas for my company, Storm Bushcraft. I knew that if he later checked its website he would see photographs of the expedition to Borneo. I told him I had left a USB stick with the media clippings on ricin with a contact in the capital and provided his address and telephone number.

When I returned to Europe I explained the situation to Jed and the Danes and gave Jed the number of my acquaintance in Sana'a so the US National Security Agency could monitor his calls.

At the end of the first week of September I received a text from my contact in Sana'a. 'The guy just called me and I'm waiting for him now at CityStar.' I called Klang so he could relay the message to the Americans.

'It's being picked up; be ready now,' I told him – explaining the rendezvous point was a shopping mall in the Yemeni capital. Less than an hour later my contact sent me a text telling me the pick-up had been successful. I imagined the Americans – by tracking the contact's calls – had monitored the handover. Maybe this time the USB stick would lead the CIA all the way to Anwar al-Awlaki – but hopefully not to Aminah.

The mission was going according to plan. Awlaki had confidence in me, and when I returned from the Far East I might be able to travel into Yemen's badlands to meet him. The next day I boarded a flight to Malaysia, on my way to the jungles of Borneo. It was a welcome escape. No one could reach me; and I had to survive on my own ingenuity.

★

But just days after my return reality intervened in the most brutal way. On a brisk late-September afternoon, I turned on the television and saw breaking news. I stared at the screen, mesmerized.

Early that day – 30 September – CIA drones had taken off from a base in the southern deserts of Saudi Arabia and spotted a group of pick-up trucks that had congregated in Yemen's north-west al-Jawf province. Hearing the faint whirring sound they had come to dread, several men who had just finished breakfast rushed back to their vehicles. One of them was Awlaki, who had come to the region because of the growing threat from drone strikes in Yemen's southern tribal areas.

Two Predator drones focused lasers at the trucks to pinpoint the targets while the bigger Reapers took aim. The Reaper 'pilots', operating their vehicles from thousands of miles away, unleashed a clutch of Hellfire missiles. Awlaki and six other al-Qaeda operatives were killed instantly, their vehicles reduced to skeletons. One of those killed was Samir Khan; the CIA had no idea he was travelling with Awlaki. He was just twenty-four.

As I watched, my phone vibrated in my pocket. It was a text message from Klang: 'Have you seen the news?'

'I don't believe it,' I replied.

'No – it's true.'

The US had finally liquidated the man it considered an urgent and present danger. Awlaki, US authorities subsequently alleged, had risen to become AQAP's chief plotter of attacks against the West and was plotting new attacks against the US and Western interests when he was killed.

'The death of Awlaki is a major blow to al-Qaeda's most active operational affiliate,' President Obama announced later that day at a speech in Fort Myer, Virginia. 'Awlaki was the leader of external operations for al-Qaeda in the Arabian Peninsula. In that role, he took the lead in planning and directing efforts to murder innocent Americans . . . and he repeatedly called on individuals in the United States and around the globe to kill innocent men, women and children to advance a murderous agenda.'

CHAPTER TWENTY-TWO

BREAKING WITH BIG BROTHER

Autumn 2011

'I'm so sorry but it wasn't us. We were so close but it wasn't us.'

The text stared at me, black on green. It was another from Klang, several hours after Awlaki's death had been confirmed.

'Tell Jed and the Americans: well done. Send them my greetings and congratulations. He's a terrorist and needed to be stopped,' I replied.

I had to be magnanimous, even if it meant giving up the prospect of $5m. As it was, I might get a nomination as Best Supporting Actor.

Even so I was irritated and disappointed that neither Jed nor any of my other US contacts reached out to me in the following days. I also felt, despite my best efforts, sad and not a little guilty that Anwar al-Awlaki, with whom I had sat and talked for so many hours, had been incinerated. Yet I knew how dangerous he was, and how much more dangerous he would have become.

I tried to focus on a brief trip with my kids, but I was restless. I needed to know what had happened.

Two days after Awlaki was killed, I picked up a copy of the *Sunday Telegraph*, the UK broadsheet.

'How America finally caught up with Anwar al-Awlaki' ran the headline on the front page. And below: 'The capture of a low-level errand-runner was the key breakthrough that led to the al-Qaeda leader's death.'

The sentence caught my attention.

'Details of how the US finally managed to track down al-Qaeda's chief mouthpiece to the West can be revealed today by the *Sunday Telegraph*, which has learned that the key breakthrough came when CIA officials caught a junior courier in Awlaki's inner circle. The man, who is understood to have been arrested three weeks ago by Yemeni agents acting for the Agency, volunteered key details about Awlaki's whereabouts which led to Friday's drone strike as his convoy drove through the remote province of Jawf, 100 miles east of the capital, Sana'a.'

I felt my throat tighten. '*Caught a junior courier . . . three weeks ago . . .*'

I read the passage again. Had the CIA tried to hoodwink me? I recalled Kevin's words in Edinburgh: 'We don't want you to get fucked over.'

I checked the date of the text message my contact had sent from Sana'a confirming the pick-up of the thumb drive. It was three weeks ago. I called him and asked him to describe the handover.[1] He said the phone call had come in at 9 p.m. They agreed a rendezvous point and half an hour later he parked outside the City Star mall. A few minutes later a dusty battered Toyota Hilux pick-up truck pulled up. Two men in tribal outfits were sitting up front: a lanky man in the driving seat and a short fat man sitting next to him. Both were chewing khat.

The driver had come over to him. He was young, according to my contact, probably in his late teens, tall, thin, dark-skinned and dressed in a light-green *thawb* and Maribi headgear.

He said the driver had been in a hurry.

'Can I have the flash stick Murad asked you to give me?' he had asked after a curt greeting. My contact handed it over.

'Thank you,' said the driver. 'We have a long way to travel so we must go now.'

The description closely resembled that of the courier who had delivered the first thumb drive message to me at the al-Shaibani taverna in Sana'a. It also fitted that of the junior errand runner described in the *Sunday Telegraph* article. I doubted whether the courier would have

---

1 I have a recording, which I provided to Paul Cruickshank and Tim Lister, of a phone conversation in which my contact confirmed the details of this handover.

been able to lead the CIA directly to Awlaki, but he would have certainly led them to the next messenger in the chain.[2]

Perhaps I was just looking for connections where none existed. I needed a second opinion.

'Do me a favour, look at the *Sunday Telegraph* article – and tell me your opinion,' I said to Klang on the phone. I was driving through heavy rain after dropping my kids off with Karima and my mood was darkening. I could cope with most things, but not with being cheated by people for whom I had risked my life.

Klang phoned back shortly afterwards.

'I cannot see why it's not ours. It really looks like our job,' he told me.

I ended the call. The wipers were struggling to keep pace with the rain. I was a kaleidoscope of emotions. I felt a grim satisfaction that I had been involved in a successful operation. But that satisfaction soon gave way to remorse – for Awlaki's family and Aminah – and then to anger that the Americans had discarded me without any acknowledgement for my role.

'I'm sorry I had to do this,' I said out loud several times, my voice breaking. I had met Awlaki's children and now I bore responsibility for the death of their father. Perversely, I suddenly felt he was the honourable one in this struggle. He would have given up his life for me, but my handlers would not have given me a second thought had I died in their governments' service.

The next day Klang and I spoke again. 'We've been trying again to ask the Americans about this, but we have no comment from them,' he told me.

By then fury had smothered sadness. 'Fuck them. I don't want to work with them any more. Actually, fuck all of you. If it wasn't my guy

---

2 There was recent precedent for such an operation. The CIA located Osama bin Laden through his most trusted messenger, Abu Ahmed al-Kuwaiti. The courier was used by al-Qaeda's leader as his single point of contact with his senior deputies. Bin Laden's way of operating was similar to that of Awlaki: he composed messages on a computer, uploaded them to a thumb drive and passed them to a courier.

who led to Anwar, then why was information leaked about him?' I shouted down the phone.

The next day I was eating dinner at a half-empty TGI Friday's restaurant in the English Midlands when two men installed themselves in a booth behind me. There was something unsettling about them. From their conversation, I could tell that one was British and the other American. The British man kept turning round. He did not look at me – that would be too obvious – but towards a couple sitting in the next booth in front.

I snapped. 'What are you looking at?' I blurted out. 'You're American, right?' I said, turning to the other man. 'Are you from the CIA or what? I'm going to expose your guys. I'm going to the media to tell them everything that your government did. I was behind that operation and your government fucked me over.'

It was not my most eloquent performance, but it was passionate, and it had the desired effect. The mask fell.

'If you say anything, it will be dangerous for you,' the American told me.

They got up and left. The family in the adjacent booth looked as if they had just seen an alien.

The next day I received a call from Klang, my Danish handler. 'What did you say in the restaurant?' he asked.

'How did you know about that?'

'The incident was reported at the local police station,' said Klang.

Bullshit, I thought.

'Listen, the Brits and Americans don't want to have anything to do with you right now,' Klang said.

The feeling was mutual.

But the Danes wanted to try to engineer some sort of reconciliation, not least because of my threat to go public. They implored me to come to Denmark for a meeting to clear the air. Reluctantly, I agreed.

It felt strange to be standing in the lobby of the Marienlyst Hotel in Helsingør again. It was where we had planned critical missions as a team. But this occasion seemed likely to be a post-mortem of recriminations. It was 7 October 2011 – a week after Awlaki's death.

My PET handlers had set this up with the Americans and told me I would be meeting an agent called Michael. Jed, I was later told, had left Copenhagen abruptly – though I was sceptical about that. The meeting would be in one of the hotel's holiday villas. Perhaps that was a sign; they wanted to avoid any public scene.

Two cars with tinted windows arrived outside the hotel. Klang and a tall, muscular man with dark-brown hair walked across to the cottages, while the 'desk-jockey' Jesper and Marianne, a thirty-something agent who occasionally attended debriefings, waited by the car.

Jesper beckoned me to join them in the car park.

Screw all of them, I thought. Without the Danes noticing I discreetly reached for my iPhone, set it to video mode, and hit 'record'. Then I strode out, trying to look as menacing as possible. It wasn't difficult.

My decision to record the meeting was spontaneous. If I was going to be duped by Western intelligence then I wanted to be able to prove my story. At the beginning of the recording there is a quick glimpse of the blue sofas and gleaming marble floors of the hotel lobby. After I tucked the phone back into my pocket the picture goes to black, but our voices are clearly audible.

We walked towards the villas. Seagulls cawed overhead. There were few people outside – the pretty blue-and-white deckchairs that adorned the beachfront in the summer months had been packed away for the season.

I took in the view. A car ferry was navigating the choppy waters on its way across to the Baltic.

'You'll have to talk to him. It's no good not to talk,' Jesper told me.[3]

'I have nothing to talk to him about,' I said. 'It's so clear what happened. They arrested a boy who went to meet my contact and pick up that USB stick. It's so clear and they have exposed themselves.'

'Yes, that's right but he needs to explain himself,' Jesper said.

'Yes,' Marianne chimed in. 'They need to have a chance to explain

---

3 The extracts from this conversation with the Danish agents are translated verbatim from my recording.

themselves.' Not for the first time I thought she looked and sounded just like a bookkeeper.

I recounted our success stories – in Somalia, Kenya and Yemen and here in Denmark. For five years I had been on the frontline; and now the CIA wanted to disown me.

When we reached the villa, Klang opened the door and made some pleasantries about the weather. He seemed apprehensive, as if he were about to witness what the professionals call a 'psychotic episode'.

'There's nothing to talk about,' I repeated.

'We are also searching for answers,' Klang said. I had rarely seen the playboy of PET so serious – as if the long and close relationship of the CIA and PET could hinge on the next half-hour.

'Michael' was all-American – square jaw, the picture of a 'GI Joe'. I gave him the curtest of nods and carried on talking to Klang in Danish.

Klang switched to English, keenly aware I was trying to be offensive, and offered to order coffee.

I looked at Michael.

'You are not going to convince me,' I said.

'Convince you? I guess I'm not here to convince you. I'm just here to talk to you,' he said.[4]

He spoke slowly and deliberately with an accent that came from somewhere between New York and Boston.

We walked upstairs to the living quarters on the top floor and sat down facing each other at a glass table. Light streamed in from the windows.

I thought I would hold out an olive branch.

'I want to congratulate you . . . Never mind what happened, but the good thing is that these evil guys have been removed, that's number one,' I said.

'That's right, that's right,' Michael interrupted. 'And it is number one for me too. I did not come here to argue with you. I came here

---

4 The extracts from this conversation with Michael are reproduced verbatim from my recording.

because I respect you, plain and simple. I know you feel upset – but I don't know why you feel upset,' he said – looking at me intently.

He gave a good impression of looking perplexed.

I continued: 'There are two reasons. First of all I will honour the guy who got killed, if you understand. We honour him for being an enemy.' But, I stressed again, he needed to be taken out.

'That's right,' Michael replied. 'He had to be taken out.'

'And that's fine. Because if *he* was not taken out a lot of innocent people would have been taken out,' I said.

'Yes,' said Michael. He was doing his best to soothe me. His words were all camomile.

'He was a good friend of mine. He was my mentor. He was my sheikh. He was a friend of mine but because of the evil in him I have done this . . . I felt it was a necessity to eliminate, to destroy this threat,' I said.

'Absolutely, and I'm gonna tell you something. These types of things happen, are necessary,' Michael interjected, emphasizing each syllable in the second sentence with outstretched hands in a slow chopping gesture. I noticed he had strong hands. He could have been a boxer, I thought. Klang told me later he was an ex-US Navy SEAL.

He then tried to sway me with flattery.

'This whole thing was a team effort – a team thing from my organization, from me being here with you guys, from Jed being here with you guys . . . We had our team, we had our whole project going forward – of which you played the highest role.'

The chopping motion again for the last three words.

'And it is because of that that there are a lot of people in my government – when I say lot of people I want you to understand a select few that . . .'

'Yeah, we know Alex, we know George and you know all the others,' I interjected – recalling my brief interactions with the senior intelligence official from Washington and the CIA Copenhagen station chief.

'Yeah, but I am not talking about Alex and George, you know. I am talking about . . .'

'Obama?'

'The President of the United States, okay? He knows you. The President of the United States doesn't know who I am, okay? But he knows about your work. So the right people know your contributions. And for that we are thankful,' Michael said with a degree of repetition that I thought overdone.

'I'm thankful too,' I replied.

Michael was now getting into his stride. Perhaps he thought he was ahead on points.

'I understand you might feel, and we'll get to this in a second, like we fucked you over, and I don't know why you would think that. You've got your own reasons and I'll listen to them, okay? But I'm telling you if we were fucking you over I wouldn't be sitting with you right now. I wouldn't need to be.'

He had a habit of saying 'okay' after each point he made, as if to seek my agreement for each step of his logic.

'You don't have a good reputation,' I replied, meaning the CIA as an institution.

'That's right. Unfortunately, because we're in the business of protecting people like you, okay?

'There is all this negative stuff we don't respond to because it doesn't do any good. People are going to read what they read and think what they think and you're not going to convince them otherwise.'

People could not understand, he said, what it meant to ask someone like me to put their 'balls on the line, day in day out', at great risk to their family.

'It's very stressful,' I replied, especially – I thought – when your commitment to a mission was overshadowed by the realization that your circus-masters had decided you were no longer essential.

Michael chose the moment to move on to the real business at hand. His voice dropped to a stage whisper.

'Look – Awlaki was a bad man and bad in a lot of ways. You know this more than me.'

'I told you even before the Americans were even interested in him. I told you guys: be careful – he's going to be a danger,' I replied.

'That's right,' Michael said. He continued: 'So, you, we had our project together to go forward – we were not the only ones, okay? There were a number of other projects that were going.'

'I agree,' I replied.

'We were very, very close,' he said. 'We were moving towards – and when I say we – I am talking about – you know – I want success.'

He paused to deliver the analogy he had clearly rehearsed.

'It's like being on the field at the World Cup, you're moving down the field and you're in the position to score, the other guy could have passed it to you but he didn't, he took the shot, he scores. And that's that. That's what happened.'

It was a polite way of saying sorry – but not one I would accept.

'Who was the boy you arrested in Sana'a? A boy between fifteen and seventeen years old?'

'I don't have any information a boy was arrested.'

I explained how an al-Qaeda courier had come to pick up the thumb drive three weeks before Awlaki was killed.

'How do you know he was arrested?' Michael asked.

'Isn't that a coincidence then – a very extreme coincidence?' I asked.

Michael clearly sensed this was an argument that was not going to be resolved.

'You either trust us or you don't. In this case I guess you don't.'

'I don't.'

Michael insisted he was briefed on the various plans to eliminate Awlaki.

'So don't you think that if a courier that was associated with your contact was arrested, I would know about it?' he said.

Listening to the recording afterwards, I was struck by how Michael seemed willing to say anything to placate me – except to concede that my work directly led the CIA to Awlaki.

Now it was my turn. The Americans, I told him with some relish, had failed in their previous attempts to track down and kill Anwar al-Awlaki. Sure, they had come close a few times, not always by design. But it was only when I had gone in, established contact with him, passed on equipment and exchanged messages through couriers that he had eventually been killed.

I began to catalogue the other breakthroughs that Michael might not know about. I had been the one who encouraged Ahmed Warsame to develop a relationship between al-Shabaab and Awlaki. I had encouraged him to go to Yemen. And, I reminded Michael, it was when he was returning from one of his visits that he was seized.

Then there was the case of Saleh Ali Nabhan, who by 2009 had become one of al-Qaeda's most dangerous operatives. He had even invited me into Somalia to see him. And it was the BlackBerry and laptop I had been given by Jed that had helped track him down.

'Boom! He was wiped out using our gear. So why don't you just say thank you?'

Michael let me carry on. Perhaps he thought the venting would do me good.

'We just want gratitude from your government, just to accept the fact. Obama can take the honour – that's fine. At least a 'thank you'; that's what we want from him.

'I've been honest with you guys all the time. I know you listen to my phone, all my house, cars, everything. It's fine. Every single [piece of] information you have from my side,' I said, striking the table, 'it's always been honest, you never find a lie in it.'

'And I've never accused you of lying,' Michael said.

'I even sent Anwar a wife. Did any of your agents manage to send him a wife?'

I realized that Michael's mission was to watch a volcano exhaust itself. He was never going to acknowledge my role in leading US intelligence to Awlaki. The job was done; it was an American victory against terrorism.

I stood up and shouted down the stairs to Klang and Jesper.

'He's just sitting there and lying.'

Denmark's initiative to make nice had aborted in spectacular fashion. Michael stood up and without looking at me or saying another word walked downstairs and out into the gardens. I would not see him again.

I faced Klang and Jesper.

'You know what? I recorded the whole conversation.'

'You can't do that,' said Klang, looking as though he was about to be physically sick. Were the tape to become public, his failure to search me before the meeting would not impress his seniors.

'But I did. And I quit,' I told him.

Later, I realized the reason the CIA would never acknowledge that I had led them to Awlaki was that to do so would expose Danish intelligence to allegations that they had participated in an assassination – which was illegal under Danish law.

The agencies had closed ranks.

CHAPTER TWENTY-THREE

BACK IN THE RING

Late 2011

The weeks after Awlaki's death were a dark time. I could not help feeling guilty about his killing. I kept imagining the grief of his ageing father, who had tried so hard to protect him, of his wives and children, and especially of the woman I had sent to Yemen to be his partner.

My sadness was compounded by an encrypted message I received from Aminah several weeks after Awlaki had been killed.

'I am sending you this mail with great sorrow and sadness in my heart but again happiness for my husband Shuhada [martyrdom.] Alhamdidullah he is now in the Jannat [paradise] and do not feel anything but joy and happines.

'I wanted to contact you in case I will go back in Europe, but I have 4 months to decide what to do. My first option is shahada . . . May Allah give us all sabr [patience] and strenght to go through this severelly difficult moments in our life.

'I ask Allah to bless you for connecting me with my husband. Our marriage was blessing from Allah and I am so proud for being his wife.'

I thought of her predicament – alone and helpless. But then I read the email again.

'My first option is shahada.'

Shahada: martyrdom. To avenge her husband's death, the young star-struck woman I had left sipping coffee in Vienna was ready to blow herself up.

In my sleep Awlaki would come to me, reprimanding me for what I had done.

My days were equally restless. I brooded incessantly over the behaviour of the Americans. They had vanished from my life. I was damaged goods, a loose cannon. I could hear the clichés echoing round Langley. I wanted to prove them wrong, to dispel the notion that I was a bit player. I wanted them to take notice of me again.

I also wanted to retire from frontline intelligence work on a high. The frustration simmered. Fadia was by turns anxious and irritated with my behaviour. I could hardly blame her; I was erratic and easily angered, but still I could not bring myself to tell her anything that had happened.

On a misty November afternoon I had an idea – a way to reconnect with PET and show that I, and they, could still sit at the top table. I might have missed out on the payday promised by the Awlaki mission but PET still had me on a retainer, and I was never the type to accept money for doing nothing. It was time to get to work again.

My time in Yemen had introduced me to a network that was far wider than just Awlaki. I had – as it were – grown up with al-Qaeda in the Arabian Peninsula, by now the most active and lethal of the terrorist network's tentacles. Awlaki had been critically important – but there was another figure whose operational skills and leadership were even more crucial: Nasir al-Wuhayshi.

A confidant of Osama bin Laden who had played a senior administrative role at his pre-9/11 headquarters near Kandahar, Nasir al-Wuhayshi had fled to Iran after the US launched Operation Enduring Freedom in October 2001. The Iranians had arrested him and extradited him to Yemen but his escape from prison in 2006 had galvanized the cause of jihad in his native country. Al-Qaeda in Yemen had become al-Qaeda in the Arabian Peninsula and Wuhayshi had become the group's emir. In August 2010, bin Laden had sent a message from Abbottabad praising Wuhayshi for his 'qualified and capable' leadership of the group.

By late 2011 Wuhayshi, who was known by his fighters as Abu Basir, had built AQAP into a powerful force. The group had exploited President Saleh's unpopularity to recruit thousands of fighters from sympathetic tribes. In April it had spun off a new group called 'Ansar al-Sharia' – partisans of the Sharia – to attract as broad a base of support as possible.

Ansar al-Sharia fighters had taken advantage of political turmoil to seize control of territory in Abyan, Marib and Shabwa provinces, including the dusty town of Zinjibar on the south coast, just forty miles up the coastal road from Aden. It was the road I had driven along that September night to see Awlaki.

An al-Qaeda mini-state was in the making, with the town of Jaar, ten miles inland from Zinjibar, its cradle and Wuhayshi its undisputed leader. This burnished his credentials within the jihadist movement. He was beginning to be seen as a potential successor to bin Laden and Ayman al-Zawahiri as the paramount leader of al-Qaeda worldwide.

I called Klang in Copenhagen; I needed a meeting. No longer was I immediately given a plane ticket; this time it was a trek across England and a ferry from Harwich.

I was contrite when I met Klang and Jesper. I knew they were my last chance to leave the game with a gold medal. I nevertheless was quietly confident: I knew what I was doing and there was no other agent – anywhere – who could get close to Wuhayshi.

'I think I can get him within a year,' I told them. Klang looked sceptical, almost uncomfortable – as if he were the barman being asked for one last drink by the local alcoholic.

Klang said he was happy for me to try to rekindle some militant contacts in Yemen, if that's what I wanted to do, but his enthusiasm hardly overwhelmed me. PET would as usual adjust my retainer – they paid a premium when I was overseas – bringing it to some $7,500 a month. But I felt I was a nuisance to them, no longer the ticket to dine with Big Brother.

My obstinacy kicked in: I would show them what I could do. But effectively I was now freelance, setting my own priorities, and without my most valuable contact, Anwar al-Awlaki.

On 3 December I returned to Sana'a – and immediately felt vulnerable. Not only had I lost the backing of my handlers, but I would be reliant on Abdul to put out feelers on my behalf. And after Malaga I was not sure where his loyalties lay. That meant another layer of danger.

Abdul showed no trace of being anxious or hiding something when we met. If he was working for the CIA he was good at displaying an air of composure. He suggested I talk to Mujeeb, who had delivered my first thumb drive message for Awlaki to al-Qaeda's religious chief, Adil al-Abab, in the tribal areas the previous summer. Mujeeb, he said, regularly met with Wuhayshi.

The three of us met on the roof of the house in Sana'a where I was staying.

Mujeeb was short and chubby and had a long beard. He always wore a scarf around his head but not a tribal one. It was clear by the type of car he drove – a newish Mercedes – that he was not your standard Salafist. He was a show-off, proud of his connections. He boasted that he was acting as a mediator between Salafis in Dammaj, where I had studied more than a decade previously, and al-Qaeda.[1]

Mujeeb told me he had recently carried a letter from the Saudis to Wuhayshi proposing a deal. They said they would pardon Wuhayshi and his group and donate weapons and money if they stopped fighting the Saudis and the Americans and focused instead on fighting Shia rebels in northern Yemen. I thought it an unlikely offer, as well as an outrageous infringement of Yemeni sovereignty, but with Mujeeb you could never be sure.

I changed the subject to my reason for being in Yemen. I had rehearsed the presentation, but only now would I find out if it had any traction.

'There are brothers in Sweden who are ready to avenge the death of

---

1 AQAP had proposed providing the Dammaj students with weapons training so they could fight the Houthis – a Shia revivalist movement – in the surrounding area. The Houthis had taken advantage of political turmoil to seize territory in northern Yemen. It was yet another reason why Yemen, despite its grinding poverty and relative lack of oil, was critical to the entire Arabian Gulf. In 2009 Saudi Arabia had sent troops across the border to confront the Houthis out of concern for its own security and (as yet unproven) suspicions that the Houthis were being supported by Iran.

Sheikh Anwar. They are also ready to take an oath to AQAP, so I would like to find a way to contact Abu Basir [Wuhayshi],' I told them. My hope was that I might be able to establish an avenue of communication through couriers as I had with Awlaki. That would give me a chance to re-establish myself as the group's point man in Europe – a source of supplies and recruits.

I was telling the truth. Shortly before travelling to Yemen I had met with a group in the Swedish city of Malmö who were looking for an overseas destination to wage jihad. Again, I had encountered them because of the many militants I had met over the previous decade. Danish intelligence had asked me to call on Abu Arab, the Danish-Palestinian who had adopted me during my visit to Lebanon back in 2007.

Abu Arab – real name Ali al-Hajdib – had spent some time in a Lebanese prison because of his role in the extremist Fatah al-Islam group. He had been tortured. The Danish government had done its duty and sent a diplomat to check on him in jail. Instead of thanking her he told her that when he came out he would kill her.

Despite his record, al-Hajdib had been allowed to resettle in Denmark. When I told him I was planning to return to Yemen, he urged me to come with him to Malmö to meet one of his brothers who lived there, yet another member of the Hajdib jihadist dynasty. I had met one brother – Saddam – shortly before he blew himself up as Lebanese security forces prepared to storm his house. Another was still languishing in jail for placing bombs on passenger trains in Germany. Their mother had produced eleven sons altogether and – as far as I knew – no daughters.

Two of the younger generation were especially keen to travel to Yemen. One was Abu Arab's nephew – a nineteen-year-old IT student who was tall, slim and fair-skinned, and had a short, wispy beard. He wore Western clothes to blend in and keep off the radar screen of security services. His cousin, who lived in Gothenburg, also enthused about going to Yemen.

The Hajdibs were afraid their residence might be bugged so we went for a walk in one of Malmö's public parks. When I told them I was returning to Yemen to re-establish contact with AQAP after the death of Awlaki, the young IT student looked elated.

'If you do re-establish contact we would like to come and to make *bayat* [an oath of allegiance to Wuhayshi]. I could offer myself to work on *Inspire* magazine,' he said.

I saw the Hajdibs as my next 'Warsame' – a conduit through whom I could learn more about AQAP, build a better picture of its intentions and alliances. I put the idea to Klang.

'These guys are very dangerous – ticking time bombs. It might be a good idea to send them to Yemen so that we can establish a new connection to the group,' I said.

Klang warmed to the prospect: 'You'd be in email contact with them without putting yourself in danger.'

But we knew this depended on me establishing contact with Wuhayshi, which PET then regarded as a long shot.

So I began to tell Mujeeb about the Hajdibs. It may sound like an absurd contradiction but I always tried to tell the truth as often as possible in my undercover work. It was the only way I could keep my story straight. Lying was easy, but remembering lies was difficult. Besides, if AQAP did connect with the Swedish militants, it would be important that they endorsed what I had said.

I told Mujeeb that I too wanted to avenge Awlaki's death; he promised he would make contact with Wuhayshi. I handed him a letter I had typed out for AQAP's leader on my laptop. It included plenty of red meat to get Wuhayshi's attention.

'My eyes are filled with tears over the great loss of my friend, my brother and my teacher, Shaheed Sheikh Anwar al-Awlaki, may Allah accept him as a pious man . . . Ameen. His death must be revenged with the kuffar's bloodshed and fear insha'Allah . . .

'Brother Anwar have requested from me to find brothers in Europe who could come over and get training with the intensions to return to their countries and work for our Deen. I have found a few and they are now ready insha'Allah.'

I had another card to play. My Kenyan friend Ikrimah, the long-haired al-Shabaab operative, wanted to establish contact with Wuhayshi now that Awlaki was no more. If I could connect them it would be an opportunity to track connections between different al-Qaeda affiliates, always a challenge for Western intelligence.

'Brother Ikrimah in Somalia has also found a few brothers with European and American citizenship, they too are clean and are ready to return after receiving the necessary skills,' I wrote. 'This brother got a special message for you from your own teacher from Afghanistan.'[2]

I also showed I was well aware of operational security.

'I cannot mention my name, my look or my nationality over this message, because it is not secure . . . Future communication should happen by a personal messenger, Adil [al-Abab] can receive my messages and forward them to you, and you can do the same in return. I do not accept any use of emails, mobiles, sms, phones etc'

A few days later Mujeeb and I met again. He told me he had just returned from meeting al-Qaeda figures in the tribal areas and had given them the letter.

'I might even be able to arrange a meeting for you with Abu Basir if you wish – perhaps in the New Year,' he said.

'Yes of course, definitely,' I said quickly, but with more than a tinge of apprehension. Such an encounter would be the most dangerous mission I had undertaken. Given the heavy fighting between government forces and al-Qaeda in the tribal areas, it also seemed very unlikely. Even as AQAP was taking on the Yemeni army in the south it had one eye on further attacks against America.

Mujeeb promised to provide me with sixteen gigabytes of unedited video footage from AQAP to circulate to their Western supporters. They had been unable to publish a new issue of *Inspire* since the deaths of Awlaki and Samir Khan and they were eager to advertise the territorial gains they were making in southern Yemen. Abdul showed me surveillance film shot recently of the US embassy in Sana'a and the Sheraton Hotel adjoining it. Unlike most top-class hotels, this one was surrounded by sandbags, and on the roof of the hotel were US soldiers, probably Marines. Abdul told me the group believed the Americans were running counter-terrorism operations from the hotel.

---

2 Ikrimah had recently emailed, asking me to deliver a long letter to Wuhayshi from an Islamic teacher who had taught the AQAP leader in Afghanistan many years previously. The teacher had recently been killed in Somalia.

Armed with the promises Mujeeb had made me, I returned to Denmark just before Christmas to brief PET. They seemed more interested than before – though we all knew a lot still hung on Mujeeb's word.

Klang suggested I travel across to Malmö again with Abu Arab to meet with the Hajdib clan. This was a risk for PET; they had no authority to send one of their agents on a fishing expedition in Sweden. PET and the Swedish intelligence agency, SAPO, cooperated in breaking up terrorist plots, but the Swedes would not be amused to find Danish intelligence running a freelance operation on their turf.

Even so the Danes saw an opportunity. The young English-speaking IT student would be the perfect candidate to succeed Samir Khan as the editor of *Inspire* magazine. I would have a key contact right at the heart of the group. The email address provided by *Inspire* was the portal through which supporters in the West could get in touch with the group. A year and a half after Aminah travelled to Yemen we were again plotting to send European extremists to join the terrorists.

The earnest IT student was still hungry. I met him and his father in a park in case SAPO were already eavesdropping.

'I've been to Yemen and passed on a message to Wuhayshi and am awaiting his reply. In the meantime you should prepare yourself,' I told him.

He was quietly jubilant, like a rookie player in the minor leagues suddenly called into the national team.

'I only wish I could go – but the *kuffar* are monitoring me too closely,' Abu Arab said. He was beaming with pride that a new generation of the Hajdib family were about to grasp the torch.

I returned to the UK for Christmas. It was not normally a time of year that I enjoyed. My childhood memories of what should have been a magical season were painful; as a father I rarely had my own children with me over the holidays. But this year Karima had agreed that they should stay with me and Fadia. Even though they had been brought up as Muslims, I spoiled them with gifts and every moment was precious. It was a bittersweet time. I knew I would soon have to return to Yemen and I found it hard to say goodbye.

I was always apprehensive before going on missions but this time I was especially uneasy. Finding Wuhayshi would truly take me into the lion's den. What troubled me most was that if I didn't come back alive, my kids might never know the truth about my life as a double agent. No doubt all they would see on the news was that another European jihadi had been killed overseas, and then my photograph would appear on the screen. Neither their mother nor their stepmother would be able to tell them that my life was not all it seemed.

Was I the veteran boxer extending his career one bout too far?

CHAPTER TWENTY-FOUR

THE LION'S DEN

January 2012

On 7 January 2012 I boarded a flight to Yemen. As I stared out from my window seat I listened to the band Metallica on my headphones. For five years their thumping tunes had helped pump me up before missions, but this time I turned up the volume extra loud.

Abdul was waiting at the airport for me, and we drove to his home, a comfortable three-storey brick building where I would stay for the next few days. Whatever businesses he had, they still appeared to be doing well.

Mujeeb visited but had neither news nor the video footage. It was time to exert some pressure.

'Do you know the brothers in different parts of Sweden collected the money for me to fly to Yemen so that I could gather this material and establish a connection with Abu Basir?' I said to Abdul angrily, channelling the role-playing lessons I had been given at the MI6 facility at Fort Monckton.

'Mujeeb is just wasting my time. I don't think he met with them. You know what – I'm going to travel down by myself to Abu Basir to tell him that Mujeeb is a liar.'

I had spoken without thinking. It was rash, committing me to a dangerous journey into the tribal areas. I checked myself. I could not let my determination to prove the CIA wrong make me do something stupid.

Abdul was anxious. He persuaded Mujeeb to call up a Yemeni militant who had connections to AQAP. His name was Hartaba. He had once worked as bin Laden's bodyguard in Afghanistan, and more recently he had been Awlaki's driver. He knew the safest – or the less treacherous – routes to territories controlled by AQAP. We could meet him on the road south from Sana'a.

The next day Abdul and I set out in his Toyota Corolla. My fears, felt so keenly in England, were not going away. Depending on whether he was a double or triple agent, Abdul could easily hand me over. What if the CIA had warned him about me?

But my immediate concern was to navigate the roadblocks out of Sana'a. I donned a Western business suit – for the first time in at least a decade – and held my iPhone to my ear, trying to make it look like I was taking calls. I was a businessman who had a meeting in Aden, and Abdul was my driver.

'Just look important,' he said.

I made my best impatient face at the soldiers. It worked.

After hours of driving, Abdul slowed down near a dusty settlement. The villagers eyed us suspiciously. This was bandit territory far from government control. My palms began to sweat; my toes curled.

A wiry young man climbed into the back of the car. I looked to see if he was armed, but tried to appear nonchalant.

'Do you know who that is?' Abdul asked me. 'It's Abu Basir's younger brother.'

He was the spitting image of Wuhayshi. I nearly hugged him with relief.

In the late afternoon we arrived at a small village just off the road from Sana'a to Aden that would not have been out of place in an Old Testament scene. Abdul pulled up outside what seemed a half-finished shack. 'This is Hartaba's house.'

Hartaba came to greet us. He was in his mid-forties but jihad had aged him. He was a caricature: a wiry frame and narrow face, big and slightly manic eyes, and a long beard. He tilted his head to hear because beatings in a Jordanian jail had left him almost deaf in one ear.[1]

Inside his bare home, Hartaba introduced us to two heavily armed Saudi fighters. We prayed together and then Hartaba told me to take

---

1 Hartaba had been captured by the Jordanians after fleeing Afghanistan at the end of 2001. He had been extradited to Yemen but escaped from jail in 2006 with Wuhayshi and other al-Qaeda members.

off my suit and put on traditional salwar kameez. He gave me tribal headgear to hide my face, though looking at my height and build he seemed to think I was beyond camouflage.

I noticed several of my new companions had mobile phones. I told them to take the batteries and SIM cards out so that US spy satellites could not fix our position. They seemed almost indifferent to the prospect of martyrdom but I was in no rush to become another victim of America's favourite weapon.

We set off in a Toyota Land Cruiser in the golden evening light for al-Qaeda's strongholds. Abdul and I sat up front next to Hartaba; the Saudi fighters and Wuhayshi's brother on the open-top cargo bed. The truck was full of weapons. I grasped a Kalashnikov which had been thrust into my hands along with an ammunition belt that was draped around me. The weapon was so long that I had to point the muzzle out of the window.

Abdul had a grenade launcher resting on his lap. 'Are you sure it's not going to go off?' he asked Hartaba after the car hit a large pothole and the top of the launcher banged against the roof. Abdul looked terrified, and I wondered again about his allegiance.

Hartaba got so annoyed that he stopped the car and explained that the weapon would only fire if levers were released. The same model had been used in an attack on the car of a senior British diplomat in Sana'a. He had been driving the getaway car used in the attack, he added, with a hint of pride.

'It missed by a few millimetres.'

Hartaba warmed to his theme and I could not help but admire the man for his sheer endurance. Hartaba said that on the day Awlaki died AQAP fighters had only been able to identify him by the skin on his forehead when they reached the carcass of the vehicle. Most of his body had been vaporized. Hartaba's eyes glistened as he told the story.[2]

He also talked about how AQAP was growing ever stronger in the southern tribal areas of Yemen. The group had raided military factories and taken machines to make their own ammunition.

---

2 Hartaba also said Awlaki had been devastated by the death of bin Laden. Hartaba had tried to cheer him up with practical jokes.

We passed through a checkpoint belonging to southern separatist fighters, who waved us on – another sign, I thought, of just how fast this country was falling apart. Villagers chanted 'al-Qaeda, al-Qaeda' as we clattered through dusty settlements. More than one policeman looked the other way. I glanced at Hartaba, who was miming along in a trance to the jihadist *nashids* blaring on a cassette player. To evade the last government checkpoint he went off-road and killed the headlights.

As the moon rose, we sped through the luminescent desert. Adrenalin surged through me and I felt a wave of exhilaration to be so deep behind enemy lines. For a few brief seconds on this perfect Arabian night I forgot all about my mission.

We reached the town of Jaar late that night. It had been transformed in the ten months since al-Qaeda fighters had seized control of it – renaming it the 'Emirate of Waqar' – or 'dignity'. It was now the capital of al-Qaeda's new statelet. The checkpoint we passed through was manned by Ansar al-Sharia fighters. The black banners of al-Qaeda were everywhere and fighters milled around the town. It was a new ground zero in the war on terrorism. Yemeni forces were positioned within firing range of the town and US, Saudi and Yemeni air power circled in the skies above. I realized that I was now in their crosshairs.

We pulled up at what passed for a restaurant and Hartaba went inside. He emerged with Adil al-Abab, AQAP's religious leader, whom I had befriended in Sana'a six years previously. His cheeks were even plumper. No wonder we had found him in one of Jaar's few functioning restaurants.

He had the same handlebar moustache above his pursed lips and still wore his beard short – probably because it wouldn't grow any longer.

'*Masha'Allah! As salaam aleikum* Abu Osama! How are you? How's your son, Osama?' al-Abab gushed.

'Fine. We are both fine.'

'We should go. You shouldn't be seen here if you want to come to meet Abu Basir. And I've got an old friend to introduce you to,' al-Abab said, with a broad smile.

We piled into al-Abab's white Toyota, a government vehicle the group had commandeered. He was a truly awful driver who had clearly taught himself after getting hold of the car. We juddered down pot-holed streets to a large house painted yellow and used for religious ceremonies. It was sparsely furnished but included a big chair with gold ornaments the militants had looted from the governor's headquarters.

The house had been requisitioned by Sheikh al-Hazmi, the nephew of the Muslim Brotherhood preacher Mohammed al-Hazmi. He had curly hair and unusually for a Yemeni green eyes. Al-Hazmi remembered me from my stay in Yemeni in 2001. He laughed to see me again after such a long time and we embraced. It was proof yet again of the value of the network I had built up over the years.

He, Abdul, al-Abab and I talked late into the night about the state of jihad in Yemen. Al-Abab said lots of Somalis had travelled to Yemen to fight with the group. Eventually Hazmi retired to join his family in their quarters upstairs, but al-Abab had one more question before he would let me go.

'Are you ready?' he asked, gravely.

'For what?' I asked.

'Will you take the oath? For al-Qaeda, for our emir Abu Basir?'

I replied I was prepared to take the oath but had certain conditions. 'I told Sheikh Anwar I don't accept civilian targets.'

'We already knew this – Abdul told me,' al-Abab replied.

I was left with no choice; I was about to become a signed-up member of al-Qaeda.

Taking his hand I made the oath: 'I will be true to Abu Basir, Leader of the Faithful, in all that obeys the will of Allah and His messenger. I will fight Allah's cause.'

'*Hamdulillah!*' al-Abab exclaimed.

I hardly slept that night – death might be around any corner. I even feared I might reveal myself to the brothers by talking in my sleep. I rose before dawn and walked out with al-Qaeda fighters to pray in the nearby mosque. As the first glimmer of dawn turned the eastern sky purple and then pink, the crack of distant mortar rounds interrupted the stillness. Yemeni military forces were bombarding the town, in one of their half-hearted attempts to retake Jaar.

The fighters hastened to the frontline, leaving me alone. Before departing they locked the heavy gates from the outside. I heard the clack of artillery fire and the roar of fighter jets overhead. Then there was the loud sucking sound of an explosion nearby, followed by a deafening roar. I could hear women and children screaming.

What if they're targeting this building? I suddenly thought. I went up to the roof but it was too high to jump. I was trapped.

I then had a sickening realization which made the aerial bombardment pale into insignificance.

I had left my North Face backpack in Sheikh al-Abab's car. Inside one of the pockets was a USB stick with the recording of my conversation with the CIA agent Michael back in Denmark.

I'd forgotten about it.

Game over.

I pictured my wife and kids back in Europe and wondered how they would take the news. I lay down on the floor and gazed up at the ceiling with a deep fatalism. I wished I hadn't watched so many of those brutal execution videos.

After several hours, Sheikh al-Abab returned to the house with fighters in tow and Abdul, who looked traumatized. I tried to appear relaxed but was ready to vomit. The Sheikh smiled.

'You forgot this in the car,' he said, handing me the bag. When I had a moment alone to look, I found the thumb drive still inside. I could have screamed with relief.

A few minutes later it was time to move on. I jumped into the back seat of a Toyota 4 × 4 next to Abdul and a young Saudi. Al-Abab rode shotgun with the driver. After a few minutes, he turned around and told us to lean forward and stare at the floor. We were on no account to look up until told to. We drove for a few more minutes.

The car stopped and a new passenger slid in next to me. I looked up and saw the unmistakable features of Nasir al-Wuhayshi – wispy beard, small, close-set eyes under his tribal scarf, and his trademark broad grin.

'*Salaam*,' he said cheerfully. He had a *miswak* – a Yemeni tooth-cleaning stick which the Prophet had recommended – in the corner of his mouth.

Somehow he was slighter than I had imagined.

'Murad, I know who you are. Anwar told me about you and I received your letter. I should tell you that Aminah is doing well. May Allah reward you for what you've done for her and Sheikh Anwar,' he said.

We set off with a car full of Wuhayshi's heavily armed bodyguards tailing us. We drove to a small farm outside Jaar, where we got out and walked across to a cornfield. Under the shade of some trees, we unpacked a meal of lamb and rice. The shade also provided some protection from drones, which could not be far away

I could not seem to eat everything in front of me. In an act of kindness, AQAP's leader was stealthily shovelling chunks of lamb towards me rather than eat them himself. No wonder he looked so thin.

At that point Sheikh al-Abab passed on a request to Wuhayshi from the young bearded Saudi fighter, who wanted to be put on a fast track for martyrdom. Wuhayshi considered for a few moments and then demurred; there were plenty who were ahead of him in the queue and he would have to wait his turn. The young Saudi looked crestfallen. I wanted to be sure I wasn't dreaming: a discussion over lunch of the suicide-bombing rota.

I was fascinated by Wuhayshi. He had the same softly spoken humility as his mentor, bin Laden, and exuded the same charisma. His fighters loved him and would do anything for him. No wonder people saw him as the leader-in-waiting of all al-Qaeda.

I had rolled up my sleeves to eat and Wuhayshi noticed one of my tattoos. It depicted the Norse god Thor's hammer but could easily be mistaken for a Christian symbol. 'Is that a cross?' asked Wuhayshi, one eyebrow raised.

'No,' I replied, laughing nervously, before telling the al-Qaeda emir that I had Thor tattooed on my forearm as a youngster. I gave Wuhayshi a quick lesson in Norse mythology. Thankfully he laughed too.

In fact the tattoo did not date back to my biker days. Late the previous year I had walked into a tattoo parlour in Copenhagen and had it inked on to my forearm. It was reckless. Had a militant noticed that I had suddenly acquired Thor's hammer I would have had some explaining to do. Perhaps at some level I was trying to escape the strait-jacket of my cover and reassert my identity.

Wuhayshi told the others to walk to the other side of the sandy field so we could talk in private.

'It is good you are here,' Wuhayshi said. 'I was about to head out of town, but I heard you were here so I delayed my trip.'

I told him I had sworn *bayat*, but as I had previously explained to Awlaki, I could not in good conscience be involved in targeting civilians.

'I know your position. But you should know: in Islam there is no such thing as civilians when it comes to the *kuffar*. They have chosen their states and governments,' Wuhayshi replied. That democracy thing again, I thought to myself.

There was a pause.

'But if I could choose I'd go after military targets,' Wuhayshi added.

Wuhayshi talked passionately about one day bringing the whole of Yemen under Islamic rule. 'The *Hadith* says Islam will be revived from Abyan,' he said, just as Awlaki had.

Wuhaysi confirmed the Saudi peace offer that Mujeeb had told me about, but said he had rejected it out of hand.

I told him about the letter my al-Shabaab contact Ikrimah wanted to send him from his former teacher, and offered to act as a bridge between AQAP and the Somali militant group. I needed to show him I could be useful.

'I was the one who sent Warsame to you,' I told him.

'Ah yes, the brother who got arrested on the sea. He was a very good brother and was always on the front. He was never scared. It is a shame the *kuffar* now have him.'

'We are actually in touch with some of the brothers in Somalia.'

I also told him about the militant group in Malmö, Sweden, and my own desire to get even for Awlaki's death.

He was particularly interested in the young IT student.

'Does he speak English?' he asked.

'Yes.'

'Then he can work on *Inspire* – we will arrange it,' he replied. We reminisced about Awlaki for a while. And then we talked about the cleric's sixteen-year-old son – Abdulrahman – who had been killed in a drone strike a month after his father. I remembered him that evening in 2006 as a young boy proudly presenting his homework to his father and looking after my son, Osama.

Although the strike was targeting other fighters it had provoked controversy in the US because of Abdulrahman's age and the fact he was an American citizen. Wuhayshi told me that Abulrahman had formally joined the group before he was killed.

I told Wuhayshi that, prior to Awlaki's death, the cleric had requested I bring him supplies. I was referring to the fridge and hexamine briquettes. The way he replied made it clear he knew what I was talking about.

'Should I carry on with this mission?' I asked.

'Yes, you should bring these things,' Wuhayshi said.

Wuhayshi wanted me to meet AQAP's chief bomb-maker, Ibrahim al-Asiri, who he said was some 150 miles away in Azzan, deep in Shabwa province.

Azzan was a desolate town halfway between the coast and Ataq, where Anwar al-Awlaki's son had died in the US drone attack some months previously. Al-Qaeda had seized the town a few weeks before the strike.

'Asiri's now the number three on the United States' most wanted list,' he added, with a note of satisfaction.

Al-Asiri was now in charge of overseeing the group's overseas attacks; he would be interested in the Swedish brothers who wanted to travel to Yemen.

The bomb-maker already had one Swedish operative working for him. Anders, the PET intelligence analyst, had told me that the suspected Swedish-Yemeni mastermind of the plot against *Jyllands-Posten* in December 2010 had escaped to Yemen and was now believed to be with al-Asiri.[3]

---

3 Al-Asiri was all the more dangerous for his knowledge of chemistry, which he had studied at King Saud University in Riyadh and was now passing on to apprentice bomb-makers. Like hundreds of other young Saudis, he had been determined to fight

Al-Asiri had sent his own brother to his death, built the underwear device that came close to bringing down flight 253 over Detroit on Christmas Day 2009, and constructed the so-called printer bombs. He was, put simply, among the most dangerous terrorists in the world.

To meet al-Asiri would surely reopen doors to the CIA, with a red carpet. But it would be tempting fate to travel to see him. The USB stick contained my only recording of the meeting with the CIA officer in Helsingør. If I threw it away I would also lose crucial corroborating evidence of my work for the intelligence services. But if I kept it I might not be around too much longer. I guessed the security around al-Asiri would be even tighter than that around Wuhayshi, and there was a real risk the USB would be discovered.

I had to think on my feet. 'Sheikh, that might not be possible. I told the soldiers at the checkpoints that I was on my way to Aden and if they don't see me there soon they may raise an alarm,' I told Wuhayshi.

It was a lame excuse but I knew the Yemeni government, under pressure from the Americans, was trying to keep tabs on the movements of Westerners.

'You will need to carry on to Aden, then. But when you get there you should set up email accounts with Abdul and Hartaba so we can communicate,' Wuhayshi replied.

We piled back into the vehicle and Wuhayshi gave me a tour of the al-Qaeda emirate. 'Make sure you keep your head wrapped up – we are worried about spies,' al-Abab told me.

The town was an alternative universe. Rusty old police cars patrolled the streets, driven by heavily bearded Islamist fighters. Strict Islamic law had been introduced and those who flouted it were punished.

Just a few days after my visit to Jaar, al-Qaeda's punishments reached a new level when an Islamic court ruled that a man suspected of spying for the Americans should be executed and crucified. According to residents his body was left hanging by a main road in Jaar for days. I would

in Iraq against the US occupation. He was arrested by Saudi security forces as he tried to cross the border into Iraq, but was released after a brief time in prison, which further radicalized him. After his militant cell in Riyadh was broken up by the Saudi security services, al-Asiri and his brother had fled to Yemen.

most likely have suffered the same fate had my true intent been uncovered.[4]

The code of laws imposed by al-Qaeda was called *Hudood*, a medieval form of justice long obsolete in most of the Muslim world. The al-Qaeda figure instrumental in setting up and overseeing *Hudood* courts in Yemen was none other than Sheikh Adil al-Abab, AQAP's amiable religious emir, whose portly frame was squeezed into the back seat next to me.

Wuhayshi would later depict AQAP's administration of justice as a model of restraint. A few months later, he wrote to the al-Qaeda group occupying part of Mali in West Africa, advising: 'Try to avoid enforcing Islamic punishments as much as possible, unless you are forced to do so . . . we used this approach with the people and came away with good results.'

As we drove around Jaar, Wuhayshi pointed out various public works projects. Al-Qaeda was handing out food, digging wells and storage tanks, driving water trucks around, bringing in free electricity to areas that had never known it, and providing other services that the central government in Sana'a had neglected for decades.

For Wuhayshi this was a means to an end. In his letter of advice to the jihadis occupying northern Mali he would write: 'Try to win them over through the conveniences of life and by taking care of their daily needs like food, electricity and water. Providing these necessities will have a great effect on people, and will make them sympathize with us.'

We stopped for a while at a cemetery for the martyrs of al-Qaeda in the semi-desert outside the town – row upon row of graves marked with little more than a stone. Their puritanical beliefs prohibited any sort of tombs. There were hundreds of fighters buried but you could walk right through it and never even know it was a graveyard.

---

4 Later that year fighters in the tribal areas beheaded a Yemeni woman they accused of sorcery and paraded her severed head. Her crime had been to work as a healer using natural herbs. In late 2012 Amnesty International documented the horrific human rights violations perpetrated by the group in Jaar on those it judged to have flouted 'Islamic law', including public summary killings, amputation and flogging.

Wuhayshi made a supplication – '*As salaam aleikum ya ahlul-qubur!* . . .' [Peace be upon you, O inhabitants of the grave] and we moved on.

I told Wuhayshi I planned to take a bodyguard course in the UK. 'Then you should become my personal bodyguard,' he replied. He told me his own team of bodyguards had not followed them after the picnic.

'They didn't notice me getting back in the car with you – you could have kidnapped me,' he said. We laughed. It bordered on the absurd.

It was time for AQAP's leader to depart and he embraced me before jumping into the car with Adil al-Abab. 'Wait here, I'll be back shortly,' AQAP's religious emir told me and Abdul.

An hour later the sound of screeching wheels announced his return. Al-Abab walked over to us with a grave expression on his face. Had someone told him about the flash drive? But he addressed Abdul.

'*Alhamdulillah*, we think your brother has just been martyred – can you come to see his body?' he blurted out.

Abdul, already affected by his exposure to the frontline in Jaar, could not summon the courage to go. He asked me if I would view the body; I had met his brother a few times in Sana'a. I was taken to a makeshift morgue to see the corpse. The man had horrific injuries. A mortar shell had entered through his cheek and blown out the left side of his brain and there were shrapnel wounds all over the chest. But the right side of his face was more or less intact, with his mouth curled up in a smile. He definitely looked like Abdul's brother. I stared at him.

I went back to tell Abdul and this time he came with me to take a look. 'It's him,' he said. He crouched beside him in a moment of silence to pay his respects and then turned on his heels. But then he hesitated and doubled back to inspect the dead man's teeth.

'This man has no fillings – it's not my brother,' he said, breaking into the first smile I had seen from him since we arrived. It seemed a fitting finale in what had been a surreal visit.

I was glad I would soon be travelling on to Aden. If a missile strike or mortar round were to kill me here I would be buried in the anonymous strip of dirt with al-Qaeda's other martyrs, and the truth about which side I was fighting for would surely be buried with me for ever.

We bade farewell to Adil al-Abab and the other fighters, including the would-be Saudi suicide bomber and Wuhayshi's younger brother. The Saudi kissed me on the forehead and then Wuhayshi's younger brother looked at me earnestly:

'Do you love the martyrs?'

'Yes,' I replied. I got the feeling he wanted to be one of them.

'May He whom you love, love me for loving you,' he said.

'*As salaam aleikum,*' I replied – peace be with you. He would never understand the irony.

I got in the car with Hartaba and Abdul for the dangerous drive to Hartaba's village, where we picked up Abdul's car. All the way to Aden, I pictured the look on Jesper's and Klang's faces at our future debriefing. I had enjoyed lunch and a few jokes with the leader of al-Qaeda in the Arabian Peninsula.

Wuhayshi's task for me in Aden was simple: create three email accounts for our future communications and hand them to Abdul, who would pass them on to Wuhayshi's men in the city.

After I created the accounts at an internet café, Abdul parked the car in a commercial street in Aden, just down the road from a call centre, the safest option for calling Wuhayshi's contacts. I watched dozens of customers walking in and out.

It shouldn't be taking this long, I thought, my suspicions about Abdul racing.

Across the street, something caught my eye. A car had pulled up and the driver was cleaning one of the side mirrors with a bucket of water and a sponge, glancing up occasionally. His surveillance training was good, except that he cleaned the same mirror time and again. And with all the dust and chaos of Aden, the exercise was pointless.

Was I about to become the victim of a set-up? I was relieved but also irritated when Abdul finally emerged.

'The emir's men will meet me here in an hour so that I can show them the email addresses – you should stay in the car.'

I had little option. When they came, Wuhayshi's emissaries did not look like jihadis. Both were clean-shaven, dark-skinned like many in Aden, and wore long *thawbs*. They greeted Abdul and disappeared inside a shop. The avid mirror cleaner was still across the street. He stared at them, his sponge dripping water.

I insisted on driving when Abdul got back in the car, and took a random route to shake off any tail. I ran through scenarios. Whose side was Abdul on? Had al-Qaeda sent somebody to monitor the pick-up? Or had Abdul spent so long in the call centre because he was calling a CIA handler to arrange for surveillance so the Americans could put a tail on Wuhayshi's representatives in Aden? As my mind raced I also wondered if this was all part of an American ploy for Abdul to take my place in Yemen. Might he have given Wuhayshi's men different email addresses so that he and not I would be in touch with Wuhayshi? He certainly had many jihadist contacts but given all the precautions taken by AQAP's leadership he was too low in the pecking order to get an audience with Wuhayshi. He had one ticket to the top table of al-Qaeda and that was through me. But that made me vulnerable.

I was relieved to leave Aden and escape Abdul's company. Maybe it was paranoia, but stranger things had happened. Back in Sana'a, I called Klang.

'I just met the big guy,' I told him in a thick Danish dialect.

CHAPTER TWENTY-FIVE

OPERATION AMANDA

January–May 2012

The one inevitable part of a successful mission was a debriefing invitation with PET. This time Klang chose Lisbon.

I was put up at the luxury Altis Avenida Hotel. Klang and Jesper had brought along a young analyst whose nickname was 'the Virgin'. It was obvious why. 'This is the biggest thing I've been part of,' he told me excitedly.

PET's spymaster, Tommy Chef, flew in later to join us, clearing his schedule. He handed me an envelope with 100,000 DKK – around $15,000. In the debriefing, I noticed how much the Danish team already knew about whom I had met in Jaar. Had they received word from the Americans courtesy of Abdul? If so, they were being very clumsy in tipping me off.

We all realized there was an opportunity to plant tracking devices in the fridge that Wuhayshi still wanted me to deliver. The fridge would most likely be sent on to Ibrahim al-Asiri, the bomb-maker, to store explosives, and thus could offer a unique chance to target him and also locate Wuhayshi. I told the agents I was willing to return to Yemen within two weeks.

'To be honest most people in the office thought you were done – finished,' Jesper told me on the balcony of our hotel after business was concluded that evening. 'Very few of us thought you could continue to work after what happened to Anwar.'

He paused. We watched the traffic drift past below on the Praça dos Restauradores.

'It's fucking good you are on our side – imagine the problems you would have caused us,' he added, slapping me on the back.

Of course, Klang organized a night out. We hit some of Lisbon's most exclusive bars and a gentlemen's club, champagne flowing freely, generating a bill of about $8,000 for the Danish taxpayer. The Danish agents all found 'companions' for the evening. Even Tommy Chef paired up with an East European woman. They were entangled on the couch when I left to return to the hotel.

Soon afterwards I travelled to Denmark to set up another meeting with the Hajdib clan, across the bridge in Malmö.

Oblivious to the raw cold of a February afternoon, Abu Arab and his nephew sat on a park bench enraptured as I recounted the details of my journey to and experiences in Jaar. It was as if I were Homer reciting the *Iliad* for the first time. The IT student wanted to know how soon they could travel. I told them I was awaiting instructions from the AQAP leadership.

What I did not know was that PET had finally come clean with Swedish intelligence about the Malmö ploy. The Swedes quashed it immediately. The idea of Swedish citizens being sent to join a terrorist group was beyond the pale.

On my return to Copenhagen I vented my frustrations with Klang: 'How the hell am I meant to maintain my networks if the rug is going to be pulled from beneath me like this?'

He had no answer; the decision had been taken higher up.

It turned out that we had missed a promising opportunity. A short while later AQAP released a new issue of *Inspire* magazine with a section entitled 'Rise Up and Board with Us'. From now on, it said, 'those who want to execute a slaughter to the enemies of Islam' should seek approval for their targets from AQAP's military committee. The magazine provided email addresses and details of how to download the Mujahideen Secrets software. It was essentially promoting itself as a clearing house for would-be terrorists in the West. Had our IT student been involved with *Inspire*, we could have had a window on AQAP's overseas recruitment drive and plots being hatched by its supporters in the West.

In any case, I had lost contact with Wuhayshi: no replies came back from the encrypted messages I sent to the three email accounts I had opened in Aden. Perhaps Abdul had deliberately passed on different email addresses to the ones I had created. I sent an encrypted email to Aminah telling her I needed to get in touch with Wuhayshi because I wanted to connect him to my contacts in al-Shabaab but received no reply. I wondered if she had already attained martyrdom.

For weeks I heard nothing from Danish intelligence, and the nightmares started to return, given fresh fuel by my eventful visit to Jaar. It was not until the beginning of March that PET finally summoned me. Klang arranged for us to meet in the same villa in the Marienlyst Hotel in which I had confronted the CIA agent months earlier.

It was good to be inside. An icy wind was blowing in from the Baltic, sending waves crashing on to the shore. Klang and I sat in the kitchen.

'We've been in touch with the Americans,' he said. 'They are prepared to offer you one million dollars if our mission leads to Wuhayshi and one million for al-Asiri.

'In addition they are offering one million dollars for Qasim al-Raymi. And if you later lead us to Ikrimah al-Muhajir they are offering a million kroner [around $180,000].'

I contemplated those on the hit list. Al-Raymi was a senior deputy to Wuhayshi. Klang would later tell me that the Americans suspected that Aminah had become betrothed to him after Awlaki's death.

Ikrimah, my long-haired Kenyan contact, had clearly climbed the ladder within al-Shabaab. His emails to me hinted he was in touch with Ahmed Abdi Godane – the shadowy and ruthless leader of al-Shabaab. The previous month Godane had formally merged the group into the global al-Qaeda network and appeared determined to transform it from an insurgent militia into a terror group ready to strike in Africa and beyond.

Ikrimah was now based in the Somali port city of Kismayo. The previous autumn Kenyan and African Union forces had launched an offensive against al-Shabaab, pushing the group out of Mogadishu and some of its strongholds in the south.

In response the group had vowed 'severe repercussions' in Kenya. In an email to me Ikrimah said he longed to take 'revenge' against the Kenyan government.

His emails had indicated he was still working closely with foreign operatives within al-Shabaab, including my American friend from Sana'a, Jehad Serwan Mostafa, known within al-Shabaab as 'Ahmed Gure'.[1]

Ikrimah was also working with perhaps the most wanted woman in the world – Samantha Lewthwaite, widow of one of the 7/7 London bombers, Germaine Lindsay. A mother of four who had been dubbed the 'White Widow' by the UK tabloids, she was on the run in East Africa after Kenyan police had come close to arresting her in Mombasa.[2]

'Kenya is getting really bad coz the kufar are doing all their effort to harm us,' Ikrimah emailed me. 'So you need to be extra carefull they dont get a single trace of anything coz they are now tracing a sister who was a window [sic] of one of the london 7/7 bomber (the jamecan brother) and they are accusing her of financing and organising terorisim.'[3]

Ikrimah was also friendly with an American who had become a prominent mouthpiece for al-Shabaab – Omar Hammami. Originally from Alabama, Hammami had won fame for posting jihadist rap songs on YouTube and calling on other foreigners to join al-Shabaab.

Hammami was eccentric and unpredictable and had recently fallen out with al-Shabaab's leader, Godane, over strategy, making Hammami fear for his life. In March he would release an extraordinary video claiming Shabaab's leadership was planning to assassinate him. Ikrimah had told me he feared his association with Hammami might place him in

1 Jehad Serwan Mostafa may have played a role in forging the February 2012 alliance between al-Qaeda and al-Shabaab. In October 2011 he had appeared in an al-Shabaab video stating he had been sent as an envoy by Zawahiri to Somalia to help distribute food aid to famine victims. It seems likely he would have carried messages between the two leaderships at the time they were negotiating the merger.

2 As of April 2014, Lewthwaite was still on the run.

3 Ikrimah added that money had grown tight after intelligence services increased their monitoring of the hawala money transfer system in Kenya, which had been used by jihadis there to transfer money to jihadis in Somalia.

danger too. In an email he had asked me to take care of his wife and daughters if he was killed.[4]

Shabaab was riven by internal conflicts and it seemed Ikrimah's climb up the hierarchy had created a new set of perils.

As Klang's words sank in, I realized I was not primarily motivated by the sums on offer for neutralizing the CIA's targets. I mainly wanted to hear that the Americans needed me again, driven on by wounded pride and the fear that Abdul might supplant me.

Klang's message about the rewards on offer came with strings attached. 'And on top of that we'd like ten per cent. Akhi, we also want to have some fun out of it. We can negotiate for you then.'

I nodded but said nothing. Now I had seen it all. A representative of Queen Margrethe's government was asking for a percentage of any reward I might receive from the US.

I wished my iPhone was recording the discussion, as it had the last time I'd sat in this villa. I wondered whether PET was altogether out of control or whether I had had the misfortune to be paired with its most dishonest officer.

Klang had sensed an opportunity and was ready to take a big personal risk.

'Big Brother doesn't want to deal directly with you any more so we would be the ones handling you from now on,' he said. I had little choice. I needed to earn the premium rate for overseas missions after spending so much to set up Storm Bushcraft.

The Americans clearly wanted to keep me at arm's length. Perhaps they didn't trust me; perhaps they thought I was high risk. Michael, sitting in the same cottage just a few months before, had surely drawn up a damning report. But I had already risked my life to meet Wuhayshi and I still wanted that heavyweight title.

'What guarantee do I have they won't screw me over this time?' I asked.

---

4 Ikrimah asked me whether he might be able to send his wife and children to Dammaj in Yemen or a similar religious institution. 'I am thinking of the future of the children i want them to have proper islamic education . . . anything can happen any time,' he wrote in an email in March 2012.

'You don't,' Klang replied, with a smugness that made me itch to punch him.

'I need to be sure that if I die my wife and kids will be taken care of,' I told him. My trip to Jaar had impressed on me the dangers that would lie ahead.

'They'd be in line to receive a million kroner ($180,000),' Klang promised.

'I'd be more comfortable if the Americans paid that up front,' I replied. I could hardly argue my family's corner from beyond the grave.

'We'll look into that.'

Klang promised that PET would also get my wife permanent residence status in Denmark before I travelled. I wanted to make sure she could continue to live in Europe if I was killed.

I went home to England to consider my options.

Against all the odds I had forced myself back into contention. As a freelancer I'd got on first-name terms with one of al-Qaeda's most important men. But still I was getting little support, and rather too many demands, from my handlers. And the situation in Yemen was far more treacherous than when I had made contact with Awlaki just a year earlier.

Two weeks later Jesper and Soren, the team leader, came to England. They had received permission from British intelligence to meet me on their patch. Klang was not with them; his security clearance had been suspended when he was arrested after a brawl at a pizzeria in Copenhagen. In another incident not likely to advance his career, he had been caught having sex with the mistress of PET's Director-General, Jakob Scharf,[5] in the toilets at the agency's Christmas party. Maybe Klang too was battling demons.

---

5 Scharf's tenure at the head of PET was to become embroiled in scandal. But at this stage he had been in the job nearly five years and was a powerful figure with deep connections throughout the Danish establishment. Before being appointed as Director-General of the Intelligence Service he had been Deputy Commissioner of Denmark's national police service.

Over breakfast in their hotel, Soren and Jesper conveyed to me the Americans' final word on the life insurance 'deposit' I had requested.

'We can get you fifty thousand dollars up front – they won't go a dollar higher,' Jesper said. The former banker had clearly been designated as the numbers guy.

It was not what I was hoping for, but I was working my way back to the summit and was still climbing in the foothills.

'I can live with that.'

Soren told me a plan was taking shape. I would drive down with Abdul as I had in January and deliver the supplies with the hidden tracking devices to Wuhayshi.

'When do I leave?'

'Soon,' Soren said.

They had brought my wife's Danish residence application and helped me fill in the paperwork.

'There won't be any difference between her and a Danish citizen,' Jesper declared.

Afterwards we drove into the countryside. I had promised to take them quad-biking. Soon we were racing along tracks, spattered in mud. It was the perfect pressure release valve. The only blemish was that Jesper broke his ankle after getting his foot caught in the track. I was stunned to see the insurance disclaimers they had signed. They had used their real names and Soren had listed an address in the vicinity of PET headquarters in Søborg as his home address. Had they been taught nothing?

Late in March, I was preparing for my most challenging and possibly final mission when an email dropped into my inbox. It was encrypted and it came from Aminah. She was still alive.

'Yes, yes,' I muttered to myself. The guilt of luring her to Yemen had never left me.

She said she had been divorced from the outside world for months and had only just received an email I had sent to her late the previous year. Her letter was long and rambling, peppered with Koranic references. Despite everything she had not lost the faith.

Aminah sent greetings to me and her 'dear sister' Fadia and talked about dreams she'd had that her husband would be killed – dreams which had continued after his death. I could empathize.

'Two weeks after his shuhadu I saw him in my dreams . . . We were talking and I told him I want to do martyrdom operation, and he said it is great idea, he was very happy about it. In my dream he was so close and yet so far away.

'He look so beautiful, in white dress, glowing and shining, he appeared above me . . . He was happy and smilling and he told me, Aminah – come to me, come to me.'

But she was still on this earth, thanks to none other than Nasir al-Wuhayshi.

'I wanted to do a martyrdom operation but Shaykh Basir [Wuhay-shi] said that sisters so far will not do the operations because it would bring a lot of problems for them and then government would start to imprisoning Ansar sisters which would be very bad. So I cannot do the operation, I am praying for shuhada, I want to be killed like my husband was. Insha'Allah.'

Instead she was put to work – a blonde waif from the Balkans now committed to al-Qaeda.

'I am in contact with brothers now as I am started to work on Inspire [magazine], alhamdidullah.'

But – and here the guilt kicked in again – Aminah felt isolated and afraid.

'I didn't here from my family for a year and I do not know what is happening. I am sending letters to my sister but she doesn't responding. I do not know is she under the preassure of government or secret service . . . I ask Shaykh Basir can I come back after he didn't approve martyrdom operation, and he said I cannot. He said that my government wanted to put me in prison. I do not know that . . . And my husband told him in a case that he is killed he doesn't want me to come back.

'Is there any chance you can check am I on CIA wanted list or no fly list?' she asked.

Despite my sympathy, she was also a possible conduit for reaching Wuhayshi again and putting the second phase of the mission into gear. She clearly had a direct line to him.

'Insha'Allah you will receive a mail from Amir [Wuhayshi], I sent message to him. Insha'Allah you will manage to connect Somalia and Yemen.'

She ended with a note of fatalism:

'So I am here for now. Untill situation change insha'Allah. Shuhada would be the best solution for me.'

I had visions of a double triumph, rescuing Aminah and at the same time putting an electronic tag on Wuhayshi.

My orders to travel to Yemen finally came towards the end of April. It wasn't before time. I'd been ready to go for more than three months, and didn't understand why PET was holding back. Not knowing had further strained my relationship with Fadia, who could not understand why I was so agitated, constantly checking my phone for texts. I was so restless at night, muttering to myself in Danish, that she asked me to sleep on the sofa.

There was time for one last outing with my children. I took them to Waterworld, a theme park not far from Birmingham. They were in their element, slaloming down the water chutes and jumping in the pools and fountains. I tried to look as though I was enjoying it, but more than once felt tears welling.

I went to Copenhagen to discuss the final details of the mission and craft a response to Aminah. 'I am still not over the Sheikh . . .' I wrote to her, 'I have lost my friend brother teacher may Allah accept him as Shaheed.

'Regarding CIA then give me some time I cannot search their website from my town. I have also forgotten your name in your passport so you need to mail it to me again Inshallah. I don't think it's a crime if they find out you have been married to Sheikh. Just tell them you have been kept hostage and had no way of escaping. You have not committed any crime and they cannot prove your marriage to him.'

I felt treacherous using Aminah as a way to reach Wuhayshi, but justified it to myself by hoping that one day – if we remained in touch – I could help her.

'I agree with Sheikh Abu Basir don't do any actions without considering it carefully Inshallah. This is very important you give this message to Sheikh Abu Basir,' I wrote. 'Tell him I got the stuff for your husband and the stuff he asked me for. The stuff is ready and I should be at his place around the 10th [of May] Inshallah.'

I had another message for her to convey – one that would show Wuhayshi the importance of keeping lines open to me.

'Somalia . . . they are nagging me again for coming over to Yemen. Tell him that Abu Musab al-Somali and Ikrimah have intentions to come ASAP it seems like it's very important.'

I might well need her help: every avenue was precious.

'I have heard that Hartaba has been killed. Is this true? Then I ask Allah to accept him. He was my only way into Sheikh Abu Basir. Now how will I enter?'

I promised I would bring clothes for her and told her to take care of herself, signing off: 'Your brother Polar Bear.'

PET clearly liked Helsingør, the resort town on the coast near Copenhagen. They invited me to a summer house nearby to discuss next steps. The lashings of winter storms had given way to a mild spring and the Baltic was a placid blue-green.

Klang was back on the team because of the importance of the mission. We sat down in the reception room.

'We've discussed the Aminah situation,' Jesper told me. 'Our feeling is that it would be dangerous for her to come back to Europe. As you wrote in your email, there's no guarantee that she would be arrested and she could be a ticking time bomb.'

I wondered if he meant a time bomb for innocent civilians or for Danish intelligence. Perhaps they had calculated that her story would implicate them in a legally questionable operation.

I asked my handlers why there had been so much delay in sending me back to Yemen. Klang said implausibly that it was because the Americans were re-purposing spy satellites previously monitoring Afghanistan.

We discussed the mission. I was to meet Abdul in Sana'a and we would drive down to deliver the supplies.

'It's really important you stick with Abdul,' Klang said.

'Don't make a mockery of my intelligence,' I retorted. 'Don't you think I know he is working for the Americans?'

Klang threw up his arms. 'Fine, yes, he is working for them but as far as the Americans are concerned – you don't know this, okay?'

Finally my suspicions were confirmed. I had tried to flush Abdul out after the Lisbon meeting with a terse email in which I told him that I had been stopped by Danish security services at Copenhagen airport and warned that they knew about my visit to the south of Yemen. Someone had told them something, I wrote to Abdul, and my guess was that it was him.

Of course, nothing of the sort had happened, but I needed to lay the bait. I had received no reply, and that was confirmation enough for me.

'I have something for you,' Jesper said, changing the subject.

He came back clutching a make-up box. 'A present for Aminah from the Americans.'

It was a large oval box, plastic. When I opened the lid there was a mirror on the underside and beneath were rows of neatly packaged lipsticks, nail varnishes and eye shadow.

'Be careful how you handle it – it's a seriously expensive piece of kit,' Klang said.

Jesper said that if Aminah was engaged or already married to Qasim al-Raymi, one of Wuhayshi's senior deputies in AQAP and the second most powerful commander, a tracking device inside the make-up box might enable the Americans to target him.

'If Abu Basir decides to crush the make-up box in front of me and finds the device what am I going to say?' I asked. I felt uneasy. Two years previously the Danes had judged it too dangerous for me to supply Aminah a similarly modified cosmetics case. Had I become expendable?

'Just blame it on Abdul and let him be the fall guy,' Klang replied.

Not for the first time, Klang astonished me with his gall. It was never his problem, always someone else's. There was a blithe answer for everything.

'No, I'd never do that,' I replied. 'You have just told me he is working for us. We are on the same side.'

He had no answer but instead handed me a new iPhone the Americans had provided.

'This will allow us to follow your movements in real time. Leave it on all the time. If anything happens you can call us for assistance but only use it in emergencies.'

The Danes also gave me a sports bag with clothing for Aminah.

I caught the television news that night in my room in the summer house. Yemen was the lead: a new plot by AQAP against US-bound aeroplanes had been thwarted. It had involved the most sophisticated device yet designed by Ibrahim al-Asiri. But the man AQAP had selected for the attack – a Saudi recruit with a British passport – was a mole working for the intelligence services.[6]

The Saudi operation had culminated with the agent and another informant – most likely his handler – being whisked out of Yemen. Perhaps that's why my own mission had been delayed: Western intelligence already had a mole close to AQAP's senior leadership. But after he was extracted they had turned to me again.

Yemen was in a fog of war, which only complicated matters. It had a new president, Abd Rabbu Mansour Hadi. What he lacked in a power base he made up for with political manoeuvring and the promise of greater cooperation with Washington.

His focus was on reversing al-Qaeda's gains in the south. The group still controlled a stretch of coastline adjacent to some of the world's busiest shipping lanes, as well as several towns inland. Unless the Yemeni army – starved of supplies and leadership – acted quickly, even Aden might fall to the fundamentalists.

Government forces aided by tribal militia had embarked on a spring offensive. Wuhayshi's fighters were resisting fiercely, but air strikes were intensifying, aided no doubt by US intelligence, and regime forces were inching towards Jaar.

As I read an account of the battles, I asked myself one simple question.

'How the hell are Abdul and I going to be able to drive down there in the middle of a war?'

The next day I asked the Danish agents about the $50,000 payment they had promised my family.

---

6 The man had infiltrated the group in early 2012 after being recruited by Saudi counter-terrorism the previous year. Before switching sides he had lived in the UK for a long time and had moved in radical circles there – just like me. His background had given him credibility and his British passport had enhanced his appeal, because it allowed him to travel without a visa to the US.

'That's being processed – you should get it very soon after you return from Yemen,' Jesper replied.

If I return, I thought gloomily.

They had me on the hook. They knew I was hungry, focused – and were taking advantage.

Jesper handed over the immigration document for my wife, but rather than permanent status it conferred the right of residence for five years. I was furious. If I died there was no assurance my wife could stay beyond that and she would be in great danger in Yemen if word leaked that I had been an informant.

'We never promised her permanent resident status,' Jesper said.

I couldn't believe my ears. More than any reward, my wife's security was paramount.

I stormed out of the villa – shouting at Jesper as I left: 'You know what? I'm done.' As always, I'd quit first and negotiate later.

I spent that evening in my mother's house in Korsør. She had known about my work but had been the soul of discretion. I told her about my frustrations.

'I bet you Abdul is not even in Yemen. And if he's not there I have a feeling they'll want me to drive down myself and be killed in the fighting,' I told her.

It was all beyond her comprehension. Why should I even want to be involved in such a scheme? She looked at me in disbelief. It was far from the first time I had seen that expression.

I called a number Abdul had given me to use in Yemen. His wife answered. 'My husband is not here,' she said.

In a fit of pique I ignored calls from Danish intelligence but after two days finally took one from Klang. I told him I'd only meet them if the boss – Tommy Chef – was present. We agreed to meet at the Scandic Hotel in Ringsted, halfway between Korsør and Copenhagen. When I arrived, Tommy Chef was outside the lobby, checking messages on his phone.

'Hello, Morten. It's good to see you again. I'm sorry for these misunderstandings. Let's go inside to talk, just the two of us.'

In his suite he sat down opposite me on a sofa and looked me straight in the eye.

'I'm sorry for the mix-up. My agents had no authority to promise your wife these documents. There are steps that need to be taken; you can't just apply straight away for a permanent residence. But I've now taken charge of this and I can personally guarantee she will receive permanent residence status. As for the money I can also guarantee you will get it when you come back.'

His voice was calm and even, as if he were clearing up after some mischievous children.

'I'm glad to hear it,' I replied. 'Abdul is not in the country. How on earth am I supposed to get down to the tribal areas?' I asked.

'Yes, we know that. Believe it or not he's in China, but he'll get back the day after you arrive in Sana'a. It's all under control.'

He paused for effect.

'Morten, this is one of the most important missions in the history of Danish intelligence. Our director, Jakob Scharf, is closely following this. It's really vital you travel down to do this.'

The counsellor had just become a coach.

I had one more request. I wanted Klang and Jesper to come to Korsør and tell my mother about the mission. I wanted an insurance policy, some incentive for them to protect me. They would know that if something bad happened to me my mother could go to the media and explain what I was really doing in a remote corner of Yemen, hanging out with al-Qaeda's leadership. What they didn't know was that she had a copy of the photograph of the three of us in the pool in Reykjavik.

'Go and do what you need to do in Korsør and then let's meet for a nice dinner tonight,' Tommy Chef told me, charm personified. He smiled and placed his hand briefly on my shoulder in reassurance.

My mother lived on a quiet street in Korsør. The back garden was perfectly manicured, with a swing set and slide for the grandchildren who – sadly – rarely visited. She had at last found a gentle, honourable man to share her life with, a man I came to like. The inside of the house was an obstacle course for the clumsy: carefully placed china, cushions and ornaments meticulously arranged.

Klang and Jesper arrived wearing jeans and T-shirts and looking uncomfortable. I was sure this was the first time they had come to explain to an agent's mother what her son was doing, like schoolboys wanting permission to go for a bike ride. My mother greeted them with reserved Danish courtesy. Her husband was confined to the kitchen – not permitted to see officials of Denmark's secret service.

They moved to the living room, picking up the decorative cushions and holding them awkwardly. Light streamed in through the French windows. It was a picture of suburban orderliness.

Klang and Jesper were trying – not very successfully – to grapple with my family background. How could this hooligan have emerged from such genteel surroundings? They did not know the long and painful backstory.

We sat in silence as my mother made coffee. Klang took a sip from one of the delicate china cups and carefully replaced it on the saucer. I was amused to see that he was terrified of breaking something.

'Mrs Storm,' he began, with a synthetic cheeriness. 'You have to know Morten is a real one-off because he knows so many Muslims around the world.'

'Is it a dangerous job?' she asked.

'Yes – but he's doing this to fight terrorism,' Jesper said. 'It's important for the whole world.'

'It's why he got the $250,000 from the Americans,' Klang interjected.

'He brought the briefcase here,' my mother said. 'You know, even then it didn't seem real to me that he was working for the intelligence services.'

'We can't tell you much more than this but he's about to go back to Yemen,' Klang said.

'Will he be in danger?' she asked, more insistently.

'There's always some risk,' Klang replied carefully.

My mother looked at me as if to remind me that I had been trouble for as long as she could remember, and now I was thirty-six. But I felt reassured when we drove away at dusk. Both Klang and Jesper had taken a step out of the shadows.

There was a further bonus awaiting me. We joined Tommy Chef at a beach restaurant beside a pretty fishing marina. The house speciality was herring prepared several different ways. Washed down with Sancerre, it was an excellent dinner on the government's tab.

Tommy Chef dabbed his mouth with a white linen handkerchief.

'We've been doing some thinking, Morten. We're going to offer you something that has never been offered before to a civilian agent. Once you come back we are going to offer you a job. Because we don't want you just to stop working after this mission. We want you to continue – not on the frontline but on the cyber jihadi front – infiltrating these guys online.

'We also thought you could work with Anders to train agents.'

I was ecstatic at the prospect of a job that would put my address book to good use. Just days after I had quit, my future suddenly seemed to be opening up. Married life and approaching middle age were – just possibly – beginning to soften me.

As we left, Tommy Chef put his arm on my shoulder.

'You are doing all of us a great service.'

'You know what? We're going to do this for Amanda,' I said, referring to the code name of Elizabeth Hanson, the CIA agent who had recruited me and had been killed at Camp Chapman near Khost in Afghanistan in December 2009.

We called the mission 'Operation Amanda'.

CHAPTER TWENTY-SIX

CHINESE WHISPERS

May 2012

11 May 2012. A perfect late-spring dawn. Driving from Helsingør to Copenhagen, I watched the tractors rumbling up and down the immaculate fields. It was the picture of rural peace, at odds with my inner turmoil. My final field trip was underway. I had the 'modified' make-up box for Aminah (and Qasim al-Raymi) in my suitcase and a camping fridge for Wuhayshi to send on to Ibrahim al-Asiri, also fitted with a tracking device. I assumed it was the same fridge the CIA had been customizing for Awlaki.

The previous evening all the Danish agents, led by Tommy Chef, had attended a dinner in my honour. It felt awkwardly like a farewell and I was in a maudlin mood. Tommy Chef handed me $5,000 for expenses.

At Copenhagen airport there was one more piece of business. Jesper filled out an official notice stating that a package of hexamine had been confiscated from me. PET were still not comfortable with me providing hexamine to al-Qaeda, but at least Wuhayshi would see that I had tried.

By the time I boarded a connecting flight to Sana'a in Doha, my stress levels were rocketing. I began to second-guess everything: Tommy Chef's soothing words, the promise of Danish residency for my wife, Abdul's loyalties and his reaction on receiving my accusatory email. Why had he gone to China, of all places? Was he on the run? And if so from whom? I felt like I was facing a steep climb up a mountain lined with crevices and dotted with loose boulders. Any one of these hazards could finish me. But reaching the summit – leading Western intelligence to Wuhayshi and al-Asiri – would bring vindication. And – not incidentally – solvency.

At the customs hall in Sana'a nobody gave the fridge a second look; officials were used to foreigners bringing in appliances. I checked into a furnished apartment I had rented on 50th Street, the thoroughfare cutting through the southern part of the city. And I waited.

Tommy Chef had assured me that Abdul would return to Yemen from China the day after my arrival. I had no idea how he could be so confident, and in fact Abdul failed to arrive on the appointed day. I felt claustrophobic, holed up in an apartment on a mission I could not execute, my key intermediary thousands of miles away.

I got hold of the phone number Abdul was using in China from his anxious wife and sent him a text.

'Come and see me here,' he wrote.

'Why don't you come to Yemen?' I responded.

'I can't, brother, but I need to see you.'

A few seconds later my phone started ringing. It was Abdul. He was agitated.

'Murad, you must come here. I can't tell you what I need to tell you over the phone.'

'So you're telling me to come to China?'

'Yes, you must come, it's very important.'

'Let me figure this out,' I replied in disbelief.

I called Soren in Denmark, taking a calculated risk with security.

'Do you think you can persuade him to come back if you go?' he asked.

'Yes,' I replied.

'Then book your ticket,' he said. 'But don't take that iPhone we gave you.'

Perhaps Abdul picked China because he wanted to be sure he was beyond the eyes and the ears of the CIA.

Hardly had I arrived in Yemen than I was on the move again, connecting in Doha for the nine-hour flight to Hong Kong. I looked down at the vast cultivated heartland of India and the mystical green hills and jungles of Myanmar and could not help but be excited, despite the unpredictability of this mission. I always relished the prospect of arriving somewhere new. And the view on approach into Hong Kong was more spectacular than I could have imagined: soaring skyscrapers hugging steep hills, and wooden junks with their orange sails navigating between the islands.

From the airport I crossed on to the mainland and walked into Shenzhen railway station, a vast glass edifice. I thought of Yemen. Sana'a was nine hours and ninety years away. The Arab world was being left behind.

The new high-speed link between Shenzhen and Guangzhou had recently opened and covered the seventy miles in about thirty minutes.

Abdul had agreed to meet me at the railway station in Guangzhou, one of China's booming megacities. Amid the thousands of Chinese commuters hurrying to and from trains, he was not difficult to find, dark-skinned and slight. We embraced. He looked tense.

'What's going on?' I asked him.

'I can't tell you yet. We have our phones with us so it's not safe,' he replied.

I dropped my luggage and the cheap mobile phone I had brought in the apartment where he was staying. He told me he had come to Guangzhou because he knew some Yemeni businessmen in the city. We walked through thronging markets and squares where roller-skaters and acrobats performed. Skyscrapers lined the wide river flowing through the heart of the city.

Our destination was a spa. Before going into the jacuzzi room, we undressed in front of each other. Abdul clearly wanted to be sure that whatever he had to say could not be recorded. When we were alone in the gurgling water, Abdul turned to me with a worried look in his eyes.

'I have something to tell you.'

I cut him off. 'Remember the email I sent you about what they told me at Copenhagen airport. *I know . . .*'

I wanted to get ahead of him. I suppose it was part of the contest I felt between us.

'But the CIA, they're . . . they're going to kill you along with the terrorists if you travel down with me,' Abdul blurted.

'*Subhan'Allah* – what?'

'Murad, they don't want to kill you in Sana'a. They want to kill you when you are sitting with Abu Basir and the other brothers,' he continued.

He told me his CIA handlers had given him $25,000 to purchase a Toyota Prado SUV. He had taken the car to a workshop used by the Agency, where it had been fitted with a satellite transmitter connected to an electronic switch under the car seat. During a test run the equipment worked perfectly.

'One click would signal you had joined me in the car. Two clicks would signal we had left Sana'a. Three clicks would tell them we are in the same location as the target. And four clicks would mean I had left you alone with the target.'

He grabbed me by the shoulder. 'That's when you were going to be killed. They'll tell the world you were a terrorist like the others.'

Only my mother would know differently. It was plausible, but I was not convinced.

He climbed out of the jacuzzi. 'Murad, you can hit me now, you can hate me, but I couldn't bear it on my shoulders if you were hurt. I was scared about driving down with you, and that's why I left the country.'

I had not yet said a word. The CIA had been avoiding me, yet wanted me to return to Yemen. They knew that I had recorded one of their agents in Copenhagen the previous year and I had threatened to go public. There was also the iPhone which I had been told to leave on at all times.

I remembered the warning from Jacob, the outdoor instructor: '*Don't sit with the terrorists because the Americans won't hesitate to kill you.*'

Abdul was not exactly the most reliable of sources. But he did seem genuinely scared. Did he fear he would be killed with me?

'How long have you been working for the Americans?' I finally asked.

'You remember when years ago I told you I was arrested by intelligence services in Djibouti? That's when they recruited me. They left me no choice but to work for them. I am sorry that I lied to you.'

'Did you tell the CIA about me?' I asked.

'All I told the Americans was that you disagreed with the brothers about targeting civilians.'

Abdul was not an easy man to read, but he did not seem to have any inkling that I too might be working for Western intelligence. I fought back the urge to tell him.

'May Allah reward you for telling me this,' I told him.

He broke down. 'Murad – I am done working for the Americans. Do you think you can help me claim asylum in Denmark?' I promised to find out but told him it would be difficult.

When we got back to his residence I prayed with him. Now was not the time to drop my guard.

That night I had trouble getting to sleep. I didn't know whether to believe Abdul or not. I now knew he had lied to me just as much as I had lied to him. One idea kept coming back: could he be trying to scare me so he could return to Yemen and deliver the supplies himself? Just by being seen with me in Jaar he had boosted his credibility with Wuhayshi. And he could claim I had asked him to deliver the supplies. That would be one way for the Americans to tunnel directly into AQAP without needing me.

Then another thought: might Abdul have flipped back to the al-Qaeda side, like the Jordanian 'triple agent', Humam al-Balawi, who had killed Elizabeth Hanson and the other CIA agents in Afghanistan? Was he testing me on Wuhayshi's orders? If I returned to Yemen and didn't warn al-Qaeda of Abdul's treachery they would know I was a spy.

It was like trying to solve a Rubik's Cube blindfolded.

The next morning I was awoken by the buzzing of an incoming text. Jesper was asking me if I had persuaded Abdul to return.

I replied: 'I don't think he will travel or come down there while there is still fighting. He's convinced that I'm going to die and he will be taken with me.'

In a follow-up text I requested a meeting with my handlers in Doha on my way back to Yemen. Jesper said the Americans would be there too, but asked me to try to change Abdul's mind. Late that night, 19 May, I texted again: 'It doesn't look good . . . the boy doesn't want to travel right now.'

Jesper's reply came in a few minutes later: 'Can you ask for the car keys?'

I stared at the screen, startled. Did the Danes also want me to drive alone to the south? Were they in league with the CIA? Or did the Americans just want their high-tech car back?

There was no way I was going to ask Abdul for the keys. I texted: 'I tried with the car but unfortunately no he ready in one or two months. Right now he wants to have a break and to travel to the EU.'

At that moment Abdul's scenario, which seemed so outlandish at first, was beginning to look more than plausible.

Two days later I was checking in at the Mövenpick Hotel close to Doha airport. Jesper and Soren had already arrived and I met them for breakfast.

I related Abdul's warning, trying to sound sceptical but wanting to test their reaction. They both dismissed it out of hand.

'Where is Big Brother?' I asked.

'They're in the hotel but they don't want to meet directly with you,' Jesper replied.

'Fantastic,' I replied.

'Look, Akhi, this mission is very important to us. Do you think you might be ready to drive the supplies down to the south of Yemen yourself?' Soren said.

'You have to be joking,' I replied, reeling at such a rash proposition. Even if Abdul hadn't unnerved me with his warning, there was no way I was going alone into Yemen's war zone.

I asked them to put another idea to the Americans – that I should arrange a courier to pick up the camping fridge, cosmetic box and other items in Sana'a.

'That method is tried and trusted – it worked with Nabhan and Awlaki,' I said.

'That sounds like a good idea,' Jesper replied. He said they would ask.

When they were gone I sat in the lobby, staring vacantly at guests arriving and leaving, smiling and chatting, travelling the world in peace.

Eventually they returned.

'Big Brother says the courier idea is not an option,' Jesper said in a matter-of-fact tone. 'They insist you deliver it to Abu Basir in person.'

'I don't think I'm comfortable doing that,' I replied with what seemed masterful understatement.

I was staggered by the US insistence that I personally deliver the equipment. Time and time again I had successfully used couriers – with the Americans' encouragement – to supply Awlaki and through him AQAP. The ploy had also worked in Somalia. The Americans' refusal to even discuss this approach made me fear a trap. I wondered if they were even in the hotel.

'You don't need to give us your answer right away – sleep on it,' Jesper replied.

The next day – 22 May – Jesper, Soren and I went for lunch at L'wzaar, an expensive seafood restaurant in Doha. Decorated floor to ceiling with a mosaic of blue marble tiles, it brought cool to the oppressive heat of the Gulf. On one side were the still waters of the Gulf and on the other a row of chefs preparing fish.

'So, did you think about it?' Jesper asked me.

I allowed a moment to pass.

'I think I'm going to call an end to it,' I told them.

Jesper and Soren looked at each other.

'It's up to you – it's your call,' Soren replied.

And so, at a fish restaurant on the shores of the Persian Gulf, the curtain dropped on a journey that had begun, in the Islamist ferment at Dammaj on the other side of Arabia, fifteen years before.

It was an anti-climactic way to end more than five years on the frontline. And it was also – to me at least – inexplicable. The US, which had put the 'War on Terror' at the top of its agenda, had walked away from an opportunity to neutralize two of its most dangerous opponents – Nasir al-Wuhayshi and Ibrahim al-Asiri – and deal a blow to the most active of al-Qaeda's affiliates.

That decision would soon appear as a major error of judgement.

I flew back to Yemen the next day, 23 May, to fetch my belongings. After I landed I received a text message from Soren asking me to return the fridge and make-up box to CIA agents in Sana'a. The last thing the Americans wanted was tracking gear falling into the wrong hands.

I told them I would drive my silver Suzuki to the Sana'a trade centre – the closest thing in Yemen to a shopping mall – with the equipment inside.

'Place the small box in the large box and place it on the back seat just behind the driver's seat,' Soren's message read.

Even in these final moments, there was a change of plan. Another text from Soren asked me to leave the box on the tarmac of the car park. I did, but I was furious. There were security guards in the area. Had they noticed me leaving a large box unattended in the car park – in a country where plenty of bombs exploded – I could have been in deep trouble.

A few minutes later Soren forwarded a message from his CIA contact.

'I can confirm its picked up. Tell our boy "good job".'

I replied: 'Roger that, my pleasure.' If only phones had a key for irony.

CHAPTER TWENTY-SEVEN
A SPY IN
THE COLD

2012–2013

In July 2013, just over a year after my last mission in Yemen, an online message stream was intercepted by the US National Security Agency at its sprawling complex in Fort Meade, Maryland, and filtered through the most powerful supercomputers on the planet. Once the message was deciphered and translated it triggered a state of high alert.

We will carry out an attack that will change the face of history.

Within hours the entire US intelligence apparatus was mobilized to discover the scope of the attack being planned. It was clear an ambitious strike had been set in motion at the top level of al-Qaeda, but precious little was known about how, when or where. The US State Department took the unprecedented step of closing down more than twenty embassies and consulates across the Arab and Muslim world.

It soon became clear that the nexus of the threat was Yemen – with the US embassy in Sana'a one of the likeliest targets. The author of the message that triggered the alert was none other than my tour guide in Jaar – Nasir al-Wuhayshi, the leader of AQAP. In one of my last reports, I had told my handlers that Wuhayshi had ordered reconnaissance of the US embassy in Sana'a. Since then he had been appointed as Ayman al-Zawahiri's deputy – the number two of al-Qaeda globally. The man who had once been Osama bin Laden's protégé was now the annointed successor to Zawahiri.

Wuhayshi's creation of an Islamic emirate in the southern tribal areas of Yemen had enhanced his reputation in jihadist circles world-wide. His men had controlled Jaar and an expanse of southern Yemen for fifteen months. They had only retreated in the face of overwhelming firepower brought to bear by Yemeni government forces and loyalist tribal militias – supported by US drone strikes.

Even after being forced to retreat to more remote areas, AQAP had continued with suicide bombings against Yemeni security forces, assassinations of senior military personnel and ambushes of Yemeni troops. As Adil al-Abab noted in one of his last missives before he was killed by a drone, a new generation of jihadis had been blooded.

Less clear to Western intelligence were AQAP's priorities: whether Wuhayshi remained focused on carving out a state based on Islamic law and at the very least denying space to the Yemeni government, or whether, newly installed as al-Qaeda's number two, he now embraced global jihad as the pre-eminent mission. Perhaps I would have gained a sense of this with another visit or two. Equally, had I been given approval to organize the delivery of the fridge early in 2012, Zawahiri would most likely have been looking for a different deputy.

Since my final mission had been aborted I had turned to cocaine as my comfort blanket. For a few hours the frustration ebbed but as I came down from each high the jitters got worse. I was stressed about money, after sinking so much into Storm Bushcraft but losing both my business partner and a base in Kenya.

For half a decade I had moved back and forth between two worlds and two identities – when one misplaced sentence could have cost me my life. I had switched identity in airport departure and arrival halls around the world, travelling between atheism and hardline Islam, English and Arabic, T-shirts and *thawbs*, between being an agent for Western intelligence and a sworn member of al-Qaeda. As my fellow passengers reclined their seats and started the in-flight movies my brain was always running in fifth gear, focusing on the mission or trying to recall every detail of the one I had just endured.

My life depended on keeping sharp. Most recently my work had entailed maintaining layers of deception: the Western agent pretending to be an al-Qaeda operative pretending to be an outdoor travel entrepreneur.

Even at home – in England or Denmark – I was still on stage, as that well-known militant Islamist Murad Storm. In London or Copenhagen, Luton or Aarhus, Birmingham or Odense, there were enough radicals on the streets to mean I could not let the mask drop for a moment. It had been easy to play the role in the early days, but the further I travelled from my days as a radical fundamentalist, the more challenging it became to play the jihadi with any conviction.

Only when I was in the deep countryside or far-flung nightclubs could I become Morten Storm and knock back a beer. They were not the sorts of places that would attract serious jihadis, I reasoned. Even then I was on edge.

This lifestyle had brought me to the verge of a breakdown. For years I had been fuelled by the need to stop the next attack, by the rush of the spy game and camaraderie with my handlers. But their insistence that I travel alone down to Yemen's tribal areas unnerved me. Abdul's warning kept ringing in my ears and I was starting to doubt whether it was worth it. I had tracked down Wuhayshi, at a level of risk bordering on the insane, and Western intelligence had dropped the ball.

I had been lucky, but luck has a habit of running out. It was time to become a backroom boy, one of the analysts who did their best to divine the intentions of terrorists the world over.

On 12 July 2012 I flew from Manchester to Copenhagen to follow up on the offer made to me by Tommy Chef in that seafood restaurant. PET had booked a room at the airport Hilton for the meeting. I was apprehensive: the Danes had broken promises and my final divorce from the Americans had been ugly. It would be prudent, I thought, to have a record. I reached into my pocket to check my iPhone was primed.

Jesper was waiting for me, and told me Klang (restored to his job after a humiliating stint checking the records of would-be refugees) and Anders would arrive soon.

'Everyone is on vacation,' Jesper told me, with an eye on the coverage of the Tour de France on a TV in the corner of the room.

He reached for his laptop case and took out a large wad of $100 bills.

'Here's $10,000,' he said to me, handing me the cash, as if it were a perfectly normal thing to do in the middle of a conversation.

'Is this from the Americans?' I asked, conscious that I was recording his every word.

'This is for the trip – that's all I could do for you, Akhi. I hope it's good enough,' Jesper replied. He could see that the cash had not placated me.

'Akhi, what are we doing?' he asked.

'I don't know – we are on holiday until the Americans get back into it,' I replied sarcastically.

I still wanted an explanation for events in Doha.

'I was ready in January. I was down with Abu Basir and ready, and was ready two weeks later to return to Yemen. Why has everything been postponed? It's not my mistake.'

'Nobody's pointing a finger at you; that's why they gave you the $10,000.'

I made clear to Jesper it would be dangerous for me to return to Yemen.

'Abdul may be playing a double game. He could also be working for al-Qaeda, as well as the CIA,' I said. 'Maybe it's a test,' I continued. 'If I go back to Abu Basir and if he asks "Why did you never tell us about Abdul?". . .'

I let the consequences of failing such a test hang in the air.

'Do you really believe Abdul would save me if he's a traitor to his own brothers in al-Qaeda?'

'I don't think the Americans will ever work again with Abdul,' Jesper offered.

I didn't believe him but his response was useful nonetheless. The PET agent had just reconfirmed that Abdul had been recruited by the CIA, and I had it on tape.

I told him I thought it possible that Abdul's warning was an American ploy to remove me from the game and have him replace me as their key informant on al-Qaeda in Yemen.

Jesper said he could not understand why the Americans had rejected my plan to track Wuhayshi using couriers.

'Jesper, I'm not just talking about Abu Basir [Wuhayshi]. I'm talking about the bomb-maker too. They know I'm the one who would get into those two guys and yet they don't want to do anything about it. I'm frustrated. It must be something to do with me.'

'The reason why they stopped it with you is because they said it was too dangerous for you,' Jesper said.

In Qatar I had been the one who had expressed concern about the dangers in Yemen – not the Americans. Had Jesper simply forgotten that? Was he trying to rewrite history? Or was he just not very bright?

There was a knock. Anders and Klang had arrived.

We called up room service and ordered some sandwiches. Klang got a beer.

I decided to ask them about the position away from the frontline that Tommy Chef had offered.

'I'd like to take up the job,' I told them.

'I'm afraid that was conditional on you fulfilling your mission in Yemen. We can't provide it to you now,' Jesper replied.

Just as I had feared they were going to renege on a promise. I felt like I had fulfilled my end of the bargain, before having the rug pulled from under me. No one had ever told me that another actual meeting with Wuhayshi was the quid pro quo for a position.

'What about my wife? What about her papers?'

'We are still working on it,' Jesper said.

I did not believe them.

Klang had come forearmed. He had another proposal, though it was unclear whether his superiors had signed off on it. I should offer myself as the point-person for al-Shabaab in Europe. If I was the one arranging safe houses for militants in Europe, Danish intelligence could have eyes and ears on any terrorist plots being hatched.

I did not take the bait.

'If I retired now, what can I expect?' I said.

'If you quit then you should expect PET would be grateful,' Jesper said, as non-committal as possible.

'And then we probably would do some sort of agreement to step back, like retirement. Yeah, I think we would be able to do that,' he added, every inch the former banker.

He and Anders indicated they could get me a year's salary in severance pay. Anders seemed to be my only true ally, conscious of the value
of intelligence from the frontline.

'You were just about to get hold of the ones who could carry out an
attack against us,' Anders said – referring to Ibrahim al-Asiri and the
AQAP operatives charged with planning attacks overseas.

'Isn't it just insane that the Americans stopped me?' I said.

He nodded.

We discussed other options, but with the possible exception of
Anders they were only humouring me.

It was time to leave. The agents embraced me. Anders lingered
longer. 'I know you got cheated over Awlaki,' he said with real emotion,
shaking my hand.

My status with PET was in limbo for weeks. A Western Union wire
transfer for £2,466 from Jesper came in on 30 July – my monthly
retainer. But of the future there was no word until a call in mid-
August.

It was Jesper. He began with some pleasantries about who was on
vacation and the English summer.

'Now,' he said briskly. 'PET has decided you are eligible for six
months' severance.'

'You said twelve,' I replied.

'That's all they are willing to approve,' he said.

I was being jettisoned. But I had some news for them.

'I've contacted the Danish newspaper *Jyllands-Posten* and they want
to meet.'

For a few moments there was dead air.

'I'm going to need to call you back,' he finally said. He sounded disturbed, no doubt conjuring lurid headlines about lap-dancing clubs in
Lisbon and champagne at the taxpayers' expense.

I had contacted *Jyllands-Posten* because I was fed up with PET's
broken promises. I burned to set the record straight on Awlaki and
knew I had the evidence to corroborate my side of the story. And I also
thought that going public would offer me protection from any foul
play. Abdul's warning haunted me.

There was another reason. Many of my acquaintances and some of

my family still believed I was a radical extremist associated with terror-
ists who ought to be behind bars. It was time they knew otherwise.
And I wanted to take a stand for other informants risking their lives for
Western intelligence.

When Jesper called me back, it was to invite me to a meeting with
Tommy Chef – troubleshooter-in-chief – at the Admiral Hotel, overlooking the Copenhagen waterfront.

The following day I flew to the Danish capital, unsure whether
Tommy would find a solution or issue veiled threats. He greeted me
warmly, but I wasn't in the mood for pleasantries.

'What about the job you promised me?' I asked.

'Oh, we can't do that,' he replied.

He looked out into the harbour at a wooden vessel bobbing gently
in the water.

'That's a nice ship. Is that what you are going to do? Do you want to
learn how to sail?'

I had mentioned that I might try to get work as a contractor in
anti-piracy.

'No, I don't want to learn how to sail,' I replied curtly.

He continued staring at the boat, then turned to look at me.

'Let's just agree you will call the journalists and tell them not to
come.'

'I'm not sure I can do that. You've cheated me and you've lied to me.
We're done.'

The meeting had lasted ten minutes.

I walked through Copenhagen, feeling a sense of freedom tinged
with apprehension. I was on my own now – and the Danish intelligence service would spare no effort to discredit me. They would
certainly renege on the promise of permanent residency for my wife.
With the sense that I had broken my chains came isolation and
vulnerability.

At least I could take solace from the panic that had clearly set in on
the top floor of PET's headquarters. In the hours before my scheduled
meeting with *Jyllands-Posten* on 27 August, Jesper made a series of ever
more desperate calls. I recorded them. They would offer me a year's
severance. Rejected. Another call – two years' salary if I kept silent.

Rejected. And finally came an offer of $270,000 – 1.5 million DKK – that the Kingdom's long-suffering taxpayers would have to fund to save the agency from embarrassment and – worse – closer political scrutiny.

'The money you get from us you don't have to declare to anyone,' Jesper said.

They were offering me a payoff tax-free. I was no tax lawyer, but that seemed to me illegal under both Danish and UK law.

'But what really annoys me is the way you treated me last year with Anwar,' I replied.

'Yes, yes, but that's what we're trying to make up for now,' he said.

Then came the not so subtle threat about the consequences of my talking to the press.

'You don't have a lot of time to think about it because there are some people who are waiting to talk to you . . . The problem is once you have spoken to them there is no way back.'

Jesper tried his pitch once more.

'The offer they are coming up with now – I have never, never seen anything like it before. And this is a confession. It is a confession they make. And you can use that positively.'

I told him I needed to think about it. I badly needed the money – an informant's CV has plenty of gaps and whatever I could wring from them would need to sustain me and Fadia – and provide for a fresh start far from my former 'brothers'. Reinventing myself would not come cheap. This was my one shot.

I devised a proposal and called Jesper. In return for 4 million DKK ($700,000) I would hand them my computers and my file of corroborating emails and recordings and never speak of my work for Western intelligence. He called back, saying PET could not improve on their previous offer.

'I just can't accept that offer. I can only say thank you to you, Jesper, and I can only tell the leadership that they should feel ashamed,' I said.

'And the same from me to you. Sometimes you have been a bit difficult but you have never been boring,' he said with more than a hint of understatement.

Somehow, Danish intelligence must have been aware that I had begun to lay out my story to three journalists from *Jyllands-Posten*, because on 19 September Jesper called again. PET would give me the equivalent of five years' salary plus a cash payment of almost 700,000 DKK: a total of almost 2.2 million DKK or $400,000.

I asked Jesper if we could draw up a contract.

'It's very, very difficult to sign something. I don't know if it would make you feel more safe to go and speak to Jakob,' he said, referring to Jakob Scharf, the director of PET.

After some haggling over the details, I called Jesper one more time.

'Done deal,' I told Jesper when I called him back.

'Thank you – that was fucking difficult,' he replied.

Not as difficult as what was to follow. That same afternoon, the journalists at *Jyllands-Posten* told me that a Danish TV station was planning to break the story about my work for PET. It seems that the station had been approached by PET as part of a damage limitation exercise: throw enough mud and throw it first. I had no idea whether wires had been crossed at PET or whether they had planned this while trying to spin out negotiations. Whatever the case, a journalist at the station later confirmed to me that he had received a call from Danish intelligence offering their take on my story.

I felt it likely that PET would backtrack on the settlement. I suspected their offer was just a ploy while they figured out a way of separating me from the cache of electronic evidence I had built up. Incensed, I called Jesper back to say the deal was off the table.

Jesper made it clear PET would not protect me if I broke my cover.

'If you go public just to get revenge you have to think, was it worth it? You won't be able to travel around freely with your kids. They won't be able to see their grandparents freely. Just because you needed that satisfaction,' he told me in a rare burst of spite.

But his increasingly desperate arguments fell on deaf ears.

Just before the first article ran in *Jyllands-Posten* on 7 October 2012, I texted Jesper.

'Just wanted to let you know I recorded all our conversations,' I wrote.

'Why did you do that?' came his reply.

'Because I'm a spy – and that's what you taught me ☺.'

EPILOGUE

Undisclosed Location in the UK, Spring 2014

The first *Jyllands-Posten* article on 7 October 2012 caused a sensation in Denmark. The piece outlined the role I played in tracking down Awlaki for the CIA and PET so that he could be targeted with a drone strike: explosive allegations in Denmark, where the government is forbidden to take part in any such assassination. The *Jyllands-Posten* journalists were later awarded the inaugural European Press Prize for their stories.

The news was picked up around the world. In December 2012 I sat down with CBS's *60 Minutes*, the celebrated US news magazine show, for an interview which focused on my role in tracking down Awlaki.

After all the years operating in the shadows it felt surreal seeing my name in newspapers and on television and my work for Western intelligence made public. It was satisfying to go public with what I perceived to be both the achievements and the failings in my work with intelligence. But away from the cameras, I felt vulnerable. And my wife, Fadia, was still coming to terms with the fact that I had deceived her for so long with so many lies.

A couple of weeks before *Jyllands-Posten* published my story, I suggested to her that we go for a long country walk. I chose a beautiful late-summer's day; the air was fragrant with the harvest of barley and wheat. We sat at the edge of a field; I had even put together a picnic.

As we watched the skylarks above, I told her everything: my recruitment, my work in Yemen and Kenya, in Lebanon and Birmingham, Denmark and Sweden, my falling-out with the CIA and PET – my role in the assassination of Awlaki, the money, the cocaine and my mission to southern Yemen to see Wuhayshi. The strain had already affected our marriage; I warned Fadia that once my story was in the press the pressure would only grow. I could expect no protection from the intelligence agencies and plenty of people would want me dead. Our world would shrink; we would always be on our guard.

Fadia was traumatized.

'Why?' she asked. 'Could you not trust me? Five years of endless lies. And have you any idea how lonely I was? You were hardly ever there, and when you were it was in body only. Your mind was always somewhere else.'

I tried to explain that I wanted to protect her, that it was better she knew nothing, that in any case I could have told her so little.

'But I'm your wife,' she said – looking at me through eyes swollen with tears.

In the autumn of 2012, the pressures generated by my 'coming out' weighed heavily on both of us and we agreed to separate – at least for a while. I was diagnosed as suffering from post-traumatic stress disorder, unable to work, unable to get a new National Insurance number in Britain, where I still lived, for fear that a militant sympathizer working in a government office would uncover and locate me.

The moment *Jyllands-Posten* went on sale on 7 October, I was a marked man. On jihadist forums and Facebook pages, animosity and threats to me and my family poured out. Among militants Anwar al-Awlaki had been a beloved figure. To avenge his killing would be an honour, an act on which Allah would smile. My bitter fall-out with Danish intelligence meant, as Jesper had warned, that I could expect no help from my own government.

One of the Americans who had been at Dammaj with me, Khalid Green, took to YouTube to denounce me for pretending to love Allah but betraying Islam.

'Someone we considered a companion and a friend,' he intoned – sitting in front of shelves full of Islamic texts – 'who was with us in one of the most esteemed places of knowledge in the camp in Dammaj studying with Sheikh Muqbil . . . we find out that this person has worked for the CIA.'

Others among my circle were shocked and even grudgingly impressed. Rasheed Laskar, the young man from Britain whom I had known in Sana'a, wrote on an Islamist blog under the name Abu Mu'aadh:

'I knew Murad personally since 2005/6 & we lived together in Yemen . . . When I was first informed about the news from Danish friends I was in shock . . . his contacts with Sheikh Anwar raheemahullah are true.

'Believe me if his – whole ex-CIA-PET agent story – is true – & it really does go back to 2006 – then he was quite honestly – back in those days – brilliant at his job.'

'Since 2005/6 I have had a lot of contact with Murad . . . and I never suspected him of being an agent. I know many brothers that have been in & out of Arab prisons, tortured, deported and hounded from coun-try to country (and even assassinated) with one common element in our stories – knowing Murad Storm.

'From the bottom of my heart – I ask Allah to give him what he deserves both in this life & the hereafter.'

His tone suggested he didn't have seventy-two virgins in mind.

More seriously, in August 2013 a group of Danes who had travelled to Syria and joined forces with ISIS released a video calling for my mur-der, along with several other high-profile Danes they considered enemies of Islam.

'It's important that we shoot with our Kalashnikovs at these *mur-tadeen* and those *kuffar* attacking Islam,' a Danish jihadi calling himself Abu Khattab said to the camera, overlooking a hilltop town in Syria. His face was familiar. I had seen him in Copenhagen. He was one of the followers of an al-Muhajiroun spin-off in Denmark.

The camera then scans along six pictures against a stone wall. My picture is the first that comes into view, followed by that of Naser Khader, a moderate Muslim politician in Denmark whose murder I had once called for, as well as Anders Fogh Rasmussen, the Danish Secretary General of NATO, and the cartoonist Kurt Westergaard. A caption comes on to the screen: 'Enemies of Islam'.

The fighters crouch and take aim – shouting *'Allahu Akbar!'* as they unleash a volley of gunfire at the posters. Another clip posted by the same band of jihadists in Syria featured Shiraz Tariq, a Pakistani extrem-ist I had gone paintballing with a decade previously in Odense.

In a follow-up video Abu Khattab was asked why they chose to include me on the execution list.

'His task was to kill our beloved Sheikh Anwar al-Awlaki.'

Sure enough a threatening message appeared on my Facebook account. Its author was Abdallah Andersen, one of the Danes convicted in relation to the 2006 Vollsmose terrorist plot. He was now out of jail but his views had hardly softened; he now called himself 'Abu Taliban' on his Facebook profile.

'How's the family? Everyone hates you. Everyone wants you dead,' he said.

I passed the comment to Danish police. Everyone on the 'execution list' not already under police protection had been offered a round-the-clock guard by PET, except me. For weeks PET did not return my emails even when the story was all over the Danish media, and they never offered protection.

But there were compensations for going public, chief among them restoring my reputation among those who had been my friends before I vanished into the world of radical Islam. Many had cut ties with me, some just thought me a lunatic. Apart from my mother – and more recently Fadia – I had told nobody that I had become an agent.

Several of my friends and family didn't believe me when in the weeks before I went public I told them the truth. To them it must have seemed one twist too many in my already improbable story.

Jyllands-Posten's series of articles gave my story the stamp of credibility. Slowly I was able to rekindle some old friendships. I was given a chance to say sorry to a lot of people. Sorry for my behaviour. Sorry for disappearing. Sorry for the lies. But above all, sorry for hating you because you did not accede to my beliefs.

Many of my former friends, including Vibeke, my first love, were astonished by my story.

'I simply never guessed,' she said. 'I thought you had become this crazy guy always vanishing overseas and spending your life praying. I felt I didn't know you any more.'

It was also a relief to be able to escape the pretence of being a hard-line Salafist. Murad Storm was finally history, and gone with him were the Islamic robes, the long beard and the pretend prayers. It felt good to wear jeans and a T-shirt and grab a beer without worrying that my cover would be compromised.

In early 2014 I went on Danish television to apologize to Naser Khader, the moderate Muslim politician whose killing I had once called for. Now we were both literally in al-Qaeda's crosshairs, as the video from Syria had made clear. After the cartoon controversy had erupted Khader had attracted further ire from jihadis by bravely defending the cartoonists' right of free speech.

I handed him a drawing I had asked my daughter, Sarah, to do. It showed me apologizing to him. 'Dude Naser. I was wrong. I am sorry!!! Forgive me,' the speech bubble said. Underneath was written 'Free Speech is not negotiable. Long Live Democracy.'

He embraced me, saying all was forgiven. 'I am very touched and think it is extremely nice of you. I'll keep this in my home,' he said. We both had tears in our eyes; we had both been through a great deal and might yet face more.

Naser told me that PET had informed him more than ten years previously that I had threatened him. He had received many death threats since. He asked me to join him in an initiative to deradicalize Danish youngsters sucked into extremism. I readily accepted. If I could help just one person turn his back on al-Qaeda's murderous world-view, the shame I still felt would be slightly less.

From Danish, British and US intelligence there was a predictable wall of silence after I went public. PET had tried to cover their tracks by dissolving their front company, Mola Consult, after I told them I planned to go public.[1]

Jakob Scharf – the head of PET – limited himself to a carefully worded statement.

'Out of consideration for PET's operational work, the PET neither can nor will confirm publicly that specific persons have been used as sources by the PET . . . However, the PET does not participate in or

---

1 According to the Central Business Registry of Denmark, Mola Consult was dissolved on 31 August 2012.

support operations where the objective is to kill civilians. The PET did therefore not contribute to the military operation that led to the killing of al-Awlaki in Yemen.'

His denial of involvement in 'the military operation' was a very precise formulation. No one was accusing the Danes of actually firing the drones that killed Awlaki, but one of their agents had been leading the hunt for him. And it wasn't to inquire after his health.

The revelations led Danish parliamentarians to demand new oversight rules for PET. In January 2013 I met with several of them. At the same time Denmark's Ministry of Justice announced it would set up a supervisory board to oversee the Danish intelligence agency. The Justice Minister, Morten Bødskov, a close friend of Jakob Scharf, said the new board would strike 'the right balance that will ensure that we have an effective intelligence agency and a good rule of law'.

In March 2013 my account received heavyweight backing from Hans Jørgen Bonnichsen, Scharf's predecessor as head of PET. He told Danish television that the corroborating evidence confirmed to his satisfaction the agency had used me to track down terrorist operatives overseas to help the US target them for assassination. 'I now have no reason to doubt that they have participated,' he said.

The establishment closed ranks. Denmark's two main parties blocked a parliamentary inquiry. It was perhaps no accident that they had both been in power while I was working for PET.[2] They seemed to believe the story would eventually go away. For a while I thought perhaps they were right. Danes take pride in the transparency of their democratic institutions but I have long believed that in the process they have become too trustful of the state – almost complacent.

My time working for PET revealed an agency with some competent, decent people, but with too many others incapable of worthwhile intelligence work. Many were ex-cops who had spent most of their lives in vice or drug squads. Handling foreign intelligence and

---

2 On 3 October 2011, three days after Awlaki was killed in a drone strike, Helle Thorning-Schmidt of the Social Democrats took over as Prime Minister from Lars Løkke Rasmussen, of the Venstre party, who served from 2009 to 2011. Prior to that Anders Fogh Rasmussen of Venstre held the top job.

understanding terrorism seemed beyond them. Others seemed to see the agency as a gravy train – and me as a source of income or expensive trips.

In late 2013 stories of impropriety within PET exploded in the Danish media. The first centred on the previous year's riotous office Christmas party. It was revealed that Director Scharf, in a rare act of transparency, had drunkenly made out with a subordinate in a glass-walled corridor in full view of everybody. Klang had at least been more discreet in his choice of rendezvous with Scharf's mistress.

Revelations followed about discord and expensive trips Scharf and senior aides made overseas. According to internal complaints leaked to the media, Scharf was 'unprepared' and 'frivolous' during meetings in Washington DC and more interested in sightseeing, leading the CIA to lose confidence in his leadership. Government insiders revealed that this trust had already been eroded after I went public. The CIA expected friendly agencies to keep their informants under control.

Finally it emerged that Scharf had instructed subordinates to obtain information on the movements of a Danish MP. The scandal forced the resignations of both Scharf and his boss, the Justice Minister, Morten Bødskov. The revelations put my story back in the public spotlight. Scharf's predecessor, Bonnichsen, sharpened his criticism of the agency, asserting that my disclosures on Danish involvement in assassination plans overseas were so serious there was a basis for a criminal investigation.

The tide seemed to be turning. At the end of the year the beleaguered agency was put under more pressure when *Jyllands-Posten* disclosed PET's refusal to offer me protection after the Syrian death threat video.

'Is it really a satisfactory way for the security services to carry out their task in that it takes three weeks before you answer a former employee who – rightly – felt threatened by Islamists?' the chairman of the Danish People's Party said to the newspaper.

Such were my jihadist networks that hardly a month went by without a former associate being arrested, martyred in the service of jihad, or identified as an emerging leader in a terror group. Kenneth Sorensen, who had been part of my circle in Sana'a, was killed fighting alongside jihadis in Syria in March 2013, one of a staggering 2,000 European militants who would travel to fight there. Jihadis in Syria released a martyrdom video to honour his sacrifice to the cause. His mortal wounds were horrendous. The video showed the congealed blood streaked across his face and then fighters bulldozing dirt over his unmarked grave.

It was a fate I too could have shared, for I was led to believe by one of my handlers at PET that by 2013 Sorensen was working as a double agent.

Abu Khattab, the Danish jihadi who had called for my murder, was himself killed fighting in Syria; so too was my former paintballing buddy Shiraz Tariq.

In February 2014 Abdul Waheed Majeed, the British-Pakistani al-Muhajiroun follower who had so assiduously taken minutes during Omar Bakri's talks in Luton, became the first British suicide bomber in Syria. He had been recruited by Jabhat al-Nusra, al-Qaeda's affiliate in Syria. A video released by the group showed him in a white tunic and black Islamist bandana cheerily speaking to other fighters beside a heavily armoured truck before the attack. Fighters cheered '*Allah Akbar!*' as he set off towards the central prison in Aleppo, where he detonated the vehicle in a huge fireball.

Only a small number of my jihadist contacts paid their debt to society. Clifford Newman, the American convert who had assisted John Walker Lindh – 'the American Taliban' – in getting to Afghanistan served five years in prison in Dubai from 2004 to 2009 for attempted robbery. He then served a three-year sentence in the United States for child abduction.

Aminah, as far as I know, remained in Yemen – still committed to her deceased husband's cause. On 18 July 2012 – just before I left the intelligence fold – I received one last encrypted message from her.

She revealed she had spent several months under Wuhayshi's protection, but with the government retaking territory across the tribal areas she had relocated to Awlaki's village, and was hoping eventually to go to Sana'a.

'You are always in my *duas* [supplications]. Sometimes I cry when I remember all things you have done for me and my dear Anwar, may Allah have mercy on him.'

How she must hate me now.

As for Abdul, he eventually returned to Yemen, and I received a message from him in which he recanted his previous accusations that the Americans had wanted me to go to southern Yemen and planned to have me killed there.

'The yanks never ever, never ever, never ever mentioned harming you at any time, never said they will kill you, the car was not for you,' he wrote.

But he maintained the CIA had warned him that I was on my way back to Yemen – an extraordinary breach of faith if true.

'They told me Morten is coming, leave everything behind and stay with him because we think he is up to no good.'

Abdul appears never to have entertained the thought that I too was an informant.

'I did not want you to come to yemen and go back to the south and get deeper with the misguided, and therfore, you might be a target one day. I made up the story just to make you stay out of yemen and out of the trouble in this miserable country.'

Abdul said his CIA handlers had been furious that he had travelled to China and then met with me – and had cut ties with him afterwards.

I will never know what the CIA's plans for me were. It is conceivable that someone at the Agency wanted me out of the way, and that Abdul's final message to me was a desperate attempt to cover his and their tracks. Perhaps Abdul was a compulsive liar. Perhaps the Americans had originally wanted us both to return to southern Yemen and complete a mission that could have helped decapitate AQAP.

Looking back at the hectic events of 2011 and 2012, I think that to the CIA I had become expendable, worth sending on one last mission to southern Yemen on my own just in case it came off – even though they and the Danes knew the risk to my safety was exorbitant.

What is beyond dispute is that a real chance to track and eliminate Wuhayshi and other leaders of AQAP was lost in the mishandling of that final mission. Despite losing territory in the latter half of 2012, the group remained a potent threat well beyond Yemen.

In September 2012 three of its operatives took part in the terrorist attack on the US diplomatic compound in Benghazi. At a large gathering in Spring 2014 Wuhayshi made clear to fighters that attacking the West was a priority and made good on another pledge by greeting several operatives recently liberated from prison.

Intelligence agencies believed Ibrahim al-Asiri was developing a new generation of explosives that would be more difficult for scanners to detect. In February 2014 the US Department of Homeland Security sent out an alert to airlines after intelligence indicated he was developing a new shoe bomb design. With every year that passed the Saudi terrorist was becoming more ingenious – and instructing apprentices in the mechanics of terror. So high was concern over an emboldened AQAP that the US and Yemen carried out a large wave of strikes in April 2014. When this book went to press a week later no key figure had been confirmed killed.

The temporary closure of US embassies in the summer of 2013 – from Libya in the west to Madagascar in the south and Bangladesh in the east – illustrated how much of the world had become unsafe for Westerners. Al-Qaeda's black banners fluttered in the deserts of Mauritania, close to the Atlantic shore, in the Sinai desert, throughout Syria, in western Iraq and in southern Somalia. In many of these places, AQAP had a role, a presence or contacts. It was the first among equals of al-Qaeda's affiliates.

Al-Shabaab too shifted its centre of gravity from insurgency in Somalia to more 'classic' terrorism after formally becoming an affiliate of al-Qaeda. And I knew some of its most accomplished operatives.

On the morning of Saturday, 21 September 2013, at least four heavily armed gunmen in jeans and T-shirts marauded through the upscale Westgate shopping mall in Nairobi. In a siege that lasted four days and appeared to have been modelled on the Mumbai attacks in 2008, more than sixty men, women and children were killed.

Al-Shabaab claimed the attack was in retaliation for Kenya's 2011–12 military offensive in Somalia which had pushed the group out of the port city of Kismayo, an important source of income for the group.

The suspected mastermind was none other than my main point of contact in al-Shabaab – Ikrimah, the long-haired Kenyan who spoke Norwegian.

Unlike the American jihadi Omar Hammami, who was killed a week before the Westgate attack, Ikrimah had survived the infighting within al-Shabaab. Kenyan intelligence believed that he had emerged as the key figure plotting attacks in Kenya because of his militant contacts inside the country.[3] One of his previous schemes, disrupted by the Kenyan security services in late 2011, envisioned multiple attacks on the Kenyan parliament, United Nations offices in Nairobi and politicians, which Kenyan intelligence learned had been sanctioned by al-Qaeda in Pakistan.[4]

Two weeks to the day after the gunmen launched their assault on the Westgate Mall a team of US Navy SEALs from the same unit that had killed Osama bin Laden raced towards the Somali coastline in a high-speed boat. It was a moonless night. Their mission was to capture Ikrimah from an al-Shabaab compound south of Mogadishu. But this time the mission went wrong. Their approach was noticed and al-Shabaab fighters emerged from the compound, guns blazing.

Reports suggested several of the SEALs had seen Ikrimah through the windows of the compound, but could not get to him. The American commandos continued to take fire while trying to find a way to get closer to their target, but soon realized that women and children (not accidentally) were inside the house. They abandoned the mission.

Ikrimah escaped alive and became more dangerous as a result. Not only was he still free to plot terrorist attacks in East Africa but by

3 Ikrimah had worked to build up a network in Kenya to plot attacks. According to a 2013 Kenyan government report he dispatched an operative to Kenya in July 2013 'to train youth, lay down the infrastructure for a major attack and await instructions'.

4 Before Kenyan police made arrests in late 2011 the planners had trained the operatives designated to carry out the attack, acquired safe houses in Nairobi and Mombasa, transported explosives from Somalia and begun to construct bombs. The 'White Widow', Samantha Lewthwaite, was believed to be connected to the cell, but escaped capture in Mombasa. The green light for the plot from al-Qaeda in Pakistan may have been communicated to Ikrimah by our mutual American friend, Jehad Serwan Mostafa, if he did indeed meet with Zawahiri in Pakistan a few months before.

surviving a Navy SEAL attack his credentials had been burnished. In our communications between 2008 and 2012 Ikrimah made it clear that his ambitions stretched further than just Africa. His goal was to dispatch Western al-Shabaab recruits to launch attacks in their home countries. If he finally suceeded in his attempt to connect with Wuhayshi, the leader of al-Qaeda in Yemen, both men could pool resources in plots to attack the West and Western targets around the world.

To some degree Western intelligence created Ikrimah. The CIA, MI6 and PET helped him rise through the ranks in al-Shabaab because the supplies and contacts I provided him with impressed his superiors. But my contacts with Ikrimah netted valuable results, including the removal of one of the most dangerous al-Qaeda operatives in East Africa – Saleh Ali Nabhan – and gave us a window into the operations of al-Shabaab. Helping Ikrimah was the price paid for a greater gain.

After the Westgate attack I wondered if Ikrimah might have been apprehended or killed had I continued my relationship with him. Had I been able to build up Storm Bushcraft in Kenya, I might have had a better sense of his place in al-Shabaab, his plans and even some of the recruits he was training. Of course, it would have been difficult and hazardous to meet with him. By the middle of 2012 Ikrimah's emails suggested he rarely ventured beyond Somalia. But it would have been possible to deliver a tracking device to him hidden in equipment – as I had arranged for Nabhan.

In my view, Western intelligence would have found it easier to remove Ikrimah from the battlefield by taking advantage of the trust he had in me. And even if we had not been able to target him it is possible that he would have shared information with me, hinting at some of the deadly attacks he was planning.

My retirement also meant that Western intelligence lost a resource in one of its most arduous challenges: detecting small-scale 'lone-wolf' attacks. These are the most difficult for counter-terrorism agencies as there is often no trail of communication. Al-Qaeda had seen the advantage, releasing a video in 2011 entitled *You are Only Responsible for Yourself*, which called for solo attacks by followers in the West.

The Boston bombings of April 2013 and the murder and attempted beheading of a British soldier, Lee Rigby, on the streets of Woolwich in

South-East London the following month signalled that such attacks could be the wave of the future. In both cases militants based in the West had carried out the attacks independently of any group. I knew their motivation and their path to radicalization because I had made the same journey.

One of the two Woolwich killers – Michael Adebolajo, a British-Nigerian convert – had once been a follower of my former group, al-Muhajiroun, and I had come across him at a talk in Luton.

Such 'lone-wolf' attacks are virtually impossible to prevent unless there is someone on the 'inside' who detects a change of behaviour or appearance, is asked a strange question or confided in. Twice during my career I had informed Western intelligence of terrorist plots by radicalized zealots determined to bring carnage to the streets of Europe – because the plotters had told me of their plans.

Awlaki's sermons and writings, even from beyond the grave, had provided the inspiration for both the Boston and the Woolwich attacks. The Boston bombers built pressure-cooker bombs from a recipe in *Inspire* magazine.[5] Since his death Awlaki's sermons have only grown in popularity among radicalized Muslims in the West, their message as simple as it is spellbinding: the United States and its friends are at war with Islam and Allah commands that Muslims must fight back by any means necessary.[6]

It was a message that had appealed to so many who felt marginalized, discriminated against, rootless – or simply lonely.

After publication of the first story, *Jyllands-Posten* put me up in a country hotel in England, both for my own safety and to keep competing media away. But I felt obliged to go to the local police station.

The well-meaning sergeant behind the desk thought I was unhinged when I told him my story and said I needed protection.

---

5 The recipe entitled 'Make a bomb in the kitchen of your Mom' featured in the first issue of *Inspire* magazine, published in June 2010, and was found on one of the Boston bombers' computers.
6 Awlaki's death triggered a New York extremist, Jose Pimentel, to plot a bombing in the city in late 2011 to avenge the cleric's death.

'Just Google my name,' I said. 'Morten Storm.'

Up popped my face splashed across the front page of *Jyllands-Posten*.

In a place where disorderly drunks were the daily fare, I was an unusual subject.

'Just a moment, sir,' the sergeant said.

An hour later, two detectives arrived and admitted that they had no idea what to do with me.

'I've never met anyone like you, nor will I again,' one of them said with a wry smile. So I was passed up the food chain, to my old friends at MI5.

The following day, a middle-aged woman with a plain face and pursed lips, her hair cut in a no-nonsense bob, arrived at the police station. She was accompanied by a man who introduced himself as Keith, a tall and genial fifty-something officer. I spilled out as much of my story as I could, saying that I believed the Americans had tried to get me killed in Yemen. The pair of them took notes but said little.

Occasionally the sergeant would pop his head around the door to see if we needed refreshments. He was quite enjoying the small circus from the world of 007 in his shop.

Neither of the MI5 officers said much until the end of our meeting.

'You must understand,' the woman said, 'that we have no obligations towards you; you are no longer working with us. This is a problem between you, the Danish government and the Americans. I can't understand why you want to drag us into it.'

I recalled that phone conversation with my MI5 handler Kevin as I had prepared to leave Birmingham airport in April 2010: '*Morten – if you travel now, you have to realize we are not going to see each other again.*'

Even so, MI5's concern at the possible fall-out from further disclosures prompted them to invite me to a follow-up meeting in a nearby city. A large and voluble Londoner called Graham, who must have been close to retirement, joined the party.

MI5 wanted to explore the outlines of a possible deal. Several detectives lurked in the hotel car park and reception as we met in a conference room. This time I was relieved of my mobile phone. The nameless woman with the sensible shoes probed about future instalments of the *Jyllands-Posten* series. To date only one story had been published. If I would tell the newspaper I wanted nothing else published and refused other requests to talk – including the appearance on *60 Minutes* – British intelligence would consider relocating me to somewhere like Canada or Australia. Alternatively, we might discuss a role as a trainer for informants inside the Muslim community or helping former agents deal with the transition to retirement. They even asked me to write papers on both subjects.

But first there would be a probation period of six months, during which I would have to vanish from the radar. I might only have limited access to my kids, and MI5 would have no financial obligation to me. I recalled the fate of the Danish informant who had helped Klang bust the Vollsmose bomb plot but was then forced to flee into unhappy exile overseas.

There was talk of cosmetic surgery and a place in the witness protection programme. But the thought of changing my appearance – to the point where my children would not recognize me – was beyond the pale.

I said that I would think over their terms, but in the meantime wanted a meeting with the security services psychologist, whom I'd met in Scotland at the team-building exercise four years before.

A couple of weeks later I was invited to a hotel in Manchester. The psychologist I knew as Luke from Aviemore was there. He gave me a hug and seemed genuinely pleased to see me again. But concern was soon etched across his face as I recounted my experiences. I was on the verge of tears.

'Do you think I am insane to believe the Americans wanted me dead? Am I paranoid?' I asked.

'Look,' he said. 'You are in a very difficult situation. Fear is not paranoia; it's based on what could have happened and what still might happen. You may have done the right thing in not going to the south of Yemen. You might well have been killed, and, yes, the Americans might not have cared. And I understand why you decided to go to the media; it's a form of protection.'

Luke made it abundantly clear that I needed help. My struggle in processing what I had been through was only just beginning, he said; and while understandable my cocaine use had to stop. He was at pains to cast himself as independent of the security services but I noticed that on occasion the 'I' slipped into 'we'. And he clearly was not at liberty to counsel me or recommend a course of treatment.

It was a long and painful conversation. At least I had been able to talk. He hugged me again at the end.

I still had to give MI5 a response to their proposal. They were already unhappy with me for leaving hotel accommodation that neither *Jyllands-Posten* nor I could afford and returning home. My pervasive distrust of the agencies held me back. I could not spend six months underground, without work, income or protection, for the outside chance of acceptance into the fold.

At a final meeting in a bland hotel conference room, I told Graham that I couldn't accept MI5's scheme; there were too many risks and I had some trust issues.

He looked disappointed but not surprised. He shook my hand firmly and grasped my shoulder.

'That's okay,' he said. 'Take care of yourself; I think you know how to look after yourself.'

As I walked home through blustery, rain-swept streets, I began to absorb the scale of the challenge.

I had made the choice to be on my own. I would no longer suffer from false expectations or be deceived by false promises. I could speak freely but would always need to look over my shoulder. I could look at my children and feel I had made some small contribution towards making the world a better place.

In a school project, my son, Osama, decided to make me his subject. He scanned a photograph of me and wrote an essay entitled: 'My Dad, the Hero'. I had to make sure he deleted the essay from the school computer, but I was also proud. All those tearful farewells suddenly seemed worth it.

Now I would have to start again and deal with my demons. I would also have to adapt to a life without the rush of travelling into terrorist heartlands, and protect my obscurity while at the same time laying out a story that should have lessons for those charged with keeping Western societies safe.

Passers-by glance at me but can't know the role I played in protecting their way of life.

With a shrug or a raised eyebrow, I read media stories of individuals I knew and the threats they posed, the attacks they were planning (or indeed had carried out) and the millions of pounds and dollars being spent trying to stop them. A group I had known in Luton was convicted in 2013 of plotting to blow up a British army base with a bomb strapped to a toy car – one incident among many.

Occasionally I reach the checkout of a supermarket with my groceries, only to see a newspaper headline about one of my former 'brothers' who has finally crossed that Rubicon from talk to terror. As I scan the article for details, the cashier presses coins into my hand and says vacantly, 'Take care.'

I smile as I leave the shop, muttering to myself, 'Take care.'

DRAMATIS PERSONAE

Bødskov, Morten	Justice Minister of Denmark 2011–13
Bonnichsen, Hans Jørgen	Former Director of Danish intelligence agency PET
Butt, G. M.	British-Pakistani kiosk owner in Milton Keynes
Cindy	My girlfriend in Luton
Cowern, Toby	Royal Marines reservist I enlisted to help me run my cover company
Fadia	My Yemeni wife. A pseudonym
Hadi, Abd Rabbu Mansour	President of Yemen since 2012
Hulstrøm, Mark	My boxing coach and smuggling boss in Korsør
Karima	My Moroccan wife. A pseudonym
Khader, Naser	Danish Muslim politician
Lisbeth	My mother
Mears, Ray	Famous British outdoor survival instructor
Nagieb	Documentary maker who travelled with me to Yemen in 2006
Osama	My son
Rosenvold, Michael	Head of the Bandidos in Denmark
Sage	Aminah's fiancé
Saleh, Ali Abdullah	President of Yemen till 2012
Samar	My Palestinian-Christian girlfriend in Korsør
Sarah	My daughter
Scharf, Jakob	Director of Danish intelligence agency PET 2007–12

Mark Hulstrøm.

Awlaki's son was killed a few months after his father in a drone strike.

Negotiating with the Masai tribe in Shompole, Kenya.

Toby Cowern in
northern Sweden,
March 2010.

Apologizing to
Naser Khader on TV.

PET director
Jakob Scharf
(Danish DR).

Stevens, Cat	The British singer now known as Yusuf Islam
Suleiman	Muslim friend I met in prison in Denmark in 1997
Tony	Head doorman at the Shades nightclub in Leighton Buzzard
Vibeke	My first serious girlfriend
Westergaard, Kurt	Danish cartoonist responsible for a controversial 2005 depiction of the Prophet Mohammed
Ymit	Turkish childhood friend in Korsør

Militants and Islamists

Abab, Sheikh Adil al-	Yemeni cleric who became religious guide of AQAP
Abdaly, Taimour Abdulwahab al-	2010 Stockholm suicide bomber I knew in Luton
Abdelghani	Islamist I knew from Denmark who sent me an invitation from the Islamic Courts Union
Abdul	Yemeni friend who worked as a courier for al-Qaeda
Abdulmutallab, Umar Farouk	Nigerian 'underwear bomber' who targeted Northwest flight 253 over Detroit
Abu Bilal	Swedish-Ghanaian room-mate in Dammaj
Abu Hamza	Radical Moroccan preacher in Aarhus
Adebolajo, Michael	Nigerian-British radical who killed British soldier in London in 2013.
Ahmed, Zohaib	British extremist convicted for plot to target the EDL in 2012
Ali	Danish convert and fellow member of Awlaki's Sana'a study circle

Aminah	Croatian convert seeking to marry Awlaki. Real name: Irena Horak
Andersen, Abdallah	Danish convert from Odense convicted for 2006 terrorism plot
Arab, Abu	Danish-Palestinian extremist I met in Lebanon. Real name: Ali al-Hajdib
Asiri, Abdullah al-	Brother of Ibrahim al-Asiri and so-called butt-bomber
Asiri, Ibrahim al-	AQAP master bomb-maker
Avdic, Adnan	Bosnian extremist friend in Denmark acquitted in terror case
Awlaki, Abdulrahman al-	Awlaki's son
Awlaki, Anwar al-	American-Yemeni terrorist cleric
Awlaki, Omar al-	Awlaki's brother
Bakri Mohammed, Omar	Syrian founder of British extremist group al-Muhajiroun
Balawi, Humam al-	Jordanian 'triple agent' responsible for suicide attack on CIA in Afghanistan
Barbi, Rashid	US army veteran who travelled to Dammaj with me
bin Laden, Osama	Al-Qaeda's founder and leader till 2011
Choudary, Anjem	Deputy to al-Muhajiroun's founder, Omar Bakri Mohammed
Geele, Mohammed	Somali convicted of axe attack on the Danish cartoonist Kurt Westergaard in 2010
Godane, Ahmed Abdi	The leader of al-Shabaab. Aka: Muktar al-Zubayr
Hajdib, Saddam al-	Brother of Abu Arab and senior member of Lebanese terrorist group Fatah al-Islam
Hajdib, Youssef al-	Brother of Abu Arab convicted of a 2006 plot to bomb a train in Germany
Hajuri, Shaikh Yahya al-	A teacher at Dammaj

Hammami, Omar	American al-Shabaab member from Alabama. Aka: Abu Mansoor al-Amriki
Hartaba	Awlaki's driver and a former bin Laden bodyguard
Hasan, Nidal	US army major responsible for 2009 Fort Hood shooting in Texas
Hazmi, Mohammed al-	Muslim Brotherhood cleric in Sana'a
Hazmi, Sheikh al-	Cleric with links to AQAP I met in Yemen in 2001; nephew of Mohammed al-Hazmi
Hussain, Anzal	British extremist convicted of plot to target EDL in 2012
Ibrahim	Algerian radical in Aarhus
Ikrimah	Somali-Kenyan al-Shabaab operative I met in Nairobi. Real name: Mohamed Abdikadir Mohamed
Ja'far Umar Thalib	Dammaj alumnus and leader of the Indonesian terrorist group Laskar Jihad
Jimmy	Owner of a gym popular with extremists in Birmingham
Khan, Samir	American editor of AQAP's *Inspire* magazine
Khurshid, Hammad	Danish-born Pakistani convicted of 2007 Denmark terror plot
Lewthwaite, Samantha	So-called 'White Widow' of a 7/7 bomber on the run in East Africa
Majeed, Abdul Waheed	Omar Bakri acolyte who became the first British suicide bomber in Syria
Masri, Hussein al-	Egyptian Islamic Jihad operative I met in Sana'a
Mehdar, Abullah	Yemeni tribal leader close to Anwar al-Awlaki

Menni, Nasserdine	Algerian friend from Luton convicted of providing funds to Stockholm suicide bomber Taimour Abdulwahab al-Abdaly
Misri, Abdullah	Yemeni AQAP financier and arms broker
Mostafa, Jehad Serwan	American member of Awlaki study circle in Yemen who became a senior al-Shabaab operative
Moussaoui, Zacarias	French-Moroccan I met in London who became the 'twentieth' 9/11 hijacker
Mujeeb	Yemeni Islamist who mediated between Salafists and AQAP
Mukhtar	French Muslim friend and flatmate of Zacarias Moussaoui in Brixton
Muqbil, Sheikh	Salafist founder of the Dammaj Institute
Nabhan, Saleh Ali	Kenyan al-Qaeda operative responsible for 1998 bombings of US embassies in East Africa
Newman, Clifford Allen	American convert I met in Dammaj along with his son, Abdullah. AKA: Amin
Ramadan, Mustapha Darwich	Fellow prisoner in Denmark who took part in the beheading of Nick Berg
Raymi, Qasim al-	Second most senior Yemeni in AQAP
Reid, Richard	So-called shoe-bomber who targeted a Paris–Miami flight in December 2001
Saheer	British-Pakistani Birmingham ex-con who plotted attack on Danish newspaper

Salim	British-Pakistani al-Muhajiroun follower whose father owned taxi company I worked for in Birmingham
Samulski, Marek	Australian-Polish fellow member of Awlaki's Sana'a study circle
Somali, Abu Musab al-	Somali terrorist operative I knew from Denmark
Sorensen, Kenneth	Danish convert to Islam who was in Sana'a with me in 2006
Sudani, Abu Talha al-	Sudanese senior al-Qaeda operative based in East Africa
Tabbakh, Hassan	Syrian refugee convicted of the 2007 UK terror plot
Tariq, Shiraz	Pakistani friend from Odense extremist circle
Tayyib, Mahmud al-	Saudi I met in Regent's Park mosque who suggested I study in Dammaj
Tokhi, Abdelghani	Danish resident of Afghan descent convicted of 2007 terror plot
Uddin, Jewel	British-Pakistani extremist convicted of 2012 plot to target the EDL
Uqla, Sheikh Humud bin	Saudi cleric who issued a fatwa in support of 9/11
Usman, Mohammed	British-Pakistani I met on the flight to Yemen in September 2009
Warsame, Ahmed Abdulkadir	Somali friend who became a senior operative in al-Shabaab
Wuhayshi, Nasir al-	Leader of AQAP and former senior bin Laden aide
Zaher, Mohammad	Palestinian from Odense convicted of 2006 terorrism plot
Zarqawi, Abu Musab al-	Jordanian founder of al-Qaeda in Iraq
Zawahiri, Ayman al-	Leader of al-Qaeda from 2011
Zindani, Abdul Majid al-	Head of Muslim Brotherhood in Yemen and founder of al-Iman University

Radicals from the West

Mohammad Zaher
(Danish DR).

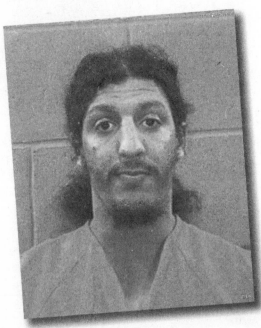

Richard Reid, my
one-time friend
in Brixton and
the so-called
shoe bomber.

Anzal Hussain
(police handout).

Abdallah Andersen
(BT.DK).

The Danish
militant Abu
Khattab (centre),
threatening my life
in 2013.

Radicals in Yemen

Mohammed al-Hazmi.

Adil al-Abab.

Abdul Majid
al-Zindani.

AQAP master
bomb-maker
Ibrahim al-Asiri.

Jehad Serwan
Mostafa
(*Guardian*).

My Intelligence Handlers

Alex	Senior US intelligence official who oversaw the 'Aminah mission'
Amanda	The CIA agent Elizabeth Hanson, who recruited me to work for the CIA
Anders	PET intelligence analyst specializing in Islamist extremism and terrorism
Andy	My senior MI5 handler; ex-British police
Buddha	One of the two PET agents who recruited me
Daniel	Weapons instructor in Denmark
Emma	My second MI6 handler
Frank	Weapons instructor in Denmark
George	CIA Copenhagen station chief
Graham	MI5 operative I met in 2012
Jed	My main CIA handler
Jesper	Danish intelligence handler who joined the team in 2010; former banker
Joshua	CIA agent I met at same time as Amanda in 2007
Kevin	MI5 handler reporting to Andy
Klang	My main PET handler who recruited me as an agent. He first introduced himself as Martin Jensen
Luke	Psychologist working for MI5
Matt	My first MI6 handler
Michael	CIA official I met in Denmark after killing of Awlaki

Dramatis Personae

Rob	SAS trainer at MI6 retreat near Loch Ness
Robert	MI5 official who approached me in Luton just before the London bombings
Soren	Team leader of the PET agents handling me
Steve	MI6 instructor at the Fort Monckton training facility
Sunshine	Female MI5 agent reporting to Andy. My main point-person at MI5
Tommy Chef	Director of Operations for PET
Trailer	One of my Danish intelligence handlers; former farmer

AGENT ARCHIVE

Jihadi Communications

Official Invitation
from the Islamic
Courts Union to move
to Somalia.

GOLAHA MAXKAMADAHA
ISLAAMIGA SOOMALIYEED
Xafiiska Arrimaha Dibadda

مجلس المحاكم الإسلامية في الصومال
مكتب الشؤون الخارجية

Date: 19/12/06
Ref: F.A.O/232/06

Semali Council of Islamic Courts
Foreign Affairs Office

التاريخ: ـــــ
الرقم: ـــــ

TO: Deeqa Construction & Water Well Drilling

FROM: Prof. Ibrahim Hassan Addou, Ph.D.
          Secretary of Foreign Affairs

SUBJECT: Permission to Enter Mogadishu

DATE: 28 Dulqa'da 1427 (December 19, 2006)

As you requested, in your letter of December 17, 2006, we have no objection for
Mr. Strom Morten Pass.NO: 101288867 (Danish) to enter the country from
Mogadishu International Airport and remain in the country two weeks from his/her
date of arrival.

Thank you for your cooperation, and should you have any question(s), please feel
free to contact us.

cc: Head, Planning   Dept.
cc: Head, Security   Dept.
cc: Head, Finance   Dept.
cc: Head, Information   Dept.
cc: Head, Health   Dept.

Awlaki email correspondence
in my Yahoo Account.

Mujahideen Secrets
Software Interface.
You can see Awlaki's
public key 'hereyougo'
which he used to
communicate with me.

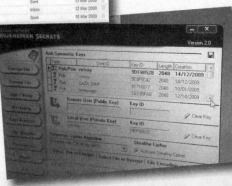

Aminah's very
first Facebook
message to me.

20:54

Aminah Muslimah Fisabilillah

Assalamu alaykom

Eid Mubarak to you and your family. Can you tell me please what do you mean specifically when you
type in your post on the wall of group od support Shaikh Anwar al-Awlaki? What kind of support and
are you in direct contact with Shaikh?

Aminah on
Facebook broaches
the possibility of
marrying Awlaki.

Aminah Muslimah Fisabilillah

No problem, I think you mixed South East Europe with South Croatia

I have one question tho. Do you know personally AAA? And if it is so, may I be so liberal to ask you
something?

11:23

Murad Al-Danimarki

Yes I do know him. Feel free to ask

11:32

Aminah Muslimah Fisabilillah

As I told you before I do not have mahram, and I sent Shaikh a letter by mail, I am not sure if I had his
correct email address, but actually I was wondering will he search for a second wife, I proposed him a
marriage, and I do not know how silly it is. But I tried. Now, as I am in contact with you there is a
possibility for you to get know me better in a way you can recommended me to s Shaikh, if you are
interested in it and if you want to help me, inshaallah. You can see I am a revert, convert on Islam
alhamdidullah. I seek a way how to get out of this country, and I search a husband who will teach me
and whom I can help a lot. I deeply respect him and the all things he do for this Ummah and I want to
help him in any way.

What do you think about that?
JazzakAllah khayrun

11:38

Murad Al-Danimarki

Waleikum Salaam Warahmatullah

Sister, I was with him for 3 months ago, and he asked the same, if I could help him getting married to a
revert sister. Subhan'Allah how Allah plans. But sister by getting married to him, means that you may
never again come to croatia as you know his current situation. I can however travel with you to him, as
there is no way for you otherwise to know his whereabout. Could I get your personal details to forward
them to him today? I will write down his requirement for marriage, as he told me to search.

garding the sister first of all thanks for keeping me in mind:) so far I am interested. I just need a few
rifications from you and then I need you to pass on a message to her:
How did you get to know about her?
Are you communicating with her in a secure manner?
I want all my communications with her to pass through you. But just in case you got cut off the internet if
I could pass on to me an email for her that I would only use if I am unable to communicate with you. My
me in any on-line communications with her should be Sami
What do you suggest in terms of how to get her here?

Extract from
Awlaki's email
telling me he
is interested
in Aminah.

Awlaki tells me in an
encrypted message he
has attached a video
recording of him for me
to pass on to Aminah.

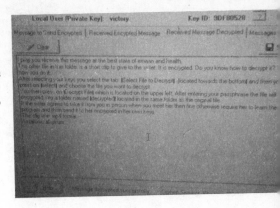

Assalamu alaykum
Alhamdulillah we got married. May Allah reward you for all what you have done. However, according to your description of her I expected something different. I am not saying that you tricked me or anything; I am just saying that I expected something different.
I do not blame you or your wife because I believe you were sincere and you were doing your best.

So she turned out to be different then what you described. Masha Allah she turned out to be better than I expected and better than you described:)

Awlaki's encrypted 28 June 2010 email giving
me the verdict on his new wife Aminah.

Sister, please can I ask you a favor. If it is possible for you to go and buy some stuff for me.
So far everybody who bought it, majority I didn't like. And it is hard for sisters here to buy
some western clothes. I give up of Yemeni clothes. All I have I don't like and it is too hot to
wear it. Fabrics are not good, synthetic, it's just horrible.
So please if you can find some European clothes. I miss it so much. I just need few dresses
(2) and skirts (2) and top (4). All simple without any glittering stuff and pleats, I hate it.
Dresses should be long, without sleeves - like top, wide but tight in top part and all in one
piece. Not 2 pieces like Yemeni dresses. Fabric should be light, non-transparent. Skirts also
should be long and light fabric, wide, solid. Tops whatever you find simple and nice. Colors
and patterns never mind, just please avoid pink and orange color. White, black, different
shades of blue and green. Floral pattern is nice, and solid is just fine. And if you can find
denim mini skirt, size 40 or L, tight and very short. ?
Next I need 10 packages of feminine pads; it's called FAM.thin, regular with wings, made in
Lebanon. Package is white and green color with sunflower. I am sure you will find it.

Extract from the reque
for clothes and beau
products Awlaki attach
from Aminah for Fadi

ome of hooks men r still interested to come here then let me know so that arrangements could be done ....
as for going to hooks place ... then i was told by hook that they want to train brothers and then send them
ck or to the west .... i told him i need advanced training so he told me its on and off so it could take long
i i have to be patient .. for me i can b patient and learn more of deen and improve arabic inshaAllah
estion 1 ... if they gonna train brothers from here what kinda traing is it gonna be?
estion 2 ... the anti tank mine that brothers got will they be willing to sell them to us and do they have
eapons that can hit a tank frm far like the ones hisbullah used to destroy israel merkeva tank? or rpg 29 etc?
estion 3 .... regarding the project how is it coming so far? how is shompole, is it a good place? how is the
gestration and paper word going on? update me inshaAllah and inshaAllah this wil b a very good project to
muslims inshaAllah
hecked the site and its really interesting for people who love nature and hicking and expedition may Allah
ess this project and keep it away from the eyes and suspicions of the kufar
hii al habib take good care of yourself especially in yemen after wat happened in usa .. and the yemen
rniture business u told me abt .. check on it if it would b worth dealing with it but let it b like something for
ustaqbal inshaAllah

o in iman

Extract from an encrypted email Ikrimah sent to me in November 2010 indicating Awlaki and he were hatching a plan to send operatives to attack the West. He also praised my Storm Bushcraft Kenya venture.

ne sandals are good. The tablets I was looking for are hexamine. The ones you sent are something else. If
ou are traveling again then see if you can get me hexamine tablets.

ease send any messages from my wife's sister.
you are going on-line please send me all what is available on the arrest of our Somali brother.
so I heard on the news that the New York Times reported that al Qaeda in Yemen is buying a lot of castor
ans to make ricin and attack the US. Find me what you can on that. You could do a search for: Yemen +
in

xtract from an encrypted email from Awlaki
sking me about a *New York Times* report on ricin.

alamu alaykom we rahmetullahi

sending you this mail with great sorrow and sadness in my heart but again happines for my husband
nada. Alhamdidullah he is now in the Jannat and do not feel anything but joy and happines. Alhamdidullah,
a grant him Shuhada what he wanted and grant him the higest rank of Jannat.

husband give me this in case something happend to him so I can contact you. Actually I wanted to contact
in case I will go back in Europe, but I have 4 months to decide what to do.

first option is shahada inshaAllah

Extract from an email from Aminah telling me she wanted to carry out a suicide attack to avenge the death of Awlaki.

Kenya is getting really bad coz the kufar are doing all their effort
to harm us. And they monitor the hawala (dahabshil ,qaran etc)
accusing them of helping and financing mujahidin. So you need to
be extra carefull they dont get a single trace of anything coz they
are now tracing a sister who was a window of one of the london
7/7 bomber (the jamecan brother) and they are accusing her of
financing and organising "terorisim" so please watchout when
you are here coz they may put you in a case that you dont know.

Ikrimah encrypted email referencing the
White Widow, Samantha Lewthwaite, March 2012.

Spy Stuff

The Ascot Hotel in Copenhagen where I had many of my meetings with Western intelligence.

Business card for Storm Bushcraft.

Business card for Alum Rock Cab Company, which I worked for.

Jesper's quad-bike insurance disclaimer.

Greetings card from Klang Trailer Buddha and Jed.

Jimmy's gym.

førshe mødested
① Gersthof S-Bahn Station
Anker bakery.

② Café "Seafredo" Gersthof Lounge
on Gersthof strasse 30, Wien 1180.

My mission notes for my
first meeting with Aminah
in Vienna. The CIA
wanted me to bring her
to a bar—restaurant, but
I changed the plan and
took her to McDonald's.

10:00 am meeting at McDonalds. Cover story, gifts, money.
Anyway
meeting up after embassy, going to buy ticket, travel security
new emails, only use it until you arrive to Y.
hghKthg11@gmail.com — Send your public key — you get number
buy a mobile phone in Y. You will get a new laptop.

Flight details to 24. +385 92 28 666 76 — mobile
white blue2010
@gmail.com
Islam 786 Islam

africansunrise2010@gmail
Islam 786 Islam

Mission notes from
the last time I met
Aminah in Vienna.

Mission notes as Aminah neared
travelling to Yemen.

Tillykke bror du er
lige blevet rig ☺
meget rig ☺

Text message from
Klang — 'You just got
very rich'.

Klang
Læg den lille boks i den
store boks og placér den
på bagsædet lige bag
førersædet.
From:Klang
23/05/12 16:57

Options   Reply   Back

'Place the small box in
the large box and place
it on the back seat just
behind the driver's
seat.' Soren texted me
in Yemen from Klang's
phone after my last
mission was aborted.

The $10 000 Jesper gave me
in my Hilton hotel room.

Paper Trail

Western Union transfer from PET. Note that the sender lists their address as Soborg, the district in which PET HQ is located.

Invoice for a hotel paid by Klang. Note his invoice address is Mola Consult, the PET front company.

Invoice for one of the MI5-authorized money transfers to Somali terrorist Ahmed Abdulkadir Warsame.

Invoice for chemical gloves also purchased for Ahmed Abdulkadir Warsame.

Visa stamps for a Lebanon
Mission in 2007.

Hong Kong and China visa
stamps on my trip to see
Abdul there in May 2012.

Signing contract to
develop Masinga Dam.

regarding the money, pls tell the sister that the hook wants her to have 3000 dollars with her which you
will provide at the next meeting in vienna.   this is perfect cover for your next trip to see her.

have a safe trip and good luck,

your brothers

Email from my CIA handlers
Jed and George before one of
my trips to Vienna.

Confiscation notice for
Hexamine, signed by
Jesper ahead of the May
2012 mission to Yemen.

Soren's quad-bike
insurance disclaimer.

ACKNOWLEDGEMENTS

Morten Storm

I would like to thank all my family members and friends in Denmark, Sweden, Norway, Holland, the UK, Kenya and around the world for their support.

Thank you, Paul Cruickshank and Tim Lister, for masterfully making sense of it all during the many weeks we spent together and for the many months you spent investigating every last detail of my story and peeling back the layers of my memory. I will always be in your debt. I first met Paul during my 'radical years', when he came to Luton in 2005 to report on the extremist group al-Muhajiroun. He is now CNN's terrorism analyst and the editor of a recent five-volume collection of scholarship on al-Qaeda. It seems like a lifetime ago we met in Luton.

Paul and Tim have reported on al-Qaeda terrorism and international security for many years, and their expertise was invaluable in providing context to this story. Tim travelled across Yemen well before I did and unlike me made it to Afghanistan, where he reported on the US bombing of Osama bin Laden's redoubt in Tora Bora for CNN.

Thanks to the *Jyllands-Posten* reporters Carsten Ellegaard Christensen, Orla Borg, Morten Pihl and Michael Holbek Jensen who broke the story about my work for Western intelligence. You deservedly won the inaugural European Press Prize. Thanks also to all the Danish journalists who have believed in and supported me.

I'd also like to thank our literary agents, Richard Pine and Euan Thorneycroft, and our editors, Joel Rickett at Viking and Jamison Stoltz at Grove Atlantic, for giving me the chance to tell the world my story. If this book makes just one person think twice about following the path of violent extremism it will have been worth it.

Thanks to the Danish politician Irena Simonsen for her huge help and backing, and thanks too to my lawyer, Karoly Nemeth, in Denmark for all his guidance and support.

There are several others I would like to thank for their support, including Nic Robertson at CNN, Mark Stout at the International Spy Museum, Frederik Obermaier at *Süddeutsche Zeitung*, Howard Rosenberg at *60 Minutes* and Bent Skjaerstad at TV2 in Norway. Thank you also Joost in Holland. There are many others I can't thank for security reasons, but you know who you are.

Thanks to the bands Metallica, Slayer and Anthrax for your great music. You helped me wind up and wind down after missions.

Finally a massive thank you to all the lovely, kind and generous people and families I met in the Middle East and in North and East Africa. They enriched me with great knowledge and taught me how to live with honour and be a generous human being.

Paul Cruickshank and Tim Lister

Thank you, Morten Storm, for making it necessary and for allowing us to burrow deep into your life during stressful times for you and your family. We were staying with you when al-Qaeda types in Syria threatened your life in an online video and were struck by your humour and poise.

Thank you to your friends and family and ex-girlfriends we met in Denmark. Thanks to the Danish politician Irena Simonsen for inviting us into her home and helping us understand the political dynamics.

A giant thank you to Richard Pine, our literary agent at Inkwell in New York, for making it all possible. Huge thanks also to Euan Thorneycroft at A. M. Heath in London for working with Richard to bring this story to the world, and for your valuable feedback.

We have been blessed in having two of the best editors in the business: Joel Rickett at Penguin and Jamison Stoltz at Grove Atlantic. Thank you for working so seamlessly together and for your brilliant edits and ideas which immeasurably improved the book. Thanks also to the team of people working with you who helped put the book

Acknowledgements

together, including Ellie Smith, Allison Malecha, Ben Brusey, Sara Granger and the copy-editor, Mark Handsley.

Thank you Eliza Rothstein and Lyndsey Blessing at Inkwell for all your assistance and getting this book translated around the globe. Thanks to Taryn Eckstein for her legal advice.

Thanks to Carsten Ellegaard Christensen at *Jyllands-Posten*. You are a pro and it was Morten's good fortune to first approach you with his story. Thanks for the help you provided when we visited you in Copenhagen and keeping us in the loop on your investigations. You and your *Jyllands-Posten* colleagues deserve all the accolades for first breaking the story.

A special thanks to the Croatian journalist Sandra Veljkovic at the Croatian newspaper *Večeřnji List* for her help on the Aminah side of the story. Thanks to Bent Skjaerstad at Norway's TV2 for sharing information on Ikrimah's time in Norway.

Big thanks to Nic and Margaret Lowrie Robertson, as well as Ken Shiffman, for their counsel on the project. We are indebted to Magnus Ranstorp, one of Scandinavia's leading counter-terrorism academics, for casting his expert eye over the text and his smorgasbord of insights on the Danish context.

Thanks to those who read various iterations of the book and provided precious feedback. Some cannot be named because of the sensitivity of their positions, but you know who you are.

Thanks to our friends and family who indulged us while we disappeared off the map for a year to write this book.

And finally thanks to our wives for their love, support, feedback, ideas . . . and transcribing.

NOTES

1. Desert Road

2 **'Come to Yemen . . . see you':** This is my recollection. This is one of the few emails quoted in the book I did not save. Unless otherwise stated all emails, text messages and recorded conversations quoted in the book are reproduced verbatim, including spelling and grammatical errors.

4 **met two of the hijackers:** The 9/11 Commission said, in its final report, that it had 'been unable to learn enough about Aulaqi's relationship with Hazmi and Mihdhar [two of the 9/11 hijackers] to reach a conclusion' (p. 221), and that its attempts to locate and interview the cleric had been unsuccessful (footnote 35, p. 517).

9 **'The ballot . . . your ranks':** 'Salutations to al Shabaab of Somalia', Awlaki blog posting, 20 December 2008.

9 **'I pray . . . or not':** Brooks Egerton, 'Imam's emails to Fort Hood suspect tame compared with online rhetoric', *Dallas Morning News*, 28 November 2009.

10 **'the blame . . . a few dollars':** Ibid.

10 **suicide attack:** The four South Korean tourists were killed in the suicide bombing in Hadramaut on 15 March 2009; 'False Foundation? AQAP, Tribes and Ungoverned Spaces in Yemen', Combating Terrorism Center at West Point, October 2011.

10 **soliciting prostitutes:** Chitra Ragavan, 'The Imam's Very Curious Story', *US News and World Report*, 13 June 2004.

2. Gangs, Girls, God

19 **third-largest illegal business:** Klaus von Lampe, 'The Nicotine Racket. Trafficking in Untaxed Cigarettes: A Case Study of Organized Crime in

Germany': guest lecture given at the Institute of Criminology, University of Oslo, Norway, 6 May 1999.

22 **killing one:** Edward Winterhalder, *Out in Bad Standings: Inside the Bandidos Motorcycle Club*, Blockhead City, 2005, chap. 24.

25 **I learned . . . God's messenger:** For one of many accounts of this event, see John Miller and Aaron Kenedi, *Inside Islam: The Faith, the People, and the Conflicts of the World's Fastest-Growing Religion*, Da Capo Press, 2002.

25 **'Proclaim . . . blood':** Koran, al-Alaq, 96:1–2.

25 **'Allah is with us':** Koran, al-Tawba, 9:40.

25 **'Our Lord is God':** Koran, al-Haj, 22:39–40.

4. Arabia

39 **what was driving:** For more on Sheikh Muqbil and the Salafist worldview, see Bernard Haykel, 'The Salafis in Yemen at a Crossroads: An Obituary of Shaykh Muqbil al-Wadi'i of Dammaj (d. 1422/2001)', *Jemen-Report*, 2 (October 2002); Bernard Haykel, 'On the Nature of Salafi Thought and Action', in Roel Meijer et al., *Global Salafism*, Columbia University Press, 2009; Quintan Wiktorowicz, 'Anatomy of the Salafi Movement', *Studies in Conflict & Terrorism*, 29:3 (2006), 207–39.

43 **US authorities . . . year before:** *United States of America v. Clifford Allen Newman*, Appeal from the United States District Court for the Middle District of Florida, 17 August 2010.

5. Londonistan

47 **'Had it issued . . . many a contradiction':** Koran, An-Nisā', 4:82.

49 **Master's degree:** 'Profile: Zacarias Moussaoui', BBC, 25 April 2006.

49 **What he . . . Chechen war:** Richard Willing, 'Westernized kid grows into 9/11 suspect', *USA Today*, 25 June 2002; 'British have file on Moussaoui', *USA Today*, 13 June 2002.

49 **one of al-Qaeda's camps:** Indictment: *United States of America v. Zacarias Moussaoui*, US District Court for the Eastern District of Virginia, 11 December 2001.

50 **Russian rockets rained down:** Amelia Gentleman, 'Russian rockets hit Grozny market', *Guardian*, 21 October 1999.

51 **He had . . . 'twentieth hijacker':** Indictment: *United States of America v. Zacarias Moussaoui*, US District Court for the Eastern District of Virginia, 11 December 2001.

51 **'shoe-bomber':** *United States v. Richard Colvin Reid*, US District Court of Massachusetts, 16 January 2002.

6. Death to America

55 **issued a fatwa:** Noorhaidi Hasan, *Laskar Jihad: Islam, Militancy, and the Quest for Identity in Post-New Order Indonesia*, Cornell Southeast Asia Program Publications, 2006.

55 **'Fight in the cause . . . not aggressors':** Koran, al-Baqarah, 2:190.

56 **'must be fulfilled . . . their minds':** The words of Ahmad Yahya Ibn Muhammad al-Najm in response to requests for guidance from Salafis wanting to fight in the Moluccas. Al-Najm was a member of the Saudi senior Ulama committee. See Hasan, *Laskar Jihad*, p. 117.

56 **In September 2006 . . . the country:** Elisabeth Arnsdorf Haslund, 'Titalt: Mit TATP var ikke farligt', *Berlingske Tidende* (Denmark), 13 September 2007; 'Denmark convicts men in bomb plot', BBC, 23 November 2007.

58 **CALES:** The Centre for Arabic Language and Eastern Studies at the University of Science and Technology in Sana'a.

58 **USS *Cole*:** 'USS *Cole* fast facts', CNN, 18 September 2013; Michael Sniffen, 'FBI: Plastic Explosives Used in *Cole* Bombing', ABC News, 1 November 2000.

58 **jihadist network:** One of the men I got to know was a Yemeni-American called Abdul Rahman al-Yaf'i from a prominent tribal family, who several of my circle told me was Osama bin Laden's 'right-hand man' in Yemen. The previous year those alleged ties had prompted his extraordinary rendition by the United States during a family visit to Cairo. He was flown to Jordan for interrogation, where he was tortured and pressured to confess to a role in the 1998 bombings of US embassies in East Africa, which he denied. After his release he visited me several times – in secret – at my house, but never spoke of al-Qaeda.

59 **none of the al-Qaeda members:** Abdul told me he spent time with the Yemeni jihadi Adil al-Abab in Afghanistan. Al-Abab did not contradict this after I got to know him.

60 **women and children:** Tim Lister reported on the battle for CNN from a location near Tora Bora.

62 **a long fatwa:** The full text of bin Uqla's fatwa can be found at http:// sunnahonline.com/ilm/contemporary/0017.htm.

62 **'When America attacked . . . terrorism?' the Sheikh asked:** Ibid.

62 **with us or with the terrorists:** President George W. Bush, Address to a Joint Session of Congress and the American People, 20 September 2001.

63 **He was referring . . . travel:** For more on John Walker Lindh's travelling to Afghanistan, see Mark Kukis, *My Heart Became Attached: The Strange Journey of John Walker Lindh*, Potomac Books, 2008.

65 **MV *Limburg*:** On 6 October 2002, in an attack allegedly endorsed by Osama bin Laden, a Yemeni terrorist cell blew up an explosive-laden boat beside the French oil tanker MV *Limburg*, near the port of Mukalla, killing the suicide bombers and one sailor: 'False Foundation? AQAP, Tribes and Ungoverned Spaces in Yemen', Combating Terrorism Center at West Point, October 2011; Sebastien Rotella and Esther Shrader, 'Tanker Blast Likely a Terror Attack, French Say', *Los Angeles Times*, 11 October 2002.

7. Family Feuds

67 **In September 2006 . . . sentence:** Elisabeth Arnsdorf Haslund, 'Titalt: Mit TATP var ikke farligt', *Berlingske Tidende* (Denmark), 13 September 2007; 'Denmark convicts men in bomb plot', BBC, 23 November 2007. For more, see Morten Skjoldager, *Truslen Indefra: De Danske Terrorista*, Lindardt og Ringhof, 2009, pp. 191–203.

71 **opened fire:** Dahr Jamail, 'Falluja's struggle after invasion,' Al Jazeera, 1 May 2008.

71 **an offensive . . . Sharia law:** Pepe Escobar, 'The Islamic emirate of Fallujah', *Asia Times*, 15 July 2004.

72 **'magnificent nineteen':** Dominic Casciani, 'Profile: Omar Bakri Mohammed', BBC, 12 August 2005.

72 **'The punishment . . . be imprisoned':** Koran, al-Ma'idah, 5:33.

72 **Several of his acolytes. . . in London:** The plot to target crowded spaces in London was broken up by 'Operation Crevice' in March 2004. For ties to al-Muhajiroun, see Peter Bergen and Paul Cruickshank, 'Clerical Error: The Dangers of Tolerance', *New Republic*, 7 August 2005.

73 **After two British men . . . their plot:** On 30 April 2003 two followers of al-Muhajiroun attacked a nightclub in Tel Aviv, killing three. See Bergen and Cruickshank, 'Clerical Error'.

73 **ultimate sacrifice:** Kiran Randhawa, Justin Davenport and David Churchill, 'Suicide bomber Brit worked as driver for hate cleric Omar Bakri', *Evening Standard*, 13 February 2014.

75 **demand for the training:** Training camps like the one I ran soon drew the attention of the security services and the UK media. See Ian Cobain and Richard Norton-Taylor, 'Training camps for terrorists in UK parks', *Guardian*, 13 August 2006.

75 **On 7 May . . . was filmed:** Maria Newman, 'Video Appears to Show Beheading of American Civilian', *The New York Times*, 11 May 2004.

76 **After his release . . . Ansar al-Islam:** Edward F. Mickolus, *The Terrorist List. Volume 1: A–K*, ABC-CLIO, 2009, p. 524.

76 **killed in Fallujah:** US Central Command statement, 8 October 2004; Hans Davidsen-Nielsen and Kjeld Hybel, 'Danmark i Krig: Krigens beskidte ansigt', *Politiken* (Denmark), 3 April 2007.

76 **'It is . . . Mighty, Wise':** Koran, al-Anfal, 8:67.

78 **'The woman . . . Last Day':** Koran, An Noor, 24:2.

79 **'Satan said: " . . . among them" ':** Koran, al-Hijra, 15:39–40.

79 **'Those are . . . forgives sins?':** Koran, 'Āli 'Imrān, 3:135.

8. MI5 Comes to Luton

80 **The magazine reported ' . . . detainee's lap':** Text of original article and retraction at John Barry, 'Gitmo: Southcom Showdown', Newsweek.com, 8 May 2005.

80 **used the story:** See, for example, Hendrik Hertzberg, 'Big News Week', *New Yorker*, 30 May 2005.

81 still available online: When this book went to press the footage was available here: http://www.youtube.com/watch?v=FG4fZNPLgWY.

9. Meeting the Sheikh

91 designated a 'global terrorist': The designation described the university as a training ground for terrorists. 'Al Iman students are suspected of being responsible, and were arrested, for recent terrorist attacks, including the assassination of three American missionaries,' it said in part: http://www.treasury.gov/press-center/press-releases/Pages/js1190.aspx.

93 '44 Ways . . .': '44 Ways of Supporting Jihad' was released in early 2009.

94 He had been born . . . vocation: Judicial Watch Awlaki FBI FOIA documents obtained in May 2013; Scott Shane and Souad Mekhennet, 'Imam's Path From Condemning Terror to Preaching Jihad', *The New York Times*, 8 May 2010.

94 'more seriously': See 'Spilling Out the Beans: Al Awlaki Revealing His Side of the Story', AQAP's *Inspire* magazine, issue 9, May 2012.

95 he scored a 3.85: Documents later obtained by the advocacy group Judicial Watch under the Freedom of Information Act provide fascinating detail into Awlaki's life in the US. A former teacher at San Diego State University wrote to the Doctoral Screening Committee at GWU to recommend Awlaki, ticking the 'Excellent' column for his maturity, self-confidence and analytical ability. His former professor said, 'Anwar brings a unique perspective to class discussions and the work he produces . . . His peers in the classes looked to Anwar as a leader . . . When Mr Al-Aulaqi completes his studies in the US he will become an educational leader in the higher education system in Yemen.' Awlaki's name was frequently spelled 'Aulaqi' while he was in the US. Judicial Watch obtained the documents in May 2013 and posted them online in July 2013.

95 wrote Woodall: Andrea Bruce Woodall, *Washington Post*, 12 September 2001.

95 interview to *National Geographic*: Brian Handwerk and Zain Habboo, 'Attack on America: An Islamic Scholar's Perspective', *National Geographic*, 28 September 2001.

97 **warrant for his arrest:** Investigators had sought the warrant as a way to detain Awlaki for further questioning on his links to the 9/11 hijackers. See ABC News, 'Investigators Blew an Opportunity to Arrest Awlaki', 1 December 2009.

97 **Tracing the . . . ' . . . coincidental':** Final Report of the 9/11 Commission, chap. 7, p. 221. Further suspicion about Awlaki's links to the hijackers is voiced on p. 230.

97 **'There is reporting . . . were terrorists':** National Commission on Terrorist Attacks upon the United States, 'Outline of the 9/11 Plot: Staff Statement No. 16', published 16 June 2004.

97 **There was . . . ' . . . group Hamas':** Final report of the 9/11 Commission, footnote 33, chap. 7.

98 **One article written:** Chitra Ragavan: 'The Imam's Very Curious Story', *US News and World Report*, 13 June 2004.

98 **character assassination:** Awlaki years later would put an elaborate spin on the police cautioning him for soliciting prositutes. He wrote in *Inspire* magazine, the online publication of al-Qaeda in the Arabian Peninsula: 'In 1996 while waiting at a traffic light in my minivan a middle aged woman knocked on the window of the passenger seat. By the time I rolled down the window and before even myself or the woman uttering a word I was surrounded by police officers who had me come out of my vehicle only to be handcuffed. I was accused of soliciting a prostitute and then released. They made it a point to make me know in no uncertain terms that the woman was an undercover cop. I didn't know what to make of the incident. However a few days later came the answer. I was visited by two men who introduced themselves as officials with the US government . . . and that they are interested in my cooperation with them . . . I never heard back from them again until in 1998 when I was approached by a woman, this time from my window and again I was surrounded by police officers who this time had go to court. This time I was told that this is a sting operation and you would not be able to get out of it.' See 'Spilling Out the Beans', *Inspire* magazine.

98 **Among the avid consumers:** Nic Robertson, Paul Cruickshank and Tim Lister, 'Documents give new details on al Qaeda's London bombings', CNN, 30 April 2012; Paul Cruickshank, 'Al Qaeda loses its English-language inspiration', CNN, 1 October 2011.

98 '. . . revved up . . .': Cruickshank, 'Al Qaeda loses its English-language inspiration'.

98 **favour of suicide bombings:** Ibid.

98 **'Constants on the Path of Jihad':** Anwar al-Awlaki, 'Constants on the Path of Jihad', 2005. The lecture was widely posted online.

99 **'Allah is Preparing Us for Victory':** By July 2006 the recording was circulating on online Islamist forums in the West. A good translation of the lecture, made when Awlaki was in prison in Sana'a, can be found at: https://docs. google.com/document/d/10SyzllD6ESWK9mUw18sOw5l2RK5QfRBAXxg pO5quKHY/edit.

100 **At morning prayers . . . in Afghanistan:** 'False Foundation? AQAP, Tribes and Ungoverned Spaces in Yemen', Combating Terrorism Center at West Point, October 2011.

100 **El Cajon Boulevard:** R. Stickney and Paul Krueger, 'Accused Terrorist Was "Kind, Peaceful Man": Friends', NBC News, San Diego, 6 August 2010.

100 **graduate to the FBI's Rewards:** http://www.fbi.gov/wanted/wanted_ terrorists/copy_of_jehad-serwan-mostafa/view.

103 **Abu Talha . . . most-wanted list:** His death was announced by al-Shabaab more than a year later. Bill Roggio, 'Senior al-Qaeda Operative Killed in Somalia', *Long War Journal*, 1 September 2008.

108 **sent troops into Somalia:** Mohamed Olad Hassan, 'Ethiopian Force Enters Somalia', Associated Press, 20 July 2006.

109 **The FBI . . . solitary confinement:** Judicial Watch Awlaki FBI FOIA documents obtained in May 2013.

10. *The Fall*

112 **push eastwards:** Jeffrey Gettleman and Mark Mazzetti, 'Somalia's Islamists and Ethiopia Gird for a War', *The New York Times*, 9 December 2006; 'Ethiopian Troops Seize Strategic Town in Somalia', *Somaliland Times*, 9 October 2006.

112 **Australians and my British friend:** The Australians arrested were my friend Mustafa Ayoub and his brother. For more on the arrests, see Cameron Stewart and Martin Chulov, 'Yemen ties terror's loose ends', *The Australian*, 4 November 2006; Abul Taher, 'UK Preacher in Secret Web Call for Jihad', *The Times*, 4 January 2007.

113 **released and deported:** Stewart and Chulov, 'Yemen ties terror's loose ends'; Taher, 'UK Preacher in Secret Web Call for Jihad'; 'Dansker Tortureret i Yemen', TV2 (Denmark), 27 December 2006; Janet Fife-Yeomans, 'Australians Placed on US Terror No-Fly List', *Daily Telegraph* (Australia), 31 August 2011.

117 **'Allah is . . . due measurements':** Koran, Az-Zumar, 39:62, and al-Furqan, 25:2.

11. Switching Sides

128 **Egyptian al-Qaeda operative:** The senior Egyptian operative was Abu Ubaidah al-Masri. See Mitchell D. Silber, *The Al Qaeda Factor: Plots against the West*, University of Pennsylvania Press, 2011, pp. 142–52.

128 **discovered in his luggage:** Morten Skjoldager, *Truslen Indefra: De Danske Terrorista*, Lindardt og Ringhof, 2009, chaps. 15–16.

128 **used a front company:** A Western intelligence source provided the information on the Khurshid investigation to Paul Cruickshank in 2013.

128 **A short while later . . . in prison:** Silber, *Al Qaeda Factor*; Morten Skjoldager, 'Portræt: Trænet til terror mod sit fødeland: Portræt, Hammad Khürshid', *Politiken* (Denmark), 10 November 2009; Paul Cruickshank, personal communication with Elisabeth Haslund (a Danish reporter who covered the trial), New York, September 2009.

12. London Calling

129 **'Send him Bak!':** *Sun*, 20 July 2005.

129 **' . . . make it a long one':** Alan Travis and Duncan Campbell, 'Bakri to be banned from the UK', *Guardian*, 9 August 2005.

131 **terror dynasty:** For more on the al-Hajdib brothers, see Hassan M. Fatah, 'German Suspects from Opposite Sides of a Lebanese Town', *The New York Times*, 29 August 2006.

131 **Youssef, had been arrested:** 'A Terrorist Gets the Judicial Middle Finger', *Der Spiegel*, 10 December 2008; '9 arrested by Denmark in reported terror plot', *International Herald Tribune*, 5 September 2006.

134 **Not long after . . . were killed:** 'Slain Lebanese Militant was Suspect in Failed German Bombing', *The New York Times*, 21 May 2007, and Hassan M. Fattah, 'Lebanese Army and Islamists Battle for Second Day', *The New York Times*, 22 May 2007; 'Dozens killed in Lebanon gunbattle between Islamic militants, security forces', Associated Press, 20 May 2007; 'Nowhere to put us', BBC, 23 May 2007. For more on Fatah al-Islam in the Nahr al-Barid camp, see Muhammad Ali Khalidi and Diane Riskedahl, 'The Road to Nahr al Barid', Middle East Research and Information Project, no. 244.

136 **Hamid Elasmar:** James Orr, 'Guilty pleas over soldier beheading plot', *Guardian*, 28 January 2008.

138 **Tabbakh was arrested:** Duncan Gardham, 'Terrorist bomb maker Hassan Tabbakh jailed for seven years', *Daily Telegraph*, 30 July 2008; for more on Tabbakh's case, see Judgment: *Regina v. Hassan Tabbakh*, Court of Appeal, Royal Courts of Justice, 3 March 2009 [2009] EWCA Crim 464; Decision: Hassan Tabbakh against the United Kingdom, The European Court of Human Rights (Fourth Section), sitting on 21 February 2012; Judgment: On the Application of Hassan Tabbakh, High Court of Justice, Royal Courts of Justice, 9 August 2013 [2013] EWHC 2492 (Admin).

13. From Langley with Love

144 **arresting more than twenty men:** For more details on the arrests, see Michael Mugwang'a, Gitonga Marete and Tim Querengesser, 'Kenya: Scores Arrested in Terror Hunt', *The Nation* (Kenya), 15 December 2007; David Ochami and Mwangi Muiruri, 'Face to Face with Dangerous Terrorists', *East Africa Standard*, 6 August 2008.

144 **real name was Elizabeth Hanson:** For more on Hanson, see Joby Warrick, *The Triple Agent: The al-Qaeda Mole Who Infiltrated the CIA*, Vintage, 2012.

146 **'Because of the flowing style . . . me directly':** Moazzem Begg, interview with Imam Anwar al-Awlaki, Cageprisoners.com, 31 December 2007.

146 **Wuhayshi . . . upper echelons of al-Qaeda:** 'False Foundation? AQAP, Tribes and Ungoverned Spaces in Yemen', Combating Terrorism Center at West Point, October 2011.

149 **sixty email accounts:** Catherine Herridge, 'American cleric used more than 60 email accounts to reach followers, including Hasan', Fox News, 15 June 2012.

14. *Cocaine and Allah*

156 **acquitted in a terrorism case:** See 'Danish teenager sentenced to 7 years in Bosnia-linked plot', Associated Press, 16 February 2007.

15. *Clerical Terror*

165 **'. . . Hearts and Minds':** Anwar al-Awlaki, 'Battle of the Hearts and Minds', May 2008.

165 **The Dust Will Never Settle Down':** The lecture was released on 26 May 2008 and can be found in full on several Islamist websites, such as Kalamullah.com, which includes a wide range of Awlaki's lectures and sermons. Many of them have been removed from YouTube.

166 **as a dog:** 'Muslims protest Swedish newspaper's cartoon of Prophet Muhammad', Associated Press, 31 August 2007.

167 **'I have gifts':** This is my recollection. I do not have a saved copy of this email.

168 **gun and car attack:** Robert Worth, '10 are Killed in Bombings at Embassy in Yemen', *The New York Times*, 17 September 2008.

16. *Killing Mr John*

173 **In another email . . . deliver it:** I do not have a saved copy of this email. I have the invoice for the chemical gloves from Aspli Safety Limited dated 13 October 2008.

174 **moustache:** Paul Cruickshank and Tim Lister, 'U.S. target in Somalia: An inside story on an Al-Shabaab commander', CNN, 7 October 2013.

176 **now in command of hundreds:** Government Affirmation: *USA v. Ahmed Abdulkadir Warsame*, United States District Court, Southern District of New York, filed 26 March 2013.

176 **most dangerous operative:** 'Profile: Saleh Ali Saleh Nabhan', BBC, 15 September 2008.

178 **'Bad news . . .':** This is my recollection. I do not have a saved copy of this email.

179 **'Mr John says thanks':** This is my recollection. I do not have a saved copy of this email.

179 **On 14 September . . . at sea:** Jeffrey Gettleman and Eric Schmitt, 'U.S. Kills Top Qaeda Militant in Southern Somalia', *The New York Times*, 14 September 2009; Nicholas Schmidle, 'Getting bin Laden', *New Yorker*, 8 August 2011.

180 **'Mr John was killed . . .':** This is my recollection. I do not have a saved copy of this email.

17. Mujahideen Secrets

184 **'Fucking good':** This is my recollection. I do not have a saved copy of this text.

187 **Hasan was armed . . . the wounded:** Eric M. Johnson and Lisa Maria Garza, ' "Hell Broke Loose," Witness Says of Fort Hood Massacre', Reuters, 12 August 2013.

187 **Hasan had written . . . in 2001:** David Johnston and Scott Shane, 'US Knew of Suspect's Ties to Radical Cleric', *The New York Times*, 9 November 2009; Carol Craty, 'FBI official: Hasan should have been asked about emails with radical cleric', CNN, 2 August 2012; 'Anwar al Awlaki Email Exchange with Fort Hood Shooter Nidal Hasan', Intelwire, 19 July 2012.

188 **In one email . . . and research:** Ibid.; 'Fort Hood report shows FBI ignored warning signs on Hasan, lawmaker says', Associated Press, 19 July 2012.

188 **'Nidal Hisan is a hero . . .':** Awlaki's comments were posted on his now defunct blog. A summary of the posting can be found on the website of the Anti-Defamation League.

189 **thirty-four al-Qaeda fighters:** 'Yemen foils "al-Qaeda plot" killing 34', BBC, 17 December 2009.

189 **But the intelligence . . . one strike:** Amnesty International, 'Images of missile and cluster munitions point to US role in fatal attack in Yemen', 7 June 2010.

190 **destroyed a Bedouin hamlet:** Gregory D. Johnsen, *The Last Refuge: Yemen, Al-Qaeda, and America's War in Arabia*, W. W. Norton & Co., 2013, p. 253; Chris Woods, 'The civilian massacre the US neither confirms nor denies', Bureau of Investigative Journalism, 29 March 2012; Michael Isikoff, 'Yemen cable gives al-Qaida new "recruiting" tool', NBC News, 30 November 2010.

190 **' . . . scored a big own goal':** This is my recollection. I do not have a saved copy of this email.

190 **statement from the Yemeni embassy:** See Nasser Atta, Brian Ross and Matthew Cole, ' "I'm Alive," Says Yemeni Radical Anwar al-Awlaki Despite US Attack', ABC News, 31 December 2009.

190 **First reports . . . been killed:** Ibid.

190 **'The tall guy is fine':** This is my recollection. I do not have a saved copy of this text.

190 **several passengers:** On passengers' role in thwarting Abdulmutallab, see Peter Slevin, 'Fear and Heroism aboard Northwest Airlines Flight 253 after Attempted Bombing', *Washington Post*, 17 December 2009.

191 **collected and driven:** Details of Abdulmutallab's movements in Yemen are included in the US Government's Sentencing Memorandum, US District Court, Eastern District of Michigan, Southern Division, filed 10 February 2012. On the timing of Abdulmutallab's trip, see Steven Erlanger, 'Nigerian May Have Used Course in Yemen as Cover', *The New York Times*, 1 January 2010.

191 **Abdulmutallab told the preacher . . . to record:** Ibid.

191 **then bring it down:** Ibid.

191 **hospital bedside:** Trial transcript: *USA v. Umar Farouk Abdulmutallab*, United States District Court, Eastern District of Michigan, Southern Division, filed 11 October 2011.

191 **More disturbing still . . . Saudi royal family:** Paul Cruickshank, Nic Robertson and Tim Lister, 'Al Qaeda's biggest threat', CNN, 16 February 2012.

192 **commandos descended:** 'Yemen forces kill al-Qaeda chief', BBC, 13
January 2010; 'ﺓﻮﺒﺷ ﺔﻳﻻﻮﻟ «ﺮﻴﻣأ» ﻥﺎﻛ ﺭﺎﺿﺤﻤﻟا' [al-Mehdar was emir of
Shabwa], Asharq-al-Awsat, 14 January 2010.

194 **Awlaki declared war:** Anwar al-Awlaki, 'A Call to Jihad', 17 March 2010,
transcribed by Al Ansar Mujahideen English Forum.

18. Anwar's Blonde

197 **As a teenager Irena . . .:** Details on Irena Horak's life in Croatia were
provided by Sandra Veljkovic, a journalist who broke exclusive details on
Irena Horak's story for the Croatian newspaper *Večeřnji List*. See also
Renata Rašović and Darko Marčinković, 'Teroristica: Irena Horak (35) iz
Bjelovara je Al-Qa'idina Amina', *Večeřnji List* (Croatia), 24 October 2012;
'Ekskluzivno: Kako je Hrvatica postala Al-Qaidina nevjesta?', RTL, 25
October 2012.

197 **posted photos:** These can still be viewed on one of her social media
profiles.

203 **spymaster, 'M':** Piers Brendon, 'The spymaster who was stranger than
fiction', *Independent*, 29 October 1999.

212 **approving the assassination:** Scott Shane, 'U.S. Approves Targeted Killing of American Cleric', *The New York Times*, 6 April 2010. Shane reported:
' "The danger Awlaki poses to this country is no longer confined to
words," said an American official, who like other current and former
officials interviewed for this article spoke of the classified counterterrorism measures on the condition of anonymity. "He's gotten involved in
plots."

'The official added: "The United States works, exactly as the American people expect, to overcome threats to their security, and this
individual – through his own actions – has become one. Awlaki knows
what he's done, and he knows he won't be met with handshakes and
flowers. None of this should surprise anyone." '

215 **'Never is a man alone . . . with them':** As narrated by the scholar
Muhammad ibn Isa al-Tirmidhi and classed as an authentic *hadith*
by Sheikh Muhammad Nasir ud deen al-Albaani in *Saheeh al-Tirmidhi*.

19. A New Cover

226 **downloading instructions from *Inspire*:** Vikram Dodd, 'Jihadist gang jailed for plot to bomb EDL rally', *Guardian*, 10 June 2013.

227 **three others I knew:** The others I knew convicted of the plot were Zohaib Ahmed, Mohammed Hasseen and Omar Khan. For details on the plot, see 'Six admit planning to bomb English Defence League Rally', BBC, 30 April 2013.

227 **established that Geele:** Paul Cruickshank, 'Al Shabaab: a looming threat', CNN, 5 October 2011.

228 **In January 2010 . . . reach him:** Ibid.; Marie Louise Sjølie, 'The Danish cartoonist who survived an axe attack', *Guardian*, 4 January 2010.

228 **When the police . . . into custody:** Ibid.

230 **suicide bombers affiliated . . . seventy people:** 'Somali militants "behind" Kampala World Cup blast', BBC, 12 July 2010.

231 **Many . . . were Kenyan:** Letter dated 18 July 2011 from the Chairman of the Security Council Committee pursuant to resolutions 751 (1992) and 1907 (2009) concerning Somalia and Eritrea addressed to the President of the Security Council.

231 **received a summons:** For more see Orla Borg, Carsten Ellegaard and Morten Pihl, 'Briten der skulle være Storms makker', *Jyllands-Posten*, 14 January 2013.

232 **A Tunisian . . . al-Qaeda operatives:** See Paul Cruickshank, 'Four convicted in Scandinavian "Mumbai-style" terror plot', CNN, 4 June 2012.

232 **The suspected Swedish-Yemeni . . . headed to Yemen:** Confirmed by Paul Cruickshank, conversation with European counter-terrorism source, 2013.

233 **A man plotting carnage . . . No one else was hurt:** Per Nyberg, 'Sweden bomb went off early, authorities say', CNN, 13 December 2010; Paul Cruickshank, Tim Lister and Per Nyberg, 'The last days of a suicide bomber', CNN, 9 December 2011.

233 **exception of Nasserdine Menni:** 'Nasserdine Menni jailed for seven years for funding Stockholm bomb attack', BBC, 27 August 2012.

20. Target Awlaki

236 Awlaki was rapidly . . . deadly cargo: Mark Mazetti and Robert F. Worth, 'U.S. Sees Complexity of Bombs as Linked to Al Qaeda', *The New York Times*, 30 October 2010; Paul Cruickshank, Nic Robertson and Ken Shiffman, 'How safe is the cargo on passenger flights?', CNN, 19 February 2012.

237 addressed the American public: 'At this stage, the American people should know that the counterterrorism professionals are taking this threat very seriously and are taking all necessary and prudent steps to ensure our security,' the President said. 'Going forward, we will continue to strengthen our cooperation with the Yemeni government to disrupt plotting by al Qaeda in the Arabian Peninsula and to destroy this al Qaeda affiliate': President Obama's Statement on Security Alert, 29 October 2010, 4.22 p.m. EDT, whitehouse.gov.

237 Al-Asiri had concealed . . . a plane: For a broader look at the growing sophistication of AQAP's bomb-making, see Paul Cruickshank, Tim Lister and Nic Robertson, 'Al Qaeda's bomb-makers evolve, adapt and continue to plot', CNN, 8 May 2012.

237 asked Rajib Karim: See Andrew Carey and Paul Cruickshank, '"Terror Planning" by Muslim cleric al Awlaki described in UK trial', CNN, 1 February 2011; Opening Note, *The Queen v. Rajib Karim*, Woolwich Crown Court.

237 'not only helped plan . . .': Letter from US Attorney General Eric H. Holder to US Senator Patrick Leahy, 22 May 2013, http://www.justice.gov/ag/AG-letter-5-22-13.pdf.

237 sermons on their iPods: See Kiran Khalid, 'Confessed bomb plotter takes stand in NYC subway terror trial', CNN, 17 April 2012.

237 Another devotee: Scott Shane and Mark Mazzetti, 'Time Sq. Suspect Drew Inspiration from Radical Cleric', *The New York Times*, 6 May 2010.

238 'How to Build a Bomb . . .': See Paul Cruickshank and Tim Lister, 'From the grave, the cleric inspiring a new generation of terrorists', CNN, 24 April 2013.

238 al-Qaeda began to take advantage: For an overview of AQAP's expansion in southern Yemen, see Andrew Michaels and Sakhr Ayyash,

'AQAP's Resilience in Yemen', Combating Terrorism Center at West Point, 24 September 2013.

239 **US military drones . . . locked on:** See Barbara Starr, 'Al-Awlaki targeted in Yemen', CNN, 6 May 2011.

239 **US intelligence believed . . . nearby village:** Margaret Coker, Adam Entous and Julian E. Barnes, 'Drone Targets Yemeni Cleric', *Wall Street Journal*, 7 May 2011.

240 **Awlaki told a comrade:** Shaykh Harith al Nadari recounted Awlaki describing the near miss to him and others in 'My Story with Al Alwaki', AQAP's *Inspire* magazine, issue 9, May 2012.

240 **The car had accelerated . . . Awlaki's group:** Coker, Entous and Barnes, 'Drone Targets Yemeni Cleric'.

240 **The swap . . . brothers instantly:** Ibid.

240 **'Something of fear befalls you . . .':** Shaykh Harith al Nadari, 'My Story with Al Alwaki'.

243 **clashes erupted:** Adam Barron, 'Chaos swirls in Yemen's capital as rivals clash', *Pittsburgh Post-Gazette*, 25 May 2011.

244 **planted in a mosque:** Robert F. Worth and Laura Kasinof, 'Yemeni President Wounded in Palace Attack', *The New York Times*, 3 June 2011.

248 **'Please find a new courier':** This is my recollection. I do not have a saved copy of this email.

248 **khat-filled cheeks:** On the importance of khat in Yemen, see Jeffrey Fleishman, 'In Yemen, chewing khat offers ritual and repose', *Los Angeles Times*, 5 January 2013.

251 **Warsame took . . . Somali fighters:** Indictment: *USA v. Ahmed Abdulkadir Warsame*, unsealed 30 June 2011; 'Guilty Plea Unsealed in New York Involving Ahmed Warsame', U.S. Attorney's Office, Southern District of New York, 25 March 2013.

251 **took him into custody:** Warsame was also accused of weapons offences; conspiracy to teach and demonstrate explosive-making; and receiving military training from AQAP. He pleaded guilty and cooperated with the authorities. See Benjamin Weiser, 'Terrorist Has Cooperated with US since Secret Guilty Plea in 2011, Papers Show', *The New York Times*, 25 March 2013.

21. A Long Hot Summer

257 Khan had been born: Khan was radicalized while living in Queens, New York, then moved to North Carolina, where from his parents' basement he ran a jihadist blog using catchy graphics that became a prototype for *Inspire*. See Paul Cruickshank, 'U.S. citizen believed to be writing for al Qaeda website', CNN, 19 July 2010.

257 Khan met with the Nigerian . . . bomb plot: US Government's Sentencing Memorandum, US District Court, Eastern District of Michigan, Southern Division, filed 10 February 2012; Paul Cruickshank interview with US intelligence source, 2013.

257 'The use of poisons': AQAP's *Inspire* magazine, issue 8, Fall 2011.

257 found the *New York Times* article: Eric Schmitt and Thom Shanker, 'Qaeda Trying to Harness Toxins for Bombs, U.S. Officials Fear', *The New York Times*, 12 August 2011

258 text from my contact in Sana'a: This is my recollection. I do not have a saved copy of this text exchange.

259 Early that day . . . just twenty-four: Mark Mazzetti, Charlie Savage and Scott Shane, 'How a U.S. Citizen Came to Be in America's Cross Hairs', *The New York Times*, 9 March 2013; 'U.S. officials warn of possible retaliation after al Qaeda cleric is killed', CNN, 30 September 2011.

259 'I don't believe it' . . . 'No – it's true': This is my recollection. I do not have a saved copy of this text exchange.

259 leader of external operations: Letter from the US Attorney General, Eric H. Holder, to US Senator Patrick Leahy, 22 May 2013, http://www.justice.gov/ag/AG-letter-5–22–13.pdf.

259 President Obama announced: Remarks by the President at the 'Change of Office', Chairman of the Joint Chiefs of Staff Ceremony, Office of the Press Secretary, White House, 30 September 2011.

22. Breaking with Big Brother

260 'I'm so sorry . . .': This is my recollection. I do not have a saved copy of this text.

260 **'Tell Jed . . .':** This is my recollection. I do not have a saved copy of this text.

260 *Sunday Telegraph:* Adam Baron, Majid al-Kibsi, Colin Freeman and Sean Rayment, 'How America finally caught up with Anwar al-Awlaki', *Sunday Telegraph*, 2 October 2011.

269 **'He's just sitting there and lying':** I do not have this on tape. I stopped the recording after the end of the conversation with Michael.

23. Back in the Ring

272 **Al-Qaeda in Yemen had become:** For details on the merger, see Thomas Hegghammer, 'Saudi and Yemeni Branches of al Qaeda Unite', 24 January 2009, at Jihadica, http://www.jihadica.com/saudi-and-yemeni-branches-of-al-qaida-unite/. On the group's expansion, see Sudarsan Raghavan 'Al Qaeda group in Yemen gaining prominence', *Washington Post*, 28 December 2009.

272 **A confidant of Osama bin Laden . . . leadership of the group:** Paul Cruickshank, 'Terror warning may be linked to choice of al Qaeda chief deputy', CNN, 3 August 2013; Eli Lake, 'Meet al Qaeda's New General Manager', *Daily Beast*, 9 August 2013; bin Laden letter to Atiyya Abdul Rahman, 27 August 2010, Combating Terrorism Center at West Point, Harmony Documents: SOCOM-2012-0000003 Trans.

272 **By late 2011 . . . as possible:** See Christopher Swift, 'Arc of Covergence: AQAP, Ansar al-Shari'a and the Struggle for Yemen', Combating Terrorism Center at West Point, 21 June 2012.

24. The Lion's Den

282 **attack on . . . a senior British diplomat:** This appears to have been the attack Hartaba was referring to: Richard Spencer, 'Britain's deputy ambassador to Yemen survives mortar attack', *Daily Telegraph*, 6 October 2010.

283 **reached the town of Jaar:** For a good description of Jaar at this time, see Casey L. Coombs, 'Land of the Black Flag', *Foreign Policy*, 9 March 2012, and Gaith Abdul-Ahad, 'Al Qaeda's wretched utopia and the battle for hearts and minds', *Guardian*, 30 April 2012.

288 **a month after his father:** Tom Finn and Noah Browning, 'An American Teenager in Yemen: Paying for the Sins of His Father?', *Time*, 27 October 2011.

288 **Al-Asiri was all the more dangerous:** For more, see Paul Cruickshank, Nic Robertson and Tim Lister, 'Al Qaeda's biggest threat', CNN, 16 February 2012.

289 **left hanging:** See 'Yemen In Conflict: Abyan's Darkest Hour', Amnesty International, 4 December 2012.

290 **Wuhayshi would later depict:** 'Letter from Abu Basir to Emir of Al-Qaida in the Islamic Magreb', 21 May 2012. This letter was discovered by the Associated Press in a house used by al-Qaeda fighters in Timbuktu, Mali, and was made available at http://www.longwarjournal.org/images/al-qaida-papers-how-to-run-a-state.pdf. See also Bill Roggio, 'Wuhayshi imparted lessons of AQAP operations in Yemen to AQIM', *Long War Journal*, 12 August 2013.

290 **'Try to win them over . . .':** Ibid.

25. Operation Amanda

295 **'Rise Up and Board with Us':** AQAP's *Inspire* magazine, issue 9, May 2012.

296 **Qasim al-Raymi:** For more on AQAP's senior figures at this time, see Gregory D. Johnsen, 'A Profile of AQAP's Upper Echelon', Combating Terrorism Center at West Point, 24 July 2012.

296 **Godane . . . determined to transform:** Tim Lister and Paul Cruickshank, 'Ruthless leader aims to extend reach of al-Shabaab, eyes the West', CNN, 24 September 2013.

297 **'severe repercussions' in Kenya:** Paul Cruickshank and Zain Verjee, 'Kenya's high stakes Shabaab offensive', CNN, 24 October 2011.

297 **longed to take 'revenge':** This is my recollection. I do not have a saved copy of the email.

297 **Lewthwaite . . . was on the run:** Jeremy Stern, 'Samantha Lewthwaite: Whereabouts of Kenya attack suspect a mystery', BBC, 3 February 2014.

297 **Hammami:** For more on Hammami, see Andrea Elliot, 'The Jihadist Next Door', *The New York Times*, 27 January 2010, and J. M. Berger, 'Omar and Me', *Foreign Policy*, 18 September 2013.

297 **extraordinary video:** Tim Lister, 'American fears fellow jihadists will kill him', CNN, 16 March 2012.

298 **internal conflicts:** For more on the divisions within al-Shabaab, see Raffaello Pantucci and A. R. Sayyid, 'Foreign Fighters in Somalia and al-Shabaab's Internal Purge', The Jamestown Foundation Terrorism Monitor, 3 December 2013.

305 **a new plot by AQAP . . . intelligence services:** See Nic Robertson, Paul Cruickshank and Brian Todd, 'Saudi agent in bomb plot held UK passport, source says', CNN, 11 May 2012.

305 **What he lacked in power . . . with Washington:** See Gregory D. Johnsen, *The Last Refuge: Yemen, al-Qaeda, and America's War in Arabia*, W. W. Norton & Co., 2013.

26. Chinese Whispers

311 **sent him a text:** This is my recollection. I do not have a saved copy of this text exchange with Abdul.

315 **'Can you ask for the car keys?':** This is my recollection. I do not have a saved copy of this text.

27. A Spy in the Cold

318 **In July 2013 . . . alert:** Barbara Starr, 'Details emerge about talk between al Qaeda leaders', CNN, 9 August 2013.

318 **change the face of history:** This was how the threatening message was reported by President Abd Rabbu Mansour Hadi of Yemen. In a speech he related: 'When I was in Washington, the Americans told us that they had intercepted a call between Ayman al-Zawahri and Wuhayshi, in which Wuhayshi told Zawahri that they would carry out an attack that would change the face of history.' Mohammed Ghobari, 'Al Qaeda plan to "change face of history" led to U.S. scare', Reuters, 23 August 2013.

318 **more than twenty embassies:** 'US embassy closures extended over militant threat fears', BBC, 5 August 2013.

318 **number two of al-Qaeda globally:** UK Foreign and Commonwealth Office: 'AQ Core is no more: the changing shape of al Qaida', October 2013; Paul Cruickshank, 'Analysts: Terror warning may be linked to choice of al Qaeda chief deputy', CNN, 3 August 2013.

319 **been blooded:** Adil al-Abab, 'Gains and Benefits of Ansar al Shariah Control of Parts of the Wiyalahs of Abyan and Shabwa', available at http://www.longwarjournal.org/images/al-qaida-papers-how-to-run-a-state.pdf; Bill Roggio, 'AQAP's top sharia official killed in recent drone strike', *Long War Journal*, 20 October 2012.

321 **'Here's $10,000':** I later took a film of the cash on a table in my hotel room.

322 **'I'd like to take up the job':** The discussion about the job offer took place during a break in my recording.

322 **He had another proposal:** Klang made this proposal after I resumed recording.

323 **He and Anders indicated . . . shaking my hand.** This part of the conversation occurred after I stopped recording.

323 **a call in mid-August:** I did not record this call.

326 **I called Jesper one more time:** I did not record this call.

326 **on 7 October 2012, I texted Jesper:** This is my recollection. I do not have a saved copy of this text.

Epilogue

328 **Khalid Green, took to YouTube:** Khalid Green, 'Darse Twelve: Nullifiers of Islam', uploaded to YouTube 17 October 2012.When the book went to press the video was available here: http://www.youtube.com/watch?v=POLWQogyEuo.

329 **wrote on an Islamist blog:** This was posted on the Islamic Awakening blog. When this book went to press the posting was available here: http://forums.islamicawakening.com/f18/morten-storm-had-undercover-company-61838/index4.html#post659177.

331 **apologize to Naser Khader:** 'Naser Khader til Morten Storm: PET sagde du ønskede at slå mig ihjel', DR, 7 January 2014.

331 **'Out of consideration . . . killing of al-Awlaki in Yemen':** Orla Borg, Morten Pihl and Carsten Ellegaard, 'Jeg kunne hjælpe CIA og PET til at

spore Anwar, så amerikanerne kunne sende en drone efter ham og få ham slået ihjel', *Jyllands-Posten*, 7 October 2012.

332 **'the right balance . . .':** Justin Cremer, 'New Controls Over PET Announced in Wake of Media Storm', *Copenhagen Post*, 11 January 2013.

332 **heavyweight backing from Hans Jørgen Bonnichsen:** Maria Malmdorf Laugesen, 'Beautyboks kæder PET sammen med drab', TV2 (Denmark), 31 March 2013. The video of Bonnichsen's remarks is available at: http://nyhederne.tv2.dk/article.php/id-66670423:beautyboks-k%C3%A6der-pet-sammen-med-drab.html.

333 **made out with a subordinate:** Kristian Kornø and Thomas Gösta Svensson, 'PET-chef jokede med affære', *Ekstrabladet* (Denmark), 7 November 2013.

333 **CIA to lose confidence:** Thomas G. Svensson, Kristian Kornø and David Rebouh, 'PET-folk: CIA stoler ikke på Scharf', *Ekstrabladet* (Denmark), 4 December 2013.

333 **Government insiders revealed:** Paul Cruickshank, phone conversation with Carsten Ellegaard Christensen, a journalist with *Jyllands-Posten*, December 2013.

333 **Morten Bødskov:** Peter Stanners, 'Morten Bødskov out as justice minister', *Copenhagen Post*, 10 December 2013; 'Leader of intelligence agency quits', *Copenhagen Post*, 3 December 2013.

333 **Bonnichsen, sharpened his criticism:** Preben Lund, 'Tvivl om PET-chefens rolle i drab på terrorleder', DR, 9 December 2013.

333 **'Is it really a satisfactory way . . .':** Morten Pihl, Orla Borg and Carsten Ellegaard, 'PET sagde nej til at beskytte eks-agent', *Jyllands-Posten*, 19 December 2013.

333 **Kenneth Sorensen . . . was killed:** Bill Roggio, 'Danish jihadist killed while fighting for Muhajireen Brigade in Syria', *Long War Journal*, 7 May 2013.

334 **Abu Khattab . . . Shiraz Tariq:** Tariq was killed late in 2013 after releasing a video he recorded in Syria. See http://www.b.dk/nationalt/martyrvideo-dansk-emir-kaempede-for-al-qaeda. On death of Abu Khattab see 'Danish Jihadist reportedly killed in Syria', *Copenhagen Post*, 13 January 2014.

334 **first British suicide bomber:** 'Video "shows British Syria suicide bomber"', BBC, 14 February 2014; 'Crawley Suicide Bomb Suspect in YouTube Film', Sky News, 16 February 2014; Kiran Randhawa, Justin

Davenport and David Churchill, 'Suicide bomber Brit worked as driver for hate cleric Omar Bakri', *Evening Standard*, 13 February 2014.

334 **Clifford Newman . . . child abduction:** *US v. Clifford Allen Newman*, 11th Circuit Court of Appeal, 17 August 2010, #09-14557.

336 **three of its operatives took part . . . in Benghazi:** Paul Cruickshank, Tim Lister, Nic Robertson and Fran Townsend, 'Sources: 3 al Qaeda operatives took part in Benghazi attack', CNN, 4 May 2013. According to a US Senate committee, fighters 'affiliated' with AQAP participated in the attack. See U.S. Senate Select Committee on Intelligence: 'Review of the terrorist attacks on U.S. facilities in Benghazi, Libya', 15 January 2014.

336 **liberated:** '14 "mostly Qaeda" inmates flee Yemen jail after attack', Agence France Presse, 13 February 2014.

336 **new generation of explosives:** Rhonda Schwartz and James Gordon Meek, 'Al Qaeda Threat: Officials Fear "Ingenious" Liquid Explosive', ABC News, 5 August 2013.

336 **new shoe bomb design:** Robert Windrem, 'U.S. Terror Warning is about Yemen Bombmaker', NBC News, 20 February 2014.

336 **instructing apprentices:** Paul Cruickshank, Nic Robertson and Tim Lister, 'Al Qaeda's biggest threat', CNN, 16 February 2012.

336 **siege that lasted four days:** Daniel Howden, 'Terror in Westgate Mall: the full story of the attacks that devastated Kenya', *Guardian*, 4 October 2013.

337 **The suspected mastermind . . . Ikrimah:** Nima Elbagir and Laura Smith-Spark, 'Norwegian may be suspect in Kenya attack', CNN, 18 October 2013.

337 **Hammami . . . killed a week before:** Paul Cruickshank, 'American jihadi reportedly killed in Somalia', CNN, 12 September 2013.

337 **Kenyan government report:** Kenya Situation Report, 26 August 2013.

337 **acquired safe houses:** Ibid.

337 **Two weeks . . . abandoned the mission:** See, for example, Henry Austin, 'SEAL Somalia target named as "Ikrima" as questions remain about aborted mission', NBC News, 7 October 2013.

338 **releasing a video . . . called for solo attacks:** The video appeared on jihadist forums on 2 June 2011. The American al-Qaeda propagandist Adam Gadahn says that 'America is absolutely awash with easily

obtainable firearms.' Anyone can 'go down to a gun show at the local convention center and come away with a fully automatic assault rifle without a background check and most likely without having to show an identification card'. He concludes: 'So what are you waiting for?'

339 **Michael Adebolajo:** 'Two guilty of Lee Rigby murder', BBC, 19 December 2013.

339 **The Boston bombers built . . .** *Inspire* **magazine:** See Indictment: *US v. Dzokhar Tsarnaev*, 27 June 2013.

339 **avenge the cleric's death:** James McKinley Jnr, 'Man Pleads Guilty to Reduced Charge in Terrorism Case', *The New York Times*, 19 February 2014.

343 **A group I had known in Luton:** 'Four "planned to bomb Territorial Army base" with toy car', BBC, 15 April 2013.

INDEX

Index

AFTERWORD

May 10, 2015

The masked killers – two brothers dressed in black – moved with deadly precision after they stormed into the Paris offices of the satirical magazine *Charlie Hebdo* during its weekly editorial meeting on the morning of January 7, 2015.

What followed would traumatize France.

The two men – Said and Cherif Kouachi – called out the name of the magazine's editor, Stéphane Charbonnier, known as "Charb," and then killed him with a short, controlled burst of gunfire from their Kalashnikovs. They turned their guns on the rest of the editorial staff, killing twelve by the time they were done.

They then calmly walked out of the building, shouting, "We have avenged the Prophet Mohammed."

"We are with al-Qaeda in Yemen," one witness heard the brothers shout before they sped away down the street. When a French police car approached they got out and fired several bursts – hitting the car's windshield at some distance, and forcing the police to rapidly reverse in the other direction.

The police officers were no match for the disciplined and well-armed killers. Around the corner the brothers encountered another French policeman, a Muslim. They shot and wounded him, then finished him off on the sidewalk in cold blood, despite his pleas for mercy.

The brothers then hijacked another vehicle at gunpoint, telling the driver their murderous spree had been to avenge the death of Anwar al-Awlaki.

I was stunned. These murderers were essentially saying that they were taking revenge for *my mission* – the one that led the CIA to launch the drone strike which killed Awlaki in September 2011.

Two days later, after a manhunt that transfixed the world, Cherif and Said Kouachi were killed in a printing plant near Charles de Gaulle airport after a seven-hour standoff with police.

At the same time police stormed a kosher grocery in Paris and killed Amedy Coulibaly, a friend of the brothers who had launched his own attack and whose victims included a French policewoman and four Jews inside the store.

Before Cherif Kouachi died in a hail of bullets, he spoke on the phone with a French television station.

"I, Cherif Kouachi, was sent by Yemen's Al-Qaeda. OK?" he told the interviewer.

"I went there and it was Anwar Al-Awlaki who financed me . . . it was before he was killed."

Several days later, al-Qaeda in Yemen – the group which I had infiltrated – confirmed in a video it was behind the attack on *Charlie Hebdo.*

"The one who chose the target, laid the plan and financed the operation, is the leadership of the organization . . . the arrangement with the amir of the operation were made by Sheikh Anwar al-Awlaki – may Allah have mercy on him, who threatens the West both in his life and after his martyrdom." Those were the words of Nasser bin Ali al-Ansi, one of the group's senior leaders.

Terrorism experts viewed the claim as credible. Back in 2011, US intelligence agencies had developed intelligence indicating that one and perhaps both brothers had gone to Yemen and likely received training in an AQAP camp.

This would have required them to swear an oath of obedience to the group and agree to any missions it wanted them to carry out. AQAP would never have offered training to somebody who didn't formally join the group. After the Charlie Hebdo attack, US intelligence officials said that Cherif likely met Awlaki during this trip.

I knew all too well that Awlaki saw the cartoons of Mohammed as a grave insult which needed to be avenged. In the spring of 2013, *Inspire*, the online magazine he had founded, had included Stéphane Charbonnier on an assassination hit list.

A recruit like Cherif would have been manna from heaven for Awlaki, who had by then become increasingly determined to attack the West.

Back in September 2009, when I met Awlaki in Abdullah Mehdar's compound deep in Shabwa province, he had tasked me to find European recruits who could be trained in Yemen to launch attacks back in their home countries. Soon afterwards he had groomed the underwear bomber Omar Farouk Abdulmutallab to blow a plane up over the United States.

According to a Yemeni journalist, Said Kouachi roomed briefly with Abdulmutallab in Sana'a in the summer of 2009.

When Cherif Kouachi trained with the group in the summer of 2011, France was already in AQAP's sights. In October 2010, Saudi intelligence had told their French counterparts they had information suggesting AQAP was planning an attack on France.

The Americans tipped the French off about the Yemen trip a few weeks after Cherif returned to France in 2011, and French security services put both brothers under surveillance. But later they lifted that surveillance – judging the brothers were no longer a threat.

Clearly nothing could have been further from the truth. The Kouachis had managed to fool the French. They were clearly following Awlaki's playbook. The ever security-conscious cleric had encouraged me and other Europeans working for him to take care to mask our radicalism when we were in Europe.

It's impossible to know if there is anything that I could have done to prevent the attacks in Paris had I continued to work as a double-agent inside al-Qaeda in Yemen. I never met the Kouachi brothers while I was there. But the attacks demonstrated the group's resilience.

My worry is that AQAP will receive a recruitment and fundraising windfall from the Paris attacks. For years, attacking the cartoonists was a key goal for terrorists worldwide because they knew it would boost their popularity among those angered by the cartoons.

After the missed opportunity in 2012 to target its leader Nasir al-Wuhayshi and chief bomb-maker Ibrahim al-Asiri, AQAP had withstood a US drone campaign and an offensive by Yemeni forces. There was also concern the group was sharing its sophisticated bomb-making technology with the Khorasan group, an al-Qaeda "A team" based in Syria plotting attacks against Western aviation.

Yemen, the country where I spent so much time for Western intelligence and which I had come to see as my second home, collapsed into anarchy in the first half of 2015. Houthi advances beyond the capital southwards, the detention and later hurried departure of President Hadi to Saudi Arabia and a renewed offensive by al-Qaeda were part of a toxic mix that led the Saudis to launch hundreds of air-strikes against the Houthis and their allies.

AQAP typically took advantage of the chaos, expanding its sphere of influence in the south and recruiting Sunni tribes to what it portrayed as an existential battle against the Shia Houthis. More than once I wondered whether the situation might have been different had I continued my work infiltrating AQAP.

The US drone campaign continued to enjoy some success against the terrorists. AQAP's top cleric and former Guantanamo Bay detainee, Ibrahim al-Rubaysh and Naser al-Ansi, who had claimed credit for the Charlie Hebdo attack on behalf of AQAP, were killed in drone strikes. Al-Ansi had viewed attacks on the US as a key priority for the group.

Al-Ansi was also prominent in AQAP's war of words with ISIS, in what threatened to become a fratricidal war among jihadists similar to that in Syria.

ISIS, the successor to al-Qaeda in Iraq, had emerged as the big beast of the global Jihadi movement and had taken control of vast areas of Syria and Iraq and declared the foundation of a "Caliphate" by the summer of 2014.

The ISIS fighters believed they had divine winds in their sails. As their extraordinary seizure of territory dominated news bulletins night after night, I recalled something Anwar al-Awlaki had told our small group during those study sessions in Sana'a in 2006. According to the prophecies in the hadith, he had told us Jihad would be revived in Syria and Iraq.

By the spring of 2015 ISIS was also openly challenging AQAP as the standard-bearer of Sunni fundamentalism in Yemen. It announced its arrival with a series of suicide bombings against Houthi gatherings in the capital, one of which alone killed some 150 people, and began producing videos of its fighters training there.

It was also helped by endorsements from several well-known figures in Yemen's jihadist firmament, including a preacher I had gotten to know. Abdul Majid al-Raymi, a leading Yemeni Salafi-jihadi scholar long admired by AQAP, announced his support for ISIS and the Caliphate in the summer of 2014 – and asked his large number of followers in Yemen to do the same. I was once his student in Sana'a, where he ran the Salafist Markaz Dawah Institute. Our relationship did not begin so auspiciously. I thought he was one of those evil innovators who dared interpret the words of the Prophet and told him so. When I later apologized, he smiled and graciously forgave me. I attended his lectures and visited his home, and as a passionate Salafi myself came to appreciate his learning and integrity.

Al-Raymi, a short man in his mid-forties when I knew him, was a cheerful and generous man to his friends, and a danger to Yemen. I saw how he influenced up-and-coming militants like Adil al-Abab, and often thought he had a charisma and learning similar to Anwar al-Awlaki's. His knowledge of the Koran and the hadith was extraordinary. Sheikh Muqbil at the Dammaj Institute offered his daughter to al-Raymi in marriage; even AQAP leader Nasir al-Wuhayshi seemed in awe of him.

I am not sure where al-Raymi is now, but he has the capacity to mobilize a new generation of Yemeni Salafis and help build a bridgehead for ISIS in a country that is as volatile and ungovernable as Iraq and Syria.

In the months after the Paris attacks, the cartoons of the prophet would provoke more attacks in the West. On the afternoon of February 14, 2015 – Valentine's Day – a gunman dressed in dark clothes with a scarf covering his head approached the entrance of the Krudttønden cultural center in Copenhagen. Inside attending a discussion on "art, blasphemy and freedom of expression" was the Swedish artist Lars Vilks, whose depiction of the Prophet Mohamed as a dog in 2007 had so angered Awlaki. With a single shot from an assault rifle, the gunman killed a

Danish filmmaker outside the venue. He then sprayed the entrance with 27 bullets, injuring three police officers inside. Only their presence prevented him from entering.

Late that night the gunman reemerged, shooting dead from close range Dan Uzan, a Danish Jew providing security outside a bat mitzvah party in a building next to a Copenhagen synagogue, before again escaping into the night. But police were by now on the gunman's trail, and in the early hours of the morning shot him dead when he opened fire on them near a residence they had under observation.

The gunman was identified as Omar el-Hussein, a twenty-two-year old Dane of Palestinian descent. He had been involved in gangs just like me and had previously been convicted of stabbing a man on a commuter train. He had just been released from prison, where he had been radicalized and had apparently been inspired by the Paris attacks. While he had no direct ties to overseas terrorist groups, just minutes before his first attack he had posted a pledge of allegiance to ISIS leader Abu Bakr al-Baghdadi on Facebook.

It was the first fatal Islamist terrorist attack in Denmark in the years after 9/11. What we had worked so hard to prevent had materialized. But it was hardly a surprise. I knew all too well just how big the terrorist threat had been all along.

And for me, it had become personal. Late the previous year, I had testified in the trial of Said Mansour, one of my former radical circle who the previous decade had been the first person convicted in Denmark for incitement of terrorism. After getting out of jail he had been rearrested in early 2014 for the same offence, but this time his target was me. He had circulated a picture of me online with a caption stating WANTED DEAD OR ALIVE that had been downloaded thousands of times across Europe. When I addressed the court, Mansour stared at me with a snarl on his lips, with no pretense of disguising his hatred. I smiled at him; I knew he was going down. He was given a four-year prison sentence for his threat against me and a similar one against the Danish cartoonist Kurt Westergaard.

There were other threats made against me. In January 2015 an extremist in Copenhagen was charged with threatening my life in a

Facebook posting. One of his more charming suggestions was "Morten Storm should be stabbed in the throat."

In Denmark and across Europe, the terrorist threat was now bigger than ever and I felt frustrated there was nothing I could do about it. More than a hundred Danes have now travelled to Syria and Iraq to fight with Jihadi groups, a ticking time bomb as they begin to return.

After the Copenhagen shooting Islamist extremists flocked to the street in which the gunmen el Hussein had been killed and laid flowers. Hundreds of them attended his burial. They clearly felt strength in numbers. One of those who visited the street where he died in homage was the dimwitted Adnan Avdic, the Danish-Bosnian extremist I had made believe I was dealing cocaine in the service of Jihad. A French television interviewer asked him why he was there.

"This man has a heart of gold . . . he's a hero," he replied.

The attacks were not confined to Europe. On the evening of Sunday, May 3, 2015, terror came to Garland, Texas. Two gunmen armed with assault rifles and wearing body armor exited their vehicle and opened fire on police guarding a parking lot of a venue hosting a drawing contest for cartoons featuring the Prophet Mohammed. They had driven through the previous night from Phoenix to get there. The event had been organized by the controversial American Freedom Defense Initiative, which had offered a $10,000 prize for the winning submission. The organization's founder Pamela Geller had invited the far-right Dutch politician Geert Wilders to give the keynote speech.

Just minutes before he opened fire, one of the gunmen – Elton Simpson, a radical convert to Islam whose Twitter profile picture was none other than Anwar al-Awlaki—tweeted under the hashtag #texasattack "May Allah accept us as Mujahideen." In the same message, just like the Copenhagen shooter before his attack, he announced that he and his comrade had pledged allegiance to ISIS leader Abu Bakr al Baghdadi.

His comrade was his flatmate Nadir Soofi, an American of Pakistani descent who was equally obsessed with Awlaki. After I led the CIA to Awlaki and he was killed in a drone strike, Soofi's passion for the American terrorist cleric's teachings had deepened, his mother later revealed. In the lead up to the attack he had been devouring his online sermons.

Only the actions of a real hero prevented tragedy. Despite being heavily outgunned by two terrorists wearing body armor, a traffic cop stationed outside the parking lot shot both gunmen dead with precise shots with a Glock pistol.

While Awlaki had clearly provided inspiration for the attack from beyond the grave, ISIS claimed responsibility – its first claimed attack on US soil.

A few hours before the attack, Simpson had urged his Twitter followers to follow a British ISIS hacker in Syria called Junaid Hussain.

In the minutes after the attack Hussain sent out a series of tweets claiming ISIS ownership of the attack.

According to investigators, Hussain had urged Simpson to launch an attack in secure private online messages. When this was revealed, I wondered whether they had been using some variant of the Mujahideen Secrets software I had used.

Investigators learned Simpson had also been encouraged to launch an attack in private online communications with Mohamed Abdullahi Hassan, an American extremist from Minneapolis believed to be with the terrorist group al Shabaab in Somalia.

There had also been public messages. Ten days before the failed attack, Simpson had tweeted an online link to the event to Hassan, stating "When will they ever learn?"

Hassan had replied "The Brothers from the Charlie Hebdo attack did their part. It's time for brothers in the #US to do their part." Simpson had then retweeted Hassan's threat.

By the time of the Texas event, the FBI was aware of some of these tweets and had sent a warning to the local police in Texas about Simpson. But they had no idea that an attack was in the works, despite the fact he was under investigation and was known to have previously harbored a desire to fight Jihad in Somalia.

By the time of the attack, the level of radical activity in the United States had started to stretch the capabilities of US law enforcement. The FBI had opened hundreds of investigations of possible extremists influenced by ISIS figures overseas. Almost two hundred Americans had travelled to Syria and Iraq, where some had been recruited by ISIS. Several dozen Americans, including several teenage girls, had been arrested before they could travel to join the group. And more than a half dozen plots by lone-wolves, some of them admittedly rather aspirational, had been thwarted on US soil.

The game-changer had been a fatwa released by senior ISIS leader Abu Mohammed al-Adnani in September 2014 which declared it was a religious duty for Muslims in the West to carry out lone-wolf attacks in retaliation for the airstrikes against it. ISIS-inspired extremists had responded by launching deadly attacks in Canada, Australia and Europe.

What most concerned counter-terrorism officials was that Western ISIS recruits in Syria and Iraq were flooding social media with calls for attacks, and increasingly reaching out directly to sympathizers in the West to groom them for terrorism.

"The siren song sits in the pockets, on the mobile phones, of the people who are followers on Twitter," the Director of the FBI James Comey said after the Garland, Texas shooting. "It's almost as if there's a devil sitting on the shoulder, saying, `Kill! Kill! Kill! Kill!' all day long."

Throughout the Middle East, a surge in terrorism has darkened the horizon – and brought the threat of contagion ever closer to Europe. ISIS has gained an affiliate in Egypt's lawless Sinai Peninsula and established a presence on the Libyan coast, raising fears that it might try to exploit the flood of migrants trying to reach Italy to send some of its fighters north. It has exported its choreographed horror videos of beheadings of Christians to the beaches of the Mediterranean.

ISIS is a different beast from al-Qaeda, with an end-of-days ruthlessness on display through its beheading of hostages, abduction and rape of Yazidi women and girls, and a remorseless application of its interpretation of medieval Islamic law where it holds territory. Its ambitions are without bounds; it has gained followers and a foothold far from its heartland in Iraq and Syria.

Perhaps as dangerous is its sophisticated outreach through social media to alienated young men, and not a few women, in Western societies. These are the individuals who spring from nowhere to carry out low-tech gun attacks on the streets of Europe and America. For Western intelligence services, they represent a new and frequently undetectable danger. Al-Qaeda, if it is to escape irrelevance, may engage in a nihilistic contest to bring as much carnage to as many places as possible.

ISIS has been open about targeting Europe. In January 2015, Belgian police broke up a major plot traced back to the group's leadership, in an operation that brought gunfire and explosions to the small town of Verviers. It seems more than likely ISIS will persist in trying to infiltrate cells into Europe, and exploit an alienated fringe of European Muslims with its sophisticated social media campaigns. By May 2015 European officials believed as many as six thousand European militants had traveled to wage Jihad in Syria and Iraq.

ISIS members and followers certainly have their targets in Europe. They include me. As I mentioned previously, a group of ISIS fighters attached posters of six Danes, myself included, on a wall and then fired at them with Kalashnikovs – a warning that we would be targets for militants. One of the group subsequently said I had made the list because of my role in the killing of Anwar al-Awlaki.

I may have helped kill Awlaki – but his influence among would-be jihadis and militant Muslims around the world lives on. It may sound perverse, but Awlaki has gained the status of a saint among al-Qaeda members and sympathizers. How much more dangerous he might have become if allowed to live.